SCHOOL OF ORIE   **S**

University of London

This book is due for return not later than the last date stamped below.
A fine will be charged for late return.
Application for renewal should be made on or before the due date,
by post or by e-mail to
LIBRENEWALS@SOAS.AC.UK or by telephone to 020 7898 4197.
Please quote the book bar code number.

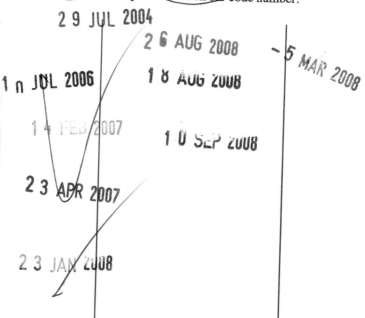

29 JUL 2004

2 6 AUG 2008

-5 MAR 2008

1 0 JUL 2006

1 8 AUG 2008

1 4 FEB 2007

1 0 SEP 2008

2 3 APR 2007

2 3 JAN 2008

POLITICAL AND ECONOMIC LIBERALIZATION

POLITICAL AND ECONOMIC LIBERALIZATION

Dynamics and Linkages in Comparative Perspective

edited by
Gerd Nonneman

LYNNE
RIENNER
PUBLISHERS

BOULDER
LONDON

Published in the United States of America in 1996 by
Lynne Rienner Publishers, Inc.
1800 30th Street, Boulder, Colorado 80301

and in the United Kingdom by
Lynne Rienner Publishers, Inc.
3 Henrietta Street, Covent Garden, London WC2E 8LU

Library of Congress Cataloging-in-Publication Data
Political and economic liberalization : dynamics and linkages in
   comparative perspective / edited by Gerd Nonneman.
   Includes bibliographical references and index.
   ISBN 1-55587-639-0 (alk. paper)
   1. Economic policy. 2. Comparative economics. 3. Democracy.
   4. Comparative government. I. Nonneman, Gerd.
   HD87.P637 1996
   338.9—dc20   96-1320
                                                           CIP

British Cataloguing in Publication Data
A Cataloguing in Publication record for this book
is available from the British Library.

Printed and bound in the United States of America

5 4 3 2 1

Contents

Tables

Preface

This book is the culmination of a project sponsored by Britain's Economic and Social Research Council (ESRC), which began with workshops in 1993 and 1994 and brought together economists and political scientists from Europe, the United States, the Middle East, and Asia.

Considerable attention has been devoted recently to the phenomena of democratization and economic liberalization. Nevertheless, for the most part this work has suffered from a number of gaps. The first gap is the lack of attention to the linkage (whether positive or negative) between democratization and economic liberalization. The second is that very little research has been comparative—at least in a form that straddles countries whose cultures and stages of development vary widely. And the third is the lack of interdisciplinary collaboration. This project was initiated to address these concerns.

Three regions were selected as sources for case studies: Eastern Europe, the Arab Middle East, and East Asia. From the first two regions, the case studies are of former state-socialist countries; from East Asia, one case represents a centrally planned economy and the second a newly industrializing country (NIC).

In Eastern Europe, Poland was an obvious choice as perhaps the most important path-breaking case, initially in politics and subsequently in economic liberalization. The second case study, Albania, was the last holdout of the model of socialist autarky in Europe before, in its turn, it succumbed to the winds of change. In the Middle East, the Algerian example is important both because of the extent of the liberalizing reforms attempted in a previously strongly authoritarian polity and centrally planned economy and because it provides perhaps the most dramatic example of a polity and economy where the liberalization process ended in crisis. The second Middle Eastern example, Syria, was also long known for both a socialist economy and strict authoritarian rule, and it is a key player in the present-day Middle East. In East Asia, the People's Republic of China was an inevitable choice—by virtue of its size, as well as the combination of political authoritarianism with stunning economic growth under economic liberalization. South Korea, the second Asian case study—often referred to as a NIC liberalization success story—features a very particular, and in many ways limited, type of economic liberalization, as well as genuine, if perhaps not yet fully "mature," democratization since the late 1980s.

This book is not simply a collection of "conference papers." Instead, it is a structured and elaborated crystallization of the themes that emerged from the work conducted during and subsequent to the workshops, including chapters by people not able to attend the workshops themselves. In Part 1, three thematic chapters highlight the main areas of debate and draw together the insights of the case studies and the existing literature on the subject. The first chapter introduces and assesses the state of the debate over the technical merits of the neoliberal paradigm, which underlies much of the economic liberalization effort of the 1980s and 1990s. Chapters 2 and 3 are devoted to explanations for the varying observed patterns of economic and political liberalization.

In the remainder of the book, two chapters are devoted to each of the six country studies: broadly, the origins of the liberalization process are examined in the first chapter of each set, while the second chapter sketches content and assesses the outcome so far. Where appropriate, however, different angles and approaches filter through this distinction.

Indeed, the differing contexts being analyzed dictate varying approaches and divisions of labor in their treatment. In Algeria, for example, the pre-1990 period of liberalizations contained little significant political liberalization, while the second period is characterized by both striking developments and dramatic reverses in that field; the chapter division reflects this. Both of the chapters on China, where by all accounts political liberalization has been faint at best, inevitably concentrate on the economic side of the liberalization programs; the first chapter analyzes the origins and the international aspect of the "opening up," while the second considers the internal dynamics and achievements.

Several differing interpretations and kinds of analysis are represented in this book, though all contributors use a similar set of questions as the backdrop to their inquiry. The gestation of the project and the interaction between those involved have, however, allowed a number of mutually enlightening conclusions and suggestions to emerge. Because these are as much about the diversity of countries' experience as about the similarities, it would be counterproductive to try to derive a single model from those experiences or to impose one on them. However, Chapters 2 and 3 do arrive at such conclusions and suggestions, which are informed by previous work on the subjects of political and economic liberalization as well as by the insights of the case studies presented here.

Both in the present volume and elsewhere, several positive or negative links have been suggested between the initiation, process, or modalities of economic liberalization and those of political liberalization or democratization. The book concludes with a brief review of such observed and potential links as emerge from the foregoing chapters.

The case studies presented here cannot claim to be a representative sample, however carefully they have been picked. Additional countries might have been included, but a larger number of case studies would have diminished the extent and depth of analysis of each. The ability to approach each case study from two angles is in our view a particular strength of this volume. At the same time, the thematic chapters give extensive attention to the general, more comprehensive picture.

The hope of all those who participated in the project is to make some modest contribution toward a better understanding of the dynamics and complexities involved in political and economic liberalization. We also wish to lay the basis for further exploration of these two, often intertwined, processes so prominent in the post–Cold War world.

* * *

The original ESRC project was formulated, and the workshops held, at Exeter University, under the auspices of RUSEL (Research Unit for the Study of Economic Liberalisation). Both at that stage and later on, many people there contributed to the eventual success of the project. They know, I trust, that they have my warmest appreciation; but three individuals need mentioning specially. Professor Tim Niblock, now at the University of Durham, was the main force behind the project's gestation and development. Neil Quilliam, now completing his doctorate at Durham, and Stephen Day, also one of the authors in this volume, performed a crucial role in chasing funds, bringing the contributors to the workshops, and ably managing the project's day-to-day administration.

Gerd Nonneman

PART 1

THEMES, DEBATES, AND EXPLANATIONS

1

Economic Liberalization: The Debate

GERD NONNEMAN

The increasing prominence of the economic-liberalization paradigm in the late 1980s and early 1990s has found itself reflected throughout the world, though this reflection has taken different forms in different places. In the academic attention the topic has received—and particularly with regard to the debate on the technical merits of the paradigm—perhaps the main problem is the newness of the phenomenon: Empirical evidence is still weak. Contrary to the fairly general agreement that political liberalization of one sort or another is a good thing in itself, such agreement is less secure when it comes to economic liberalization—even if the 1980s saw an expanding apparent consensus in this regard (what has been called the "Washington consensus"[1]). Given the extent and the significance of the debate, as well as the persistent controversiality of the neoliberal policy prescriptions in vogue in the 1980s and early 1990s, this first chapter will be devoted to a review of the main arguments about the paradigm itself. The following two chapters will explore possible explanations for its increased acceptance by policy advisers and policymakers; the causes for the variation in extent or manner of implementation; and the issue of political liberalization and its possible linkages with economic liberalization.

The widespread—though by no means complete—consensus in favor of liberalization is essentially a phenomenon of the late 1980s and early 1990s; it therefore represents a very recent and drastic change from the previous climate, especially that prevailing from the 1950s to the 1970s. Its most prominent and forceful advocates have been the World Bank and the IMF, along with a number of high-profile neoliberal economists who, in several cases, occupied senior positions in these institutions. Before exploring the origins of this consensus and the ways in which it has been, or in places has failed to be, turned into policy (Chapter 2), it is necessary first to consider its actual content and the arguments that have been put forward for and against it. It will be suggested that by the mid-1990s a new consensus, or at least a new

3

dialogue, might be emerging that would eschew [*sakinmak*] the extremes of either the free-market or the statist school of thought.

The Neoliberal Paradigm

Definition and Content: The Neoliberal Case

Economic liberalization is, of course, wider than privatization. In fact, boosting the private sector can imply the opposite of liberalization if it is achieved by controlling foreign trade. Essentially, economic liberalization means a reduction in the direct involvement of the state in economic activity (state enterprises); a reduction of state control of economic processes and activity (prices, production directives, etc.); giving leeway [*hareket serbestligi*] and encouragement [*müsaade*] to the private sector; and liberalizing foreign trade. The latter includes not only the reduction of trade barriers for imports, but also the halting of policies that favored import substitution over production for export.

These prescriptions derive from the tenets of neoclassical economics (a return to pre-Keynesian themes), and in their particular antistate focus of the 1980s, more specifically from that strand that has been referred to as neoliberal.[2] Neoliberal economists have gone much further than, for instance, Adam Smith, or one of the main early exponents of the neoclassical school, Bela Balassa, in rejecting any role for the state in the economy.[3] Both schools assume that the market is much better at creating short-term allocative efficiency than is the state, but whereas other neoclassical economists add several other variables when considering the conditions for long-term growth, the neoliberals conflate the two processes: Market-led, short-term efficiency will lead to long-term growth.

The main exponents of neoliberal economics are Bauer, Little, Krueger, and Lal.[4] Their interpretation has had a broad influence, and contributions on specific issues within the neoliberal case have been made by several other economists, but these four are perhaps the most widely recognized standardbearers. The following, admittedly generalized summary of the neoliberal case is based mainly on their writing.

The neoliberal case rests on a twofold argument: (1) The ultimate aim of development—reduced poverty and improved welfare—is best achieved through economic growth; well-meaning measures directed at the former while holding back the latter will be futile at best and most likely counterproductive. (2) In order to achieve economic growth it is better to rely on free-market forces than on state intervention. The free market will on average allocate resources much more efficiently than will the state, and this in turn will promote economic growth.

According to this view, the main reason for developmental difficulties and slow growth in the past is that the state or public sector was too big, too pervasive, and too inefficient, and was employing the wrong methods. This situation often brought about a crisis, while at the same time inhibiting the necessary flexibility and adaptation that might have helped counter the effects of such a crisis. Underlying the liberalizing consensus is "the recognition of the importance of flexibility of response to changing economic conditions and of the importance of private initiative to this end"[5]—on the assumption that private initiative tends to be more efficiently guided by market signals.

That the state sector in the developing world (and worldwide) had grown in unprecedented fashion in the two decades prior to 1975 is well attested. In the early 1970s thirteen countries of those monitored by the IMF were spending as much as 30 percent of their GDP in the public sector; by the end of the decade over forty were spending more than a third of GDP there. Over the two decades of the 1960s and 1970s the number of state-owned enterprises grew from 150 to over 400 in Mexico, from 150 to over 600 in Brazil, and from 50 to around 400 in Tanzania.[6] In many instances these enterprises proved to be failures, due in part to a lack of skilled labor but more importantly to their social function and their use as "sponge employers." The public sector's poor performance is also explained by the argument that signals to enterprises are either "distorted or non-existent and have been replaced by government command motivated by narrow political interest"; a distinct but equally valid factor tends to be that "the system of management (classically described as bureaucratic) provides neither incentive nor reward."[7]

The new consensus noted the failure of state interventionism in the style prevalent for over two decades, and of public enterprises more specifically. The model did not produce a viable economy; the enterprises did not generate revenues and had in fact proved, on the whole, a drain on the state's resources; even in terms of social equity and structural change of the economy the results were meager. The deciding factor was that the whole system by the 1980s was simply no longer affordable—witness the debt crisis.

Liberalization of the economy was argued to be helpful in three ways. First, it would allow the input of new resources from foreign investment and from domestic liquidity that had so far remained untapped. Second, it would allow economic dynamics to emerge that, because of more accurate signals (from the market) and more responsive and flexible reactions (by private initiative unencumbered by state controls), would help produce more wealth and, generally, an economy with long-term viability. Third, the opening up not only to domestic but also to international competition would sharpen competitive skills and thus reinforce the entire process and promote economic growth.

The attendant belief that private is inherently better and more efficient than public, and opening up better than protection, gradually became received wisdom—with rather less rigorous testing of the hypothesis than might have been desirable. Some more recent efforts in that direction will be reviewed later.

The neoliberals do not, of course, claim that the market is perfect but only that, on average, government intervention is even less so. They concede that some instances of intervention may conceivably offer some benefits, when seen in isolation, but that the costs associated with even such instances are likely to be much greater. (The branch of economics called "welfare economics" looks into precisely this question, trying to measure the welfare effects of various measures and their interaction.) One of the main reasons put forward for the less impressive performance of governments, as compared to markets, is the phenomenon of rent seeking,[8] along with the propensity for corruption. These are nonproductive—indeed, not oriented in the first place at production at all, let alone efficient production—and thus result in lower growth and lesser welfare overall. The more state intervention there is, according to this argument, the more chances there will be for this kind of behavior. In addition, it becomes increasingly difficult to wean a system off these dynamics once they have become entrenched, which is another reason for preventing rather than curing them.

Neoliberal policy prescriptions, which have become very much part of the mainstream since the 1980s, have therefore focused on the following: (1) The state should provide for prudent macroeconomic management (reducing budget deficits, keeping inflation low, etc.), basic infrastructure, and a legal framework within which private property is safeguarded and the market can do its work; (2) the market should, in the main, be left to function unhindered (no direction, no subsidies, no protection); (3) private enterprise should be the engine of economic life and growth; and (4) foreign trade should be liberalized and exports fostered. It will be noted later, however, that the mainstream has in the 1990s gradually been absorbing some additional elements as well.

The argument for exports and liberal trade is based on the theory of comparative advantage. This holds that it is more resource efficient for a country to concentrate on producing in fields in which it has a comparative advantage, and sell the produce through exports to pay for the import of other goods in which it does not have such an advantage. The general theoretical formulation, simply put, is that increased competition and trade end up creating more wealth overall; protection and trade wars, while aiming at an individual country's interests, in effect result in reduced wealth creation, or even outright depression. Liberal trade policies combined with liberal domestic policies will, in the neoliberal case, promote exports, and these will in turn boost growth.[9]

The view that threatened industries must be kept alive by protection or subsidies suffers, in the eyes of neoliberal economists, from the mistaken belief that an industry can get strong without the spur of competition. When governments guarantee an industry's survival regardless of performance, that performance is almost certain to worsen. Policy-makers may start by protecting a weak industry, but quickly find themselves having to protect an even weaker one.[10]

It is added that, whether or not there may have been the odd instance of apparent success, those defending protectionism "ignore the fact that protection has costs which, if honestly accounted for, would be regarded as pro-*fahis* hibitive."[11] Some of the empirical evidence on these issues will be reviewed later.

The push for privatization, for example in the post-Communist states of Eastern Europe, would seem to follow logically from the combination of arguments above. However, even if one accepts the importance of market-driven competition as an engine for growth, it is possible at least in theory to question whether private ownership really is a necessary component of a market system. In Eastern Europe, reformers (often disciples of the neoliberal school) have generally answered this question in the affirmative, on a number of grounds. First, without private ownership and property rights, "it is seen as impossible to allow the emergence of an entrepreneurial class, and to reward private innovation." Second, "in its absence, one cannot form efficient capital markets." As Estrin says, drawing together this and other aspects of the liberalizing option:

> The most convincing argument that private ownership and competition are both needed for economic efficiency is . . . empirical[:] the alleged failure of the market socialist experiments in Yugoslavia, Hungary and Poland. . . . [A]lthough the state had, in principle, withdrawn from operational management of the enterprise, in practice it continued to influence every aspect of decision-making. . . . The best-documented case is that of Hungary, where . . . enterprise was better served by negotiations with the bureaucracy over the setting of prices, credits, subsidies, taxes and international trading conditions than in innovation, marketing or sales.[12]

The policy ingredients referred to above have usually been included in the last fifteen years' stabilization, adjustment, or restructuring programs for indebted developing countries, imposed or inspired by the IMF and/or the World Bank. Various combinations of these elements have been implemented in different countries; but there has been a growing degree of similarity in the apparent underlying philosophy—regardless of a regime's ideological orientation—along the lines of the Washington consensus. Whatever the reason for this trend, the influence of the Bretton Woods institutions is glaring; before expanding on this it is worth considering more closely the key elements of IMF and/or World Bank programs, as they relate to the neoliberal paradigm.

These programs and conditions have been aimed at breaking the cycle of underdevelopment, debt, and economic crises spinning out of control. The prescribed remedy has varied over time, moving from a focus on stabilization (in the face of acute adversity in terms of trade, interest rates, and currency fluctuations in the 1970s) to more intrusive structural adjustment in the 1980s, including macropolicy reform, and further toward more attention on institutional reform, capacity building, and governance at the turn of the decade. World Bank lending and projects have increasingly had IMF-like conditions imposed on them; in fact, "by the end of the 1980s, nearly one third of new World Bank lending was devoted to programme loans which contained specific policy reform conditions."[13]

Although an overall reorientation toward the private sector was not initially the overriding aim of stabilization measures, the need to cure spiraling government budget and balance-of-payments deficits, along with the search for new ingredients of economic regeneration, entailed an increased reliance on the private sector in terms of both domestic enterprise and foreign investment. Such reliance, in turn, implied the necessity of more economic openness. In the course of the 1980s the stress on opening up the economy, toward both domestic private enterprise and foreign trade and investment, became a more central and fundamental plank of IMF/World Bank policy.[14]

As summarized by Richards and Waterbury,

> Successful structural adjustment will require at a minimum reduced government spending, a shift of investment resources from the urban to the rural sector and from the public to the private sector; a move away from a planned economy to one in which the market plays a major role in allocating resources; and, in the most general sense, a move to an economy in which equity concerns may be "temporarily" sacrificed to those of efficiency. The process is inevitably painful: Standards of living for people on fixed incomes and/or low- and middle-income urbanites may decline; privileged labour unions may find their wages and benefits eroding; educated and skilled youth may face an economy generating very little employment. Short-term economic contraction, it may be argued, is the price that must be paid to assure future sustained growth, but getting from the short to the longer term may prove politically impossible.[15]

Richards and Waterbury thus reveal some of the reasons behind the policy's controversiality. In addition to a recognition that implementation can at times be politically impossible, some (including, prior to the 1990s, recipient governments) have charged the IMF with being insensitive to countries' circumstances and being ideologically driven to abolish any state intervention in the economy. However, by the early 1990s, the Washington consensus actually profiled itself as somewhat more balanced than such charges indicated. The World Bank in its 1991 *World Development Report* identified the four linked elements of this consensus. They have been summarized as follows:

1. *Sound macroeconomic policies.* This requires governments to moderate their public spending, raise adequate revenue, keep firm control of public borrowing and the creation of money, and maintain a competitive exchange rate.
2. *Measures to promote microeconomic efficiency.* Governments need to free prices, deregulate markets, allow free entry and exit for businesses, dismantle industrial licensing systems and so on. They should invest in new infrastructure, and make sure that existing infrastructure is properly maintained. They must define and protect property rights, to create an environment within which commerce can flourish.
3. *Liberal trade.* This means reducing or eliminating protection for domestic industry, opening up to imports and foreign investment, and ensuring that trade and other economic policies do not discriminate against exports.
4. *Social investments.* Markets in developing countries cannot be relied on to provide essential social services like primary education or health care. Such investments are fully justified on humanitarian grounds—but it happens that they also yield exceptionally high economic returns.[16]

often

The oft-heard criticism of the emerging consensus of the early 1990s, namely that it was ideologically and rigidly (and therefore wrongly) opposed to state involvement in economic matters,[17] clearly needs qualifying. Although the balance certainly tilted in that direction during much of the 1980s, the consensus was never absolute and it became increasingly sophisticated as evidence and studies accumulated. It is now recognized within the organizations and by most economists that

> markets cannot operate in a vacuum—they require a legal and regulatory framework that only governments can provide. And, at many other tasks, markets sometimes prove inadequate or fail altogether. That is why governments must, for example, invest in infrastructure and provide essential services to the poor.[18]

Governments are also responsible, of course, for setting macroeconomic policy. Yet the neoclassical position is reflected in the added qualification that

> for many years these tasks were not high among third-world governments' priorities. Instead governments were doing the things that the new consensus regards as utterly misguided: commanding industries what to produce and how much to charge, extracting punitive taxes from farmers to subsidise urban civil servants, keeping the outside world at bay. That was what "correcting market failure" turned out in practice.[19]

There remains a definite reluctance to recognize any degree of "interventionist" state action in the economy as being anything other than potentially harmful. Nevertheless, since 1991 the very gradual recognition has begun to creep into World Bank thinking that in some circumstances the state might contribute something positive after all; evidence to that effect will be looked at later in the chapter ("Toward a New Consensus?").

Positive Evidence for the Liberal Paradigm?

The contentiousness of the liberalization paradigm, its very newness, and the impact it is bound to have as a comprehensive developmental strategy have led to concerted efforts to assess its actual effectiveness—not least by the IMF and the World Bank themselves. Some critical commentators have drawn attention to the fact that the evidence has been mixed at best. Indeed, no clear verdict seems to emerge from much of the available studies, varying as they do from the positive to the negative to the simply inconclusive.[20]

Perhaps the most important macroassessment of the new paradigm's effectiveness must be whether or not it promotes growth. One criticism of structural-adjustment programs has been that although they may achieve adjustment, they might do so at the expense of growth (because their aim of deficit reduction usually calls for policies that reduce demand and output). A 1990 IMF study found no clear, significant correlation between the adoption of an IMF program and achieving growth.[21] But the World Bank came to a different conclusion. In a study of 78 countries it compares the performance in growth, savings, and exports of 25 "early adjusters" (who received at least two structural-adjustment loans before 1985), 25 "late adjusters" (since 1985), and 28 "nonadjusters." By the latter half of the 1980s, early adjusters outperformed the others on growth, savings, and exports, though they lagged behind on investment. Even after controlling for external and other factors, the conclusion emerges that after four years of a Bank-supported adjustment program, a country would expect to have a GDP on average 8 percent higher than otherwise; its savings and exports would have grown faster; but investment turns out to be lower.[22]

An independent study published in 1991 arrives at conclusions that lie somewhere between these two. Mosley, Harrigan, and Toye found at best a small positive impact of World Bank policy–based lending on growth.[23] The finding of comparatively lower investment might be put in perspective by the valid assumption that investment in the new context may be of a better quality, while substantial amounts of inefficient public investment had been cut (which would be confirmed by the finding that growth is at least not negatively affected).

That the conclusions, so far, are less than wholeheartedly positive on the link between structural adjustment and growth might be ascribed to a number of factors. It might simply be too early to come to a definitive judgment: even though the *ideas* have been around for a long time, committed and comprehensive reform has appeared only since the late 1980s. For instance, even where adjustment loans were granted earlier, countries often failed to comply with the imposed conditions.[24]

What evidence is presented for the case that government intervention in directing the economy (*dirigisme,* in a word) has generally negative results? Considering the decades of the 1950s to the 1970s, it is not difficult to find a plethora of failed experiments; relatively few economies have succeeded in such a strategy. Some neoliberal economists argue (admittedly without providing hard evidence) that even the apparent exceptions—the NICs of East Asia—only did well under government intervention because of other factors, and that they would have done even better without it. "The dirigiste strategies of industrialization are presented as mistakes that required further government intervention to offset them (such as export subsidies to offset import protection)."[25]

Turning to smaller-scale measurements of the impact of economic policy (more liberal versus less liberal), the *World Development Report 1991* assesses the rate of return of 1,200 projects supported by the World Bank or the affiliated International Finance Corporation, and relates this rate to the policy environment of the economy in which each project is based. The four measures of policy are: (1) trade restrictions; (2) exchange rates (how large is the black-market premium on foreign exchange?); (3) interest rates (negative or positive in real terms?); and (4) the budget deficit. The picture that emerges is striking. The average rate of return for projects—whether in the private or public sector, agricultural, industrial or other—was consistently and considerably higher where trade restrictiveness was low rather than high; where the foreign-exchange premium was low rather than high; where real interest rates were positive rather than negative; and where the fiscal deficit was low (less than 4 percent of GDP) rather than high (8 percent or over). This holds for each of the measures individually as well as in combination. By any standards these results would seem to be a convincing victory of the policies of the Washington consensus over their rivals. It should be noted that the study also confirms the positive effects of institution building, and investing in infrastructure.[26]

Specific evidence has also been published since 1990 on the question of privatization—the buzzword of the 1980s and early 1990s. Until recently there was very little hard evidence based on consistent studies of privatizations in different countries. A 1992 study (published in 1994) by a team from the World Bank, however, has begun to fill this gap.[27]

The study considers three privatizations in each of four countries (Britain, Chile, Malaysia, and Mexico)—most having taken place between 1984 and 1988 and therefore offering sufficient comparative perspective on their performance before and after. The performance of each privatized firm is compared with a carefully constructed projection of how it would have performed if it had stayed in the public sector. The gains and losses are then calculated for (1) the firm's employees, (2) the country's taxpayers and consumers, (3) consumers abroad, (4) the governments concerned, and (5) the shareholders. Special caution was exerted to exclude effects that were not clearly due to privatization (such as a general economic upswing coinciding with the privatization). The striking finding is that in eleven out of twelve cases privatization produced a net increase in wealth—averaging for all twelve a yearly increase of about 26 percent of the firms' turnover in the year before privatization. The factors the authors identify as responsible for these gains are (in varying degrees from case to case) the freedom to increase investment, managerial innovation, better pricing of the firm's services, and the cutting of surplus labor. Even though prices were often raised (to more "realistic" levels) consumers were found to be net losers in only five cases, and gained in four. Although performance was often boosted by drastic labor cuts, workers sometimes gained as well. In fact, on balance workers lost in none of the twelve privatizations (where necessary because of generous redundancy deals), and in most cases actually gained, for instance through the opportunity to buy shares in their own firm, whose value tended to rise after privatization.

Another important finding at this micro scale is that, rather than privatization resulting in less investment, it is in fact the governments that tend to be the worst underinvestors, although it is not clear why this should be so.

As to the concern that most of the benefits of full-scale privatizations will go to foreign investors, the study found that in three cases foreigners did indeed benefit more than all domestic groups combined. But, the study argues, this still left substantial benefits to be reaped by others. As *The Economist* put it: "Foreign capital can make the difference between some gains, enjoyed partly at home and partly abroad, and no gains at all."[28] Perhaps equally important, even those privatizations that do not in the first instance benefit domestic groups directly can have the demonstrative effect needed to attract foreign capital into the economy in large volumes. The same paper commented:

> In individual cases, sceptics will be able to unearth a crucial investment-choice here, a marketing campaign there, that could just as easily have been undertaken by the public sector. In principle, yes. In practice, though, not one of those crucial decisions was taken while the firms were in public ownership.[29]

If this kind of evidence were to find further confirmation, it would also be possible to answer the charge (made, for example, by Ayubi—see page 17) that the most efficient enterprises are not always the most conducive to national development. Although there are undoubtedly such individual cases, they do not detract from the larger point that, on the whole, widespread privatization would result in more wealth being created and more capital attracted, and would lend the economy long-term viability.

The study also stresses, however, that for the positive effect of privatization on welfare to be realized, "credible and effective regulatory institutions" are necessary. This leads the authors to add the caveat:

Caution must be exercised in extrapolating our results to other countries, which lack some of the institutions and markets our sample countries possess. The same caution applies to the former socialist countries, [which] . . . almost completely lack private sector institutions and the kind of market mechanisms taken for granted in mixed economies.[30]

In regard to trade liberalization, the evidence from the study of project returns referred to earlier would seem to be a significant, though indirect, indicator of the positive impact of a liberal trade regime on economic success. Beyond this there is a variety of empirical evidence, but it is either fairly limited or less than clear. The first of these is the historical record. Proliberalization commentators point out that

Overall, the evidence suggests that the industrial countries grew with somewhat lower tariffs and substantially fewer nontariff barriers than those employed today by developing countries. . . . Since the beginning of the nineteenth century, tariffs in industrial countries have averaged less than 25 percent. . . . In 1987, the average tariff in developing countries was more than 30 percent, and that was after a decade of extensive reforms.[31]

The World Bank finds that statistically "the majority of the evidence . . . available [in 1991] shows a positive relation between openness—however defined—and growth," but adds that "the difficulties in isolating the impact of trade *policies* per se and establishing causality suggests that the debate is not fully resolved."[32] This is notwithstanding the efforts expended on trying to establish this link by the neoliberal economists.[33]

A massive study undertaken for the World Bank on the short-term impact of trade liberalization (often feared to be damaging even if beneficial in the longer term), has also put forward generally supportive conclusions. Papageorgiou, Choksi, and Michaeli summarized the findings of a large series of World Bank studies of individual country experiences with trade liberalization, covering virtually every significant attempt at trade reform by developing countries from 1945 until 1984. Where such reforms were successfully implemented, they found that even the transitional costs of liberalization are smaller than often feared (yet it must be noted that this study has itself attracted serious criticism).

Growth.   "Even in the short run, liberalization went hand in hand with faster, rather than slower, growth. This was especially true of the stronger programs for which the rigidities to be overcome—and thus, it might have seemed, the costs of transition—were greatest."

Balance of payments.   "In most of the reforming countries, exports increased faster than imports and the foreign-exchange reserves grew larger—not smaller, as feared by many policy-makers—after the reforms were launched."

Employment. "Trade liberalization did not, as a rule, raise unemployment even in individual sectors of the economy such as manufacturing or agriculture."

Distribution of income. "Because the reforms tended not to increase unemployment (even in the short run), they posed no direct threat to the distribution of income. There is no evidence that trade liberalization hurts the poor."[34]

Before winding up the case for the neoliberals' interpretation, it is worth referring briefly to their use of the East Asian NICs as examples to demonstrate the correctness of their approach. They have argued that it was the unshackling of exports, and international competition of private enterprise, together with the provision of political stability and a sound macroeconomic environment, that explained the success stories of these countries.[35] This view has been attacked by those who point out that most of these states have in fact been very interventionist. The neoliberal and mainstream response to this has been to argue that (1) even where *dirigisme* was in evidence, it did not try to counter the trends of the market, and it did not imply unconditional protection; (2) overall, "economic policies . . . distorted prices less than was the case in other developing countries";[36] (3) the strong outward orientation (i.e., the absence of a bias against exports) and openness to foreign technology are key ingredients in the observed success; (4) they would have done even better without the interventionist policies;[37] (5) some of these countries (such as South Korea) are now themselves attempting to liberalize the economy further and are finding it very difficult; and (6) past policies are creating serious problems for the more interventionist of these economies today, whatever the past benefits may have appeared to be (as, for instance, the overwhelming position of the Korean *chaebol* and their potentially dangerous mountain of debt).[38]

Whatever the validity of its liberalizing prescriptions, the neoliberal consensus is geared toward correcting perceived economic imbalances and their attendant economic problems. The growing acceptance of the consensus in the 1980s and early 1990s must therefore find its explanation, at least in part, in those very difficulties—even if other important forces may have been at work. This subject will be dealt with in the following chapter.

At this point we turn to a brief review of the criticism directed at the neoliberal school.

Critique

The neoliberal economists were aiming their arguments essentially against the "structuralist" approach of those who maintained that many more international and domestic factors conditioned a state's chances of development than just sound, "hands-off" domestic policy, and that the state should play an active role in addressing these factors. Structuralists, reasserting their own insights, in turn began to build a critique of the neoliberal consensus; critical or qualifying sounds came also from sources not necessarily based on a structuralist perspective. It must be noted from the outset that this critique was not simply a return to pre-neoliberal or pre-neoclassical positions. Some critics concentrated on deficiencies in statistical methods used; others on the historical record of the role of states in development throughout the world; some found fault with the internal coherence of neoliberal theories; yet others blame neoliberal writings for using partial evidence only; and most refer especially to the case of the East Asian NICs to disprove the neoliberal axioms.[39]

The General Critique

Much of the criticism comes down to the accusation of dogmatism:

> Compared with the pre-packaged solutions which have been advocated as desirable policy reforms . . . during the 1980s, the structuralist literature is markedly more eclectic and less dogmatic. This follows from the basic building blocks of the structuralist approach: an emphasis upon the importance of initial conditions, of national resources, of the size of the country and its relations with the international economy, as variables which must influence the appropriate balance and composition of policies. . . . What may be appropriate in one case may be highly inappropriate in another.[40]

The New Political Economy of the neoliberals is viewed as partial because it treats the domestic political economy as closed. ("As long as sound pro-market policies are adopted domestically, development will follow.") Toye comments that

> No one feels the need to test [the Washington consensus] empirically because the facts are too obvious; no one really wants to delve into welfare economics because its results are vulnerable to a whole raft of academic quibbles. . . . We are . . . in the realm of the Empowering Myth.[41]

Shapiro and Taylor label the central tenets of neoliberal economics "ahistorical," and add: "Historically, no country has entered into modern economic growth without the state's targeted intervention or collaboration with large-scale private-sector enterprises."[42] Having reviewed the history of European development and industrialization, Weiss and Hobson conclude that

> states, not merely markets, are central to an historical understanding of national economic development, and that this applies to "early" and "late"

industrializers alike. Strong states have historically been successful states. That is, they have promoted, not hindered, economic development. Moreover, they have done so by seeking to collaborate with, rather than work against, the dominant economic groups.[43]

The discrepancy between this historical record and the neoliberal analysis is not surprising, in the view of the critics. Taking their conclusions on trade policy (arguably the central element in neoliberal policy prescription), Colclough points out that they omit important variables from their analysis because they "attribute export and output success to a fairly narrow set of policy instruments being manipulated in a tightly defined way." This

> ignores all of the other policies utilized by successfully industrializing exporters, many of which have been highly interventionist in neo-liberal terms . . . [and] it implies that both the initial conditions of these countries immediately prior to their export success and the international environment within which they were beginning to trade had few if any implications for the success of their endeavours.[44]

The assessment of the costs and benefits (welfare gain/welfare loss) of intervention versus market imperfections is based upon the methodology of welfare economics. Given that this would require a very careful examination of all the variables in each case in order to be able to generalize, the neoliberal assertion that "imperfect markets are better than imperfect states" could only be accepted as established after "a fairly formidable empirical treatment covering a large number of country cases in considerable detail." Such a comprehensive empirical treatment, says Colclough, "does not exist, and would even in principle be difficult to achieve."[45]

The issue of trade liberalization, referred to earlier as central to the neoliberal schema, is perhaps the area on which most empirical research has been concentrated. Some apparently positive evidence was reviewed in the previous section, but the cautious approach to those conclusions taken by even the World Bank indicates the difficulty of arriving at clear results. Regarding the linked propositions that free markets will increase short-term efficiency and that this in turn will result in better long-term performance, Shapiro and Taylor state that "solid support . . . is difficult to find."[46] And Colclough correctly stresses that the causal linkages between trade policy, exports, and growth have not been proven.[47] The major empirical studies undertaken on this issue in the 1970s and 1980s—involving Little, Balassa, and Krueger, among others—did indicate a correlation between these various factors, but proved less than satisfactory in their attempt to establish causal links. The methods used in these studies and in the more recent review by Papageorgiou et al.[48] have been criticized on technical grounds.[49] Moreover, some of the positive conclusions by Balassa do not necessarily support strictly neoliberal prescriptions: What he terms a liberal trading regime is actually allowed to include a degree of state involvement that others would call interventionist, as long as it is oriented toward higher exports (e.g., compensating for market imperfections, and protecting infant industry to allow production to start from a base in a small market before the dynamic benefits of trade create economies of scale).[50]

There has been limited empirical testing of the hypothesis that greater size of the state is detrimental to development. The historical evidence referred to earlier, however, seems at least to qualify the hypothesis. In addition, a 1986 study "shows that across the world government size is *positively* associated with economic growth performance. This is so in the overwhelming majority of country cases . . . especially in developing countries."[51]

The acceptance of the axiom that private is better than public has also been challenged by a fairly limited number of economists and political economists.[52] Ayubi claims there is scant information on the actual productivity and efficiency of the private versus the public sector, and adds that "the most profitable enterprises are not always the most conducive to overall national development."[53] Stevens concurs that "there are no empirical grounds to assume that private enterprise is automatically superior to public enterprise"[54]—although this finding would need to be qualified by reference to the World Bank study on privatization referred to in the previous section.

The experience of structural adjustment in the developing world has been used to illustrate some of these criticisms. The key criticism is probably, again, that the neoliberal approach is too dogmatic in its insistence on simplistic policy prescriptions regardless of the individual country's circumstances. Mosley concludes from an empirical analysis of the results of structural adjustment during the 1980s:

> Whereas there is indeed a statistically significant payoff to "structural adjustment" considered as a package, certain elements of the package appear to be vital—notably exchange rate policy and the rationalisation of government investment—and other elements—notably privatisation and foreign trade liberalisation—are irrelevant.[55]

This does not mean that the latter two are necessarily always irrelevant, but that an assumption that they always are relevant, regardless of the circumstances, is not tenable. This is an unsurprising finding in light of another of Mosley's conclusions, namely that "such effectiveness [of the structural adjustment programs] as can be observed is acutely sensitive to a cluster of intermediate variables"—some relating to the country's political economy, some to "the relationship between the structural adjustment effort and the success of the government's mobilisation and long-term development policies."[56] Since these and other variables are likely to differ considerably across countries, a less uniform set of policy prescriptions may be called for.

This may also be desirable because in some countries it might be extremely difficult to implement the full "bag of tricks" at all. For one thing, "exchange rate and public expenditure reforms, being administratively simpler and politically less visible, are easier to implement than liberalisation and privatisation." Mosley concludes that "the liberalising brand of structural adjustment fashionable in the 1980s appears to have more relevance to richer than to poorer LDCs and least of all to those which are in absolute decline."[57] This corresponds with the conclusions of a study by Harvey on reforms and their problems in sub-Saharan Africa, which are interpreted by Colclough as showing that

> liberalization might work better only where the adjustment challenge is small and where the redistributive changes needed are not acute. Thus, one of the critical differences between liberalization as applied in South-East Asia and as it has been applied in Sub-Saharan Africa, lies in the initial conditions. Introducing a liberal regime in the context of impoverishment is very different from a setting (or early prospect) of dynamic growth.[58]

It is undeniable that in some cases economic-liberalization policies have been closely followed by instances of political unrest. The actual implementation of such reforms remains fraught with difficulties and political risks. Quite apart from the sub-Saharan examples, the cases of Russia, the new states of Central Asia, and even eastern Germany may serve to confirm this. Particularly dramatic instances have been provided in the Middle East (see, for instance, the case of Algeria).[59] In an assessment of the applicability, advisability, and feasibility of liberalizing reforms, therefore, the context must be a prime consideration.

The Case of East Asia

The question of why the East Asian NICs (Japan, South Korea, Taiwan, Hong Kong, and Singapore) were able to make such spectacular economic progress, apparently disproving the contention of dependency theorists that it would be impossible for states in the "periphery" to escape their underdeveloped status, has naturally received special attention from economists and political economists of all hues. The contrast with the rest of the developing world has, indeed, been striking. As mentioned in the previous section, the neoliberal analysis initially claimed these cases as proof of its own arguments. The reason for the NICs' success was said to be that they better obeyed the prescriptions of neoclassical economic theory, distorted the market less, and thus obtained better resource-allocation efficiency, which in turn led to higher exports and economic growth.

Work by Amsden, Wade, Weiss, and Hobson,[60] among others, has convincingly debunked this interpretation. They demonstrate that these states (especially Japan and South Korea) have been very interventionist indeed; if their success is, therefore, either the result of, or compatible with, such interventionist policies, then the generalized statement of the neoliberal approach no longer holds.

Neoliberal authors cannot, of course, deny the existence of some of these interventionist policies. But

> while the fact of "government intervention" . . . is acknowledged, it is given scant analysis; the effects of intervention are asserted with virtually *no* basis in evidence. . . . Key challenges, such as the combination of Korea's admitted high protection with its admitted good performance, are ignored. The dirigiste strategies of industrialization are presented as mistakes that required further government intervention to offset them (such as export subsidies to offset import protection); the idea that those dirigiste strategies might have *helped* industrialization is not even entertained.[61]

The neoliberal commentators on East Asia are criticized for using selective and partial data, and for failing to examine the detail of the range of policies rather than, for instance, just the *average* level of protection. Selective protection or subsidies intended to promote certain sectors is clearly interventionist and against neoliberal principles—even if it means that other sectors are not thus supported, and that therefore the average level of such support may well be fairly low. It is the dispersion around the average that is significant—and in the case of East Asia this is much higher than in, for instance, Latin America or India.[62] All the above-mentioned authors show how strongly and extensively the state in Korea, Japan, and Taiwan has been involved in directing the economy, both domestically and in their export drive, and how close the relations between government and private sector have been.

Amsden explains the adoption of these policies as a necessary reaction to being in the position of a "late industrializer," with the world market already dominated by the companies and technologies of the developed world. The initial condition from which these states had to begin their effort to compete and develop industrially and technologically was very different from that of the early industrializers. (But it will be remembered that Weiss and Hobson showed that state involvement was important also in the case of the early industrializers, even if in different ways.) The entry of these countries into industries in which they were not thought to have a comparative advantage at the time should have resulted in disaster, according to neoliberal theories. Instead they proved, on the whole, very successful, even if in individual industries severe problems were encountered as a result of the 1979 oil shock and growing indebtedness. Such difficulties, the "neointerventionists" would argue, do not invalidate the whole policy; even where there were problems, the overall, often indirect effects might still be beneficial. This would largely be due to the improvement of the human resource base and infrastructure, which went hand in hand with the directed industrialization push.[63] The policy, in other words, was to *create* comparative advantage.

The question remains, however, why these states should have done so much better than others, where subsidies and government intervention badly backfired. One answer can be shared with the neoliberal account: political stability and a highly educated population. Another is the strong export orientation of these economies. Although this appears at first sight as a confirmation of the neoliberal case, Weiss and Hobson point out that the reforms in Korea did not create a neutral trade regime (by eliminating bias against exports) but "one very strongly biased in favour of production for exports."[64] Subsidies for exports, however, depended on good, competitive export performance: The discipline of the market therefore still applied, albeit implemented via the government. The East Asian economies, Weiss and Hobson point out, "certainly manage their trade *differently* from many developing countries, but not less."[65]

Amsden for Korea, Wade for Taiwan, and Weiss and Hobson for the East Asian NICs in general, all develop a variation on the theme of vibrant private enterprise supported, directed, and disciplined by the state. Amsden's "disciplined market," Wade's "guided market," and Weiss and Hobson's "governed interdependence" all address this phenomenon. Amsden's view of the dynamics of the Korean case are summarized as "industrializing through learning, learning through reciprocity between government and diversified business groups, reciprocity through price-distorting subsidies in exchange for performance."[66]

Amsden adds: "Growth has been faster in Korea not because markets have been allowed to operate more freely but because the subsidization process has been qualitatively superior."[67] Weiss and Hobson then go on to argue that the reason state capacity in this respect was so great in the East Asian economies lies in the "governed interdependence" between the state and the market, where "the authoritarian-corporatist form of power gradually and more closely approximates a more collaborative and potent form. . . . The peculiar strength and capacity of such states resides less in their authoritarian use of power . . . than in their unusual combination of bureaucratic autonomy and collaborative linkaging with the economic sector."[68] Information flows between the government and the market, in both directions, and institutions link the two—among other things enabling the state to arrive at sound decisions. Although this relationship has been recognized by several authors since the 1980s, Weiss and Hobson refine the recognition to suggest that "government and industry are indeed highly interdependent, but the rules for establishing and maintaining that interdependence make it a highly managed affair, in which the state takes the role of senior partner."[69]

The foregoing account has demonstrated that, although at least the 1980s version of neoliberalism must be considered intellectually passé, the neointerventionists do allocate a very important place to the market. Together with developments in the 1990s among the mainstream, this contribution seems to indicate that the debate is beginning to be redefined away from the extremes.

Toward a New Consensus?

Notwithstanding the striking gap between the two sides of the argument, and the sometimes blunt language in which such differences have been expressed, the 1990s have seen a tentative rapprochement between the neoliberal and interventionist ends of the spectrum.

In a recent study on the NICs of East Asia, Chowdhury and Islam argue that neither of the two schools provides a sufficient base for understanding the success of these countries. In reality, they say, there is an overlap: "A broad-based, eclectic approach is more useful in understanding the nature of East Asian development."[70]

> The extreme versions of the statist as well as the neoclassical models of East Asian success lack analytical and empirical credibility. . . . The truth probably lies in a synergistic interaction between the state and the market. . . . While the state in East Asia may not have played the role of an "engine of growth," it has certainly played the role of a "handmaiden of growth."[71]

tamamlayici

Mosley's criticism of the neoliberal approach to structural adjustment was referred to earlier. It will be recalled, however, that he also concludes that "the liberalising brand of structural adjustment fashionable in the 1980s" *does* appear to have had some relevance for the richer LDCs (less developed countries). A similar shift may be noted in Woodward's otherwise highly critical analysis of the prevailing structural-adjustment prescriptions. While highlighting the damaging effects that existing prescriptions have often had in the given international context, his conclusions indicate not only that structural adjustment may be inevitable in many countries, but that it may even fulfill its intended function—on three conditions. The first is that the programs are designed with great attention to country specificity; the second is that care is taken to protect the more vulnerable sections of the population; and the third—crucially—is that the international economic context is made to *allow* the economic restructuring inside these countries to bear fruit. The third condition refers mainly to reducing the debt burden and opening the markets of the North.[72] (It is worth noting that especially the latter point— liberalizing access to Northern markets—is now being advocated strenuously by the World Bank itself, as well as by many in the neoclassical camp.)

The writings of Wade and others[73] clearly demonstrate that the interventionist case has been reformulated—hence my use of the term "neo-interventionist." They now recognize the importance of the market, and intend to use price as well as nonprice methods to channel investment away from unproductive uses, expand technological capacity, strengthen links with foreign firms, and give a directional thrust to selected industries. The overall economic indicative plan this is based on, they argue, must be open to feedback from the market; temporary protection, though useful in some cases, must be conditional on performance. Taiwan, Japan, and South Korea are put forward as examples of such a policy. Even more strikingly, Wade also recognizes that "in some political conditions . . . the risks of selective intervention are likely to outweigh the benefits. This is true where state authority is rudimentary (as in much of Africa) and where the state elite is fused with the business and landed elites (as in the Philippines). Here, neoliberal prescriptions are the least bad starting-point for policy."[74] This is true because such systems lack the institutional prerequisites of an autonomous, capable, and incorrupt bureaucracy, as well as collaboration and information flow between government and industry.

The neointerventionists recognize the important role of private rather than public enterprises as the main vehicle of development; they go along with the neoclassical point that bad public policies have inhibited development in many developing countries; and they agree that "markets allocate resources better than do central decision makers without markets."[75] (Their point is that these are not the only alternatives: The state *with* the markets may do an even better job.) The first factor Wade himself lists in explaining why positive initial conditions in the East Asian NICs led to such success is "the discipline of the market and private property"[76] (along with a highly technically educated workforce, the geopolitical situation and threat, and the collaborative "governing-the-market" system established between government and industry). Underlying the neointerventionist case is the observation (as by Lall) that "the bulk of the most dynamic manufactured exports of developing countries today comes from industries that underwent a 'learning' process behind protective barriers" (including the development of human capital). Although outward orientation is very important, and "the non-selective, non-economic [protective] interventions practised by most import-substituting regimes in the past" are condemned, they present a case "for selective intervention within the broad framework of outward-oriented policies, based on market failure in product, factor and technology markets."[77]

"As more and more comparative research makes clear, states active in dynamic industrial economies are not replacing markets but strengthening them." Weiss and Hobson expect

> to find more and more attempts to build the public–private forms of coordination that combine market orientation with state guided development. "Governed interdependence" . . . invokes this idea of a strategic capitalism in which institutions enable flexible responses to a new world of international competition.[78]

While the interventionist wing of development economics has moved toward a market-friendly approach, somewhat more state-friendly views have also been in evidence in what has become a changing neoclassical camp in the 1990s.

An illustration of this was provided when *The Economist*—which has been explicitly supportive of neoliberal analyses and prescriptions—in 1991 published an extensive, favorable review of Robert Wade's book *Governing the Market*,[79] and in one issue the following year gave him the whole page of its Economics Focus feature for an exposition and defense of the "new interventionism."[80] The review comments that the East Asian experience "makes it implausible to argue . . . that 'aggressive' intervention is always a bad thing."

Perhaps even more surprising is that in 1987 Jeffrey Sachs—one of the key "big push" advisers to reforming governments around the world—had already written of his belief that the Asian experience suggested "that successful development might be helped as much by raising the quality of public sector management as by privatizing public enterprises or liberalizing markets"[81]—and this in a publication of the IMF and the World Bank.

On the question of privatization it is worth remembering that the study by Galal et al. referred to in the previous section, though clearly positive about the effects of privatization in the cases studied, stressed that caution was needed in extrapolating these results to other countries, where the institutions and market mechanisms the case studies possessed might not be available.

Two other studies for the World Bank, in the series on "The Political Economy of Poverty, Equity and Growth," are also worth mentioning. In the study on Brazil and Mexico, the authors conclude that neither case confirms the neoliberal claim that countries in which the state played a major, *dirigiste* role would do badly. Growth and factor productivity were perfectly respectable until the 1980s, they point out, and "the catastrophic slowdown in both economies in the 1980s did not derive from . . . the micro-inefficiency of *dirigisme*." (They blame it instead on "attempting to push growth too fast and ignoring the canons of fiscal responsibility," in addition to the debt crisis and worsening terms of trade.)[82] The study on Hong Kong, Singapore, Malta, Jamaica, and Mauritius concludes that, though a market-oriented policy was the key factor in explaining differential rates of success, and free trade was an important condition, this did not necessarily imply total laissez-faire—not even in Hong Kong, which is often given as a typical example of a noninterventionist regime. Even when comparing the "freer" regime in Hong Kong with the more activist one of Singapore, the authors comment that "there is no a priori reason why either strategy should be preferred. The choice would depend on the circumstances in each case . . . the choice appears to be guided mainly by political factors."[83]

Against this background an increasing shift in policy conclusions in the Bretton Woods institutions would not be wholly surprising. The World

Bank's Development Reports have begun to reflect this to some degree, as has a special World Bank study on the success of the East Asian Tigers.

Probably the first significant shift could be noted in the World Bank's *World Development Report 1990,* which focused on the fight against poverty. The report essentially relied on a neoclassical set of prescriptions, but added a strong emphasis on the need for the state "to provide basic social services to the poor. Primary health care, family planning, nutrition, and primary education are especially important." A strategy that does not include this as an essential part, the report states, will not adequately reduce the level of poverty. Even where an adequate strategy of this kind is adopted, the World Bank recognizes that "many of the world's poor will continue to experience severe deprivation. . . . A comprehensive approach to poverty reduction, therefore, calls for a program of well-targeted transfers and safety nets as an essential complement to the basic strategy."[84] All of this veers away from the typical neoclassical reliance on market-spurred growth as a solution to poverty.

The 1991 report, titled *The Challenge of Development,* remained essentially within the neoclassical consensus, but shifted in places toward a somewhat more state-friendly approach. It also gave an airing to more interventionist arguments, even if not, on the whole, supporting them. In its own words, the report

> stresses the complementary ways markets and governments can pull together. If markets can work well, and are allowed to, there can be a substantial economic gain. If markets fail, and governments intervene cautiously and judiciously in response, there is a further gain. But if the two are brought together, the evidence suggests that the whole is greater than the sum. When markets and governments have worked in harness, the results have been spectacular, but when they have worked in opposition, the results have been disastrous.[85]

The East Asian NICs, the report adds, "refute the case for thoroughgoing dirigisme as convincingly as they refute the case for laissez-faire."[86] Investments in human capital are recognized as highly important for development and growth (a point interventionists might expand to include "learning by doing"), and the government is said to have a large potential role in technology policy and information services: Research and development is one such role, along with education. "Government agencies and industry associations can make a valuable contribution by coordinating the exchange of information among importers."[87] All of this is clearly inspired by the East Asian experience and different from the neoliberalism of the 1980s. The government has, moreover, a role to play in the provision of safety nets for the poor and those hardest hit by reforms, and even in trying to achieve a more equitable distribution of wealth—which in itself, says the report, is beneficial for, rather than counterproductive to, growth.[88] The report admits that the debate over the link between trade policies and growth is not yet fully resolved. It also acknowledges that, although it claims there to be an aggregate correlation between lower intervention and higher growth, there is in fact very considerable variation; and that the Asian NICs have proved successful interventionists.[89] The report even points out the existence of efficient state enterprises in many economies. "These show that SOEs can be run as efficient commercial concerns responsive to consumers. In many developing countries, improving the performance of SOEs is as urgent as privatization in its own right."[90]

World Bank acknowledgement

Such insights led the World Bank to undertake its own in-depth study of the East Asian NICs, published in 1993, in which the existing literature from the neointerventionists is also taken into account. This study concludes that neoclassical fundamentals are still the key to success, but it also breaks new ground by confirming that "in some economies, mainly those in Northeast Asia, some selective interventions contributed to growth."[91] Such growth, the report finds, was higher and more equal than would have been the case without this intervention. The prerequisites for success, however, "were so rigorous that policymakers seeking to follow similar paths in other developing economies have often met with failure."[92] Apart from a capable and fairly politically insulated bureaucracy, these prerequisites are the existence of "contests" (competition-based resource allocation by the state), successful deliberation councils that allow coordination and information flow between government and industry, and a pragmatic mix of policies flexible enough, for instance, to halt subsidies when a particular recipient industry does not perform. This is not far removed from the analysis offered by Wade and other neointerventionists. The effect of performance-based directed-credit mechanisms, which the structuralists have accused the neoliberals of ignoring, are judged by the report "to have improved credit allocation, especially during the early stages of rapid growth."[93]

Equally striking is the general point made by the report that there are multiple paths to growth, and that pragmatism and flexibility are essential. The report accepts contest-based competitive discipline as being as valid as market-based competitive discipline, although it doubts the capacity of many other governments to manage the system as successfully. The East Asian development approach, it points out, is very institutionally demanding; moreover, it is doubtful whether the new international trade regime would allow more recent beginners the protective/managed leeway that the earlier NICs adopted for themselves. Again, however, these are conclusions that need not be intellectually irreconcilable with those of the new interventionists.

As a final illustration of the shift in IMF and World Bank policy, two recent developments are worth mentioning. The *IMF Survey* in April 1995 explicitly stressed the need for social safety nets along with the implementation of structural adjustment.[94] And the World Bank's 1995 Report stressed

the importance of greater equality, stronger trade unions, better work standards and practices, and greater employer–trade union collaboration. The
report also returned to the point made in the 1991 report that large inequalities are a barrier to rising prosperity and should not be viewed
simply as inevitable side effects of a developing market economy.[95] The
shift away from the 1980s-style neoliberal policy prescriptions is well under
way.

Notes

1. A term coined by John Williamson; see his *Latin American Adjustment*
(Washington, D.C.: Institute for International Economics, 1990), Chapter 2; and id.,
"In Search of a Manual for Technopols," in J. Williamson, ed., *The Political
Economy of Policy Reform* (Washington, D.C.: Institute for International Economics,
1994), pp. 11–28.
2. The term is defined by R. Wade, "East Asia's Economic Success:
Conflicting Perspectives, Partial Insights, Shaky Evidence," *World Politics,* Vol. 44,
No. 2 (1992), pp. 270–320: pp. 270–271. In addition to the literature listed in notes
3 and 4 below, see also the discussion by J. Toye, *Dilemmas of Development,* second
edition (Oxford: Blackwell, 1993), Chapters 3 and 4.
3. B. Balassa and Associates, *Development Strategies in Semi-Industrialized
Economies* (Baltimore: Johns Hopkins University Press, 1982); id., *The Structure of
Protection in Developing Countries* (Baltimore: Johns Hopkins University Press,
1971).
4. P. Bauer, *Equality, the Third World and Economic Delusion* (London:
Weidenfeld and Nicolson, 1981); id., *Dissent on Development* (London: Weidenfeld
and Nicolson, 1972); id., *Reality and Rhetoric: Studies in the Economics of
Development* (London: Weidenfeld and Nicolson, 1984); A. Krueger, "The Political
Economy of Rent-Seeking Society," *American Economic Review,* Vol. 64, No. 3
(June 1974), pp. 291–303; id., *Foreign Trade Regimes and Economic Development*
(Cambridge, Mass: Ballinger, 1978); id., *Economic Policy Reform in Developing
Countries* (Oxford: Blackwell, 1992); id., *The Political Economy of Reform in
Developing Countries* (Cambridge, Mass.: MIT Press, 1993); D. Lal, *The Poverty of
Development Economics* (London: IEA Hobart Paperback No. 16, 1983); id.,
Development Economics (Aldershot: Edward Elgar, 1992); I. Little, "An Economic
Renaissance," in W. Galenson, ed., *Economic Growth and Structural Change in
Taiwan* (Ithaca: Cornell University Press, 1979); id., *Economic Development:
Theory, Politics and International* Relations (New York: Basic Books, 1982).
5. E. Penrose, "From Economic Liberalisation to International Integration:
The Role of the State," in T. Niblock and E. Murphy, eds., *Economic and Political
Liberalisation in the Middle East* (London: British Academic Press, 1993), pp. 3–25:
p. 8.
6. E. Berg, "Privatization: Developing a Pragmatic Approach," *Economic
Impact,* Vol. 57 (1981), No. 1, pp. 6–11.
7. P. Stevens, "The Practical Record and Prospects of Privatization
Programmes in the Arab World," in Niblock and Murphy, *Economic and Political
Liberalisation,* pp. 114–131: pp. 118–119.
8. See World Bank, *World Development Report 1991* (New York: Oxford
University Press, 1991), p. 131.
9. See Chapter 5 of the World Bank's *World Development Report 1991.*

10. *The Economist,* 16 May 1992.

11. *The Economist,* 16 May 1992.

12. All quotes from S. Estrin, "Privatisation in Central and Eastern Europe," RUSEL Working Paper No. 4 (Exeter: RUSEL, Exeter University, 1991), p. 5.

13. T. Niblock, "International and Domestic Factors in the Economic Liberalisation Process in Arab Countries," in Niblock and Murphy, *Economic and Political Liberalisation,* pp. 55–87: p. 55.

14. See also R. Cassen, "Policy Reform and Conditionality," *Development Research Insights,* Spring 1991, pp. 1–2; Penrose, "From Economic Liberalisation to International Integration," p. 7.

15. A. Richards and J. Waterbury, *A Political Economy of the Middle East,* (Boulder: Westview, 1990), p. 230.

16. "Sisters in the Wood: A survey of the IMF and the World Bank," *The Economist,* 12 October 1991, p. 47.

17. E.g., N. Ayubi, "The 'Fiscal Crisis' and the 'Washington Consensus': Towards an Explanation of Middle East Liberalisations," in L. Blin and F. Clément, eds., *L'Economie Egyptienne: Libéralisation et Insertion dans le Marché Mondial,* (Paris: L'Harmattan, 1993) [pre-publication manuscript obtained from the author, mimeographed; page references refer to this version], p.11.

18. World Bank, *World Development Report 1991,* p. 1.

19. "Sisters in the Wood," *The Economist,* p. 47.

20. See J. Kay and D. Thompson, "Privatisation: A Policy in Search of a Rationale," *Economic Journal,* No. 96 (1986), pp. 18–32; M. Aylem, "Privatisation in Developing Countries," in C. Johnson, ed., *Privatisation and Ownership* (London: Pinter, 1988); M. Khan, *The Macroeconomic Efects of Fund-Supported Adjustment Programs,* IMF Staff Papers 37 (2), June 1990; P. Mosley, J. Harrigan, and J. Toye, *Aid and Power: The World Bank and Policy-Based Lending* (London: Macmillan, 1991); P. Stevens, "The Practical Record and Prospects"; and Wade, "East Asia's Economic Success." See also the studies referred to in the following section.

21. Khan, *The Macroeconomic Effects of Fund-Supported Adjustment Programs.*

22. World Bank, *Adjustment Lending Policies for Sustainable Growth,* Policy and Research Series, No. 14 (Washington, D.C.: World Bank, 1990).

23. Mosley, Harrigan, and Toye, *Aid and Power.*

24. Ibid.

25. Wade, "East Asia's Economic Success," p. 274; Wade is, of course, critical of this interpretation.

26. World Bank, *World Development Report 1991,* p. 82.

27. A. Galal et al., *Welfare Consequences of Selling Public Enterprises,* (Washington, D.C.: World Bank, 1994).

28. "Sisters in the Wood," *The Economist,* p. 84.

29. *The Economist,* 1 June 1992, p. 17.

30. Galal et al., *Welfare Consequences of Selling Public Enterprises,* p. 563.

31. World Bank, *World Development Report 1991,* p. 98.

32. Ibid., p. 99.

33. See note 3.

34. D. Papageorgiou, A. Choksi and M. Michaeli, *Liberalizing Foreign Trade in Developing Countries: The Lessons of Experience* (Washington, D.C.: World Bank, 1990), p. 4.

35. See, for instance, the collection edited by H. Hughes, *Achieving Industrialisation in East Asia* (Cambridge: Cambridge University Press, 1988).

36. Ibid., p. xvi.

37. E.g., Lal, *The Poverty of Development Economics,* p. 46.

38. See, for instance, "The House That Park built: A Survey of South Korea," *The Economist,* 3 June 1995. See also Chapter 13 in this volume.

39. For an extensive general critique of the neoliberal school, see C. Colclough, "Structuralism Versus Neo-Liberalism: An Introduction," in C. Colclough and J. Manor, eds., *States or Markets? Neo-liberalism and the Development Policy Debate* (Oxford: Clarendon Press, 1991), pp. 1–25. See also Toye, *Dilemmas of Development.* On both the historical record and the case of East Asia, a stimulating and thoughtful work is L. Weiss and J. Hobson, *States and Economic Development: A Comparative Historical Analysis* (Cambridge: Polity Press, 1995). With regard to the case of East Asia, two further key names are those of Alice Amsden and Robert Wade. See A. Amsden, *Asia's Next Giant: South Korea and Late Industrialisation* (Oxford: Oxford University Press, 1989); and R. Wade, *Governing the Market: Economic Theory and the Role of Government in East Asian Industrialisation* (Princeton: Princeton University Press, 1990).

40. Colclough, "Structuralism Versus Neo-Liberalism," p. 5.

41. J. Toye, "Comment," in J. Williamson, ed., *The Political Economy of Economic Policy Reform,* pp. 35–43: p. 39.

42. H. Shapiro and L. Taylor, "The State and Industrial Strategy," in C. Wilber and K. Jameson, *The Political Economy of Development and Underdevelopment,* fifth edition (New York/Singapore: McGraw Hill, 1992), pp. 432–464: p. 433.

43. Weiss and Hobson, *States and Economic Development,* p. 135.

44. Colclough, "Structuralism Versus Neo-Liberalism," p. 11.

45. Ibid, p. 8.

46. Shapiro and Taylor, "The State and Industrial Strategy," p. 439.

47. Colclough, op. cit., p. 8.

48. Papageorgiou et al., *Liberalizing Foreign Trade in Developing Countries.*

49. See, for instance, D. Greenaway and D. Sapsford, "What does liberalisation do for exports and growth?" Discussion Paper EC4/94, The Management School, Lancaster University (1994).

50. Balassa and Associates, *Development Strategies in Semi-Industrialized Economies,* pp. 68–69.

51. R. Ram, "Government Size and Economic Growth," *American Economic Review,* Vol. 76, No. 1 (March 1986), cited by Colclough, "Structuralism Cersus Neo-Liberalism," p. 16.

52. For instance, Penrose, "From Economic Liberalisation to International Integration"; Ayubi, "Political Correlates of Privatization Programs in the Middle East," *Arab Studies Quarterly,* Vol. 14 (1992), Nos. 2–3, pp. 39–56; Ayubi, "The 'Fiscal Crisis' and the 'Washington Consensus'"; Stevens, "The Practical Record and Prospects of Privatization Programmes."

53. Ayubi, "The 'Fiscal Crisis' and the 'Washington Consensus,'" pp. 7–8.

54. Stevens, "The Practical Record and Prospects of Privatization Programmes," p. 118.

55. P. Mosley, "Structural Adjustment: A General Overview," in V. Balasubramanyam and S. Lall, eds., *Current Issues in Development Economics* (London: Macmillan, 1991), pp. 223–242: p. 225.

56. Ibid.

57. Ibid., p. 241.

58. Colclough, "Structuralism Versus Neo-Liberalism," p. 13.

59. See D. Seddon, *Free Markets and Food Riots* (Oxford: Blackwell, 1994); D. Pool, "The Links Between Economic and Political Liberalisation," in Niblock and Murphy, *Economic and Political Liberalization in the Middle East,* pp. 40–54; and D. Seddon, "Austerity Protests in Response to Economic Liberalisation in the Middle

East," in ibid., pp. 88–113.

60. See note 39.

61. Wade, "East Asia's Economic Success," p. 275.

62. Weiss and Hobson, *States and Economic Development,* p. 144.

63. See, for instance, Wade, *Governing the Market,* Chapter 10.

64. Weiss and Hobson, *States and Economic Development,* p. 144.

65. Ibid., p. 145.

66. Amsden, *Asia's Next Giant,* p. 141.

67. Ibid., p. 145.

68. Weiss and Hobson, *States and Economic Development,* p. 162.

69. Ibid., p. 169.

70. A. Chowdhury and I. Islam, *The Newly Industrialising Economies of East Asia* (London: Routledge, 1993), p. 42.

71. Ibid., pp. 55–56.

72. This is my interpretation of Woodward's conclusions, rather than his own words. See D. Woodward, *National and International Dimensions of Debt and Adjustment in Developing Countries* (London: Pinter/Save the Children, 1992).

73. In addition to Amsden, and Weiss and Hobson, see also Colclough and Manor, *States or Markets.*

74. R. Wade, in *The Economist,* 4 April 1992, p. 91; id., "East Asia's Economic Success," pp. 317–318 (footnote 93); see also his *Governing the Market.*

75. Wade, "East Asia's Economic Success," p. 275.

76. Ibid., p. 312.

77. The case presented by Lall, as summarized in V. Balasubramanyam and S. Lall, "Introduction and Overview," in Balasubramanyam and Lall, *Current Issues in Development Economics,* pp. 1–9: p. 5.

78. Weiss and Hobson, *States and Economic Development,* p. 253.

79. *The Economist,* 1 June 1991.

80. "State and Market Revisited," *The Economist,* 4 April 1992.

81. J. Sachs, "Trade and Exchange Rate Policies in Growth-Oriented Adjustment Programs," in V. Corbo, M. Goldstein, and M. Khan, eds., *Growth-Oriented Adjustment Programs* (Washington, D.C.: IMF and the World Bank, 1987), pp. 291–325: p. 294.

82. A. Maddison et al., *The Political Economy of Poverty, Equity and Growth: Brazil and Mexico* (New York: Oxford University Press for the World Bank, 1992), pp. 3–10.

83. R. Finlay and S. Wellisz, eds., *The Political Economy of Poverty, Equity and Growth: Five Small Open Economies* (New York: Oxford University Press for the World Bank, 1993), pp. 304–305.

84. The other element of the strategy is "to promote the productive use of the poor's most abundant asset—labor. It calls for policies that harness market incentives, social and political institutions, infrastructure and technology to that end." *World Development Report 1990,* p. 3.

85. *World Development Report 1991,* p. 2.

86. Ibid, p. 5.

87. Ibid., pp. 90–91.

88. Ibid. pp. 10, 138, 147.

89. Ibid., pp. 99–102.

90. Ibid., p. 145.

91. *The East Asian Miracle: A World Bank Policy Research Report* (New York: Oxford University Press for the World Bank, 1993), p. vi.

92. Ibid., p. 6.

93. Ibid., p. 20.
94. *IMF Survey,* 17 April 1995.
95. See *The Guardian Weekly,* 9 April 1995.

2

Patterns of Economic Liberalization: Explanations and Modalities

GERD NONNEMAN

Following the review in Chapter 1 of the debate over the merits of the neoliberal paradigm, this chapter explores possible explanations for its increased acceptance by policy advisers and policymakers, as well as the causes for the variation in extent or manner of its implementation. As I have indicated, the neoliberal policy consensus of the 1980s and early 1990s represented a drastic change from the previous climate, especially that prevailing from the 1950s to the 1970s. Efforts to explain this change in both global and in region-specific terms have multiplied, their relevance heightened by the very contentiousness of economic liberalization as a developmental strategy.

The IMF and the World Bank have been, over the past decade and a half, the most prominent and forceful advocates of liberalization in the developing world—as well as its major enforcers. Yet this in itself is not a sufficient explanation for the emergence of the neoliberal consensus—and certainly not for the sudden increase in its popularity in the late 1980s. Contributing factors range from domestic economic crisis, political upheaval, or the interests of certain classes or groups, to the shifting international context—politically, economically, and intellectually—and the role played by state and nonstate international actors. The case studies in this volume and elsewhere demonstrate that, just as the forms and extent of liberalization programs have varied, so have the combinations of factors underlying their initiation.

Origins and Explanations

Three types of explanations for the spread of the economic-liberalization paradigm have generally been put forward: (1) those focusing on the perceived failure of the previous policies, and/or economic crisis; (2) those referring to the international environment, both economic and intellectual; and (3) those drawing attention to domestic politics.

31

Explanations in the first group have been formulated in ways that vary along with their authors' ideological or academic perspective. The mainstream essentially points to the general failure of the economic development model that prevailed from the 1950s to the 1970s. Others have focused on the "fiscal (or financial) crisis of the state," originating in the impossibility of sustaining import-substituting strategies at the same time as the politically legitimizing imperative of "welfarism," "except in unusual times of exceptional growth and/or availability of liquid capital."[1] This fiscal crisis, of course, could be argued to result precisely from the failure of the previous model. Other commentators have given special weight to the debt crisis that resulted in part from the fiscal crisis and in part from the international conjuncture. These explanations need not be mutually exclusive, and linkages can be perceived between this group and the two other groups of explanations.

The "failure of the model" school takes as its starting point the observation of the failures of many past state-led development efforts, which have usually led to some form of economic crisis. On the basis of neoclassical and neoliberal interpretations, the assumption is that the main reason for these failures was excessive state involvement, and that, consequently, liberalization was the obvious solution. The previous chapter demonstrated that neoliberal precepts have been powerfully challenged. Of importance at this stage, however, is not the objective validity of the liberalization paradigm, but its increasing perceived validity among the relevant political elites. They too have observed previous failures, and could be expected to draw, or be led to draw, similar "obvious" conclusions.

A variant on this theme does not blame previous policies so much for failing altogether as for having become "outdated" at a certain stage of a country's development. Kong in this volume, and Hamilton and Kim in a separate article,[2] suggest an explanation of this kind for South Korea, arguing that it was in part the country's very success that led to domestic as well as international pressures for change.

Many commentators argue that this group of explanations, which stresses the failure or inadequacy of the previous set of policies, is not sufficient—or, more precisely, that it can only be understood in its international context. There is, in this view, "an international context favouring economic liberalisation." Hamilton and Kim, bringing in both the international and the domestic context, summarize their framework for the analysis of the phenomenon of economic liberalization as follows:

> Within a global context of increasing economic integration, the major contextual factor influencing economic integration is the position of a given country within the world economy, including its model of development [outward- or inward-oriented], its level of development, its degree of trade concentration, and the level and type of foreign capital dependence. Major international actors include core state governments, multilateral and uni-

lateral lending agencies, and multinational corporations. Domestic actors include the state, in which different groups or factions may be ascendent; the private sector, which may be divided among pro-liberalisation and anti-liberalisation groups; labour; and other groups affected by the liberalisation process.[3]

This aptly encompasses the categories to be considered below, which also feature in the country studies that follow.

One theoretical perspective on the international context is that "the integrative tendencies in contemporary international capitalism . . . make it increasingly difficult for states to pursue an autonomous form of economic development."[4] Ayubi puts it as follows:

> The integrative tendency of capitalism in its current phase mitigates against national boundaries, in its search for a more "rational" and "profitable" globalization of the production process and the labor market. It is natural under these circumstances that small, late-industrializing economies, over-burdened with accumulating economic and financial problems, would find it difficult to resist the pressures and/or the temptations of contemporary world capitalism in its current globalizing phase. Populist states with declining economic and financial resources are most vulnerable. In conditions of overall contraction, they find it extremely difficult to continue simultaneously with their twin developmentalist and welfarist roles.[5]

What tends to happen as a consequence is viewed, in Ayubi's perspective, not so much as deregulation and withdrawal of the state, but as "a process of *re-regulation* in the direction of increased international competitiveness, which frequently—but not always—includes an important privatization component."[6] This would apply to the cases of Taiwan, Japan, and South Korea, and to the peculiarities of liberalization programs in some other countries. However, in many instances actual liberalization has gone further than this particular interpretation would allow for. In many reform programs deregulation has featured prominently, at least at some stage—explicitly deviating from the East Asian path.

Pressure and influence from the IMF and the World Bank, as well as from other Western creditors and especially the United States, have had an enormous impact. Such pressure might take the form of withdrawal of traditional support, as well as active pressure for reform. Examples of the former are the refusal (and/or inability) of the Soviet Union to continue underwriting the socialist experiments around the world (since the mid-1980s), or France's decision to do likewise in its former African colonies and stop, for instance, supporting the unrealistic exchange rate of the African Franc (finally devalued in 1994). Such actions left these countries little choice but to reform. It is important to distinguish, however, between the factor of pressure on the one hand, and more general influence on the other: They need not always be related. As to the former, it is clear that the more dependent on foreign inputs in finance and technology a country is, the more amenable to such pressure it is likely to be. Debt can function as one important point of pressure.

The debt crisis was referred to earlier as a key component of this international configuration. The double shock of the oil-price increases and the relative world recession drastically exacerbated the difficulties of the developing countries; these difficulties combined with the surplus of petrodollars in the world financial system to produce mounting debts on the part of these countries, in turn worsening their overall status. Niblock and others have argued that it was often specifically this acute indebtedness that allowed the IMF to impose its liberalizing conditions on countries in need of its loans.[7]

It could be pointed out, however, that not all countries that adopted IMF-inspired reforms have been so indebted to the international banking system; the Washington consensus has in fact spread much more widely. (One might also argue that in any case the essential factor was the general financial and developmental crisis resulting from unsustainable policies, that underlay these debts.)

Although such external pressure is an explanatory factor in its own right, it must *itself* be explained at least in part by the contextual picture of domestic economic crisis, and the perception that a new and different approach must be tried. In other words, the "external pressure" and "debt crisis" explanations for the liberalization phenomenon can to some extent be reduced to the first group of explanations—essentially, the apparent failure of the previous development paradigm.

However, this failure *alone* cannot form an adequate explanation for the particular response various states have chosen. Why select the neoliberal prescriptions, rather than, for instance, a "social market" solution—which had after all proved successful in Germany? Why did certain states *not* effectively liberalize? The answer to the latter question lies mainly in the realm of domestic politics, which will be considered later. The particular choice of the neoliberal model is to be explained by a combination of two interrelated factors: (1) the political and intellectual environment of the post–Cold War world; and (2) the influential position of neoliberal economists in senior posts in the Bretton Woods institutions,[8] along with the fact that local economists and decisionmakers were often trained in Western (often U.S.) universities[9] so that, when advice was given and/or pressure applied, it was of the neoliberal variety. At the same time, the collapse of the socialist states, and the liberalization of their political systems, firmly discredited the socialist economic project. This was set against the freedoms and economic success of the Western capitalist states, just as Thatcherism was in its heyday. Fukuyama's phrase, "the end of history," however flawed, did reflect a reality of *perceptions* in both the West and the former socialist states. The perceived utter bankruptcy—economically, politically and morally—of the old systems left little appeal or dynamism for the left in the intellectual contest with the right.[10] China's position in this context was of course different, but there, too, liberalizing measures were inspired at least in part by the example of the results private enterprise (albeit hand in hand with state guidance) was achieving in neighboring Taiwan, Hong Kong, and South Korea.

Many of the policymakers in liberalizing countries wished to move decisively away from the policies they perceived to have failed. Specifically, the introduction of "a little" privatization in an essentially state-controlled and -directed economy did not seem a fertile alternative. The example of the Soviet Union, and the social-market experiment in Hungary, could be interpreted as showing that, unless encompassed in an environment that as a whole is conducive to long-term viable private enterprise, such privatization would have little chance of getting off the ground at all, and that even indirect state control still often results in suboptimal efficiency.[11]

None of this is to argue that pressure based on countries' indebtedness did not play a role (where such indebtedness was a major issue), but it *is* to say that the reason for governments' increased embrace of IMF-style reforms may be based as much on those governments' own conviction of the validity of the IMF's arguments.[12] This would explain why the liberalizing climate has extended beyond the reach of IMF pressures, as demonstrated by governments' genuine enthusiasm in pursuing the prescriptions of the new consensus. Indeed, the IMF Director-General Camdessus, has remarked that "whereas his predecessor had to spend all his time persuading governments to reform, he spends all of his listening to how much they themselves want to change"—and indeed observing several of them moving faster than the IMF had envisaged.[13] The experience of Poland, as described by its reform architect Balcerowicz,[14] confirms the importance of this domestic conviction and initiative, as do the cases of China and, for different reasons, Korea, as described in Chapters 12 and 14.

Both types of explanation—the failure of the model (or domestic economic problems) and the international conjuncture (economic and intellectual)—interlink to form part of the striking liberalizing trend in the late 1980s and early 1990s. The eagerness of key domestic actors themselves to pursue this path might also, however, lend credence to the third type of argument that has been advanced to explain the trend toward liberalization—that of domestic politics.

The category of domestic politics may contain forces both in favor of and against economic liberalization, as has been indicated in the quote by Hamilton and Kim.

How might domestic political forces be ranged behind liberalization? The first variant of this line of reasoning has been formulated most clearly by Niblock with reference to the Middle East (though he has later argued against it).[15]

The revolutionary state established after the demise of colonial rule, the argument runs, is typically transitional. Groups that might want to resist economic liberalization are repressed, while the state bureaucracy that is bred in the context of this state develops its own anti-egalitarian interests and, specifically, accumulates funds for which it begins to look for investment opportunities. This state, therefore,

> is gradually transformed into a bourgeois-bureaucratic state—built on the linked interests of the state bureaucrats and the commercial bourgeoisie, and having a strong interest in opening up the economy and providing opportunities for investment.[16]

Empirical observation, however (especially in the Arab world), indicates that there is not necessarily such a clear distinction between the public and private sectors' interests, because the commercial bourgeoisie is often dependent on the state for protection and opportunities.[17] "The bourgeois-bureaucratic state, in short, does *not* have a strong interest in the structural transformation of the economy; only in a limited opening up of trade and investment opportunities"[18] (emphasis added). The evidence of this is that consistent support for economic liberalization tends to come from a narrow section of the population only, including key decisionmakers.[19] In the case of Egypt, for instance, reform in part reflects pressure from the outside, but equally, Hinnebusch has pointed out, the state "has adopted for its own a semi-liberal project which favours international and at least one wing of domestic capital." This does not mean, however, that reform has grown from the interests of the population at large: "The other condition making for reform is the simultaneous decline in the state's autonomy from international forces and the increase in its internal autonomy of the mass public."[20]

The link between domestic and foreign interests as pictured by the concept of the "comprador bourgeoisie" (a dominant class whose interests are based on cooperation with, and profit in, the external, metropolitan markets, and which has the ability to shape domestic policies accordingly) may seem a tempting explanation for instances of liberalization. Although such dynamics have at times been in evidence, neither the cases studied in this volume nor the majority of the literature suggest that this particular type of explanation is adequate. The mosaic of class interests is generally too complex to allow for such neat dynamics; there is competition between different classes or groups, and different sections of the same class often prove to have varying interests, whether for political or economic reasons, in the short or long term. Moreover, the extent of dominance by the groups labeled "comprador" in the political systems around the world has probably shrunk; if the model were valid, this phenomenon would be inconsistent with the increased liberalization trend of the 1980s and 1990s. Indeed, if comprador dynamics were a significant factor, economic liberalization would long have been a familiar and continuous phenomenon rather than the striking development it is.

Economic self-interest by dominant groups may be one explanatory factor in the adoption of liberalizing measures, but as often as not it is the political interests of the regime (usually fairly narrowly based) that can be served by such measures. Thus, it might be useful to co-opt (or preempt the potential opposition of) the existing commercial bourgeoisie if it is felt to be a potentially useful ally (Syria might be a case in point). Alternatively, the aim may be actually to create a new constituency that will allow the circumvention of existing bases of power (here Iraq's controlled liberalization program of the late 1980s comes to mind).[21] Even though examples of such dynamics can be found, they are not the rule and therefore cannot be considered an essential part of the general explanation—except in their confirmation that the economic-liberalization phenomenon need not be monocausal. In any case, the instances of liberalization based on such domestic dynamics will not usually extend as far as opening the economy up to foreign competition.

Nevertheless, domestic political calculations may lead a regime or a leader to opt for a policy of economic liberalization as a symbol of distance from the preceding regime. It may, in other words, be a way of garnering legitimacy as a "new broom." This would seem to be what South Korea's President Chun had in mind when he introduced reforms reversing some of the measures of his predecessor, Park. Chun's moves were made with an eye on the student demonstrations of 1980, and to an extent represented concessions to their demands. He also was mindful of the fact that, having become president through a coup, he initially had a very narrow constituency.[22]

Finally, it must be remembered that the context in which economic reform was introduced in Eastern Europe and the former Soviet Union was very much a political context. The existing political system had undergone a crisis, and these societies were in a period of what Balcerowicz has called "extraordinary politics."[23] In such circumstances, committed groups of decisionmakers are apparently able to push through quite radical programs that might otherwise not get the necessary popular support or even acquiescence.

The conclusion must be, then, that the key explanatory factors in the wider trend of economic liberalization are the perceived failures of previous development models, in a context of an increasingly internationalized capitalist economy, and the perception on the part of the relevant decisionmakers that an economic policy based on the insights of the Washington consensus was indeed superior. Such factors have, of course, been reinforced and hastened by the leverage and forcefulness of the large Western creditors and the IMF and World Bank, and by the post–Cold War zeitgeist that almost precluded an effective voice for proponents of less liberal economic solutions.

The extent to which these factors worked, in varying combinations, to bring about the liberalization phenomenon of the late 1980s and early 1990s has greatly differed between countries. The country studies in the following chapters make clear that the *kinds* of programs adopted also varied and fluctuated, while in some cases liberalization did not go very far at all.

Limiting Factors: Domestic Politics

The limited willingness of some states to let liberalization proceed freely, and the low success rate of some such limited openings, may be ascribed largely to political factors. These limitations are rooted in (1) specific regime calculations and fears, and (2) investors' perceptions; both derive directly from the political context. The precise dynamics at work depend on the nature of the particular regime. In autocratic regimes with narrowly based ruling groups, the key element is the unwillingness to loosen political control and the consequent reluctance to allow much leeway for significant autonomous economic action. The limitations and contradictions of the economic liberalization measures in Iraq provide a clear illustration of this, as does the case of Syria presented by Hinnebusch in Chapter 8. One particular form of this dynamic of control is rentierism.

The political context in such states also implies that the stage and direction of the development of civil society and the rule of law remain highly uncertain; associated with this is a general lack of political transparency and predictability. Taken together, these characteristics deter domestic and foreign investors alike, even where limited opportunities for such investment *are* offered. The virtual failure of Iraq's drive to attract Gulf investment in the late 1980s must be explained in these terms.[24] Investor confidence is further eroded by the possibility, in a political context of this nature, of sudden upheaval.

These regimes share a further consideration with other, more widely based regimes: Most tend to fear the social (and hence political) consequences of sudden economic reforms. Their fears are justified by the riots and political tensions that in several countries have followed, for instance, the inevitable price rises, especially when these extended to staple foods.[25] It is the recognition that this is a genuine problem that has led to the recent reappraisal by the IMF and the World Bank of the usefulness and desirability of providing adequate safety nets, and of poverty-reducing measures in general.

The rentier state argument referred to earlier describes another dynamic that may cause a regime to limit the extent of economic liberalization. This argument holds that in states in which the main source of revenue is derived from outside the domestic economy (e.g., from aid, or from the sell-off of oil reserves), the essence of the economy and the political system becomes one of getting access to the circulation of this rent (from the viewpoint of the population), and allocating it for purposes of political stability (from the viewpoint of the rulers).[26] In developing states in which the politics of rentierism has become part and parcel of the system's dynamics (the rich oil producers would be an obvious example, but such rent has spread much more widely, from them and from other sources), these dynamics and the regime's calculations are also likely to inhibit far-reaching liberalization.

Not only will those parts of the population (including a state-dependent private sector) that benefit from the allocation of such rent resist drastic change, but the regime itself is unlikely to let go easily of the means of power and patronage that a politically stabilizing allocation system affords it. The imperative of distribution and control over the rent circuit may therefore remain more important than that of efficiency and productivity. Even if one does not subscribe to the rentier argument in full, there is no denying that state apparatuses and public bureaucracies, especially in developing countries, are often used as much as "sponge employers" for sociopolitical reasons and for engendering the dependence of their employees, as for their official purposes. The option of slimming down the public sector therefore becomes politically loaded, implying socially and politically destabilizing unemployment and a loss of regime control. In the end the outcome will depend on the available resources and on their balance with increasing demands. The skillful allocation of rent is likely to become insufficient to maintain Huntington's "performance legitimacy" even in such extreme examples as the rich Gulf states. At that point the imperative for even these countries to disassociate the state from lackluster economic performance may put them on the way to some kind of economic liberalization.

It is not just the regime or the state that may harbor obstacles to liberalization: Important groups within society may also resist it. Where state institutions have not been discredited, labor may resist deregulation of the labor market as well as the lifting of protection on domestic industry; the latter may also be resisted by domestic manufacturers; landowners and farming interests are likely to resist reducing protection (where it exists) of the farming sector (for example, resistance to change in the European Union's Common Agricultural Policy). Such resistance from various groups—whether within or outside the regime's structures—will not be uniform, however. The often contradictory efforts will target different elements of liberalization programs: Some groups may favor privatization while opposing the liberalization of foreign trade, for instance, thus clashing with the interests of other exporters and importers.

Conditions for Successful Reform?

Where attempts at thoroughgoing reform *have* been made, the rate of success or failure has varied greatly. As pointed out earlier, many of the reform programs introduced before the second half of the 1980s were either not actually implemented or only patchily so. Sometimes this was due to the kind of political considerations outlined above; sometimes to serious problems inherent in the environment and circumstances of the country concerned. Krueger, for instance, studied various attempts in ten countries between 1950 and 1972; the only wholly successful case was that of South

Korea.[27] What lies behind this variation? What are the prerequisites for successful implementation of economic liberalization programs? Some of the answers have already emerged in this chapter, but it is worth lifting out a few specific elements that are confirmed by some of the country chapters in this book as well as by other studies.[28]

The first condition of successful reform is political stability. Without this the benefits of liberalization (such as investor confidence) are unlikely to materialize, nor may there be the will to push reforms through. This would indicate that politically destabilizing reforms—however sound in economic theory—would be counterproductive. Instability would also tend to reduce the extent to which the institutions of the state and the market can function. The existence of adequate institutions for the safeguarding of the rule of law, the protection of private property, and the regulation of the market is another crucial prerequisite for successful liberalizing reforms. In apparently paradoxical terms, therefore, a strong state and regime, whether authoritarian or democratic, are much more likely to carry through economic reform than an undeveloped, truly minimal, or unstable political and state system.

If these conditions are fulfilled, a number of further conditions (not in any particular order of importance) also seem highly relevant.

The existence (or otherwise) and nature of the middle class is an important determinant. If an entrepreneurial middle class exists, the next question is how dependent it is on state patronage, as discussed in the previous section. This often ties in with another factor, namely the extent of the country's history of private, capitalistic activity. This seems to have been important, for instance, in the revival of such activity in China's Special Economic Zones (see Chapter 15).

Another condition pertains to the available resources—natural, technical, and human. As Colclough puts it, "Introducing a liberal regime in the context of impoverishment is very different from a setting (or early prospect) of dynamic growth."[29] Indeed, the problems of vulnerable groups would then be likely to be much higher, and the difficulty of avoiding political problems and potential upheaval much greater. Similarly, a context in which great inequality prevails—which in itself has now been recognized by the mainstream (as represented by the World Bank) as a brake on growth—will also make the adoption of liberalizing reforms without compensatory programs much more politically and socially unsettling. If reforms end up increasing such inequality they will be counterproductive in terms of long-term growth. For liberalizing structural reforms to succeed in such circumstances, they must be designed in tandem with programs to protect the most vulnerable (through social safety nets), and to reduce inequality (through basic services, education, and possibly land reform, among other measures). The question of available resources is also relevant to one of the usual aims of liberalization: the mobilization of available domestic private capital.

This discussion also indicates a further crucial factor: Political acceptance must be acquired for the reform program. This acceptance might result from one or a combination of the following: a crisis ("extraordinary politics"); a new, popularly supported regime's "honeymoon"; effective selling of the program by the government and the reformers; measures to win the support or acquiescence of influential groups in society; and the protection of those potentially most vulnerable to the effects of the liberalization program.

There is a consensus, also, about the need for the reforming country to "own" its program: It should as far as possible be designed by, or with the full involvement of, local economists and decisionmakers. This will improve both the commitment to carry it through and the chances of its political acceptance. From the results of a wide-ranging collaborative study project on the political conditions for successful economic reform, Williamson and Haggard also conclude that of major importance are (1) a leadership with a clear vision, able and willing to look beyond short-term political sensitivities; and (2) a strong, coherent group of reformers behind the reforms.[30]

If none or very few of these conditions are fulfilled, external aid in support of a reform program is probably pointless; but where the country rates better in respect to the above determinants, and especially when the reforms emerge from a financial crisis, such aid can be very helpful. It can smooth over initial financial and debt problems and help supporters of reform win the day over their opponents (one such example being Poland, as confirmed by the architect of that country's reform plan).

The chances of a reform program's success, therefore, seem to depend very much on whether the attempted reforms were appropriate to the particular situation in the first place. "Fully robust empirical generalisations" on the conditions for success, as Williamson and Haggard also confirm, are not possible. The same is true for the content, speed, and extent of the program itself: "The important element is not simply whether a program is rapid or comprehensive, but whether it is appropriate to the needs of the situation."[31]

Is an authoritarian regime a prerequisite for successful implementation of an economic liberalization program? A number of academic and other commentators have suggested that this may be the case, and a similar impression may also be given by some of the material in this book. Such an impression would be erroneous. Much depends on the *degree* of authoritarianism, on the regime's other features, and on other contextual factors. The record, in any case, demonstrates that democratic government is not an obstacle to success: "Profound economic reforms have been accomplished by democratic governments, even those in a simultaneous transition from authoritarianism."[32] This conclusion can be illustrated by, among others, the

Polish case as depicted by Gowan and Day in Chapters 4 and 5. At the same time, the evidence of authoritarian regimes around the world shows that the dynamics of autocracy, though they do not rule out some economic liberalization, tend to imply severe limits on its extent.

Notes

1. N. Ayubi, "The 'Fiscal Crisis' and the 'Washington consensus': Towards an Explanation of Middle East Liberalisations," in L. Blin and F. Clément, eds., *L'Economie Egyptienne: Libéralisation et Insertion dans le Marché Mondial* (Paris: L'Harmattan, 1993) [pre-publication manuscript obtained from the author, mimeographed; page references refer to this version], p. 9. See also R. Owen, *State, Power and Politics in the Making of the Modern Middle East* (London: Routledge, 1992), p. 140.

2. N. Hamilton and E. Kim, "Economic and political liberalisation in South Korea and Mexico," *Third World Quarterly,* Vol. 14, No. 1 (1993), pp. 109–136.

3. Ibid., p. 111.

4. T. Niblock, "International and domestic factors in the economic liberalisation process in Arab countries," in T. Niblock and E. Murphy, eds., *Economic and Political Liberalisation in the Middle East* (London: British Academic Press, 1993), pp. 55–87: p. 56.

5. Ayubi, "Political correlates of privatization programs in the Middle East," *Arab Studies Quarterly,* Vol. 14 (1992), Nos. 2–3, pp. 39–56: p. 40.

6. Ibid.

7. Niblock, "International and domestic factors."

8. For instance, Balassa, Berg, Krueger, and Lal.

9. On this, and generally the intellectual influences, see J. Williamson and S. Haggard, "The political conditions for policy reform," in Williamson, ed., *The Political Economy of Policy Reform* (Washington, D.C.: Institute for International Economics, 1994), pp. 257–296.

10. This was forcefully argued by Maurice Glassman, in "Unnecessary Suffering: Why Was the Social Market Ignored in Europe?" paper presented to the Political Economy Seminars series, Lancaster University, 25 April 1995. He argues that Poland had all the makings of a state and society suited to the social market, and that only this overwhelming intellectual climate could explain the actual path chosen.

11. See S. Estrin, "Privatisation in Central and Eastern Europe," RUSEL Working Paper No. 4 (Exeter: RUSEL, Exeter University, 1991), p. 5.

12. H. Bienen and J. Waterbury, in their "The Political Economy of Privatization in Developing Countries," in C. Wilber and K. Jameson, *The Political Economy of Development and Underdevelopment,* fifth edition (New York/Singapore: McGraw Hill, 1992) pp. 376–402, also stress that the impetus for privatization in LDCs is as much an *internal* recognition of the failings of public enterprises as it is external pressure.

13. "Sisters in the Wood: A survey of the IMF and the World Bank," *The Economist,* 12 October 1991, p. 47.

14. He stresses that, although there was external pressure, this was more important for giving the reformers the wherewithal to keep their opponents at bay than for imposing the reforms in the first place. The group of technocrat reformers, conversant with neoclassical economics, were themselves wholly convinced of the urgency

of implementing these measures. See L. Balcerowicz, "Poland," in J. Williamson, ed., *The Political Economy of Policy Reform,* pp. 153–177.

15. T. Niblock, "The State of the Art in British Middle Eastern Studies," in T. Ismael, ed., *Middle Eastern Studies: International Perspectives on the State of the Art,* New York: Praeger, 1989) summarized and argued against in Niblock, "International and Domestic Factors."

16. Niblock, "International and Domestic Factors," p. 57.

17. See J. Waterbury, "Twilight of the State Bourgeoisie?" *International Journal of Middle Eastern Studies,* Vol. 23 (1991), pp. 1–17; Ayubi, "Political Correlates"; and Niblock, "International and Domestic Factors."

18. Niblock, "International and domestic factors," p. 57.

19. See, for instance, Bienen and Waterbury, "The Political Economy of Privatization."

20. R. Hinnebusch, "The Politics of Economic Reform in Egypt," *Third World Quarterly,* Vol. 14 (1993), No. 1, pp. 159–171: p. 170.

21. See I. al-Khafaji, "State Incubation of Iraqi Capitalism," *MERIP Middle East Report,* September 1986, pp. 4–9, 12.

22. See Chapter 12 in this volume, as well as Hamilton and Kim, "Economic and Political Liberalisation in South Korea and Mexico," p. 117.

23. Balcerowicz, "Poland."

24. See G. Nonneman and A. Ehteshami, *War and Peace in the Gulf* (Reading: Ithaca Press, 1991), p. 71.

25. See D. Seddon, *Free Markets and Food Riots* (Oxford: Blackwell, 1994); D. Pool, "The Links Between Economic and Political Liberalisation," in Niblock and Murphy, *Economic and Political Liberalization in the Middle East,* pp. 40–54; and D. Seddon, "Austerity Protests in Response to Economic Liberalisation in the Middle East," in ibid., pp. 88–113.

26. See G. Luciani, "Allocation vs. Production States: A Theoretical Framework," in Luciani, ed., *The Arab State* (London: Routledge, 1990), pp. 65–84.

27. A. Krueger, *Foreign Trade Regimes and Economic Development* (Cambridge, Mass.: Ballinger, 1978).

28. Especially Williamson, ed., *The Political Economy of Policy Reform,* and the studies collected therein, particularly Williamson and Haggard, "The Political Conditions for Policy Reform," pp. 527–596, which provides an extensive and thoughtful overview of a number of these conditions for success, along with a useful summary of individual country experiences.

29. C. Colclough, "Structuralism Versus Neo-Liberalism: An Introduction," in C. Colclough and J. Manor, eds., *States or Markets? Neo-liberalism and the Development Policy Debate* (Oxford: Clarendon Press, 1991), pp. 1–25.

30. Williamson and Haggard, "The Political Conditions for Policy Reform," pp. 577–579.

31. Ibid., pp. 562–589.

32. This is one of the "firm conclusions" of Williamson and Haggard's comparative project. See ibid., p. 592.

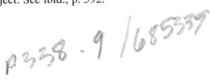

3

Patterns of Political Liberalization: Explanations and Modalities

GERD NONNEMAN

Definitions and Concepts

The term "political liberalization" used in the title of this book is meant to encompass any movement or development from a system with less popular participation, or less accountability, to one with more of either. It might be rephrased as "the shift away from autocracy or authoritarianism." It includes, therefore, both democratization—the transition toward a democratic system—and less thoroughgoing measures to loosen some political controls or grant more rights. Many would reserve the term political liberalization for the latter, more limited process. When the term is used in the remainder of this volume it will be in the more general sense, except where explicitly chosen in contrast with democratization.

Democracy and democratization are themselves less than straightforward terms. If democratization is the process of transition toward democracy, then what precisely is democracy? One answer would identify it with liberal democracy, as practiced in the "liberal democracies" of the Western world and elsewhere, with functioning political parties able to compete for the population's votes in regular general elections for a legislative assembly. Two problems arise here. The first is that those forms may be officially employed, but in such a fashion and under such conditions that the intended aim of genuine accountability and popular participation remains unfulfilled. Examples of this abound: it was precisely such a situation that enabled Alberto Fujimori in Peru not only to gain power but then to destroy, with popular support, the old democratic structures. The second is that the actual aims of participation and/or accountability may conceivably be reached through other means. "Direct democracy" through referenda, people's councils, or some form of telecommunications or cybertechnology are some of the variants that come to mind, along with traditional systems of consultation, tribal or otherwise. Pinkney, for instance, distilled five main ideal types

45

of democracy from the existing literature: radical democracy (focusing on the rights and interests of individuals); guided democracy (where the state is meant to assure the achievement of the general will); socialist democracy (equally guided, but with the focus on equality and social justice); consociational democracy (which aims at consensus between, and representation of, different groups); and finally liberal democracy (where the representation and protection of diverse individual and group interests is the aim).[1] This list again illustrates the problematic nature of the field: Not only is it less than complete, but there will be questions as to the guided and socialist types' democratic credentials.

A variety of definitions has been put forward (varying, among other things, by type of democracy described), some concentrating on the necessary institutions, some on the essence of widening political participation from small ruling groups—or indeed individuals—and potentially arbitrary rule, to the population at large. This may be achieved through continuous active participation, or via a system of accountability in which the governed periodically judge the performance of the governor.[2]

Regardless of the precise form or institutions, the essential formula for the purposes of this volume is precisely that laid out at the opening of this chapter. If the development ("transition") toward such a system is far enough advanced to have become not easily reversible, it is often termed "consolidation." This is not to say that a consolidated democracy is unchangeable—or that it may not in some circumstances be swept away again by an undemocratic system. But, as Barrington Moore recognized, democracy is in any case a continuing, incomplete process—even if certain principles within it are accepted and anchored in institutions.[3]

Whatever the precise shape or content of "democracy," "participatory politics," or "political accountability," it is recognizably distinct from a situation in which a narrow ruling group or individual maintains the reins of power essentially uncontested by the governed, but "opens up" the system from above, grants some rights, and perhaps consults appointed "representatives." Such a scenario would be covered by the narrower definition of political liberalization. At the same time, the more liberalized end of this spectrum may begin to blur into the less developed end of the "democratic" spectrum—where, for instance, elected assemblies with little legislative power are able gradually to assert themselves more powerfully. The dividing line would perhaps have to be drawn on the basis of whether or not the ruling group or individual retains the realistic ability to suspend any such representative body and practices at will.

This book is concerned with both phenomena in all their variations, recognizing that liberalization in the strict sense is a necessary condition or element of democratization, and that it may itself sometimes lead to the latter.

Origins, Conditions, and Explanations

Political liberalization in both its limited and its broader sense has been very much in evidence in the past twenty years or so. After the democratic changes in southern Europe (Greece, Portugal, Spain), the most striking example was the opening up of the political systems of the Soviet Union and Eastern Europe in the late 1980s and early 1990s, but the phenomenon has been almost worldwide—though it remains far from complete, and the level of liberalization has varied greatly. In Latin America authoritarian regimes have been giving way to more democratic successors since the 1970s.[4] More recently a wave of political liberalization has swept over sub-Saharan Africa—the case of South Africa being only the most remarkable. In Asia, too, regimes have opened up (Thailand, the Philippines, Taiwan, and even Singapore, for example), and even in the Middle East and North Africa elements of democratic life have gradually been emerging—although this particular region remains perhaps a better illustration of the obstacles the process can encounter. It is not surprising that, especially since the events in Eastern Europe, there have been renewed attempts to analyze the phenomenon, to discover the possible preconditions for such dramatic shifts away from authoritarianism, and to explain the striking similarity of the forms of democratization encountered (largely on liberal democratic lines). The focus of the book and this chapter is on the waves of political liberalization of the last two decades (rather than the early democracies of Europe and the United States), and especially of the 1980s and 1990s in the Third World and Eastern Europe.

The Issue of Explanation

It is ironic that the surge of liberalization in recent years has led to less, rather than more confidence in political scientists' understanding of the phenomenon. Although a possible collapse of these systems had been the subject of some speculation since the late 1970s, hardly anyone had foreseen the speed, timing, and nature of the changes that took place in Eastern Europe; old models therefore seemed to have lost credibility. Moreover, these Eastern European states were not the "developing states" that had traditionally been studied through modernization theory.[5] Neither this theory nor, for most, Marxist analysis, appeared fruitful avenues any longer—at least not if the aim was to find a general theory of democratization or of transition. A variety of approaches has been attempted, but clear conclusions of worldwide applicability are proving elusive. As Parry and Moran point out, "despite a generation's systematic social science research we now seem less certain than ever about how to create and sustain democratic political institutions."[6] Although some themes are emerging that seem of general relevance, such as that of civil society, not only is there a variety of sometimes incompatible theories and approaches, but the one conclusion that can be drawn is that different dynamics may be involved in different countries, let alone in different regions.

There may be a thirst for explanation but such explanation is proving a problematic endeavor. This is partly due to the inherent nature of political science: It can never be an exact science, based on absolute laws. Not only are regularities in human and societal behavior less lawlike than is necessary for building a general and absolute explanatory model, but the number of such regularities as can be observed is inevitably small—the (incomplete) historical record being their only source.[7]

This need not mean that it is futile to try to determine the dynamics at work in different cases, and whether some might recur more often than others. Edwards, in a sharp critique of virtually all efforts to explain democratization so far, virtually dismisses "empiricist" attempts to arrive at general models by cross-country evidence, defining the problem as follows: "The empiricist has to choose between a strong requirement for necessity and sufficiency which will prove impossible to satisfy, and a weaker sense that will not provide the sort of knowledge desired."[8] On the other hand, he finds the "realist response" equally inadequate. This response, comments Edwards, posits that "in so far as democratisation is a prime example of a complex conjunctural causation within an open system . . . cannot plausibly be explained as a general phenomenon. . . . [The implication of this is that] no general explanation of democracy will be provided."[9] In fact, however, the divide described by Edwards need not be (and indeed *is* not) so extreme; moreover his criticism of attempts at explanation and prediction is somewhat overdrawn. Pridham and Vanhanen, faced with the varying findings in their edited volume on democratization in Eastern Europe, and the difficulty of arriving at a list of agreed and generally valid explanations, conclude that

> universal, regional, and local explanations do not necessarily contradict each other, because universal factors and hypotheses may explain one area of the variation in democratization, regional factors and hypotheses another, and various local and historical factors and hypotheses a different part of variation. The basic problem is that we cannot be sure precisely how much of the variation in democratization has been explained by certain hypotheses and factors because most variables used . . . are qualitative. This means that we are restricted in measuring the relative significance of different explanatory variables and the explanatory power of different hypotheses. Only rough estimations are possible. Besides a part of variation in democratization ultimately remains unexplained for the simple reason that random factors always play a role in politics.[10]

The findings of previous studies and in the chapters of this book can only be qualified explanations, in the sense of a twofold recognition: first that they are rough estimates, the validity and relative combinations of which will vary from case to case and from region to region; and second, that those engaged in such explanation often ask their questions (and may arrive at different answers) on the basis of usually unspoken qualifiers, "imposed by pre-theoretical commitments"[11] and underlying axioms (such as Marxist-materialism, or modernization theory).

Qualified Findings

From the evidence of the case studies in this volume, as well as the literature that has accumulated on the subject particularly since the late 1980s, four groups of conditions emerge that help explain the phenomenon of political liberalization (including democratization). The first category is the presence of appropriate structural conditions in the country or society concerned (relating to economic development, technology and education, the [re]creation of civil society, the position of the middle class, etc.).[12] The second refers, broadly, to a supportive international environment[13] (including political acts by outsiders, inducements, examples, conditionality, and the intellectual climate). To these two, broadly "domestic" and "external," groups must be added two less measurable or predictable categories. The third category is that of the historical background, which will almost by definition be different for each case (including experience of social organization, of external domination, of particular events, or of particular ideologies). The fourth is a catch-all category of accidental or conjunctural factors other than the ones already subsumed in the above categories. It must be noted that the factors, events, or forces covered by any of these groups are not necessarily isolated to one group; the different groups, and the varying combinations of factors, interact to varying degrees. The above categorization therefore is mainly a matter of intellectual convenience (as are most other categorizations found in the literature).

A brief overview of some of these factors is offered below. They concern the *initiation* of the process of liberalization and democratization (why it occurred, in whatever form). Those factors that may be specifically involved in determining the *type* or *extent* of the liberalization process will be referred to in the following section; those that help explain the limitations of, and obstacles to, political liberalization and democratization in some cases are covered in the final section. Again, however, there exists a large overlap between the latter two areas of explanation and the groups of factors summarized above.

That domestic and external factors cannot be neatly disengaged is immediately obvious when one considers the first important set of factors: the (varying and interrelated) combination of globalization, technological developments, and economic development. Information technology, the role of the mass media (both international and domestic),[14] the spread and increased sophistication of education, the changing dynamics involved in developing economies, and the inexorably increasing integration of the

world economy have all tended to nudge systems toward, or to open opportunities for, political liberalization and democratization. Commenting on the
case of Eastern Europe, Pridham and Vanhanen conclude that

> the most fundamental causes of democratization . . . can probably be traced
> to technological inventions that changed social conditions and structures,
> i.e., the domestic and international environment of the communist systems.
> The regimes were ultimately unable to control the consequences of tech-
> nological change [that] . . . created new forms of wealth and furthered the
> spread of education and knowledge. Economic and intellectual resources
> became more widely distributed within societies, and it became increas-
> ingly difficult for governments to control people's activities and ideas
> effectively.[15]

Vanhanen and Kimber's "distribution of power resources" in society, which,
if spread sufficiently widely, helps explain democratization,[16] is related to
this technological evolution as well as to economic development. One example of economic development, and the success of authoritarian industrialization, leading to increased power and autonomy of nonstate actors is supplied
by the large industrial conglomerates (*chaebol*) in South Korea
(see Chapter 12). These, along with other developing forces in society (students, workers, etc.), acquired both the desire and the ability to press for
political (as well as a degree of economic) liberalization. It is more economic *change* than economic growth or expansion per se that is of key
importance here. Lipset's identification of the latter as a factor in the growth
of democracy is based on a different argument, which is in any case less than
convincing as a stand-alone explanation. In essence he argues that the
greater wealth that comes with economic development reduces the fierce-
ness of competition for resources, thereby allowing a more consensual and
peaceful form of politics to develop.[17] Increased wealth, by itself, can in fact
sometimes have the effect of impeding democratic development. It is only
through the change-inducing aspects of economic and other development
that the dynamics referred to earlier can come into play. As Pinkney has put
it:

> Economic changes, whether in the direction of industrialization, austerity,
> structural change or collapse, are likely to disturb current political arrange-
> ments. If a democratic government is already in place it will face the strain
> but, if the current rulers are authoritarian it may be their power base that is
> undermined as old centres of power crumble as groups outside the elite
> acquire new or additional resources, whether in terms of economic sanc-
> tions, organizational ability or increased support from key elements in
> society. This does not pave the way for an inevitable transition to democ-
> racy, but it creates opportunities that would not exist if the economy had
> remained static.[18]

What these kinds of dynamics entail is the (re)emergence of civil society, through the intrinsically linked processes of a wider distribution of power resources on the one hand, and the undermining of existing power structures on the other. This is perhaps the most widely accepted condition for the more advanced forms of political liberalization, and certainly for democratization.[19] Once such autonomous expression and organization have a chance to form and assert themselves—whether as a result of those processes or specifically of limited liberalization measures by an authoritarian regime—they often grow into a powerful force for further change. This was true in South Korea,[20] in Eastern Europe (Poland, Albania, Romania, Czechoslovakia, and elsewhere),[21] and to some extent in Latin America.[22]

The expression of civil society can come in a variety of ways. A growing middle class with increased autonomy and expectations is one of these. It is of course the middle class (or more precisely the bourgeoisie) that has been associated historically with Western evolution toward liberal democracies; this is the centerpiece of Moore's analysis of the genesis of democracy in Europe and the United States.[23] None of this is to claim that there is a clear and one-directional line of causation from economic development to political liberalization. Indeed, it can be argued that some key economic changes (such as the industrial revolution in Europe) could in part be explained by political circumstances (such as the economic weakening of the aristocracy through war).[24] The term "middle class" is vague and can cover a variety of meanings; thus, some types or segments of a middle class may be state-dependent and therefore less inclined and able to press for liberalization; and some—whether state-dependent or not—may be unwilling to press for the depth of liberalization that would bring in the potentially conflicting interests and demands of the working class.

Aside from this particular category, other cases of autonomous expression include both such expression and organization *within* the structures or orbit of authoritarian regimes (in part brought about by the processes summarized earlier), and instances of counterculture—expression and organization quite outside the system and society created by such regimes. Examples of the former would be the increasingly autonomous debate within the mass organizations of Eastern Europe's Communist structures, or the residual autonomy of the Catholic Church in Poland. Instances of the second type are the counterculture of the youth movements in Hungary, Czechoslovakia, and East Germany; Charter 77 in Czechoslovakia; and the trade union Solidarity in Poland.[25] Even in the notoriously undemocratic environment of the Middle East, such expression is increasingly a force to be reckoned with.[26]

The account by Gowan of the Polish experience in Chapter 4 demonstrates, however, that the re-emergence of civil society cannot be the whole story. There are two sides to his argument. On the one hand, not all expressions of civil society, nor all internal debate within the Communist structures, had been wholly eradicated; on the other hand, the crisis for these regimes came at a time of (and must be partly explained by) increasing divisions and weakness within themselves. Such weaknesses can be traced back to the technological and economic changes referred to earlier, but they are also linked with external factors. This can be reconciled with Waller's interpretation that some of these weaknesses were inherent in the Communist (and presumably other autocratic) systems:

> The collapse of the communist system in both the Soviet Union and Eastern Europe revealed the extent to which that system was beset with problems in information flows. Viewed in systemic terms, the power monopoly was choking off inputs of information, whilst generating its own messages within the core system. The result was oversteering; the centre put out ill-informed decisions, and equipped itself with the means of enforcing these decisions regardless of their social efficacy or their acceptability to the population.[27]

Given the domestic and international changes in the environment discussed earlier, it was perhaps inevitable that "the absence of democracy quite simply brought collapse."[28]

Just as in the discussion of the dynamics of economic liberalization, the factor of economic nonperformance or crisis must also be reckoned with, in part because this is one special subtype of the "economic change" factor discussed earlier; it may contribute to a change in the relative distribution of power resources, and thereby disrupt established power structures. In addition it may force the regime to allow some political liberalization in order to soften resulting political discontent (as in the case of Algeria and in much of Eastern Europe). Finally, and more dramatically, when the total collapse of the totalitarian economic system, accompanied by other contextual factors, discredits and effectively sweeps away the existing regime, a sharp turn toward a more open political system (however ill-defined or qualified) appears inevitable. This was the pattern in the Soviet Union and most of Eastern Europe; in the present volume the case of Albania is instructive in this respect.

An authoritarian regime's interest in allowing some liberalization—or "decompression"—as in the above context, is an example of the political conditions for liberalization. It is a conscious decision by the regime or the elite itself to institute such measures, for a range of political calculations. If such liberalization from above is combined with pressures from below (civil society), this may lead to more far-reaching liberalization and democratization,[29] but the regime's *intention* generally is to maintain the essential controls itself. In a context of economic hardship or increased international exposure to ideas, a selection of liberalizing measures may aim at legitimizing the regime. In the context of the Middle East, for instance, Pool writes:

> The sequence is one of economic crisis . . . , the introduction of economic reforms, and a process of political reforms involving new constitutions and electoral and party laws, which permit the registration of opposition polit-

ical parties, and seem to have the goal of legitimating new leaders and/or reforms, as well as diffusing opposition.[30]

One specific reason for introducing limited political liberalization, then, may be as a means for economic reformers to push through their reforms against the opposition of antireform factions within the regime. This appears to have been a factor in the political liberalization in Algeria (see Chapter 11), as well as, to varying degrees, in Egypt, Jordan, and Tunisia.[31]

External factors, which have already featured in the discussion, are also of major importance. The increasing globalization of political and economic life, referred to earlier, is one such factor. Another is the zeitgeist or intellectual climate—itself a result of the perceived failures of totalitarianism and the successes of Western-style democratic systems—which feeds into and is fed by such globalization. The world, in short, has become much more interdependent, and, as Ionescu and others have pointed out, this has made it more difficult for states, or more precisely regimes, to opt for deviance. In the climate of the 1980s and 1990s it has become increasingly difficult to resist at least pretending to join the trend toward democratization (and even pretend gestures may develop their own momentum, as argued earlier).[32] Specifically, the increasing integration of the world market, and authoritarian states' own resulting interests, meant that in most cases

> the autarky of the system had to give way to an opening to the world market. This affected indirectly the question of democracy in numerous ways: the image of [these] . . . governments became important . . . ; this affected policing and conformity with international agreements (on human rights for example); exit could no longer be denied to people, just as goods . . . had to be allowed to flow across the frontier.[33]

The examples of Korea and Mexico are instructive here.[34] In Korea, hopes of hosting the Olympic Games in 1988 would have been dashed by harsh reprisals against the student demonstrations, and in the end the regime gave in to some central demands. In Mexico the lead-up to the signing of the NAFTA agreement also brought increased international attention to bear on the country.

Beyond this general international integration and climate, specific external events and pressures also played a major role in a number of instances of political liberalization. In the case of Eastern European states in the orbit of the Soviet Union, the latter's withdrawal, under Gorbachev, of support for these regimes was obviously a crucial factor. To various degrees this also played a role throughout the erstwhile Soviet clients or protégés in the Third World. The examples of Syria, South Yemen,[35] and a number of sub-Saharan states come to mind. In the case of Poland, the role played by the Vatican (see Chapter 4) was significant (although this role very much tied in with the particular domestic context of the country).

Pressures by international institutions and individual countries (for instance, the United States) were also, here as for economic liberalization, of major importance. Hyde-Price, commenting on the case of Eastern Europe, finds that especially the European Community, the CSCE, and the Council of Europe played a role in encouraging the region's transition toward democracy.[36] The role of the EC in particular can be viewed as twofold: On the one hand there was explicit as well as implied pressure from the EC and its member states; on the other hand, and equally importantly, there was these states' own desire—once the old regimes had collapsed—to become associated with, and part of, the EC.[37] Selective U.S. support for democratization around the world, through conditionality in aid and economic agreements, is well attested to; Washington also supported the liberalization of the political system in South Korea, for instance, although such support was as much reactive as initiating. France's role in the wave of political liberalization in francophone sub-Saharan Africa since the late 1980s, after decades of support for the authoritarian regimes of these states, equally proved of crucial importance. Such interventions, however, must perhaps themselves be seen in the context of a changing international climate, which involved the recognition that there were more than moral advantages to political liberalization—whether they be the longer-term interests of France in Africa, or the avoidance of state collapse under autocratic mismanagement. This view is confirmed by the incorporation of the conditions of open and accountable government, and respect for the rule of law and human rights, into the concept of "good governance" the World Bank has since the late 1980s increasingly introduced as a condition for some of its assistance (the other component is, of course, sound economic policies).

In introducing this section, conjunctural or accidental and historical factors were also listed as important categories of determinants. Some of the external events and interventions may serve as examples of these: The election of a Polish pope can hardly fit into a general predictive model. Neither can the decisions of leaders such as Gorbachev, or domestic figures such as King Juan Carlos in Spain. Other possible examples include a natural disaster that either worsens economic conditions and/or necessitates foreign assistance. Country-specific conditions also may not fit easily into any general framework: Abundant resources may create exceptional dynamics (one possible example being the Gulf oil states); so could cultural characteristics, such as an Islamic ethos in the Middle East that may in certain circumstances militate against the implementation of democratizing reforms. (It will be pointed out later that where this is so, it is in fact very much the result of those political and historical circumstances rather than inherent in the faith.)

Historical factors are almost by definition country- or region-specific. The legacy of previous political traditions and systems, both indigenous and introduced from outside, is likely to influence the direction of developments;

so will the effect of a society's previous experience with outside actors and their ideologies, or with previous domestic models. For instance, Pinkney has attempted to set out the potential differentiating implication for democracy of variations in colonial rule.[38] He suggests that colonization in the pre-democratic era is likely to have left the colony without democratic foundations (as in Latin America), whereas later colonization by democratic powers of some description may imply that democracy is seen as the ultimate destination (as in India and Africa). He further suggests that democratic legitimacy may be more difficult to establish depending on the depth, and especially the destructiveness, of the colonial penetration. Settler colonialism may mean the settlers later resist majority rule. On the other hand, if there is an attempt at assimilation between colonizers and colonized, nationalism may be blunted and opportunities for consensus (and hence potentially democratic politics) may emerge. Yet history, it must be stressed, is not deterministic; it forms only part of the overall context.

Factors Influencing Processes and Types of Political Liberalization

The extent and type of political liberalization (including whether or how democratization reaches the stage of consolidation) have been influenced by a number of factors, varying from case to case and including, again, both domestic forces and structures, and external actors and influences—as well as conjunctural and historical factors.

The extent to which civil society has been effaced, and the degree to which it has been able to re-emerge (or perhaps, in the case of Russia, for example, emerge in the first place), will influence the extent and shape of the process. In the same vein, the existence, strength, and role of various groups in society (organized or otherwise; parties, associations, movements, etc.) will affect the process's nature and outcome.[39] The precise result of this is by no means predictable—although in general most instances observed so far have evolved in the direction of liberal democratic institutions. Some would argue that the reason for this is that, in practice, the liberal democratic model has proved to be the only realistic model available.[40] This is perhaps only, or especially, true in the context of the increasingly interdependent world as highlighted in the previous section, including the intellectual climate in favor of democratization, and of this model in particular. It seems to an extent to parallel the choice of the neoliberal model in economics.

The factor of the intellectual climate, or political psychology, may also work in a less clear-cut manner. For instance, Ionescu suggests that some of the apparent lack of enthusiasm to be found in Eastern Europe for the democratic political process (voting, etc.) after the initial euphoria, may be ascribed to a prevailing "collective psychological phenomenon" among the peoples of these countries. This, he argues, includes a "psychological nausea" with concepts and expressions such as party, parliament, or even democracy—because all of these had become associated with the cynical, empty use they were put to under the previous regimes. The resurgent political cynicism in some of the Eastern European states, according to this argument, must in part be explained by this phenomenon.[41]

This idea fits in with the observation that history forms an important conditioning background for the way the process of liberalization develops, as particularly Waller, Pridham, Cotta, and Pinkney have stressed.[42] As noted earlier, however, history is not deterministic: Even if certain historical traits of a country's society and culture, for instance, might render it potentially more likely to develop in one particular direction, such influence may be drowned out or channeled by other determinants.

It does seem obvious that the extent and type of liberalization very much depends on the precise circumstances in which the change takes place, including the way in which the old regime had declined.[43] Huntington points out that the *type* of authoritarian regime that was in place before liberalization occurred (military, single-party, personal) also is likely to influence the type and speed of transition, as well as its subsequent depth or chances of survival[44]—but this cannot be considered a wholly independent variable (the types of regimes usually being related to the rest of the country's history, circumstances, and dynamics). Another of the elements making up those circumstances is the socioeconomic position from which the country started its process of political liberalization. Thus, the shape and conditions of reform in the southern European countries (Greece, Portugal, Spain) were very different from those in Eastern Europe: In the latter, the process happened simultaneously with the introduction of a market economy, while the former were already part of the capitalist world.[45] The process for nonindustrialized and impoverished countries will likely be different again.

The level of economic success achieved under the authoritarian phase of development is equally likely to influence the type of transition. As Kong points out in Chapter 12, the transition may take either a discontinuous or a continuous path—collapse of the regime, or regime-induced and -controlled change. He argues that

> the principal determinant of whether a continuous or a discontinuous transition is made . . . is economic performance. Rapid political disintegration is normally associated with economic failure and deteriorating living standards. By contrast, those regimes that preside over economic success are in a better position to take the continuous path of gradual reform.

Returning to the external dimension, the role of outside pressure identified for the *initiation* of political reform continues to be important in the subsequent shaping of the process. This, again, goes hand in hand with the general intellectual climate, with the existence of an available model, and with specific sources of pressure and incentives—such as conditional economic assistance from multilateral or bilateral donors; or the implicit and explicit pressures emanating from, and the attractions of joining with, the European Union.

Other conjunctural or accidental factors must be recognized as necessarily influencing developments, making for a degree of country—or system—specificity, as well as a level of unpredictability. One instance of this is the role that may be played by individual personalities, whether abroad or in the country concerned. This role will vary greatly in relative importance, however, often being dwarfed by other factors.[46] Significant examples of individuals' impact on the path and form of political liberalization include the role of Lech Walesa in Poland, Vaclav Havel in Czechoslovakia, King Juan Carlos in Spain, and (as shown by Hinnebusch in Chapter 8) Hafez al-Asad in Syria, to name but a few.

Obstacles to Political Liberalization

The factors and dynamics that may limit the extent of liberalization follow fairly straightforwardly from the discussion in the preceding sections, but it is worth lifting out a few of particular interest.

Given the argument presented earlier, it is unsurprising that the absence of certain structural prerequisites, or "appropriate structural conditions," in a society will lessen the likelihood of liberalization proceeding very far. A low score on Vanhanen and Kimber's index of the distribution of power resources would, other things being equal, be an indication of a lesser chance of democratization. Expressed in terms of the civil society question, the absence of development potential of a viable civil society would restrict any sustained moves toward an advanced form of liberalization, at least in the short to medium term. This is also the argument applied to the case of China by Christiansen, who refers to the "structural constraints" on democratization in that country.[47]

In particular, the absence of a significant middle class appears to be an important retarding factor. Even where a middle class exists but is largely dependent on state patronage—or indeed is integral to the state apparatus— this militates against the emergence of any serious pressures for democratization. Hinnebusch's discussion on Syria in Chapter 8 is instructive in this respect. More generally, certain sections of the middle class, even when not state-dependent, will in some cases have an interest in resisting the extent of political liberalization that would give a voice to those opposed to measures (for instance, privatization or economic restructuring) that benefit such middle class groups.

A particular case in which the state of society impedes the establishment of democracy may be found when it is difficult to speak of a national society at all—that is, where agreement on, and identification with, the current incarnation of the state, with its given structures and boundaries, is lacking. This, almost by definition, rules out the development of anything resembling the "civic culture" referred to by Almond and Verba.[48] On the one hand, there may be little consensus among the population on ways to organize the polity, or even a basis to develop a consensus on. Group identification (substate and cross-state), and conflict both among the groups and with the state, will often overwhelm any project of building a polity at the level of the territorial state, let alone one based on a democratic consensus. On the other hand, the perception on the part of the regime will, perhaps correctly, be that political liberalization in such a context would bring only anarchy and violence. The consequent unwillingness to allow any such liberalization may, for the same reason, well be condoned by the outside world.[49]

Historical factors may also limit the extent of the trend toward political liberalization. The "alien state" problem described in the previous paragraph is in large measure a consequence of historical events. Pinkney's observations on the impact of colonial rule, paraphrased in the section "Origins, Conditions, and Explanations" above, are relevant here.

> The relative subordination of political institutions to the "strong state" which antedated them in Latin America, or the problem of social cohesion in African states where the boundaries of "traditional" kingdoms had been replaced by arbitrary European-imposed frontiers, weakened attempts at democratic development.[50]

Again, however, the wide variation in the extent of political liberalization even among countries that appeared to start from similarly unfavorable conditions demonstrates that such historical influences can only be one part of the much wider context that determines whether or not—and to what degree—liberalization will occur.

The combination of historical factors with cultural ones, among others, may be illustrated by the case of the Middle East. It has been pointed out that in this region the ideal of liberal democracy has not become the norm even among the intelligentsia or the middle classes. Reference is often made to the influence of Islam as a nondemocratic value system. Although it is true that nondemocratic interpretations of Islam are possible, it must be stressed that there is no inherent reason why this faith and social system should be incompatible with a political system that incorporates the essence of a democratic system: representation and accountability. The main reason that in recent decades the evidence has seemed to point in a different direction lies in the population's experience of imperialist involvement by the states associated with Western liberal models, and of the quasi–liberal-democratic regimes installed in the region in the aftermath of foreign domination or kept in place by foreign protection. Where such regimes were overthrown, the priority was nationalist assertion, rather than imitation of democratic models that had become discredited by association.[51]

Foreign protection through security assistance or aid deserves mention in its own right as one of the factors limiting the extent of political liberalization in a good many countries. This needs little elaboration: not only is it self-evident, but it has also become less prevalent since the ending of the Cold War. There has been a decline in the number of cases in which the maintenance in power of an autocracy is overwhelmingly more important to an outside power than the potential benefits of allowing a more representative system to emerge (or the hazards of stifling such trends). The lifting of such almost unconditional support has been directly responsible for forcing a whole range of regimes at least to begin liberalizing, among the erstwhile protégés of the United States, the USSR, and France. Nevertheless, the reflex of trying to contain instability in a key friendly state by bolstering the regime (such as, for the United States, Egypt, or even more so the conservative Arab Gulf oil producers) remains a powerful one—even if such regimes are at the same time being given friendly nudges toward very gradual liberalizing gestures.

A final type of explanation for the limits that might be imposed on political liberalization comes in the form of the rentier state argument referred to in the previous chapter. In this analysis, the essence of the political system in a rentier state and economy is the quest for access to the circulation of this rent (from the viewpoint of the ruled), and its allocation for purposes of political stability (from the viewpoint of the rulers).[52] Provided there is sufficient rent to go around, popular energies might be directed more toward getting such access than toward political reform, and the rulers would do their utmost to keep control of the allocation process. (In the case of the states of the Gulf Cooperation Council, virtually no taxes are imposed—thus potentially making the "no taxation without representation" maxim irrelevant, at least for the time being.) Although, as Pool has pointed out, "paralleling the logic of allocation of welfare, . . . the rulers . . . of rentier states [may] . . . devolve some power to ensure their survival,"[53] this would be likely to remain limited. Nevertheless, Hinnebusch in Chapter 8 shows that the extent of such available rents is not usually high enough to form a sufficient explanation for the limitations on liberalization, and that the fluctuations in the level of authoritarianism do not, at least in the Syrian case, coincide with the levels of rent available to the regime.

Much, in the end, appears to come down to the skill of the particular authoritarian regime in balancing the various forces and groups in society (Syria being a striking example). Yet almost everywhere, the contrast between increasing economic burdens and political aspirations on the one hand, and regimes' relatively declining resources and international pressures and influences on the other, would seem to hold out the prospect of further, if perhaps very gradual, liberalization.

Notes

1. R. Pinkney, *Democracy in the Third World* (Buckingham/Philadelphia: Open University Press, 1993), pp. 6–13.

2. See, for instance, R. Dahl, *Polyarchy* (New Haven: Yale University Press, 1971); C. Gould, *Rethinking Democracy* (Cambridge: Cambridge University Press, 1988); N. Hamilton and E. Kim, "Economic and Political Liberalization in South Korea and Mexico," *Third World Quarterly,* Vol. 14, No. 1 (1993), pp. 109–136; D. Held, *Models of Democracy* (Oxford: Polity Press, 1987); B. Moore, *Social Origins of Dictatorship and Democracy* (London: Allen Lane, 1967); G. Parry and M. Moran, eds., *Democracy and Democratization* (London: Routledge, 1994); Pinkney, *Democracy in the Third World,* pp. 1–17; G. Sartori, *The Theory of Democracy Revisited* (Chatham, N.J.: Chatham House, 1987). Also, see the four-volume set edited by L. Diamond, J. Linz, and S. Lipset, *Democracy in Developing Countries* (Boulder: Lynne Rienner, 1988–1989).

3. Moore, *Social Origins of Dictatorship,* p. 414.

4. P. Cammack, "Democratization and Citizenship in Latin America," in Parry and Moran, *Democracy and Democratization,* pp. 174–195.

5. See K. von Beyme, "Approaches to a Theory of the Transformation to Democracy and Market Society," in G. Parry, ed., *Politics in an Interdependent World* (Aldershot: Edward Elgar, 1994), pp. 126–145.

6. In their "Introduction" to Parry and Moran, *Democracy and Democratization,* p. 10.

7. This point is made by J. Habermas, *On the Logic of the Social Sciences* (Oxford: Polity Press, 1988), p. 38.

8. A. Edwards, "Democratization and Qualified Explanation," in Parry and Moran, *Democracy and Democratization,* pp. 88–106: p. 91.

9. Ibid., p. 93.

10. G. Pridham and T. Vanhanen, "Conclusion," in Pridham and Vanhanen, eds., *Democratization in Eastern Europe* (London: Routledge, 1994), pp. 255–263.

11. Edwards, "Democratization and Qualified Explanation," p. 102.

12. See M. Waller, "Voice, Choice and Loyalty: Democratization in Eastern Europe," in Parry and Moran, *Democracy and Democratization,* pp. 129–151; id., "Groups, Parties and Political Change in Eastern Europe since 1977," in Pridham and Vanhanen, *Democratization in Eastern Europe,* pp. 38–62; and T. Vanhanen and R. Kimber, "Predicting and Explaining Democratization in Eastern Europe," in ibid., pp. 63–96.

13. See P. Schmitter, "Introduction," in G. O'Donnell, P. Schmitter, and L. Whitehead, eds., *Transitions from Authoritarian Rule: Prospects for Democracy* (Baltimore: Johns Hopkins University Press, 1986).

14. See the chapter by Pridham in Pridham and Vanhanen, *Democratization in Eastern Europe.*

15. Pridham and Vanhanen, *Democratization in Eastern Europe,* p. 261.

16. Vanhanen and Kimber, "Predicting and Explaining Democratization."

17. S. Lipset, "Some Social Requisites for Democracy: Economic Development and Political Legitimacy," *American Political Science Review,* Vol. 53 (1959), No. 1, pp. 69–105.

18. Pinkney, *Democracy in the Third World,* pp. 109–110.

19. See also Schmitter, "Introduction."

20. Kong in Chapter 12 of this volume; Hamilton and Kim, "Economic and Political Liberalization in South Korea and Mexico," p. 131.

21. See the chapters on Albania and Poland in this volume; Waller, "Voice, Choice and Loyalty."

22. For the example of Mexico, see Hamilton and Kim, "Economic and Political Liberalization in South Korea and Mexico," p. 132.

23. Moore, *Social Origins of Dictatorship,* pp. 413–432.

24. See Pinkney, *Democracy in the Third World,* pp. 20–21.

25. See Waller, "Voice, Choice and Loyalty," pp. 136–139.

26. See A. Norton, *Civil Society in the Middle East* (Leiden: Brill, 1995).

27. Waller, "Voice, Choice and Loyalty," p. 135.

28. Ibid.

29. Hamilton and Kim, "Economic and Political Liberalization in South Korea and Mexico," p. 113.

30. D. Pool, "Staying at Home with the Wife: Democratization and Its Limits in the Middle East," in Parry and Moran, *Democracy and Democratization,* pp. 196–216.

31. Ibid., pp. 211, 214–215.

32. G. Ionescu, "The Painful Return to Normality," in Parry and Moran, *Democracy and Democratization,* pp. 109–128.

33. Waller, "Voice, Choice and Loyalty," p. 134.

34. As pointed out by Hamilton and Kim, "Economic and Political Liberalization in South Korea and Mexico," p. 130.

35. See G. Nonneman, "Yemeni Unification: The End of Marxism in Arabia," in H. Jawad, ed., *The Middle East in the New World Order* (London: Macmillan, 1994), pp. 53–69.

36. A Hyde-Price, "Democratization in Eastern Europe: The External Dimension," in Pridham and Vanhanen, *Democratization in Eastern Europe,* pp. 230–252.

37. See von Beyme, "Approaches to a Theory of the Transformation to Democracy," pp. 130–131.

38. Pinkney, *Democracy in the Thrid World,* pp. 40–48.

39. For a discussion of various ways in which this may be the case, see ibid., pp. 124–128.

40. See Parry and Moran, *Democracy and Democratization,* p. 6.

41. Ionescu, "The painful return to normality," pp. 123–124.

42. See Waller, "Voice, Choice and Loyalty"; the chapters by Waller, Cotta, and Pridham in Pridham and Vanhanen, *Democratization in Eastern Europe;* and Pinkney, *Democracy in the Third World,* Chapter 3.

43. von Beyme, "Approaches to a Theory of the Transformation to Democracy."

44. S. Huntington, "How Countries Democratize," *Political Science Quarterly,* Vol. 106 (1991), No. 4, pp. 579–616: pp. 582–583.

45. Pridham and Vanhanen, *Democratization in Eastern Europe,* p. 5.

46. See, for instance, the conclusions arrived at by Pridham and Vanhanen, ibid, pp. 257–258.

47. F. Christiansen, "Democratization in China: Structural Constraints," in Parry and Moran, *Democracy and Democratization,* pp. 152–173.

48. G. Almond and S. Verba, eds., *The Civic Culture* (Princeton: Princeton University Press, 1963).

49. It should be stressed that this is a description of an aspect of reality, not a prescription for holding off political liberalization indefinitely: Indeed, for democratization to have any genuine chance in this situation, it might well be argued that it is those very structures and/or boundaries that must be allowed to change, even if the transition entails violent upheaval or secession. This, of course, will be little consolation to the incumbent regimes.

50. Pinkney, *Democracy in the Third World,* pp. 81–82.

51. See Chapter 8 by Hinnebusch; Pool, "Staying at Home with the Wife," pp. 204–208.

52. See G. Luciani, "Allocation vs. Production States: A Theoretical Framework," in Luciani, ed., *The Arab State* (London: Routledge, 1990), pp. 65–84.

53. Pool, "Staying at Home with the Wife," p. 201.

PART 2

EASTERN EUROPE

4

Poland's Transition from State Socialism to Capitalism

Peter Gowan

A sudden transformation, first of the political regime and then of the socio-economic order, was launched in Poland in 1989. The transformation began with a decision by the ruling party's Central Committee[1] early in 1989 to enter negotiations with the political opposition grouped around Lech Walesa, the former leader of Solidarity (*Solidarnosc*). This was, in effect, a decision for *democratization*. These negotiations were swiftly concluded on 5 April 1989; they led to partially free elections in early June that were won by Walesa's Citizens' Committees.[2] As a result of defections on the part of the Communist Party's allies, the United Peasant Party and the Democratic Party, a government led by non-Communists under the liberal Catholic intellectual Tadeusz Mazowiecki was formally sworn into office in early September. At the start of the following year, this government introduced a plan for both economic stabilization and radical systemic change toward a full-fledged capitalist social system. The resulting socioeconomic transformations then fed back into further institutional changes in all spheres of Polish society.

This internal systemic transformation in Poland was integrally linked, in complex ways, with a transformation of both the country's external environment and its external orientation. In a very short time span Poland's external linkages swung, so to speak, 180 degrees from being deeply embedded at all levels in the Soviet bloc to being progressively integrated into the Western alliance's institutional infrastructures. This reorientation is not yet completed and consolidated, but it has reached an advanced stage in the economic and political fields.

One can thus distinguish the Polish turn from transformations in other parts of the world that are considered in this book:

1. It began with a change of political regime initiated by the ruling party, in cooperation with the political opposition.
2. The political regime change took the form not of liberalization but of

65

democratization, and this threw up a new national political leadership publicly committed to destroying the country's social system and replacing it with a new one.

3. The economic transformation initiated by the new leadership was a comprehensive structural change of the entire economy. It was not a program for reform or liberalization of the state-socialist economy; nor was it a program for creating a dual system—a state-socialist sector parallel to a private capitalist sector. The program envisaged a thoroughgoing systemic transformation to capitalism to be carried through from above by public policy.

4. The domestic transformation was integrally linked with the transformation of the country's geopolitical and geoeconomic environment and ties.

I will call the Polish combination of regime change and socioeconomic transformation a *systemic change*. My goal here is to explain why this change took place and why it took certain forms rather than others. I will seek to challenge theories of this transition that assign a central explanatory role to the idea of "civil society" and its rise in a conflictual relationship with Communist totalitarianism. Before exploring other possible avenues of explanation, some conceptual clarifications must be made.

Conceptual /Theoretical Issues

Systemic Change and Related Notions

The notion of systemic change presupposes the existence of social systems in the sense of patterned structures common to large groups of countries despite the varieties of institutional forms unique to each. The most obvious such commonalities are those that link the countries of the Organization for Economic Cooperation and Development (OECD) on one side and those that link the Eastern European Soviet-type systems on the other.

Some authors dispute the existence of such patterned structures.[3] Others implicitly reject their analytical centrality.[4] But following Sachs and others[5] we will give analytical priority to the notion of social systems and systemic change. The concepts we will employ for comparative purposes are those of state-socialist systems and capitalist systems.[6]

The differences between these systems operate at all levels but most crucially for our purposes at the level of economic and state-political organization. Forms seemingly common to both systems—product markets, labor markets, enterprises, trade unions, political parties, judicial systems, etc.—in fact have radically different dynamics in each system. Phenomena within each of these systems captured by concepts of liberalization or democratization will thus also be seen as conditioned by their systemic context.

Employing the concept of social system then makes it possible to distinguish various species within a single systemic genus. I shall argue that Polish state socialism possessed features that distinguished it from others, such as those in Czechoslovakia or Romania, and that these species varieties are of great importance in explaining change in Poland.

The concepts of liberalization and democratization can be applied to developments in both capitalist and state-socialist societies, but the end products of such developments remain very different under each system. In the sphere of economics, state-socialist liberalization can take two forms. One is a decentralization of decisionmaking concerning the allocations of factors of production or their prices in the direction of market socialism. The alternative is the creation of a dual economy—a state-socialist centralized sector existing alongside a subordinate private sector.[7]

In politics, state-socialist liberalization takes the form of the emergence of ideological pluralism and/or institutional pluralism, with or without the emergence of independent political groupings, within a polity where public policy is still to be monopolized by the ruling party and its satellite allies.

An important feature of state-socialist experience has been a tendency for liberalization to grow into democratization.[8] The latter refers to a process whereby sovereignty is transferred from the ruling party to the electorate. Yet in the Soviet bloc democratization in this sense was precluded by the Soviet alliance. During the 1970s all the constitutions of the Warsaw Pact region were altered to enshrine the "leading role of the Communist Party" as a constitutional principle, thereby effectively excluding democratization in the sense of a shift from party sovereignty to popular sovereignty. Thus, democratization within Soviet bloc state socialism would provoke a constitutional and an alliance crisis. This, however, would change under Gorbachev at a doctrinal level: The 19th Communist Party of the Soviet Union (CPSU) conference of 1988 would open the way to the possibility of popular sovereignty by making the leading role of the party a goal to be achieved by winning popular support, rather than a constitutional principle.[9]

A third, conceptually distinct political change within state socialism should also be noted: *constitutionalization.* This is the attempt to turn the state into a genuinely functioning *Rechtsstaat,* in which citizens are assured that the constitutional rights in law are respected in fact. Given that state-socialist authorities have always claimed the constitutionality of their institutions, this process is a difficult one to track; nonetheless it is very important. It involves the replacement of Friend/Enemy criteria with behavioral criteria as the dominant juridical concepts for dealing with dissent or opposition.

There remains, however, a striking gap in our conceptual apparatus and vocabulary for describing and explaining change within Soviet bloc state socialism: There is very little in the literature to assist analysis and explanation of ideological and political change within the ruling Communist parties themselves.[10] There is a tendency to present such parties as being the property of an undifferentiated nomenklatura with little or no intellectual or political internal variation or development. This gap has, of course, resulted in Western students of state-socialist politics being taken by surprise by developments within the CPSU under Gorbachev. Similar problems, I will argue, applied in the case of the ruling party in Poland.

The Limits to the "Civil Society" Approach

The turn of 1989 was, of course, driven by both internal and external factors. We will look at both, but will do so from the angle of discussing various analytical constructs used by Western scholars for explaining these events.

The most influential theory of the internal forces of change is one that assigns a central role to the emergence of an independent civil society in Poland. This explanation has been most trenchantly argued by Timothy Garton Ash in a series of books on developments in Poland and within the East-Central European region.[11] He in turn has drawn upon the writings of Adam Michnik and other dissident intellectuals from the region in the 1970s and 1980s.[12]

The theory emphasizes the crumbling of totalitarian structures and forces of control through the overcoming of totalitarian atomization at a societal level. This is captured by a concept of "social self-organization." As Ash explains:

> The party-state will be compelled to adapt to these *faits accomplis,* if only by grudgingly accepting an incremental *de facto* reduction in the areas of its total control. But what is *de facto* today may eventually become *de jure* too. The *pays réel* will finally shape the *pays légal.*[13]

Ash sets up a conceptual polarization between a totalitarian party-state whose drive was "to rule over an atomised society"[14] and an emerging civil society that could not be crushed and eventually engulfed the party-state, producing the turn of 1989. Thus, the decision of the Polish United Workers Party (PUWP) leadership to enter negotiations with the opposition was a capitulation to the pressures of this autonomous civil society.

The strength of this theory lies in its focus on an institutional crisis of the regime. But I will argue that it contains the following serious weaknesses:

1. The theory obliterates the role of ideas, values, and political communication within state socialism in general and Poland in particular, both at the level of party-state interaction with society and within the party-state networks themselves.
2. It locates the source of the institutional crisis in an autonomous rise

of new institutions of civil society, rather than in a withdrawal of support from state-socialist institutions. It thus mislocates the source of institutional crisis.

3. Its concept of totalitarianism obliterates the specific features of the state-socialist polity in Poland, including the changes and the structural flaws in that polity.

4. The theory obscures the relationship between the post-1989 government policy of socioeconomic transformation and the revival of civil society.

5. Finally, it fails to grasp the nature of continuities and discontinuities in Polish politics in the early 1990s.

The Role of Consent, Communication, and Participation in State Socialism

While totalitarian theory rightly stresses monocentric forms of social organization in state socialism and the party-state symbiosis, it ignores the consensual, communicative, and participatory elements that are as important, if not in some respects more important, in state socialism than in other systems. As a result, it does not focus attention clearly enough on the consequences of the weakening or breakdown of these elements in the system. It also diverts us from the task of identifying the differences in the ways in which various Communist parties in various countries at various times have sought to constitute these forms of linkage with society; these are key aspects of the political differentiations within state socialism.

Totalitarian theory applied to Communist regimes has taken a number of different forms. Shapiro's theorization, which views it as a crisis regime marked by leaderism and terror, would exclude not only Brezhnev's USSR but also Poland from the label.[15] Early writings by Karl Friedrich and Zbigniew Brzeszinski would also tend to exclude Poland.[16] The concept deployed by Ash and Michnik in fact draws more on Max Weber's theory of the inexorable rise of rationality as societies develop, with a tendency toward total bureaucratization, than on classical U.S. totalitarian theory. Its distinguishing feature is the emphasis on total state control over the economy and on bureaucratic compliance mechanisms. A corollary of this view is that of totalitarianism as bereft of attachments to substantive values and goals: Administrative apparatuses are driven only by the rationality of technical control and compliance.

I will advance an alternative hypothesis, namely that European state-socialist polities depended for their stability to a significant degree upon their ability to achieve agreement with decisive social forces on substantive values bound up with the socialist project and not simply upon the bureaucratic domination of a passive, atomized mass. I will argue that the key social group that had to be won over to the values of state socialism was the bulk of the industrial workers. Consent from this group was required not

only for ideological reasons but for the stable reproduction of state socialism, above all in the economic field.

Without the disciplines of a capitalist labor market and attendant unemployment, and without the material incentives of wage-consumption relationships in a capitalist society, the economic reproduction of state socialism
involved the capacity to win social participation on the part of workers not
only through political coercion but also through elements of consent and
communicative interaction. At an institutional level this involved drawing
large minorities of workers into the Communist Party itself and drawing
other layers of employees into satellite organizations such as trade unions.
These tasks in turn required the support of the intelligentsia for the goals of
the state-socialist regime. This support could not be gained only through
repression; it required the ability to convince strategic groups of intellectuals that the state-socialist project was both historically justified and historically feasible.

Explaining the Polish Turn

The Specificities of Polish State Socialism

Without the Soviet army's advance across Poland to Berlin, and the subse-
quent division of Europe, Communism would not have triumphed in Poland.
Wladyslaw Gomulka, the leader of the Polish Workers Party constructed in
Poland during the Nazi occupation, informed Moscow toward the end of the
war that the party could not win acceptance of its program by a majority of
Poles even if it were led by the Virgin Mary herself! In the postwar condi-
tions of Cold War, Poland was of central strategic importance to the USSR;
Stalin was not prepared to risk Soviet security to a Polish capitalist society
most of whose leaders would not accept either Poland's new frontiers or
Soviet tutelage.

The interwar Polish Communist Party had won strong support only
among ethnic minorities, notably the Jewish and Ukrainian communities,
and was minoritarian within the small industrial working class. Its leadership was executed in the USSR in the late 1930s and the party itself was
closed down by the Comintern in 1938.[17]

The Polish Workers Party, formed in 1942, confronted a society whose
main political forces from left to right were strongly inflected with various
kinds of nationalism, most of which, and not least on the Socialist left, contained a strong element of anti-Russian sentiment. The party also faced a
population whose sense of national identity was intertwined with
Catholicism.[18] The country contained a large peasantry, strongly attached to
the church; urban workers and intellectuals possessed a strong tradition of
loyalty to the Polish Socialist Party. Such were the conditions under which

the Communists, after a brief flirtation with International Communist identities in the period from 1949 to 1955, returned to the basic stance developed by Gomulka during and after World War II. They sought to integrate themselves into Polish society and establish their political authority through the following key planks:

1. defense of the alliance with the USSR on the basis of defending the new Polish state against German revanchism
2. a demonstration of the readiness of Polish Communists to defend Polish interests and independence against Russian bullying
3. making the ruling party the united expression of the traditions of Polish socialism
4. achieving economic progress for the bulk of the population
5. becoming the defender of secular, liberal values against Catholic social conservatism and religious obscurantism
6. respect for the religious attachments of Polish people and establishment of a modus vivendi with the church hierarchy.[19]

This program was championed by Gomulka from 1956 until his fall in 1970 and revived by his successor, Edward Gierek, during the 1970s. The decisive turning point in the postwar history of Polish Communism came with the collapse of Gierek's efforts in 1980 as Solidarity came onto the scene, and the declaration of martial law on 13 December 1981.

Both in the late 1940s and with Gomulka's return to power in 1956, the Gomulkist program had a substantial degree of support within Polish society, and its liberal channeling mechanisms seemed viable.[20]

From 1956 onward the bulk of Polish agriculture was in the hands of a private, noncapitalist peasantry. The Catholic Church had institutional autonomy, and religious practice was not interfered with. The Catholic intelligentsia was allowed its own clubs and its own newspaper as well as representation in Parliament. Pluralism was allowed in student organizations. Nonpolitical scouting organizations were tolerated. The PUWP evidently embraced varying ideological and political trends and appealed, to some extent successfully, as broader than a merely Stalinist organization, and the allied Polish Peasant Party was more than just a cipher.[21]

This by no means made Poland a liberal, pluralist state in a Western sense; far less a liberal democracy. The PUWP firmly monopolized public policy, there were strict ground rules governing all nonparty institutions, and there was careful surveillance of social developments by the security services. Attempts to challenge publicly the legitimacy of the party-state in writing would be suppressed; under Gomulka attempts to build independent political groups outside the framework of officially approved institutions would not be tolerated. Nevertheless, the model in totalitarian theory of total state domination of an atomized society fails to capture the sociopolitical character of state socialism in Poland. At the level of everyday life, there was a wide measure of free communication within the country from the mid-1950s to the 1980s.

The Polish polity therefore contained a substantial degree of *liberalization* from at least 1956. It did not, however, contain a democratic underpinning. The result was a tension within the system that would repeatedly surface: The very success of liberal channeling efforts to convince the population of its ability to influence public policy could promote a democratization that could plunge the polity into crisis.

This structural tension was heightened by an unmistakable process of constitutionalization of the political and administrative systems in the country. This is perhaps a controversial area, since there were evident cases of lawlessness on the part of the police and security forces, not least on the Baltic coast during and after the strikes and riots of 1970–1971.[22] Yet such instances occur in most states considered to be rule-of-law states. There is, moreover, a large body of evidence to suggest that during the 1970s the Polish population considered that they did enjoy a minimum of constitutionality.[23]

This leads to another very important issue, that of collective as well as individual rights. Most students of state-socialist regimes recognize that the populations to a large extent absorbed the official social values of the state-socialist order: egalitarianism, social security, the right to a job, and so on. But the Polish experience shows that the population did not only subscribe to these values; they considered them as constitutional rights and treated attempts by anyone, including the government, to remove or weaken those rights as illegitimate. They believed they had the right to resort to collective action in defense of these rights if they seemed to be infringed.[24]

The Political Crisis of Polish State Socialism

In 1980–1981, state socialism in Poland entered a political crisis from which it never recovered. The roots of this crisis lay in the failures of the Gomulka government and in the contradictions of the subsequent Gierek government's attempts to reestablish the authority of the PUWP.

The Gomulka government failed to retain the allegiance of an important segment of the younger intelligentsia in the 1960s and blundered into a disastrous and bloody confrontation with workers on the Baltic coast in December 1970.[25]

The 1968 events involved the crushing of a student protest movement in the universities; the rise of a populist, anti-Semitic campaign within the PUWP, which led to the emigration of a large part of the small Jewish intelligentsia that had survived the war and remained in Poland; and the participation by Polish troops in the invasion of Czechoslovakia. This last event was of particular importance because the hopes of the Polish socialist intelligentsia, like those of the intelligentsia throughout Eastern Europe, had been pinned on a revival of the socialist project throughout the Soviet bloc through the triumph of the reform-Communist project in Prague.

The events of December 1970 were in many ways more serious. The government mishandled a combination of price rises and changes in work practices in the Baltic shipyards. Resulting strikes and riots produced brutal intervention by the security forces and the killing of a number of workers. This crisis brought the fall of Gomulka himself, while the new Gierek leadership took months to establish its authority in the face of working-class discontent in many parts of Poland.[26]

The Gierek project. Edward Gierek assumed office in the midst of the Baltic crisis. He was able to reestablish the PUWP's authority only by making very substantial concessions to the working class. In direct negotiations with striking textile workers in Lodz in April 1971 he pledged to maintain frozen consumer prices and to substantially improve living standards over the following years. He also set up new lines of communication with the industrial organizations in the main plants in the country, the so-called socialist bastions, in order to prevent the kind of communicative breakdown that had resulted in the Baltic confrontations.[27]

Gierek embarked upon a Western credit–led growth strategy with the goal of rapidly modernizing the economy and raising consumption. He borrowed heavily from the West to introduce new industrial production facilities that would pay for themselves through renewed exports. Gierek also sought to improve agricultural output by consolidating the fragmented peasant holdings into larger, more productive farms. His emphasis in cultural policy was liberal-technocratic and geared toward consumerist modernization with an appeal to the young.

During the first five years of the 1970s rapid growth was achieved, but at the cost of a deteriorating payments position and ever-larger slices of the state budget being devoted to consumer price subsidies. Rising incomes were being spent on large increases in food consumption, especially meat and meat products.

In the summer of 1976 the government attempted to increase food prices to correct these imbalances. The day after the prime minister announced the increases on television, strikes began in a number of important plants, notably at the Ursus Tractor plant and in Radom.[28]

The government responded by immediately canceling the price increases. But its authority was shaken, economic imbalances were bound to become more severe, and a new phase in Polish politics began. The key new development was an attempt by critical intellectual activists to forge a new coalition for change.

The challenge of dissent.   The 1976 price conflict spurred the creation of a serious challenge to the effort of the PUWP to build its authority along Gomulkist lines.

A group of political activists led by Jacek Kuron took the initiative in 1976 of creating the Committee in Defense of Workers (KOR). Though it remained small and did not gain the active support of the bulk of the Polish liberal and socialist intelligentsia, the KOR mounted a powerful symbolic challenge to the Gierek government. In particular it challenged the PUWP's claim to speak on behalf of all of Poland's workers and all strands of its broad socialist tradition. Secondly, and more startlingly, it claimed that the cause of the workers and of civil rights could be furthered by cooperations between secularist forces and the Catholic world.[29] Finally, by organizing openly as an independent group, it challenged the government to respect its constitutionality.

The KOR was a very small group, actively supported in the late 1970s only by a few hundred mainly young people. If the party-state had been totalitarian it would have crushed the group, but the political basis of the Gierek regime precluded arbitrary arrest and lawless imprisonment of such intellectuals merely for engaging in the KOR's activity. Although the bulk of the Polish intelligentsia did not actively support KOR, it would have challenged any roundup and show trial. That challenge would have come not only from outside but also from within the PUWP. In addition, opposition would have come from the Catholic Church, which remained a very important public institution.

Changes within Polish Catholicism.   Polish Catholicism can be likened to Irish Catholicism in that it identified the destiny of the nation with that of the church. It was also rooted above all in the countryside. Its leader, Cardinal Wyszynski, was, in theological and political terms, an antimodernist reactionary for whom Western-oriented liberal democrats were no more appealing than Communists. Wyszynski treated the Catholic intelligentsia with a mixture of contempt and suspicion, ruled the church with an iron hand, and favored an anti-intellectual peasant variety of Catholicism bordering on superstitious cult worship. A man of great courage and independence, Wyszynski had been placed under house arrest during Poland's brief Stalinist interlude, and he openly flouted Rome when Pius XII (notoriously pro-German) refused to recognize Poland's western territories as part of the territory of the Polish episcopate. Wyszynski simply appointed bishops to these territories himself. Under Gomulka, provided the government did not try to interfere with church activities, Wyszynski was prepared to make sure that Polish Catholics did not embarrass the regime.

Two events changed the equations in church–state relations under Gierek. The first and most important was a consequence of Wyszynski's ultraconservatism. At the end of the Second Vatican Council, Wyszynski, in front of the entire Polish episcopate, made two points to Pope Paul VI:

first, that no part of the universal church was as loyal as the Polish Catholics; and second, that His Holiness could not expect the Polish church actually to implement every aspect of Vatican II. Rome reacted by swiftly searching for a Polish bishop who would be prepared to defend Vatican II as a whole. It found the Bishop of Cracow, Karol Wojtila, and made him a cardinal.

Though very much on the conservative wing of international Catholicism, Wojtila was a progressive in Polish terms. First, he was an intellectual and led a very dynamic theological and intellectual regeneration in Cracow. Instead of putting up the shutters against the post-Enlightenment world, Wojtila was eager to engage in ideological contestation and debate with Communism. The PUWP leadership at first even saw him as a potentially valuable interlocutor because of his readiness to engage in a Marxist–Catholic dialogue. But as the 1970s progressed it was clear that Wojtila was eager to transform the dialogue into a public root-and-branch intellectual challenge to Communism. When the KOR came into existence, Wojtila encouraged young Catholics to become involved in the movement and provided some measure of protection to its activists.

The second development was increasing anger and suspicion on Cardinal Wyszynski's part toward the Gierek government for two main reasons. In the first place, both the Vatican and the PUWP leadership became interested in exploring the possibility of establishing direct diplomatic relations. Wyszynski saw this as a tactic on both sides to undermine his own firm grip on Catholic Poland. In the second place, Gierek's activities in the countryside were viewed as a major threat to the church. Although the Gierek government did not question the right of peasants to private ownership, its desire to consolidate landholdings and to encourage the large number of semiproletarian peasants to cut their ties with the land were seen by Wyszynski as the threatened loss of over two million of his peasant flock to the cities. At the same time, the continuing depopulation of the countryside led the government to propose the creation of larger, better-provisioned schools with a wide catchment area, replacing hundreds of small village schools. Wyszynski denounced this proposed change as the greatest threat to Catholicism in Poland for decades. Although the school system was formally secular, the local priest would enter the state school at the end of the school day and provide religious education to the pupils. The reform would mean that pupils would have buses to catch and would not wait for the priest.

The result of these developments was that the KOR activists were able to hope for a new alliance of lay, secular activists with Catholics that would champion human rights against the Gierek government.

The Gierek government did not ban the KOR, and although its activists were harassed, their activities were not actually prevented. To have banned the group would have alienated the party intelligentsia. Gierek, however, sought to make his peace with Cardinal Wyszynski through holding a high-profile meeting and seeking his cooperation to maintain political stability in the country. These efforts were, however, reduced to ashes by the shock appointment of Cardinal Wojtila as Pope in 1978. The latter's official visit to Poland in 1979 brought millions of Poles out to religious gatherings to meet their Pope, and the entire country was filled with enormous excitement and national pride that one of their countrymen could become head of the universal church.[30]

Wojtila's appointment as Pope and his Polish visit the following year were problematic for the government. But the fact that Gierek officially welcomed both the appointment and the visit indicates how far removed the regime was from totalitarian efforts to impose ideological conformity on the population.

The Crisis in the PUWP and the rise of Solidarity.   In form, the rise of Solidarity may seem to resemble the emergence of civil society, breaking free from atomization under totalitarian control. Yet Solidarity was a syndicalist political organization that did not leap into existence fully grown. It emerged out of the organic crisis within Polish state socialism itself, not least within the PUWP. Solidarity unified within itself radically contradictory currents; out of the attempts of its leaders to maintain the unity of these currents there emerged the conception of a self-managed society and of civil society pitted against the totalitarian party-state.

The political tensions in the country first surfaced in a dramatic way at the PUWP Congress at the beginning of 1980, when the prime minister was forced to resign without warning in the middle of the congress. Following that event, the official trade unions drew up a series of demands for economic change. These would subsequently find a prominent place in the demands raised during the August strike. There was a ferment of discontent within the industrial organizations of the PUWP.

When the government attempted once again to raise prices in the summer of 1980, the eventual result was a strike in the shipyards of Gdansk. A group of activists in the Lenin shipyard, led by Lech Walesa and sympathetic to KOR, launched the Gdansk strike. This has led most Western accounts of the rise of Solidarity to view it as a linear outgrowth of the KOR's activities. The role of the KOR sympathizers in Gdansk as triggers and as articulators of the initial demands is undoubted. But what gave the strike its decisive political importance was the fact that it rapidly spread in a highly organized way through Gierek's socialist bastions: to the shipyards of Gdynia, to those of Szczecin, then to Wroclaw, and finally into the mines of lower Silesia, the old power base of Gierek himself. This transmission was not the fruit of the work of KOR activists in these centers; it was largely carried out by PUWP activists and even officials.

Szczecin's strike broke the isolation of Gdansk and in Gdynia the lead was taken by PUWP members and trade union officials. The spread of the strike into the mining areas, which forced the government to back down, began at Walbrzych. One in three miners there was a Communist and many had been in the Communist Party since their youth in Belgium and northern France, like Gierek himself. Thus the rise of Solidarity was to a very large degree a crisis *within* Polish Communism rather than one between the society and a totalitarian power.

At the same time, the Polish intelligentsia tended to support the new movement, and the church sought to play a role in the symbolic expression of the movement and at the same time to offer itself as a mediating force capable of speaking over politics for the whole nation.

The PUWP leadership proved incapable of either reestablishing its ascendancy over the movement or defeating it. Instead, the PUWP itself underwent a process of ideological and political fragmentation as a very large part of its membership broke with Soviet Communist orthodoxy and adopted social-democratic platforms. Some important regional leaders of the party sought to base themselves on Solidarity itself.

The declaration of martial law on 13 December 1981 had a double effect: General Wojciech Jaruzelski not only crushed Solidarity but also removed the PUWP from real political control of the country. Power shifted into the hands of a group of military officers, as well as the managers of state enterprises and officials in the economic ministries. Attempts to rebuild the authority of the PUWP through constructing a new platform for gathering together the Polish left and industrial workers were subordinated to the principle of order and to a pragmatic attempt at economic crisis management.

The 1980s: The PUWP Discredited, Divided, and Disempowered

Even though the PUWP was subsequently revived and officially given the "leading role" in the state, the real politicoeconomic power source of party rule—the integration of decisive sectors of the factory workers into the party—was by now fatally weakened. At the same time, the party leadership was unable to communicate effectively with the intelligentsia because the latter had begun to turn its back on state socialism.

Opinion surveys carried out in 1984 showed that only 25 percent of the population supported the political leadership of the PUWP; another 25 percent were opposed and 50 percent either had no opinion or did not wish to express it.[31] This was a catastrophic decline in support for the PUWP. The sole basis for communicative integration was the need for order to evade the risk of a Soviet invasion. This message was continually communicated to the population. But it contained a subtext: State socialism is historically finished in Poland; its husk survives only for geopolitical reasons—because the USSR requires it.

Within the PUWP an ideological fragmentation that had begun in the days of Solidarity continued with social-democratic currents of thought gaining increasing strength. The PUWP was, in fact, tending to become what totalitarian theory always claimed it had been: the political expression of the managerial groups within the country.

Polish society during the 1980s was not marked by the flourishing of a newly vibrant civil society, but far more by pathological symptoms of decay and demoralization. The networks of Solidarity disintegrated not only as a result of repression, but also because of a spreading social apathy and retreat into private life. Funds from the West helped Western-oriented and Catholic intellectuals to earn a living by writing for unofficial journals and publishing houses, but this was an ersatz form of civil society based on Western—particularly Vatican and U.S.—state funding and grants from private foundations.

Government policy was thus driven not by any coherent project for reviving state socialism, but by a pragmatic search for ways to stabilize the economy without flagrantly breaching the ideological underpinning principles of the Soviet bloc. It sought to maintain economic life partly by allowing an expansion of private and cooperative activity and partly by seeking to connect with some of the syndicalist trends of thought in Solidarity, especially the notion that the factories should belong to their employees. The government transferred quasi-proprietary rights to "self-management councils" composed of management and elected representatives of employees. It also relaxed plan indicators and later in the 1980s even made arrangements for the legalization of foreign capital to operate in Poland. This was a kind of decentralizing economic liberalization, coupled with the encouragement of a dual economy involving an expanding private sector. It also encouraged a form of agricultural capitalism—the so-called Red Kulaks—allowing owners to employ labor for profit. But the central concern of economic policy was a desperate and increasingly vain effort to maintain debt servicing by limiting imports and boosting exports to the West.

By 1988–1989 the government was losing its battle to maintain debt servicing and the economy was facing an increasingly unmanageable crisis. The government desired to deepen substantially the processes of both liberalization and of "dualization" of the economy. Unable to use collective political appeals to the working class through the PUWP, it sought to stimulate economic activity by widening pay differentials and inequalities, and to carry out further reforms that would heighten such social differentiation. To legitimate such new measures in the absence of an authoritative PUWP the government turned to the device of a referendum on further economic reform. But it lost the referendum and thus its authority for implementing its own economic program.

Yet the result was not a strengthening of the authority of Solidarity. In 1988 the government sought to use Lech Walesa to channel wildcat strikes by workers protesting deteriorating conditions, but the strikers in the autumn of 1988 showed themselves unwilling to follow the lead of such unofficial

representatives of civil society. In other words, the kinds of institutionalization of social action that had developed in the 1970s in Poland, and reached
their peak in 1980–1981, had been eroding. Civil society was in this sense
in decline and the threat was of a more chaotic social explosion.

The decay was visible in the 1989 elections. The Solidarity Citizens'
Committee won all but one of the seats for which free contests were allowed.
Only 12 percent of the voters were prepared to vote for the PUWP; this was
a clear plebiscite on the ruling party after ten years of economic crisis and
after martial law. Yet the turnout, 65 percent for the first round, dropped to
25 percent for the second. The exercise was still far from being a vibrant
assertion of a new civic consciousness, let alone a popular revolution.

The Nature of Change in the PUWP:
The Necessary Condition for the Turn of 1989

The decision of the PUWP leadership in February 1989 to opt for a regime
change cannot, therefore, be explained solely in terms of the threat from
civil society to a totalitarian power. Nor, for that matter, can it be interpreted as the result of a *diktat* from the Soviet leader Mikhail Gorbachev. While
the role of the latter and other external factors was important, as will be
illustrated in the following section, it remains insufficient as an explanation
for the move. The decision derived, ultimately, from the crisis of the PUWP
as a result of a loss of popular support, particularly on the part of strategic
groups, and from the political evolution within the PUWP as a consequence
of this crisis. The dominant trends within the PUWP became those of social-
democratic and market-socialist orientation. The regime embarked upon a
process of economic liberalization that entailed the erosion of the social values and perceived rights of large parts of the working class. It attempted to
legitimate the deepening of this liberalization through a referendum but was
rebuffed by the electorate. This left only two options: a turn toward a new
type of authoritarian regime, perhaps on the Ceausescu model; or full
democratization. The PUWP leadership was able to choose the latter in early
1989 because of the Gorbachev reforms.

There was a wide variety of ideological and political trends within the
ruling parties of the Soviet bloc. The Polish variants were very different
from, for instance, those of Romania or Czechoslovakia. Nevertheless, it is
possible to detect certain general, cross-regional trends that affected different ruling parties to different degrees. One such trend consisted of market
socialism and political liberalization. Another was authoritarian "workerist"
nationalism. A third, which became more prominent in the 1980s, took its
lead from the Italian Communist Party and looked toward a systemic transformation and integration into the Western system. All these currents were
present to some degree inside the PUWP. The dominant currents by the late

1980s were those favoring market socialism and those favoring social democratization and an opening to capitalism.

In theory, a party leadership might have existed in Poland in the late 1980s that would have rejected the turn the PUWP chose to make. In practice, the political tendencies that were dominant within the party chose the course of democratization.

The domination of Western research on comparative Communism by various strands of totalitarian theory has meant that the kinds of research that would reveal why certain trends rather than others became dominant in ruling parties is still in its infancy. The result was that Western social scientists specializing in the region were as taken aback as everyone else by the emergence of "Gorbachevism" in the USSR. The same puzzlement was apparent over the PUWP's turn in 1989. Ash's use of the term "refolution" to describe the turn papers over this problem instead of analyzing it.

The Role of External Factors

It is clear that the turn of 1989 was by no means prepared *solely* by the interaction of domestic forces. The roles of Warsaw Pact alliance politics, of Western diplomacy and economic statecraft, and of Vatican politics (the choice of the Polish Pope) were crucial shaping factors.

The Soviet alliance: Pre-Gorbachev.   The role of the USSR was absolutely central not only to the formation of the Polish People's Republic but to the framework of political and economic life in the Republic's entire history.

The Brezhnev leadership's post–Prague Spring policy for the Warsaw Pact area established the framework of permissions and restrictions that drove the internal contradictions of Gierek's policies to the point of explosion in 1980–1981. In the context of European détente in early 1980s, Brezhnev allowed Polish and other Eastern bloc governments to seek to modernize their economies through Western borrowing and the import of Western technology as a substitute for domestic economic liberalization in the direction of market socialism. At the same time the Brezhnev regime gained support from party leaderships throughout the Warsaw Pact for enshrining the doctrine of the leading role of the party. The economic crisis that resulted in Poland from the attempted credit-led modernization generated a political crisis that could not be resolved through political and institutional development while the doctrine of the leading role of the party was maintained.

The domestic political crisis in Poland became a Warsaw Pact crisis in the autumn of 1980 because of the Soviet insistence that Solidarity must recognize the leading role of the PUWP before it could be legalized. The PUWP leadership fudged this issue with a compromise formula and this, in turn, led to demands within the CPSU (and within the Soviet Armed Forces political administrations) for a Soviet military intervention in Poland. Brezhnev and the politburo rejected this option but prepared, instead, for the imposition of martial law. This move may have restored the constitutional principle of the leading role of the PUWP, but it proved fatal to the capacity of the real existing PUWP to restore its authority within Polish politics.

U.S. policy and economic statecraft toward East-Central Europe. Gierek based his strategy for reviving the fortunes of the PUWP upon a stable international détente and a continuing economic boom in the West. Both these assumptions proved to be disastrously mistaken. The failure of the Polish government to turn its credit-led boom of the early 1970s into an export boom that would pay back the debts gave Western policymakers a lever on Polish domestic developments with profound consequences for the internal dynamics of state socialism. At the same time, Gierek's readiness to center his internal efforts in food-market supply on cheap U.S. grain credits was to prove fateful.

During the détente of the early 1970s the U.S. government pursued a policy of so-called selective engagement with the Soviet bloc.[32] This entailed favoring countries that showed some independence from Soviet orthodoxy in either their domestic or foreign policies. Under both Gomulka and Gierek, Poland qualified partly because its domestic polity was far more open and pluralistic than most others in the Soviet bloc, and partly because its governments had shown some attachment to economic experiment, for example with private agriculture.

For the U.S. government, selective engagement was designed to exert influence, via the satellite states of Eastern Europe, upon the USSR itself. But for Poland the effect was to open Western capital markets and to offer the prospect of gaining a relatively stable relationship with the Western-dominated world economy. The food-price crisis of 1976 led the Polish and U.S. governments to agree upon a means of tackling the problem of Polish consumer supply. The low prices of meat were leading to an ever-larger demand that outstripped Poland's livestock production. The latter faced a crippling bottleneck of feed grain. The U.S. government took a purely political decision (over the criticism of both the Commerce and Treasury departments) to supply Poland with credits on favorable terms for grain imports.

In 1979 U.S. policy took a dramatic turn that had fateful consequences for Gierek's efforts at stabilization.[33] Federal Reserve Chairman Volker's sudden switch to a high dollar and high interest rates enormously increased Poland's debt-servicing burden. And in the spring of 1980, the U.S. government informed Warsaw that it was ending grain credits. These changes were combined with a general change in U.S. policy toward the USSR and therefore Eastern Europe. The Carter administration turned from seeking to loosen up the USSR through selective engagement in Eastern Europe, toward a direct political confrontation, an arms race, and the use of economic embargoes.

Following the imposition of martial law, the Reagan administration's vigorous response in calling for Western economic sanctions against Poland, while at the same time assisting the liberal wing of the Solidarity intelligentsia, greatly increased the impact of U.S. policy on ordinary Poles. U.S. support was also very important in spreading free-market ideas within the intelligentsia; such ideas became increasingly fashionable, as was demonstrated in the publishing programs of the unofficial press.

Gorbachev and Poland.   From 1985, the international situation facing the PUWP leadership began to change in fundamental ways. The emergence of Gorbachev's reform program had itself been spurred by the Polish crisis, which demonstrated to the Soviet leadership how extremely vulnerable it had become in the most important of its Eastern bloc–allied states; after the German Democratic Republic, Poland had the greatest strategic importance to the USSR in the context of Cold War confrontation. The Soviet leadership had also been made aware of its own economic weakness in the face of the Polish crisis: The costs of producing a strong revival of the Polish economy were simply too great for the USSR of the 1980s to bear.

The Soviet leadership quickly established a priority for advancing significantly toward the integration of the USSR into the world economy. One of Gorbachev's first acts as general secretary was to indicate to the European Community (EC) his desire to break the deadlock in relations that had existed since the early 1970s. At the same time, the Soviet leadership was becoming increasingly insistent upon ending the situation in which it was subsidizing its Eastern European satellite economies not only with cheap energy and raw material sales but also by providing their industries with captive export markets with inadequate quality controls.

For the Polish and other Eastern European leaderships the message from Moscow was clear: Seek new paths toward economic prosperity, including efforts to deepen relations with the economies of Western Europe. The breakthrough came with the EC–Soviet agreement on a joint declaration between the EC and Comecon (Council for Mutual Economic Assistance), issued in the summer of 1988. The EC thereby exchanged a formal recognition of Comecon for a Soviet acceptance that individual Eastern European countries could thereafter establish their own bilateral links with the EC.[34] A trade and cooperation agreement with Hungary quickly followed and negotiations on a similar agreement with Poland began in early 1989.

In the autumn of 1988 Gorbachev followed this up with an announcement of unilateral Soviet cuts in its armed forces in Eastern Europe. These cuts demonstrated unmistakably that the USSR was abandoning its strategy of readiness to use Eastern Europe as a launchpad for rapid advance westward in the event of a war with NATO. This change of posture showed that

Eastern Europe was losing the strategic value assigned to it by the USSR since the late 1940s. Gorbachev was signaling to all that he was prepared to consider a qualitative loosening of Soviet links with East-Central Europe. The path was cleared, in other words, for the Polish government to embark on its leap into the unknown in the spring of 1989.

The Processes of Systemic Change:
Economic Content and Consequences

The elections of 1989 and the negotiations that followed them opened the way for the formation of the first non-Communist government in Eastern Europe since 1948, under the prime ministership of the Polish liberal Catholic intellectual Tadeusz Mazowiecki. I will briefly survey some aspects of the events that followed, in particular (1) the economic consequences of the policies for systemic change and (2) the forms of political evolution.

"Shock Therapy" and Civil Society

The Mazowiecki government came into office within a civil society whose genetic codes were those of state socialism, albeit a state socialism in decay. The media, the publishing world, cultural institutions, welfare organizations, economic enterprises, and religious institutions were all still shaped by a state-socialist environment. Even the activities of the private peasantry and private entrepreneurs in the cities were shaped by their relationships with state-socialist institutions.

The one apparent exception to this rule, Solidarity, was in fact also a product of state socialism in its inner identity structure, in that it combined roles that are normally differentiated in Western capitalist societies—those of a political movement and those of a trade union.

Within these institutions a large majority of Poles supported the new government in its intention to transform Polish society rapidly into a free-market society, although what such a slogan actually meant varied enormously across the population.[35] This support for change was reinforced by the population's experience with the high inflation rate that soared in 1989, but the consensus was largely negatively integrated. Regarding the substance of a free-market society there were sharply diverging trends, especially within the very heart of Solidarity. For the majority of the intellectuals who had been gathered around the KOR, a free-market society meant a particular institutional form of capitalism we may describe as "neoliberal": a drastically reduced role for state social protection, a reliance on market forces for welfare, and an economy open to free trade and free movement of capital. But for the sector of Solidarity active in the industrial enterprises, a free market meant that they could take over their enterprises without interference from the party-state and run them with proprietary rights—a development prefigured by the decentralized control of enterprises that already existed to some extent in the second half of the 1980s. For the peasants linked to Solidarity, the break with state socialism was supposed to mean a stronger and more secure position for their private farms.

All these contradictory aspirations were represented among the members of the Mazowiecki government. But its policies were governed by what may be called the neoliberal wing, which envisaged sweeping social engineering from above through government action to achieve free-market capitalism. This would, in other words, be a statist intervention in the society to restructure purposefully economic institutions toward predefined public-policy goals. In adopting this course the government was well aware that it risked alienating the bulk of the population and provoking dangerous levels of protest from civil society. Their strategy was therefore geared toward political demobilization and shock tactics that presented society with faits accomplis, rather than attempts to include, negotiate with, and achieve consensus-building compromises with the leaders of existing social institutions and networks.[36] The task of developing and consolidating other institutional infrastructures between the level of economic organization and that of political organization was assigned to the latter stages of the transformation.[37]

The Balcerowicz Plan for Systemic Transformation: Implementation, Results, and Failings

The Mazowiecki government adopted a plan that was designed to achieve four goals more or less simultaneously:

1. End the financial crisis.
2. Introduce capitalist disciplines through swiftly introducing world prices, through imposing hard budget constraints on enterprises, and establishing a capitalist labor market (via the creation of unemployment). This would lead swiftly on to large-scale privatization.
3. Establish the basis for Poland's integration into the world economy, breaking with Comecon; a free-trade regime protected only by low tariffs was to be introduced and current account convertibility was to be swiftly established.
4. Lay the basis for economic growth led by trade and foreign direct investment (FDI).

In practice the effects of the Balcerowicz Plan were not fully in line with predictions. We will trace the extent to which outcomes matched the plan's various objectives, briefly suggesting reasons for the discrepancies.

The shock depression and fiscal crisis. As a result of its measures of January 1990 the Balcerowicz-IMF Plan expected a contraction of industrial production and a rapid growth in unemployment, but no significant drop in overall GDP. The sudden introduction of world prices for most products would change relative prices within the economy. The effects of this should have been that rises in the value of factors and products that had been underpriced would be counterbalanced by falling values of other factors and products, leaving total values in the economy little affected. Instead, GDP fell 11.6 percent in 1990 and a further 7.6 percent in 1991, while industrial production fell 26.1 percent in 1990 and a further 11.9 percent in 1991.[38] The IMF had predicted rapid rises in the savings rate and in investment, but here again the outcome was very different. Gross fixed investment dropped by 24.8 percent in 1990, 14.2 percent in 1991, and 2.6 percent in 1992.[39]

In 1992, IMF economists suggested that the predictions had not been fulfilled because wages had not been flexible enough. Although in neoclassical theory any collapse in profitability can always find a solution in further cuts in wages, the explanation for the slump cannot be found in wage rigidities: Wages dropped very substantially, very fast in 1990. Jeffrey Sachs, an adviser centrally involved in the construction of the Balcerowicz Plan, has suggested that the problems lay in the collapse of Comecon. He has claimed that "the decline in industrial production in 1991, and to some extent in 1990, was the result of the collapse of trade with the former Soviet Union, not the result of economic reforms in Poland."[40] Yet this collapse took full effect only in 1991, whereas the plunge into depression occurred in 1990; furthermore, the loss of exports to the USSR in that year was almost entirely offset by a surge in exports to the West.

Others have suggested that the problem lay in the fact that Polish industry as constructed under Communism was simply a hopeless case; yet its performance in exports to the West in 1990–1992 demonstrates that this simply was not true. Exports rose 43.4 percent in 1990, 17.5 percent in 1991, and 9.7 percent in 1992. They dropped back only in 1993. These gains were not confined to traditional export sectors (which were in any case more diversified than typical middle-income country exports), but applied across the market. As Richard Portes says, "The explosive growth of Central and East European exports to the West in 1990–1992 does conclusively refute those who claimed that these countries couldn't compete—that quality was unacceptable, marketing was poor and so on."[41]

The two principal causes of the slump lay in the collapse of the domestic consumer markets, which fed back into producer-goods markets; and the very fierce credit crunch that resulted partly from the plan's imposition of high real interest rates and credit ceilings and partly from the absence of a proper financial system within the country.

The very high levels of inflation were reduced in 1991, but the government's budget deficit, which the plan had been expected to tackle, reappeared in a more acute form, as a result of the slump, in 1991 and 1992. (Inflation rose from 6.1 percent of GDP in 1989 to 7 percent of GDP in 1991 and 6.8 percent in 1992.)[42]

The failure of the turn in trade policy.   The government radically dismantled trade protections in 1990, leaving Poland a more open trade regime than most others in the world. It lacked significant nontariff barriers, antidumping and other safeguard instruments, and export-promotion instruments, and it relied upon low tariffs. The justification of the radical opening to imports was to prevent oligopolistic state enterprises from taking advantage of price liberalization by charging monopoly prices. State enterprises would be subjected to stiff competition from Western imports; openness would enable them to re-equip with new technologies to assist modernization and a stronger export performance.

This policy seems to have been unwise. It led to an invasion of the Polish market by Western European exporters, strongly assisted by export-promotion subsidies from Western European governments (export credits and credit guarantees, presented misleadingly as aid loans for Poland). Imports rose by only 17.9 percent in 1990 when the zloty had an artificially low exchange rate, but in 1991 they rose by no less than 46.9 percent and the rise continued, by 6.1 percent in 1992 and by 17.7 percent in 1993. The effect of this Western European state-supported export bonanza into Poland is generally agreed to have been very damaging for Poland's domestic industries. President Lech Walesa publicly accused Westerners of trying to destroy Polish industry.[43] As a result, the government increased tariffs by more than 100 percent and imposed other trade restrictions.

The arguments for the opening to imports seem to have been flawed. Prices in 1990 actually rose furthest not in the industrial sector, but in the service sector where private companies predominated. Polish state industry was oligopolistic only by a theoretical yardstick of perfect competition. As Alice Amsden and her colleagues have shown, it was not particularly oligopolistic by Western standards: The degree of concentration was on a par with the United States, even though small economies far more trade dependent than the United States could be expected to have higher levels of concentration in key sectors. Amsden's view is that the real problem for much of industry was too much fragmentation, rather than too little.[44]

At the same time, the Balcerowicz Plan expected recovery to come through export growth, so it depended crucially upon the EC's dismantling of its Cold War embargoes on Polish exports. Sachs had predicted that this would occur at the time the plan was launched, yet there was no reason that it should. Poland's traditionally strong export sectors were ones in which there were overproduction and high levels of protection in the EC: agricultural products, iron and steel, coal, textiles, and apparel. If there had not been an investment slump in Poland there might have been the possibility of a rise of new centers of export strength, but given the investment collapse, as Rollo and Stern's work has made clear, export growth could be sustained only in sectors with low capital-output ratios—that is, the traditional export sectors.[45]

In 1990 the EC did open up its market to some extent, particularly through the granting of its Generalized System of Preferences to Poland, but the Association Agreement signed in December 1991 was in some respects a step back from this. Although the EC presented the results as asymmetrical in Poland's favor, this claim referred only to the tariff aspects of the agreement; the EC side relied heavily on nontariff barriers for blocking key imports from Poland. The EC's Common Agricultural Policy (CAP) was not significantly modified. The Balcerowicz liberalization of prices had largely removed subsidies of Polish agriculture, but the CAP enabled the EC to subsidize its exports to Poland very heavily while maintaining insurmountable barriers to many Polish agricultural exports to the EC. The textile and apparel regime was also quite unfavorable to Poland because it involved a form of managed trade that could be controlled by EC producers. Steel was subject to pricing agreements, and cars to so-called voluntary export restraints; pig iron was blocked, and so on. As the EC plunged into recession in 1993 it subjected the Association Agreements to a tough set of interpretations that used rather arbitrary antidumping and other nontariff barriers against Polish products.

The result was that the initial Polish export surge petered out and Poland's trade with the EC in 1992 and 1993 swung sharply from its traditional positive toward a negative balance. In 1994 the EC textile industry's biggest export surplus anywhere in the world was in its trade with Poland: It stood at over ECU 1 billion.[46]

A macroeconomic policy at odds with a consumption-led recovery. The IMF expectation of an export-led recovery in Poland justified its insistence on maintaining a strong deflationary stance involving fiscal retrenchment, continuing tight credit, and a tough wage-control policy in the state sector. These were wholly inappropriate policies for an economy that would be able to recover only through domestic consumption growth. The recovery that became visible in 1993 and continued into 1994 emerged precisely from such growth. Only in 1993 did the IMF show signs of reinterpreting the situation and relaxing its drive against inflation.

Privatization, FDI, and restructuring: Aims and problems. The Balcerowicz Plan envisaged the rapid privatization of state enterprises for cash. Because the social group of money capitalists was only in its infancy in Poland, foreign buyers were seen as central to the success of privatization. Such participation by Western transnational corporations (TNCs) would also, it was thought, fit Poland's microeconomics into the Western division of labor, partly by offering TNCs the prospect of relocating production from Western to Eastern Europe to take advantage of very low Polish wages and relatively highly skilled labor.

At the same time, the international financial institutions (IFIs) sought to use their political leverage to ensure that the restructuring of Polish industry would take place only after privatization and would be carried out by the new private owners. The World Bank therefore sought to ensure that restructuring efforts before privatization would be limited to the efforts of individual enterprise managements to cope with the effect of the budget constraints imposed by government policy. The tight control of wages and the credit crunch would push enterprises threatened with insolvency toward shedding labor and nonprofitmaking assets and roles (for example, their often extensive social welfare functions).

In contrast to the pattern in Western Europe, where minor recessions produce large government subsidies to loss-making sectors, the IFIs made strenuous efforts to end Polish government subsidies in the midst of the slump by threatening to withhold loans. Such subsidies were reduced to a mere 2.4 percent of budget expenditures by 1991, substantially below western German levels.[47]

The World Bank has also blocked governments from restructuring state-owned enterprises *before* privatizing them, explaining that "such physical restructuring is best done by private owners."[48] It therefore required Poland's Industrial Development Agency (IDA) to be effectively emasculated. Its agreement with the Polish government on this matter explains:

> IDA's existing financial portfolio will be transferred to financial institutions. Loans to enterprises will be sold or transferred to financial entities capable of managing credit risks. . . . IDA's equity investments in enterprises will be transferred to equity holding entities, such as independent companies, private funds, privatisation funds or private equity holding companies. It was confirmed during negotiations [between the World Bank and the Polish Government] that transfer of IDA's financial portfolio will be completed by June 30th, 1992.[49]

The World Bank similarly sought to weaken the role of the Polish Development Bank, which was set up by the government in 1990 to lend funds to enterprises on a long-term basis. The World Bank intervened and ruled that this body must limit such lending to 15 percent of its capital; the rest of its lending should be only to commercial banks.[50]

The logic of these policies was that modernizing restructuring should be left largely to foreign capital because although state enterprises were offered for sale at very low prices, the social groups in Poland able to mobilize money capital for purchasing state assets were limited. The IMF calculated in 1990 that total private savings in Poland at that time could purchase only about 5 percent of state assets. The OECD, like the IFIs, has stressed the centrality of foreign capital in restructuring, saying that it is "crucial to the process of transition to a market economy."[51] The OECD adds that "the privatisation process must extensively rely on FDI [foreign direct investment]."[52]

However, the hope that large flows of FDI would enter Poland, on the basis of an attractive institutional structure and IMF-approved government policies, proved illusory. Large inflows of FDI are attracted above all by economies undergoing rapid growth, as is illustrated in the case of China.[53] The FDI that flowed into Poland and the rest of the region in the early 1990s was overwhelmingly market seeking rather than production seeking.[54] Statistical analysis by the OECD Secretariat has confirmed this fact for East-Central and Eastern Europe.[55]

The larger investors in Poland typically sought a monopoly position in the market. General Motors required the right to export its cars duty free into Poland as a condition for investing in Warsaw, and demanded high tariffs on non-GM cars.[56] The funds flowing in were usually for the purchase of assets rather than for the upgrading of fixed capital. The Central and Eastern European country average of the amounts of money invested in foreign-equity capital has been a mere fraction of the equivalent in the developed-country affiliates, reaching considerably less than one-tenth of even the developing-country average.

The EC has provided substantial public subsidies to its own economic operators to encourage them to purchase assets in Poland and other Visegrad countries. The PHARE (Poland-Hungary Aid for Reconstruction) program has largely funded Poland's privatization agency; it has paid Western investment banks and accounting companies to make detailed studies of various sectors of Polish industry. PHARE units staffed mainly by EC nationals have operated in the relevant Polish ministries, and the EC has offered direct top-up funds for EC companies that buy Polish assets.

The result has been that the great bulk of privatized state enterprises have been bought by Western capital rather than by Polish entrepreneurs. Both public opinion and government in Poland have become increasingly unenthusiastic about various aspects of this campaign, worrying that it has more to do with serving Western industrial interests than with strengthening Poland's supply side for effective insertion into Western markets. It is not surprising, then, that a major aspect of the Balcerowicz Plan that has not yet been implemented is the rapid privatization of the bulk of Poland's large state enterprises. The reason for this has been, at bottom, political.

One of the key reasons that industrial workers in Poland had supported the Mazowiecki government and the Balcerowicz Plan was their belief that the result would be their gaining proprietary rights over their own enterprises. Yet for the international financial institutions and the neoliberal current in the Mazowiecki government, privatization into the hands of the employees of companies was not acceptable. Given their preference for privatization for cash, they had to opt for direct sales to foreign companies, and/or for a voucher scheme that would give all citizens a nominal stake while effectively transferring ownership to holding companies, which would usually require capitalization by foreign capital.

A corollary of the Western approach was that the regime change was followed by a largely successful attempt to recentralize control over the state enterprises, which undermined the power of the works councils and placed the enterprises directly under the authority of a government agency. The government then drew up a scheme for mass privatization, but since 1991 the implementation of the scheme has remained in political deadlock.

The IMF and the World Bank have sought to use their conditionality to engineer powerful incentives for both workers and managers to accept privatization on their terms. The IMF won agreement that the private sector would be provided with a tax holiday during the transition, as would those state enterprises that entered collaborative relationships with foreign companies. This placed extra tax burdens on the state-enterprise sector. The World Bank required that the penal tax on pay increases in the state sector would continue, while private-sector companies would be exempt; this was designed to give state employees a strong incentive to seek rapid privatization. Neither of these arrangements has broken the deadlock, however.

A second political aspect has played an important role in this impasse: a nationalist suspicion of plans to hand large swathes of Polish industry over to foreign capital whether as owners or as lessees. These worries are fed not only by disillusionment with the EC's approach to trade issues, and by some examples of predatory Western buyouts, but also by memories of Poland's interwar experiences in this area. A further factor has been Polish worries over the possibility of domination by German capital, fueled by Chancellor Kohl's less than enthusiastic approach to the signing of the 1990 Polish–German Treaty accepting the country's current borders. These concerns have not, of course, been uniformly felt across the political spectrum, but they have had sufficient effect to block progress on privatization.

Achievements: The installation of capitalism, and debt forgiveness. Against this setback for the Balcerowicz strategy has been the substantial growth of the private sector to the point where it is generally calculated to account for about half of Poland's GDP. The state-enterprise sector, despite the heavy discriminations placed against it by public policy, does remain of central importance to Poland's economic future. In the spring of 1994, 60 percent of Polish exports were still being accounted for by state enterprises.

Nevertheless, overall the economic organization of Polish society has been transformed during the last five years and the basic institutions of capitalism have taken root. There is a full-fledged capitalist labor market with substantial unemployment, and a new social group of capitalists has emerged with a growing influence upon public policy. A capital market is growing, and the tax system has been restructured along capitalist lines that tie the resources of the state increasingly to the profitability of an economy rooted in private ownership. The state enterprises themselves are increasingly subject to the disciplines of capitalist labor and product markets. The level of economic activity in Poland is increasingly in tune with the rhythms of the Western economic system and no significant political forces in the country are calling for a return to state socialism. Even if the Balcerowicz Plan route to this transformation may not have been optimal in a number of respects, its goal of rapidly installing capitalism has largely been achieved.

The plan had an additional positive result. It managed to gain the support of the U.S. government and then of the Western European governments for a halving of Poland's debts both to public and private creditors in the West. This debt forgiveness has transformed Poland's external payments position, its creditworthiness, and the equations of the government's financial and fiscal policies. Such Western action with regard to Poland stands in stark contrast with the inaction toward other Eastern European states.[57]

Political Evolution Since the Regime Change

An explanatory framework for Poland's political transformation that presumed there to be, on one axis, a polarization between totalitarian forces and institutions, and on the other the emergence of civil society, would imply a sharp break in the contours of Polish politics after 1989. Such a sharp break did occur in postfascist Europe after the war and also in post-Franco Spain, but it has been far less marked in post-Communist Poland. This is all the more remarkable given the radical *economic* discontinuity in Poland as compared with the relative continuity in Spain.

The pursuit of rapid systemic change has brought with it a great deal of political turmoil, involving rapid changes of government as initial strong support for the Mazowiecki government ebbed in the face of the economic crisis. Two features of political change are nevertheless striking. First, public policy has remained effectively anchored on the course set out in 1990. This is partly explained by the phased implementation of the country's debt cancellation, with movement through these phases being dependent upon Polish governments' agreeing to terms for domestic macroeconomic policy with the IMF. No Polish government has been prepared for long to risk forgoing the debt-cancellation packages. The second reason is that no Polish political force has been able to advance a coherent alternative to the international politicoeconomic orientation toward Western Europe. The alternative that might have existed on an economic level in 1989–1990, of replacing Comecon with a new regional economic framework, disappeared—not least as a result of the Polish government's decision at that time to go it alone with shock therapy. The 1991 Association Agreement with the EC further deepened the rift between the Polish economy and those of its eastern neighbors. The rules of origin that make up an important part of these agreements have the effect of weakening the possibilities of strong production linkages between former Comecon members while privileging such linkages with EC economic operators.

The second striking feature of post-1989 Polish politics has been the extent to which the forces within the political system have retained a continuity with the forces operating under state socialism, even though the substance of their programs has significantly changed under the impact of Poland's progressive integration with the West.

The three main components yoked together within Solidarity—the liberal intelligentsia, the industrial workers, and the church—have tended to break apart, while the leader of the 1980s who had sought to stand above those components and integrate them charismatically continues to seek to project himself as a quasi-Bonaparte or, in a Polish cultural context, Pilsudski. The dominant forces within the PUWP of the 1980s—a combination of social democrats and market socialists—have continued to claim the mantle of the traditions of the Polish left. The Polish peasantry, too, has maintained its tradition of political organization.

The relationship between the Catholic hierarchy and the liberal intelligentsia in the last decade of state socialism was never more than a marriage of convenience; the regime change brought about a sharp polarization between the Mazowiecki-led Democratic Union and the new political force reflecting the ideology of the Polish Primate, the Christian Nationals. This latter trend, in the form of the Olszewski government, did attempt to mount a challenge to the Western-oriented secular-liberal program of the Democratic Union, but it failed ignominiously and collapsed in an effort by some of its ministers to stage something approaching a coup in 1992.[58]

The central axis of conflictual political development in the first half of the 1990s has been the separation between the liberal and the syndicalist forces emerging from Solidarity. This fissure has been driven by conflict over privatization and the wage-control policies, but also over the perception that the government was not prepared to consult with or accommodate the views of important institutions of civil society. This conflict eventually brought down the second government led by the Democratic Union in 1993, opening the way for the ex-Communist Socialist Party to become the strongest electoral force and return to office in the subsequent election.

The extent of the reorientation within the syndicalist current from Solidarity was demonstrated by examples of cooperation between the Solidarity trade union and the PUWP-created official union, the All-Polish Alliance of Trade Unions or OPZZ, which had been Solidarity's bitter enemy in the 1980s and which is now the largest trade-union center in Poland. At the political level, cooperation between Solidarity and the ex-

Communist socialists actually brought down the Suchocka government in the summer of 1993.

In some ways the most surprising development has been the emergence of the old satellite party of the PUWP, the Peasant Party, as the voice of Poland's private peasantry. The Balcerowicz Plan, with its neoliberal hostility to state support for agriculture and its strong orientation to opening Poland's market to Western European imports, stood in radical contradiction to the interests of the private peasants, who were the main expression of private enterprise in the country. The peasantry regarded EC humanitarian aid to Poland in the form of food surpluses as a move to destabilize the Polish market, particularly as it was followed by a surge of subsidized food imports from the EC while subsidies for Polish agriculture were being abolished. An important factor in the reorientation of those parts of the peasantry that initially supported Solidarity has been the perception that the Solidarity-derived governments were unwilling to respect or even seriously listen to the demands of their civil associations. The result has been a strong electoral showing for the Peasant Party, which under its leader Pawlak was the most skeptical of the main political parties over Poland's relations with the European Union.

President Walesa's attempts to project himself as a force above these political conflicts, as well as above parliamentary authority, took an electoral form in 1993 when he attempted to build a political bloc above the parties—a move reminiscent of Pilsudski's authoritarian populism in the interwar period. Although his effort failed, Walesa has remained a powerful force within Poland's political institutions, a force that has tended to destabilize governments and weaken the possibility of forming stable coalitions at a parliamentary level.

The efforts of Poland's first four governments, all derived from Solidarity, to demobilize civil society were partially successful. A great increase in political passivity was demonstrated by very low voter turnout and by the fact that only the ex-Communist Party and its allied Peasant Party maintained significant levels of membership. At the same time, this apathy was punctuated by bitter social revolts that have mainly taken the form of strike waves.

Conclusion

I have argued that the transformation process in Poland cannot be adequately described or explained by the concept of totalitarianism versus civil society. We still lack adequate instruments for understanding the complexities of official politics in state-socialist societies and of the relationship between official institutions and social groups within those societies. But we have argued that the starting point for an analysis of the origins of the turn of 1989 must be a search *within* the institutions of Polish state socialism as well as in errors of economic policymaking. Larger failures of the Soviet bloc as a whole to compete effectively with the Western world must be included in any adequate account; the unity of the West and the combined exclusion of the bloc from the Western-led world economy, along with the more general containment pressure on the bloc, contributed fundamentally to these failures.

The strategy for systemic change adopted by the Mazowiecki government did not in fact promote the flourishing of a strong, institutionalized civil society. To have done so would have involved slackening the drive to complete systemic change and may well, as Sachs has argued, have led to a reversal of the transition to capitalism,[59] and toward a mixed system of capitalism and state socialism, or a "third way."

Such a third way did retain a base within Polish society in the value-orientations of strategic social groups, notably within the syndicalist wing of Solidarity as well as in some trends within the PUWP. What the formula lacked was any ideological and political energy in 1989, as well as an articulation in public policy terms. The electoral swing toward the ex-Communist Socialist Party and its allied Peasant Party in 1993 expressed a wider trend in Polish society than simply numbers of votes for these parties.[60] The swing reflects the experience of bitter disappointment with the shock therapy program and a desire to turn back toward some kind of third way.

The continuation of the shock therapy, against the trend of popular sentiment in large parts of Polish society, was possible in large part because of the anchoring of the processes by the international financial institutions, especially through the positive incentive of debt reduction. Poland's inherited financial problems and the very depression involved in the policy of shock therapy led public policy to be highly constrained by the conditionality of the Western multilateral institutions. There has been an evident tension between the latter's requirements and popular sentiment in the country as expressed both on the nationalist populist right and on the left. This tension has been a prominent feature in other post-Communist countries in the region.

Various Western aid programs have been bracketed together under the heading of supporting the development of civil society in Poland. Michael Ignatieff, among others, has argued for a "civil society strategy" of this sort on the part of the West, directed against the threat of authoritarian populism and involving the funding of political oppositions, the media, the judicial system, and the police.[61] Such programs are already being sponsored by the EU through PHARE, among others, but their attempt to generate changes administratively in perceptions and behavior are unlikely to play more than a minor role. Indeed, they could easily become counterproductive if perceived as yet further forms of Western intervention.

Future consolidation of civil society and pluralist democracy in Poland will depend in large part on economic performance and on the capacity of public policy to address the social concerns of very large parts of the population. Success in these areas will in turn continue to be affected by the forms of integration into the Western European economic and political structures that Poland is offered. On current levels of GDP growth, average living standards should return to their 1988 levels by about the year 2010. Following current political trends in Poland, such a growth rate, based on the unlikely assumption that Western Europe will avoid another recession in 1997–1998, does not seem sufficient to assure political stabilization. The West would then be required to reassess its entire approach to the transformation in East-Central Europe and perhaps to its more general plans for the reorganization of the world economy.

Notes

1. The Communist Party in Poland was in fact called the Polish United Workers Party (PUWP). We shall refer to it as such, but will also use the term Communist.

2. The elections for the upper house (the Senate) were entirely free, but those for the lower house were genuinely competitive for only 35 percent of the seats; 65 percent were reserved for the PUWP and other parties allied to it.

3. See R. Dahrendorf, *Reflections on the Revolution in Europe* (London: Chatto, 1990).

4. The literature on comparative democratization that treats the political processes of transition to democracy in Southern Europe and in East-Central Europe as being essentially the same genus does this. For one example of this literature among many, see R. Bova, "Political Dynamics of the Post-Communist Transition. A Comparative Perspective," *World Politics* Vol. 44, October 1991.

5. See, for example, J. Sachs, *Poland's Jump to the Market Economy* (Cambridge, Mass.: MIT Press, 1993).

6. Marxists of various kinds would argue that what we call state socialism was not a full-fledged system counterposed to capitalism, but rather transitional toward such a system. This is an important debate but not central to our discussion here.

7. Both decentralization within the state-socialist sector and a "dualization" could, of course, occur simultaneously.

8. The classic example of this tendency was, of course, Czechoslovakia in the spring and summer of 1968.

9. For further elaboration see P. Gowan, "Liberalism and Democracy: The Contest of Ideas at the 19th CPSU Conference," *Labour Focus on Eastern Europe,* Autumn, 1988.

10. Thus as late as 1984 Samuel Huntington was arguing that "the likelihood of democratic development in Eastern Europe is virtually nil" in Huntington, "Will more countries become Democratic?" *Political Science Quarterly,* Vol. 99 (Summer 1984). The standard account was to suggest that authoritarian regimes differed from

Communist totalitarian regimes precisely in that the former could evolve toward democracy from within while the latter could not. This view is strongly argued in, among many examples, the work of Juan Linz.

11. See T. G. Ash, *The Uses of Adversity* (Cambridge: Granta/Penguin, 1989); and *The Polish Revolution: Solidarity,* second edition (London: Hodder & Stoughton, 1985).

12. See, in particular, A. Michnik, *Letters from Prison and Other Essays* (Berkeley: University of California Press, 1985).

13. T. G. Ash, *In Europe's Name* (Jonathan Cape, 1993), p. 282.

14. Ibid.

15. See L. Schapiro, *Totalitarianism* (London, 1970).

16. See, for example, Z. Brzeszinski, *The Permanent Purge* (New York, 1955) and his work with Friedrich in the early 1950s, which stresses the centrality of terror and purges. Friedrich attempted to reformulate his theory in 1969 in such a way as to make partocracy and Brezhnevism the apogee of totalitarianism, though these later criteria might suggest that Stalin's rule was not totalitarian.

17. A valuable though unsympathetic account of the history of the party is to be found in M. Dziewanowski, *The Communist Party of Poland,* 2nd ed., (Cambridge, Mass.: Harvard University Press, 1976). On the interwar Polish party, see I. Deutscher, "The Tragedy of the Polish Communist Party," in T. Deutscher, ed., *Marxism in Our Time* (London, 1972).

18. Against Prussian Lutheranism in the West and Orthodoxy in the East.

19. On Gomulka, see N. Bethel, *Gomulka* (London: Penguin, 1970). On Poland in the 1960s, see M. Gamarnikow, "Poland: Political Pluralism in a One-Party State," *Problems of Communism,* July–August 1967.

20. On the Poznan Uprising and other events in the background to Gomulka's return to power, see J. Maciejewska and Z. Trajanowiczowa, eds., *Poznanski Czerwiec, 1956* (Poznan: Wydawnictwo Poznanskie, 1981).

21. On the history of peasant politics in Poland up to 1970, see O. Narkiewicz, *The Green Flag, Polish Populist Politics, 1867–1970* (London: Croom Helm, 1976).

22. Notably the repression directed against some of the strike leaders.

23. Dramatic evidence of this was provided in 1975 when the government published draft amendments to the constitution to bring it in line with post–Brezhnev Doctrine Soviet demands. This produced many thousands of hostile responses from the population and these in turn led the government to withdraw many of its original formulations on the key amendments. Neither the popular protests (through legal channels) nor the government response would have been likely in other Soviet bloc countries. See, for example, N. Ascherson, *The Polish August* (Harmonsdsworth: Penguin, 1981), p. 112. Opinion surveys carried out by the Academy of Sciences in the 1970s indicate that while abuses of authority and attempts to suppress criticism were concerns of sections of the population, they were not very widespread, and less salient than concern about waste, bureaucracy, and nepotism. For one such survey of the views of young people, see B. Golebiowski, "The younger generation's aspirations and orientations," in J. Turowski and L. Szwengrup, eds., *Rural Social Change in Poland* (Warsaw: The Polish Academy of Social Sciences Press, 1976), pp. 279–291.

24. Jacek Kuron, a close colleague of Adam Michnik and a Solidarity leader, has recently stressed this: "Scholarship on the communist impact on Polish society has tended to stress learned attitudes: passiveness, dependence on the state, insistence on numerous entitlements, treating our governors as aliens. Accurate as far as they go, these generalisations are one-sided. The claim to entitlements means not only passiveness, but also awareness of one's rights. Sometimes that awareness

breeds the will to fight and in fact bred large social movements. . . . On a more individual and local level, acts of social solidarity were commonplace." J. Kuron, "Manifesto: Phase Two of a Program for Poland," *Common Knowledge,* Vol. 4, No. 1, Spring 1995.

25. On the events on the Baltic coast, see P. Barton, *Misère et Revolte de l'Ouvrier Polonais* (Paris, 1971) and the transcript of the negotiations between Gierek and the Szczecin strikers in *New Left Review,* No. 72, March–April 1972.

26. On the conflicting political groupings within the PUWP at this time, see A. Bromke, "Beyond the Gomulka Era," *Foreign Affairs,* April 1971.

27. For a detailed analysis of the period from 1970 to 1976 in Poland, see P. Green, "Third Round in Poland," *New Left Review,* Nos. 101–102, February–April 1977.

28. See Green, "Third Round in Poland," on these events.

29. For English translations of the early documents of the KOR, see *Labour Focus on Eastern Europe,* Vols. 1–3, 1977–1979. See also P. Raina, *Political Opposition in Poland, 1954–1977* (London: Poets and Painters Press, 1977).

30. It should be said, however, that the excitement almost certainly stopped at the front door of the Primate's palace in Warsaw.

31. Cited by L. Kolarska-Bobinska, "Myth of the Market, Reality of Reform," in S. Gomulka and A. Polonsky, eds., *Polish Paradoxes* (London: Routledge, 1990). This important article brilliantly maps the complexities of public opinion in Poland in the 1980s.

32. For a useful overview of this aspect of U.S. policy, see T. Baylis, *The West and Eastern Europe: Economic Statecraft and Political Change* (New York: Praeger, 1994).

33. For American policy in these years, see J. Hough, *The Polish Crisis: American Policy Options* (Washington, D.C.: The Brookings Institution, 1982).

34. On EC policy at this time, see P. Gowan, "The European Community and East-Central Europe, 1989–1991," *Labour Focus on Eastern Europe,* Vol. 43, 1992.

35. See Kolarska-Bobinska, op. cit., for an analysis of what she calls the market myth.

36. See the impressive analysis by the sociologist Wlodzimierz Wesolowski in his "The Nature of Social Ties and the Future of Postcommunist Society: Poland After Solidarity" in J. Hall, ed., *Civil Society: Theory, History, Comparison* (Cambridge: Polity Press, 1995).

37. Timothy Garton Ash has noted that "the social dimension of transition is a neglected third dimension" in contrast to political and economic dimensions. Yet he means by this "a particular social structure, with a substantial middle class." In other words, his social dimension still collapses back into being the end product of social engineering through a Balcerowicz Plan approach, rather than an enhancement of the salience of civic institutions and of the efficacy of civic action in the transition. See "An Interview with Timothy Garton Ash," *The Oxford International Review,* Vol. 6, No. 1, Winter 1994.

38. European Bank for Reconstruction and Development (EBRD), *Transition Report,* October 1994, p. 165.

39. Ibid.

40. J. Sachs, "Reply to Jan Adam," *Economics of Planning,* Vol 26, 1993.

41. C. Henning et al., eds., *Reviving the European Union* (Washington, D.C.: Institute for International Economics, April 1994), p. 173.

42. Ibid.

43. Cited by J. Adam, "The Transition to a Market Economy in Poland," *Cambridge Journal of Economics,* 1994, No. 18, p. 613.

44. Amsden takes sectors where East-Central European economies have had growth potential and demonstrates the overfragmentation problems. In detergents, 80 percent of the market is controlled by two companies in the UK and by three in Germany. But in Poland there were seven, none big enough for scale efficiency. In crude steel output Poland ranked 17th in the world, yet the biggest Polish steel enterprise (Huta Katowice) ranked only 32nd in size. UNIDO reported in 1991 that the steel industries of the region generally faced the problem of undersized plants. The same fragmentation problem has existed in machine tools and in pulp and paper. (See Amsden et al., op. cit., pp. 94–95.) Sachs was also aware of this, saying that "the giant firms in Poland are small players in the European market" (J. Sachs, *Poland's Jump to the Market Economy* [Cambridge, Mass.: MIT Press, 1993], p. 50). Yet it did not lead him to propose further concentration in key sectors.

45. J. Rollo and J. Stern, "Growth and Trade Prospects for Central and Eastern Europe," *The World Economy,* Vol. 15, No. 5.

46. See J. Luesby, "Sharp Rise in Exports Lifts EU's Textiles Output," *Financial Times,* 4 May 1995, page 7.

47. A. Amsden et al., *The Market Meets Its Match: Restructuring the Economies of Eastern Europe* (Cambridge, Mass.: Harvard University Press, 1994), p. 116.

48. Quoted by Amsden, op. cit., p. 117. In this case the World Bank was dealing with Hungary.

49. Ibid.

50. Ibid., p. 121. Another field of economic policy where Western public bodies have been decisive has been in seeking to end significant subsidies to agriculture in target countries. The impact of this in the trade field was noted above.

51. OECD, *Integrating Emerging Market Economies into the International Trading System* (Paris: OECD, 1994).

52. Ibid. The OECD does not explain the force of the "must" here except to say that foreign companies will be central "in restructuring the state-owned industries." This, as we have seen, is because the World Bank in Poland and Hungary would not allow industry ministries to restructure before privatization.

53. China, whose government has not defined property rights clearly and lacks even reliable contract law, attracted over $11 billion of FDI in 1992 alone. This was more than that attracted to the entire former Soviet bloc between 1989 and 1993. In 1993 the inflow of FDI into China doubled again to over $22 billion.

54. On this point for developing countries see UNCTAD, *World Investment Report 1994* (Geneva and New York: United Nations, 1994), p. 20.

55. "The major objective for FDI in Central and Eastern Europe was 'markets'." *OECD Working Paper No. 43: Market Access–FDI/Trade Linkages in Eastern Europe* (Paris: OECD, 1994), p. 5.

56. R. Parker, "Clintonomics for the East," *Foreign Policy,* No. 94, Spring 1994, p. 60.

57. Hungary, with higher per capita debt, has failed to gain even debt relief, much less debt reduction, and has been mired in desperate financial strains throughout the 1990s. These strains do much to explain the depression continuing in Hungary throughout the first half of the 1990s.

58. See L. Vinton, "Olszewski's Ouster Leaves Poland Polarised," *RFE/RL Research Report,* Vol. 1, No. 30, 19 June 1992.

59. See Sachs, *Poland's Jump to the Market Economy,* p. 5. Polemicizing with Dahrendorf's insistence on the priority of consensus and institutional stability, Sachs

says that if this philosophy had been followed, "I doubt that the transformation would be possible at all, at least without costly and dangerous wrong turns."

60. This point is affirmed strongly by Jacek Kuron, op. cit.

61. M. Ignatieff, "On Civil Society," *Foreign Affairs,* March/April 1995, Vol. 74, No. 2.

5

Poland: Significance and Limitations of the Democratization Process[1]

STEPHEN DAY

The year 1989 was undoubtedly an annus mirabilis that set Eastern and Central Europe firmly on the path of transition and established the region as part of Huntington's "third wave of democratization."[2] Since 1989 Poland has become renowned for pioneering post-Communist reform; it was the first to adopt economic "shock therapy" in the form of the Balcerowicz Plan, the first Visegrad country to elect a realigned post-Communist government, and at the same time a nation that has witnessed apparent political instability, which, as of 1995, had given the country its seventh prime minister in six years.[3] This chapter will assess the state of affairs in Poland following the election of September 1993, which brought to power the post-Communist coalition of the Democratic Left Alliance (SLD) and the Polish Peasant Party (PSL). Through the combination of a theoretical framework based on a synthesis of existing transition literature, and an analysis of current events, I hope to shed some light on the dynamics of the transition process. I will examine the process from two angles: first the dichotomy between the forces and processes associated with the ancien régime, the Polish People's Republic (PRL) and the Polish Republic (RP), and second the notion of *consolidation.* The theoretical framework will encapsulate a number of interdependent and interwoven variables: the political parties, their relationship with the trade unions, relations within the coalition itself, and the relationship with President Walesa. I will point out a number of contradictions within the coalition that could result in some sort of realignment of the political spectrum, possibly in the form of a "historic compromise" between specific post-Solidarity and post-Communist forces, despite the obvious symbolic divide.

From the outset the dynamics of change in Poland have been constantly shifting. Initially change was constrained by the mode of transition during the historic Round Table talks of February 1989, a pactmaking process in which authoritarianism was replaced by cohabitation. The declarations of April gave a favorable position to forces of the ancien régime, including a guaranteed 65 percent of the lower house (*Sejm*) seats and the ministries of defense and internal affairs. In July General Wojciech Jaruzelski was elected president with the support of Solidarity. According to Sabbat-Swidlicka,

> Walesa saw the agreement as a chance to begin a gradual transformation of the political system to make it fully democratic and nationally independent, whereas the authorities were, rather, counting on enlisting the cooperation of parts of the opposition movement in reforming the existing political institutions. The two sides sealed an electoral pact that they hoped would facilitate the realization of their aims.[4]

Following the semifree June 1989 election, the inappropriateness of the "limited democracy" that had emerged from the Round Table settlements became apparent. In September the opposition was handed power without any adverse reaction from the Communists. According to Przeworski, a "democracy that results from the *ruptura pactada* is inevitably conservative economically and socially."[5] The transition was then constrained by the desire to rejoin Europe. This entailed a procedural minimum style of democracy, heralded as the only alternative, with an emphasis on elections;[6] and a new mode of conflict resolution between political elites, namely consensus and compromise, which remained essential for coalition formation.[7] In the economic sphere the transition called for a neoliberal economic agenda. These processes had three corresponding effects. First, the modus operandi of the polity became one of competition, consensus, and compromise. Second, questions relating to mass participation were of little concern—in fact, a demobilization of the masses was seen as a necessary step. Finally, policy choices for any electoral victor, especially in the economic sphere, were severely limited.

There can be no doubt about the importance of political elites in undertaking the *initial* stages of democratization. They have been the designers of Poland's institutional architecture, which has included a semipresidential system, a corporatist arrangement to foster economic stability, and an electoral system that underwent extensive changes. This institutionalization has been achieved at the expense of civil society, which has lacked a definitive voice in the policymaking process (perhaps with the exception of the church's influence on social policy during the Olszewski government). Agh has termed this "overparliamentarization" and "overparticization,"[8] a phenomenon that has had its own impact on democratization. It seems that centralization has only a certain shelf life before it begins to undermine the democratization process. The lack of any sort of institutional link with society, low membership levels, or a developed network of societal interests has until now meant that an incumbent has failed to retain power. The automatic response of many parties in this situation is to adopt populist and unrealistic policies that further diminish levels of trust when they cannot be fulfilled. Declining legitimacy, as hope and tolerance give way to alienation and cynicism, increases the overall instability of any regime.

In the present climate, the process of change is evolving around two variables. The first is the dichotomy of forces associated with the past, that is, the PRL, and the forces of discontinuity, that is the RP. It is possible that a symbolic dichotomy between these forces, and hence instability, may be maintained. The 1995 presidential elections can be used as a barometer to measure the present strength of this divide. The second variable is the notion of consolidation, "which is distinguished by the increasing dominance of competition and co-operation as the prevailing means of conflict resolution."[9] If this remains the ultimate goal of democracy, then two outcomes must be achieved. First, "democracy . . . will be self-enforcing, when all the political forces have some specific minimum probability of doing well under the particular system of institutions."[10] Therefore, based on the minimalist definition of democracy, this requires the institutionalization of democracy whereby strategic actors accept the rules of the game, not only symbolically but as a matter of principle, and where none conspire to bring down the institutional architecture of democracy. Second, at some stage (timing is not as crucial as in the initial stages) civil society must be integrated into the democratization process. This optimally brings about a firm commitment to democracy and a corresponding increase in legitimacy. In this way, the governing parties and the opposition, the church and the government, the president and the government, Solidarity and the formerly Communist trade union OPZZ, and civil society all come into the equation, all contributing to a process that may or may not lead to the second stage of transition, consolidation.

It has always been assumed that new democracies are very fragile and prone to breakdown, through either an inability to meet popular pressure or an authoritarian backlash by forces from the ancien régime. Ironically, at least in the short term it seems to be in everyone's interest to demobilize the masses, negotiate, and wait for apparently evolutionary processes to set in that will undo many of the initial agreements of the transition. If the ancien régime was unable to stipulate constitutional safeguards, as in Chile,[11] then the sheer process of governing, often through trial and error, results in a marginalization of the ancien régime. Those forces must either modify, as in the case of the Polish United Workers Party (PZPR), which underwent a realignment and re-emergence, or fade away.

The Third Election

The October 1991 election was based on hyperproportionality and resulted in the representation of some twenty-nine political forces.[12] The political fragmentation and the blockage of the legislative process that followed led to the introduction of new electoral laws for the September 1993 election. Hyperproportionality gave way to a 5 percent threshold for single parties and an 8 percent threshold for coalitions. This would cover the 391 seats in the fifty-two electoral districts; the remaining sixty-nine seats would be divided among those parties that gained over 7 percent of the national vote, which favored the stronger parties.[13] On 19 September, with a turnout of 52 percent, the former center/center-right regime[14] lost power to the post-Communist left of the Democratic Left Alliance (SLD) and the Polish Peasant Party (PSL), who showed impressive gains with 35.8 percent of the vote and 66.1 percent of the seats.[15]

The reasons for victory were numerous, including a response to the economic hardships of transition; disillusionment with and lack of trust in the incumbents; the reformed voting system; a backlash against the church; the inability of the right (both conservative and nationalist) to unite—often due to personality rather than ideological reasons—and thus surpass the new electoral hurdles;[16] and, according to Kubiak, the "spontaneous social-democratisation of people who lost the feeling of security."[17] He goes on to argue that the elections have reflected a search for values: In 1989–1990 the issue was internal and external sovereignty; in 1993 it was societal security.

The results (see Table 5.1) produced a considerable consolidation of the *Sejm* in terms of party representation, which went from twenty-nine to six parties, but at the same time they obscure the fact that the 38 percent who voted for the right remain unrepresented. The SLD (on a platform of pragmatism, egalitarianism, and capitalism with a human face) and the PSL (advocating neoagrarianism and protectionism for its peasant constituency) emerged victorious. They were billed as the post-Communist left by some, but others were not so sure: "Although each had just finished comprehensively refurbishing its facade, the old colours still peeked forth from beneath the fresh paint."[18] Waldemar Pawlak (the coalition's first prime minister and the leader of the PSL) stated: "We are set apart from our predecessors, not by the general goals but primarily by the methods and means of attaining these goals."[19] While the PSL remained essentially a peasant-based party,

Table 5.1   1993 Election Results in Poland

Parties	Abbrev.	No. of seats	Share of the vote (%)
Democratic Left Alliance	SLD	171	20.4
Polish Peasant Party	PSL	132	15.4
Democratic Union	UD	74	10.6
Union of Labor	UP	41	7.3
Confederation for an Independent Poland	KPN	22	5.8
Nonparty Movement for Supporting Reform	BBWR	16	5.4
German Minorities		4	—

taking 46 percent of the farmers vote, the SLD obtained a plurality in all categories (except farmers) across all levels of social criteria: age, educational attainment, blue collar (19 percent), white collar (24 percent), entrepreneur (17 percent), skilled, unskilled, and self-employed workers, and pensioners (22 percent).[20]

The coalition was formed on 21 October after several rounds of talks. It was agreed that the SLD would control privatization and finance while Pawlak's more protectionist and populist PSL would take responsibility for agriculture, foreign trade, central planning, and administration. Janusz Jankowiak stated that it was a contract that did "nothing to bind the partners . . . more than respect each other's sphere of influence."[21] Although both forces emerged from parties of the PRL, it is misleading to label them left-wing according to the traditional left–right dichotomy. The PSL remains conservative, religious (although it does have a small anticlerical wing), hostile to the free market, and tied to its rural electorate. Numerous factors contributed to the stormy relationship between the partners, including the economy, local government reform, and the renomenklaturization of politics by the PSL through partisan appointments in local government, public administration, and government agencies.

The divisions relating to economic policy led to numerous antagonisms during the first incarnation of the coalition. Many within the PSL look to agriculture as the motor for economic progress, thus protecting the party's natural constituency. There were believed to be internal divisions within the PSL between forces loyal to Roman Jagielinski, the minister of agriculture and deputy prime minister, who wanted a modern large-scale farming sector, and forces around Pawlak, who maintained the idea of neoagrarian small-scale, family-oriented farms.[22] The PSL also remained uneasy with privatization, although on 19 October 1994, Prime Minister Pawlak finally approved the Mass Privatization Program (MPP) following internal and external pressure. The irony of these events, however, was that Pawlak became one of the country's most popular politicians:

> His skilful volley tactics in dealing with the unpopular excess wages tax . . . have earned him credit with the industrial working class, while the SLD's economists, opposed to freeing wages, have lost credit among their traditional constituency. He has raised pensions, disability payments and wages in the service sector . . . he has elicited funds for his own farming lobby and convinced farmers that the prospects for agriculture will continue to improve as long as the PSL is in office.[23]

The SLD's primary concerns lay in the industrial sector and in continuity with the Suchocka government's emphasis on free enterprise. The dichotomy of opinion led to the resignation of Finance Minister and Deputy Prime Minister Marek Borowski (SLD) in February 1994, as a result of PSL incongruence.

The second incarnation of the coalition, with eight new ministers, was signed on 15 February 1995. Its stated aims included continued economic growth, reform of public administration and local government, and the pursuit of integration into European structures. This was meant to address the mistakes of Pawlak's government, which had been accused of putting the brakes on reform. Pawlak's removal as prime minister resulted in the SLD reasserting control of the economic agenda in the form of Kolodko's *Strategia dla Polski*.[24] The SLD, however, has many difficult issues to tackle, especially the need to cut back welfare and pensions, which amount to some 23 percent of GDP. Kolodko has been reported as saying, "there are significant inflationary threats resulting from the incompatibility of the coalition's social policies with economic realities."[25] Whether this incompatibility will result in internal fragmentation of the SLD remains to be seen.

The SLD[26] is made up of some twenty-eight different groups, including the Social Democracy of the Polish Republic (SdRP)—the direct successor of the Polish United Workers Party (PZPR)—and the formerly Communist trade union OPZZ (see the section on trade unions), as well as the Polish Socialist Party and individuals who had no links with the previous regime. One can identify at least sixty-two OPZZ deputies, and the Polish Socialist Party claims (without foundation) that up to seventy deputies are sympathetic to its philosophy. According to Adam Michnik, the SLD is a "Noah's ark where unrepentant communist hard-liners co-exist in apparent harmony with pragmatic social democrats resolved to make the best of capitalism."[27] The SdRP, which claims to have the support of at least two-thirds of the deputies, can be further broken down into at least three different wings: those centered around Prime Minister Oleksy and Aleksander Kwasniewski, often labeled liberals: those centered around Leszek Miller, who espouses the idea of worker participation (and is often but misleadingly labeled a traditionalist); and a final group connected with the former nomenklatura. Continuity with the past stems from the fact that members of the SLD, primarily the SdRP, had nowhere else to go—hence it is often accused of harboring a desire for a "PRL mark II."

For the time being all these groups and factions consider the SLD as the best means to serve their interests. Despite the difficulties of government, a poll published in *Gazeta Wyboroza* on 6 June 1995 gave the SLD 25 percent support while its nearest rival, the UW, had 9 percent.[28] Splits within the Democratic Left Alliance may or may not transpire, but it seems certain that the coalition will face continued antagonism. Divisions have appeared over numerous issues, including the economy (as already mentioned), the constitutional debate, the role of the church, and possible future political realignments.

The program of the SLD would not be out of place in any Western European social-democratic manifesto. Its leader Kwasniewski has gone on record apologizing for past injustices; yet some of the party's actions[29] initially kept it firmly outside the doors of the Socialist International (unlike the recently elected Hungarian Socialist Party [MSZP], which at present has associate membership and is pushing for full membership). Their pragmatism vis-à-vis economic reform has to be paralleled with a need to lessen the costs of reform for the most vulnerable members of society—such as the nine-and-a-half million pensioners, who are potentially one of the strongest pressure groups in Poland.

The Polish Peasant Party (PSL), which emerged from the remnants of the United Peasant Party (ZSL) and elements of Rural Solidarity, is the only party to represent all of Poland's regions. Primarily a cleavage-based party, agrarian class-based and pro-Catholic, the PSL has attempted to transcend the confines of the cleavage space and broaden its appeal; thus, Pawlak called it a "peoples party."[30] It has pursued this campaign through its connections to nongovernmental organizations such as the Voluntary Fire Brigade (with over a million members) of which Pawlak is chairman, and the Farmers' Wives Association (with over 600,000) and housing cooperatives. There is also the Union of Rural Youth (ZMW), which has business and financial interests and boasts a considerable influence on Pawlak. According to Moszczynski,

> The ZMW has a wide choice of local notables in each electoral rural region which encompasses people who are not necessarily part of the PSL, but who, through their local knowledge and local social standing, as teachers or doctors, administrators or farmers, present a useful cross section of the more prominent people who normally give colour and substance to life in the countryside or in a smaller provincial town. . . . It is one of the methods that the PSL has for maximising its votes in these areas during local and national elections.[31]

Many of these organizations stem directly from the groups associated with the ZSL and thus highlight the structural and organizational continuity of the post-Communist forces, which gives them a distinct advantage over most of the post-Solidarity forces.

The Union of Labor (UP) also shared in the victory of the left.[32] The UP was formed during the summer of 1992, bringing together former Communists, socialists, and Solidarity activists with the aim of becoming a traditional European Social Democratic party. In its founding statement adopted on 7 June 1992, the party spoke of the need to learn from the experience of the West, in particular with regard to the role of social welfare and the active state, "which have proved in practice that it is possible to reconcile economic efficiency with the requirements of social equilibrium."[33] Such an agenda managed to secure the UP forty-two deputies and two senators and a potential role in any future coalition. Although the party played an important and influential role in the PSL–SLD coalition agreement it decided not to join;[34] it nevertheless remains a potential coalition partner. The UP has been taking a pragmatic/populist line in the *Sejm,* sometimes voting with the SLD, for example over the Concordat with the church, and sometimes against, as in the case of *popiwek*.[35] It remains committed to the idea of some sort of workers' state and it views economic change in quite orthodox terms, favoring nationalization over privatization. It has also advocated greater use of direct democracy in the form of referenda. The party, however, seems to be very "*Sejm*-centric," which perhaps explains its poor performance in the June 1994 local elections.

In June 1994 Poland held its second local elections. Local government has been a contentious issue, with critics of the government claiming that planned decentralization measures introduced by the Suchocka administration are being blocked. The PSL is especially blamed for this because its rural strength precludes any interest in reforming the status quo. Pawlak as prime minister was accused of politicizing the personnel of the provincial governors through partisan appointments.

The electoral system took the form of both a proportional and a majoritarian system. The SLD emerged as the largest single force, doing particularly well in the urban areas despite the very low turnout. The Union of Freedom took many of the major cities, including Warsaw, Gdansk, and Krakow, while the newly reconciled right did well in Poland's eastern border. According to Sabbat-Swidlicka,

> The results confirmed the popularity of the two partners in the ruling "post-communist" coalition: the Democratic Left Alliance and the Polish Peasants Party; reinforced the position of the Freedom Union as a party of the centre; and last, but not least, returned to institutional politics the newly reconciled parties of the fragmented Catholic right. . . . The emergence of three major blocs of similar strength may help to clarify Poland's political landscape, but building a consensus is likely to be just as difficult as before.[36]

Turnout declined to below 35 percent, perhaps pointing to increased levels of cynicism, as Kramer argues.[37] The most significant factor was the success of the right, which on a platform of anti-Communism, Christian nationalism, and local issues secured numerous power centers. This was achieved primarily through the formation of coalitions such as the Alliance of Poland, which was made up of the Christian National Union, the Movement for the Republic, and the Peasant Alliance.[38] The voting figures indicate that each of the main blocs has a limited core base of support that is not enough to give any one overall control. Parties will generally need to forge coalition agreements, which would call for increased levels of consensus and compromise and could lead to increased consolidation.

Trade Unions: Friend or Foe?

Since 1989 grassroots trade unionism in Poland has been relegated to the periphery, where it is still attempting to define a role for itself in the post-

Communist era. Should they represent their members and protest against the costs of the transformation, which seem to have fallen disproportionately on the workers? Or should they help the government to introduce changes by not striking or by keeping wages down? Research carried out by the Labour Research Group[39] in both the public and private sectors found that workers could be classified into three groups:

1. The traditionalists or egalitarian-statists, who have declined from approximately 25 percent to 12 percent of the workforce
2. The liberals, that is, supporters of the whole modernization package who accept the social costs; these have declined from approximately 6 percent to around 3 percent
3. The moderate reformers, who constitute approximately 50 percent and support the idea of the market economy and privatization in exchange for employment and a decent living standard. Where privatization is concerned many look to the idea of small cooperatives, workers' shares, and the use of Polish capital acquired by honest work rather than speculation.

Since 1991 there has been a huge growth of the private sector, which is being heralded as the cornerstone of the Polish recovery. In 1993 it employed some 60 percent of the workforce and contributed approximately half of the country's GDP. The workers, however, seem far from jubilant: Only 4 percent in 1993 wanted to work in the private sector. The main unions can therefore be found in the declining public sector, a phenomenon symptomatic of neoliberal economics (see Table 5.2). In terms of impact the two most prominent unions in Poland are the All-Polish Alliance of Trade Unions (OPZZ), which was established in 1984 as a state counter to Solidarity; and Solidarity itself. OPZZ is made up of 128 different unions, which for administrative ease have been streamlined into twenty-four branches. Following the 1993 election it had sixty-two deputies. The OPZZ is led by Ewa Spychalska, a popular figure within the movement who

Table 5.2   Trade-Union Membership in Poland, 1993

Trade Union	Membership
OPZZ	4,752,000
Solidarity	1,790,000
National Union of Farmers, Farming Circles & Organizations	1,700,000
Rural Solidarity	400,000
Miners Trade Union Federation	230,000
Solidarity 80	156,000

Source: "The State of the Unions: Business As Usual," *The Warsaw Voice,* 10 October 1993, p. 5.

remains adamant that the present coalition is the only one capable of moving Poland forward. The strategic role of the unions and especially the OPZZ, which makes up a substantial part of the SLD, would seem to indicate that forces other than political parties have a say in the decisionmaking process. In reality, however, the OPZZ remains an uncritical ally/appendage of the SLD, which is playing an important stabilizing role for the ruling coalition by discouraging strike action.

In February 1993, the Pact on State Enterprise in a Time of Transformation[40] was negotiated between the government and the OPZZ, NSZZ Solidarity, and Solidarity 80. This contained measures for accelerating the privatization program, giving employees the right to 15 percent of the shares in privatized companies, representation of up to 30 percent on boards of directors for privatized companies, and some say in the method of privatization. Those who lost their jobs through privatization, for example, would be eligible for additional welfare packages. The cost was to be the abolition of the Workers Councils. The pact was heralded as the ideal model of corporatism for the transformation of the post-Communist economies, but as a result of the dissolution of the *Sejm* on 31 May 1993 it was never formally ratified.

The thorn in the side of the present government has been Solidarity,[41] which remains strong among public-sector Polish workers, especially within the coal and steel industries; has its own mass circulation paper, *Tygodnik Solidarnosc;* and maintains strong links with the church. Although Solidarity failed to gain representation in the *Sejm* (gaining 4.9 percent of the vote) it did obtain nine senators. This lack of a political voice in the *Sejm,* however, has probably led to its radicalization as a populist, virulently anti-Communist movement. Its biggest targets are the OPZZ, which it accuses of harboring Stalinists; those benefiting from nomenklatura privatization; and the present finance minister, Grzegorz Kolodko. Solidarity has adopted a very populist platform calling for a popular shareholding democracy, where economic policy would emerge through a tripartite commission involving unions, employers, and the government. It also demands state subsidies for heavy industry and increased spending on welfare, education, and pensions. Many of its aims remain similar to those of the UP, but collaboration is thwarted by the UP's secularism. Since October 1994 Solidarity has begun to reestablish links with President Walesa[42] that would have obvious benefits for each. Walesa was hoping for support in the presidential elections of late 1995, in which he would be championed as a force against the forces of continuity; Solidarity looks for presidential support in its ongoing dispute with the government. A statement released during its June 1995 congress read, "In Poland a re-communisation offensive is underway. This is the main reason the country is sinking into moral, economic and sociopolitical crisis."[43]

Solidarity has launched a number of protests during the past two years.

In February 1994, over 40,000 protesters called for the fulfillment of the Pact on State Enterprise in a Time of Transformation; in April it called a general strike; in May unionists once again marched in the streets of Warsaw. A similar pattern of events prevailed in 1995 when miners, steelworkers, and workers from the Ursus[44] tractor plant took to the streets, often engaging in violent clashes with the police. Maciej Jankowski, chairman of the Mazowsze regional board of NSZZ Solidarity, says that part of the reason for these activities is that "while there is a conflict between capital and labor the state is on the side of capital instead of acting as an arbiter in between."[45]

The government upon coming to power, and wishing to continue the corporatist approach of the previous government, set up a tripartite Social Economic Commission on 24 February 1994. At the time of writing it was attempting to start up a Center for Social Dialogue under the auspices of the Ministry of Labor and Social Security. This was another bid to institutionalize some sort of corporate structure for Polish society in the hope that any social pact would reduce the potential for conflict and thus increase Poland's attractiveness for foreign investors.

Potentially Divisive Issues

No country or political system is devoid of tensions and contradictions; Poland is no exception. There remains a number of ongoing problems stemming from the democratization process that may or may not have an impact on consolidation. Two of the most prominent are the constitutional debate and the role of the church.

The Constitutional Debate

As of 1995 Poland has been unable to adopt a post-Communist constitution, due to the fierce debate that the subject has aroused. The "Little Constitution," which remained an interim document, has resulted in a system of dual presidential and parliamentary power. This document enables the president to veto or block legislation; designate the prime minister, the defense and foreign secretaries, and the minister for internal affairs; call a national referendum with senate approval; and ask the Constitutional Tribunal to deliberate on the constitutionality of legislation.[46] It will be interesting to see if the SLD maintains its traditional support for a parliamentary-cabinet model of government after its victory in the presidential election. The PSL, however, has remained silent on the issue, leading to speculation that Pawlak and Walesa were involved in some kind of mutual understanding.[47]

The legislative process began when, on 21 September 1994, seven draft proposals, sponsored by numerous groups and including a Solidarity church-backed draft, were put before the National Assembly.[48] The new constitution is being drafted by the National Assembly's Constitutional Commission, which is composed of forty-six deputies and ten senators and chaired by Kwasniewski until his election victory. It must be passed by both houses with a two-thirds majority. The president is then entitled to survey the final outcome, and he has the prerogative to send it back to the National Assembly for further consideration; the Assembly need not take heed of his views. Ultimately the final draft must be put to the people in the form of a referendum. This is likely to become a long and often bitter struggle. In terms of consolidation the constitution can provide the essential glue to bind the polity and the nation together, yet it could equally become the source of sharp divisions. The church wants references to God; Walesa wants the right to issue decrees. Przeworski posits an interesting fourfold typology concerning the effectiveness of constitutions: One can find "a constitution that is long-lasting and observed, one that is long-lasting and ignored, some that are changed often and respected serially, and others that are modified frequently and remain irrelevant—historical experience is not very informative."[49]

The Church

The role of the church[50] is another divide that has become apparent over the signing of the Concordat. The church has always been in the forefront of resistance to the Communist regime, but after 1989 it began to assume a moral dogmatism and a corresponding moral social agenda. During the Olszewski premiership, through the National Christian Democrats (ZChN), the church was able to implement a moral social and cultural program in areas such as abortion, and religious teaching in schools. This led to fears of a clerical state and cost the church a great deal of prestige.

There remain figures within the church who believe that they should be playing a much stronger role in Poland's developing democracy, and that the separation of church and state increases the likelihood that totalitarianism will reappear. The church hierarchy connected with Cardinal Jozef Glemp fears the anticlericalism of the SLD (primarily the SdRP), which it views as continuing the traditions of the Polish People's Republic. In his recent visit to Poland, Pope John Paul II spoke of a growing intolerance and an attack on Christian values.[51] Many of the bishops, however, believe that Cardinal Glemp is the cause for concern: They feel that by taking the Catholic Church into confrontational politics with the government he is undermining the position of the church throughout society, as demonstrated by the rejection of church-backed parties such as The Fatherland during the general election. While Kwasniewski has argued that "compromise with the church is proof of wisdom and strength not weakness" at a council meeting of the SdRP, many of the rank and file continue to advocate a hard line toward the church.[52] The PSL, however, remains much closer to the church, with perhaps the goal of becoming a Christian Democratic party that will bring the church back into the political arena.

Political Realignments?

The possibility of a realignment of the political spectrum prior to the next election seems unlikely, although there remains a possibility of a coalition, especially between the SLD and the Union of Freedom (UW), which would undoubtedly have a corresponding effect on the rest of the party system. The March 1995 election of Leszek Balcerowicz to the leadership of the UW increases the position of the pragmatists within his party, who have a great deal in common with the pragmatists of the SLD. If such a realignment does not happen prior to the next election, a postelection pact of the SLD and the UW (similar to the Hungarian Socialist Party's pact with the Alliance of Free Democrats) remains a possibility under pressure from the pragmatists of both sides. Zubek called the SdRP and the UD (Democratic Union, UW prior to its unification with the Liberal Democratic Congress) the main social-democratic parties;[53] in October 1991 they were both passed over as potential coalition partners despite their being the two largest parties. In conversations with the author a number of UW politicians, while not advocating such a formation, did not categorically rule out the possibility of some sort of historic compromise. This would mean a final elite settlement between forces connected with the PRL and the PR. Nevertheless, symbolically the two groups remain at opposite sides of the spectrum, especially at the grassroots.

From the outset "it was clear that the two 'post-communist' forces [the SLD and the PSL] were not natural allies, despite their shared genealogy. . . . The PSL–SLD coalition is more of an unholy alliance than a compatible partnership."[54] In an interview with Radio Zet in February 1994, Pawlak said that "it was necessary to start building a coalition based on essential agreement." Many speculated that the subtext of this statement was the formation of a new coalition possibly consisting of the PSL, the Confederation for an Independent Poland (KPN), and the Nonparty Bloc for Reform (BBWR), along with the OPZZ.[55]

In November 1994 the Freedom Union and the SLD came together to unseat the PSL mayor of Warsaw, while in the *Sejm* they ousted Bogdan Pek, the PSL chairman of the Parliamentary Privatization Commission. Kwasniewski told journalists that the UW was a potential coalition partner, though both parties had "not yet matured" for such a role.[56] It remains to be seen whether these events amount to anything more than a purely pragmatic response to a particular situation. This author is inclined to view them as evidence that certain members of the SLD, tired of the continuing dominance of the PSL (which had left the SLD outmaneuvered in areas such as finance), were sending signals to the PSL indicating that it was dispensable.

The official removal of Prime Minister Pawlak following the "constructive" vote of confidence on 1 March 1995, and his replacement by the SLD's Jozef Oleksy, former speaker of the *Sejm,* undoubtedly signaled a turnabout in the fortunes of the SLD. At the same time the PSL was quick to warn Oleksy that it could leave the coalition any time that it felt threatened, in the belief that no one else would form an alliance with post-Communists.

The Walesa Factor

President Lech Walesa, despite his declining popularity, remains a cunning, Byzantine, and strategically important force in Polish politics. His time in office has been colorful, controversial, and often unpredictable. He played a part in the downfall of three prime ministers: Mazowiecki, Olszewski, and Pawlak. After the vote of no confidence in the Suchocka government, the president dissolved Parliament instead of asking the *Sejm* to form a new government. Prior to the general election he was instrumental in setting up the Nonparty Movement for Supporting Reform (BBWR).[57] He even stated that Kwasniewski's idol was Stalin. Walesa has spent much of his time in office advocating presidential rule and, by implication, destabilizing Poland's party-based democracy. To justify this position he cited governmental ineffectiveness, as in 1995, or said that the coalition was unrepresentative of the Polish people and was in any case bound to collapse sooner or later.[58] As the 1995 presidential elections approached, increasing calls for "de-Communization"[59] echoed through the corridors of the Presidential Palace.

Walesa sometimes condemns the right but he considers himself to be of the right. When asked about his future role he said, "It all depends on how things go. If it goes on as present, I have no choice, and I have to build a bloc which will take complete power, including presidential and government power."[60] The historical parallels with Marshall Pilsudski are striking. Pilsudski launched a coup in 1926; dismayed by the ineffectiveness of parliamentary government, he had been quoted as saying that "a *Sejm* deputy is a creation that can only ask stupid questions and provide stupid answers. He is a despicable phenomenon, his actions stink and contaminate the air."[61] Prior to the restricted 1928 election he set up a BBWR (Nonparty Bloc for Cooperating with the Government).

Often written off as yesterday's man, Walesa reasserted his prominence in Polish politics in 1995. His struggle over the 1995 budget, the ongoing "veto wars," his threats to dissolve Parliament (which brought worldwide media attention and much condemnation), his success in removing Pawlak as prime minister, and his getting his way over the presidential ministries in the new coalition, all did much to remind the Polish people that he remained a real force. According to Adam Michnik, "Walesa has a peasant view of property. A peasant has a house, a barn, a cow. Anyone who wants to take them away is a thief who has to be chased away with a pitch-fork. Walesa has his presidency. He thinks he owns it. And he thinks he can turn a pitch-fork to anyone who wants to take his post away."[62]

Many believed that his ousting of Pawlak was an attempt to bring Kwasniewski in as prime minister and thus remove a potential opponent in the presidential elections, which were due to be held in the autumn of 1995. Events did not proceed in that direction, however. Walesa, attempting to harness the support of a post-Solidarity coalition, portrayed himself as the natural counterweight to the post-Communist left—the main figure of which became Kwasniewski. It was Walesa and Kwasniewski who faced each other in the second round of the elections on 19 November, with strong church backing going to the former, but with Kwasniewski nevertheless emerging victorious.

Consolidation or Not?

Unlike *democratization,* in which I believe the genetic approach—a focus on the role of political actors and their choices—is of primary importance, *consolidation* takes more time and requires consideration of the ideas of both the genetic and functionalist schools of thought.[63] Valenzuela writes that a "consolidated democracy would be one that does not have perverse elements undermining its basic characteristics."[64] In terms of the party system, organizations that have their roots in the ancien régime have accepted their new role, and Parliament is viewed as the legitimate lawmaking forum. The September 1993 election certainly consolidated the *Sejm* in terms of party representation, giving the impression of party stabilization vis-à-vis the highly fragmented October 1991 Parliament. As Rose writes,

> The successful institutionalisation of a competitive party system would raise current satisfaction and popular expectation, leading to an equilibrium in which both become highly positive, with the great majority endorsing representative government and expecting the system to remain as it is, the condition in most western nations today.[65]

Although there remains a considerable right-wing bloc inhabiting an extraparliamentary environment, it advocates a return through parliamentary means. The president, however, often uses authoritarian rhetoric, which undoubtedly undermines the stability of democracy. According to Morlino,

> There are at least two different patterns of consolidation: one achieved through legitimation and a limited control of society and another through a stronger control that compensates for the limited legitimation. It also suggests that the stabilisation of the party system is partially related to con-

solidation. That is, consolidation may be achieved with low stability and broad legitimation.[66]

In terms of legitimacy and trust the picture seems somewhat confusing. Life has obviously changed for many people—a walk through the streets of Warsaw demonstrates this visibly enough. At the same time, Gardawski and Zukowski point out that as of 1993 only 20 percent of workers felt that the years of transformation had brought a change for the better, and pessimism ran even higher in the rural areas. In the same survey, 50 percent agreed with the proposition that socialism is a good idea.[67] Among Eastern Europeans, Polish people had the lowest regard for political parties and the institution of Parliament, but at the same time they scored highest in the category of those considering themselves "hopeful authoritarians." Compared with the rest of Eastern and Central Europe, only the people of Romania remained more antimarket.[68] The long-term significance of this in terms of democratization and consolidation remains to be seen; in the short term, at least, it has not resulted in the rise of extremist, populist, or antisystem parties. A poll carried out by the Center for Public Opinion Polls (OBOP) showed that the highest levels of trust lay with the public radio and nondemocratic organizations such as the army and the police. The negative image of political parties and governments remains a continuing trend (see Table 5.3).[69]

Table 5.3   Levels of Trust in Polish Institutions, April 1995

Institution	Percentage
Public radio	81
Army	79
Public television	74
Police	71
Prime minister	60
Supreme Chamber of Control	60
TV and Radio State Commission	56
Government	46
Sejm (lower house)	43
Senate (upper house)	43

Source: "Polacy najbardziej ufaja radiu publicznemu [Poles trust public radio the most]," *Polityka,* 31 May 1995.

Putnam[70] argues that trust is an element of what he terms social capital; the further trust is developed, the more it is available and the sooner the system operating on the basis of trust becomes consolidated. The antithesis of trust is distrust.

> Deep distrust is very difficult to invalidate through experience, for either it prevents people from engaging in the appropriate kind of social experiment or, worse, it leads to behaviour which bolsters the validity of distrust itself. . . . Once distrust has set in it soon becomes impossible to know if it was ever in fact justified, for it has the capacity to be *self-fulfilling*.[71]

Although the poll is not exactly a ringing endorsement of political parties or the government, it can be read as an acceptance of the principles of free speech and a free press, essential elements for a consolidated democracy.

Increased levels of legitimacy and trust seem to require the development of civil society and its acceptance by the polity. Though it remains elusive in terms of a definitive definition, the concept of civil society is recognized by many. Dahrendorf wrote: "Civil society is the key. It pulls the divergent time scales and dimensions of political and economic reform together. It is the ground in which both have to be anchored in order not to be blown away. The hour of the lawyer and the hour of the politician mean little without the hour of the citizen."[72] Putnam argues that "it is a dense network of secondary associations" that makes democracy work.[73] I believe civil society is the arena in which democratic norms are not only acquired but experienced. As a part of the conflict-resolution mechanism it channels social interests to and from the gatekeepers, that is, political parties. It should remain outside the domain of the party and hence maintain the ability to actively criticize the party, but should also have a channel to the party. It is an ensemble that is constantly changing and includes, among others, pressure groups, trade unions, employers' associations, the media, and universities. Civil society does not just happen; it must be established through the strategic choices of ordinary people and institutions. But these groups, according to Lipset, "must legitimate themselves by encouraging the rights of other groups to oppose them, thus providing a basis for democracy."[74] Civil society can be further broken down into domestic society and political society; "domestic society represents the domain of purposeful action restricted to the private sphere and organised in terms of material needs and self interest."[75] Political society in Forment's words refers to "a place or realm where people congregate to debate and act on the burning, public issues of the day."[76] The present relationship between political parties and civil society in Poland seems to be one of domination of the latter by the former. This relationship could be responsible for the high level of apathy and cynicism toward the government and political parties that causes people to return to the domestic sphere, which many of them occupied during the Communist era.

According to Krol, "We Poles, therefore await some movement or programme that will give us a feeling of a community but without in any way limiting our individual freedom."[77] Wesolowski would appear to be justified in believing that "in the coming years doctrines with strong communitarian aspects have a greater potential for producing legitimating beliefs."[78] Such a movement could be built upon the ethos of 1989 and the progressive social teachings of the church. It could offer the philosophical foundation the SLD needs to reform the welfare state.

Conclusion

The outcome of Poland's transition remains far from clear, in that the path from democratization could take one of several directions. From an institutional point of view political parties have been formed, elections have been fought and won, and the party system has survived a fundamental realignment from a Solidarity, to a post-Solidarity, to a post-Communist government. At the same time Poland lacks an accepted constitution and a proper interest-mediation structure. Until mid-1995 the country had witnessed three elections, seven prime ministers, six cabinets, and a highly fragmented *Sejm* between 1991 and 1993. Combined with the low level of legitimacy enjoyed by political parties and leaders, the situation has hardly been conducive to consolidation. Yet neither has democratization degenerated into a populist quagmire. People have not been persuaded by extremists or lone presidents offering easy solutions, and the majority of political elites have apparently accepted the rules of the game.

Political parties, then, at present are still the torchbearers of democratization. By their choices and strategies they oversee the transition process through a series of policy goals. ("New policies affect the social identities, goals, and capabilities of groups that subsequently struggle or ally in politics.")[79] They also have the responsibility of widening the transition by opening up the political process to the forces of civil society and nurturing the democratic ideal. Thus elite action remains paramount for the consolidation of a procedural democracy.

The recent turnabout in fortune for the SLD, including its increased popularity in the opinion polls, may well increase the group's cohesiveness and hence lessen the need for a national agreement with the Union of Freedom before the next election. Nevertheless, increased cooperation between the two forces at the local level may be expected. The PSL, which as a homogeneous entity remains an unknown quantity, appears to have been able to portray itself as a necessary component of any future coalition, of whatever political complexion. The unions continue to play a role, although it should not be overestimated; as in much of the Western world, unions are in decline. In a corporate context they are generally called upon to institutionalize the demands of the workforce, tame wage demands, and most importantly, act as an ally of the government. While OPZZ seems to be performing the latter two functions, Solidarity is once again aiming to gain a political voice in a bid to institutionalize the demands of its members.

While the "hour of the politician" is already well upon us, the same cannot be said for the "hour of the citizen."[80] Conventional wisdom has it that the longer that hour takes to arrive, the greater the likelihood that the population will come to view voting and the legislative process as worthless. This in turn could lead to a decline of the legitimacy of democracy, resulting in a "cynical democracy" in which people accept that a party-oriented democracy is the only game in town but refuse to endorse it fully.[81] At the same time it seems clear from the polls and the author's own interviews that a return to the past is not on most people's minds. In this respect the present does have a certain amount of legitimacy vis-à-vis the authoritarian past. It remains to be seen whether a cynical political culture is able to sustain the political structure.

Yet a cynical political culture would appear to have developed a momentum of its own, as if people are dealing with the whole process outside the party-political arena and political civil society, and have withdrawn into the private sphere and the informal economy. People seem unsure of the appropriate role for the state and where they fit in. This is where communitarianism could provide some potential solutions. Much of its ethos fits in with the philosophy of the SLD and the UW.

In terms of laying the foundations for a consolidation, parties have a number of choices. They can embark upon the process of forming sociopolitical pacts, especially if they wish to remain as incumbents. Parties need a core of support so that they don't have to make populistic and unrealistic appeals at every election to gain votes; at the same time they need to gain the people's trust. One intermediate way of achieving this is through the formation of sociopolitical pacts. Communitarianism through the formation of a SLD–UW merger could perhaps serve the best interests of Poland and indicate another step on the road to consolidation.

If one attempts to construct a checklist of indicators to assess the significance and limitations of the democratization process, one would need to look at (1) the nature of multiparty elections and the subsequent design of the institutional architecture (achieved); (2) the nature of the parties themselves (primarily elitist); (3) their willingness to accept input from beyond the polity (presently low); and (4) the level of legitimacy the regime achieves among the people (presently low). Consolidation remains a path-dependent phenomenon that relies heavily on the institutional architecture and the ability of political actors to fully endorse the electoral aspects of democracy and open it up to the rest of society. However, just as there is no magic formula for democratization, neither is there one for consolidation. As Valenzuela put it, "Consolidation is reached as an *ex post facto* realization; any deliberate plan to advance it will, by virtue of its stated goal, indicate to all those concerned its absence."[82]

Notes

1. The author would like to express his thanks to Professor Hieronim Kubiak and Grzegorz Pozarlik of Jagiellonian University, Krakow, for numerous conversations relating to this chapter; Frances Millard, University of Portsmouth; and Paul G Lewis, Open University, for their helpful comments on an earlier draft.

This chapter has also drawn implicitly on the following sources not referred to in subsequent notes: Y. Chu, *Crafting Democracy in Taiwan* (Taipei: Institute for National Policy Research, 1992), pp. 1–15; S. Kowalski, "Poland's new political culture: The relevance of the irrelevant," *Economy and Society,* Vol. 22, No. 2, 1993, pp. 233–242; C. McClintock, "The Prospects for Democratic Consolidation in a 'Least Likely' Case: Peru," *Comparative Politics,* Vol. 21, No. 2, 1989, pp. 127–148; G. Munck, "Democratic Transitions in Comparative Perspective," *Comparative Politics,* Vol. 26, No. 3, 1994, pp. 355–375; G. Sorensen, *Democracy and Democratization* (Boulder: Westview Press, 1993), pp. 25–63; J. Wiatr, "The Dilemmas of Re-organizing the Bureaucracy in Poland during the Democratic Transformation," *Communist and Post-Communist Studies,* Vol. 28, No. 1, 1995, pp. 153–160.

2. See S. Huntington, *The Third Wave: Democratization in the Late Twentieth Century* (Norman, Okla. and London: University of Oklahoma Press, 1992).

3. In chronological order they were: Tadeusz Mazowiecki (August 1989–December 1990), Jan Krzysztof Bielecki (January 1990–December 1991), Jan Olszewski (December 1991–June 1992), Waldemar Pawlak (June 1992–July 1992, could not form a cabinet), Hanna Suchocka (July 1992–October 1993), Waldemar Pawlak (October 1993–February 1995), and Josef Oleksy (from March 1995).

4. See A. Sabbat-Swidlicka, "Poland in 1989," *Radio Free Europe/Radio Liberty (RFE/RL) Report on Eastern Europe,* Vol. 1, No. 1, 5 January 1990, pp. 24–27: p. 25.

5. A. Przeworski, *Democracy and the Market: Political and economic reforms in Eastern Europe and Latin America* (Cambridge: Cambridge University Press, 1992), p. 98.

6. See R. Dahl, *Polyarchy: Participation and Opposition* (New Haven: Yale University Press, 1971), who stipulates a number of conditions that define a procedural democracy, including popular sovereignty, individual rights, free and fair elections, and the rule of law. Lipset defines the rule of law as (1) that people and institutions will be treated equally by the institutions administering the law—the courts, the police, and the civil service; and (2) that people and institutions can predict with reasonable certainty the consequences of their actions, at least as far as the state is concerned. S. Lipset, "The Social Requisites of Democracy Revisited," *American Sociological Review,* Vol. 59, 1994, pp. 1–22: p. 15.

7. Debates relating to a minimalist or maximalist interpretation of democracy, while interesting, are not overly useful, primarily because it is unfair to judge Eastern and Central Europe by an ideal type that has yet to be attained in the West. At the same time it is necessary to take the situation as it is, rather than speculate on what might have been had an alternative approach been adopted. A minimalist interpretation of democracy can be found in, among others, F. Fukuyama, *The End of History and the Last Man* (Penguin, 1992); and J. Schumpeter, *Capitalism, Socialism and Democracy,* 3rd ed. (New York: Harper Bros., 1950).

8. See A. Agh, "The Premature Senility of the Young Democracies: The Central European Experience," *Budapest Papers on Democratic Transition, No. 67* (Budapest: Hungarian Centre for Democracy Studies Foundation, 1993).

9. H. Welsh, "Political Transition Processes in Central and Eastern Europe," *Comparative Politics,* Vol. 26, No. 4, 1994, pp. 379–394: p. 380.

10. Przeworski, *Democracy and the Market,* pp. 30–31.

11. See ibid.; and J. Valenzuela, "Democratic Consolidation in Post-Transitional Settings: Notion, Process and Facilitating Conditions," in Mainwaring, O'Donnell, and Valenzuela, eds., *Issues in Democratic Consolidation: The New South American Democracies in Comparative Perspective* (Indiana: Notre Dame Press, 1992) for numerous examples of how General Pinochet achieved a remarkable number of safeguards for the military.

12. Many of these forces were in fact made up of one member. This led to the term "sofa parties," i.e., all of their members could fit on a sofa. One of the most colorful parties at this stage was the Polish Beerlovers Party, which had 16 seats.

13. The election for the Senate was held on a first-past-the-post basis, with two seats for each *voivodship* (except Warsaw and Katowice, which had three). It's interesting to note that the post-Communist left was equally successful under this electoral procedure. The SLD gained 37 seats, PSL 36, Solidarity 9, Independents 5, UD 4, BBWR 2, UP 2, others 5.

14. This was composed of the Democratic Union (UD), the Liberal Democratic Congress (KLD), the Christian National Union (ZChN), the Polish Economic Program, the Peasant Alliance, the Peasant Christian Alliance, and the Party of Christian Democrats.

15. For a fuller normative explanation of the election results, see S. Day, "Poland's Post-communism," *The Chartist,* January/February 1994. For a comprehensive empirical understanding and numerous charts relating to voting breakdown, see F. Millard, "The Polish Parliamentary Election of September 1993," *Communist and Post-communist Studies,* Vol. 27, No. 3, 1994, pp. 295–314. H. Ka-Lok Chan, "Poland at the crossroads: The 1993 General Election," *Europe-Asia Studies,* Vol. 47, No. 1, 1995, pp. 123–145, attempts to explain the victory of the post-Communist left.

16. Even those that did unite, such as the Catholic Electoral Committee, which was made up of the ZChN, the Conservative Party, the Party of Christian Democrats, and the Agrarian Christian Party (SLCh), failed to surpass the 8 percent threshold. In the latter part of 1994 there was a considerable consolidation of the right with the formation of the November 11 Agreement, which included the Party of Christian Democrats (PChD), the Peasant Christian Party (SChL), the Conservative Party (PK), the Real Politics Union (UPR), and the National Democratic Party (SND) and the Covenant for Poland Coalition, which was composed of the Center Alliance (PC), the Christian National Union (ZChN), the Movement for Republic of Poland (RdR), the Peasant Agreement (PL), and the Conservative Coalition (KK). Although these forces are united in their support for the church (albeit to differing degrees) and in their anti-Communist stance, they remained divided over the issue of Walesa.

17. H. Kubiak, "Regularities of multi-party system formation in today's Poland," May 1995, privately circulated paper, p. 11.

18. A. Smolar, "A Communist Comeback? The Dissolution of Solidarity," *Journal of Democracy,* Vol. 5, No. 1, 1994, pp. 70–84: p. 70.

19. Pawlak, quoted in "Pawlak Policy Speech: Disaster Unlikely," *The Warsaw Voice,* 14 November 1993, p. 4.

20. See H. Tworzecki, "The Polish Parliamentary Elections of 1993," *Electoral Studies,* Vol. 13, No. 2, 1994, pp. 180–185.

21. Quoted in A. Sabbat-Swidlicka, "Pawlak to Head Poland's Post-communist Government," *Radio Free Europe/Radio Liberty Research Report (RFE/RL),* Vol. 2, No. 43, 29 October 1993, pp. 24–32: pp. 27–28.

22. The power struggle is hinted at in "Familiar Faces and Newcomers," *The Warsaw Voice,* 12 March, 1995, p. 5.

23. A. Sabbat-Swidlicka, "Pawlak Builds Up Peasant Power," *RFE/RL,* Vol. 3, No. 24, 17 June 1995, pp. 13–20: p. 20.

24. G. Kolodko, *Strategia dla Polski* (Warszawa: Poltext, 1994).

25. See "Polish Minister Puts Job On Line," *The Financial Times,* 19 May 1995, p. 3.

26. See "Don't Worry Democracy: An Interview with Aleksander Kwasniewski," *The Warsaw Voice,* 3 October 1993, p. 9.

27. Quoted in L. Vinton, "Poland's Political Spectrum on the Eve of Elections," *RFE/RL,* Vol. 2, No. 36, 10 September 1993, pp. 1–7: p. 7.

28. This continues a series of polls that have shown the SLD increasing its support since a low of 16 percent in June 1994. See CBOS, *"Silny Sojusz" Gazeta Wyborca,* 17 November 1994.

29. At the same time that many within the SLD have done little to endear themselves to the populace, their actions include a refusal to condemn martial law and speaking highly of the old system without commenting on its defects.

30. During a speech at the forum of the Future of Europe Trust and the British-Polish Parliamentary Group at the House of Commons on 8 November 1994.

31. See Viktor Moszczynski, "Assessment Visit to Poland 19 March, 27 March 1994," report made to the Labor Party (passed to the author), p. 13.

32. The UP emerged from the left of Solidarity, sections of the Polish Socialist Party, the Liberal intelligentsia, and reformists from the PZPR.

33. Union of Labor Statement, *Labour Focus on Eastern Europe,* Vol. 42, No. 2, 1992, p. 33.

34. Although Marek Pol, one of its most prominent members, joined the government in an individual capacity as the minister of trade and industry. For further information, see A. Sabbat-Swidlicka, "Pawlak to Head Poland's 'Post-communist' Government," *RFE/RL,* Vol. 2, No. 43, 29 October 1993 pp. 24–32.

35. This was a tax on excess wages aimed at stemming pay rises in the public sector and undermining the position of the workers' councils.

36. A. Sabbat-Swidlicka, "Local Elections Redress Political Imbalance in Poland," *RFE/RL,* Vol. 3, No. 27, 8 July 1994, pp. 1–8: p. 1.

37. M. Kramer comments: "The extent of this cynicism became apparent during Poland's local elections in June 1994, when the turnout, though sparse everywhere, was especially low in urban industrial areas, indicating that the vast majority of blue collar workers saw little point in voting." In "Polish Workers and the Post-Communist Transition," *Communist and Post-Communist Studies,* Vol. 28, No. 1, 1995, pp. 71–114: p. 105.

38. For an elaboration on the situation, see Sabbat-Swidlicka, "Local Elections," pp. 1–9.

39. See Gardawski and Zukowski, "What the Polish Workers Think," *Labour Focus on Eastern Europe,* No. 46, 1993, pp. 35–38. They interviewed 4,811 workers in 461 enterprises.

40. For two critical articles see the introduction by David Holland and the articles by Kazimierz Kloc, "Industrial Conflicts in Poland 1991–92," *Labour Focus on Eastern Europe,* Vol. 44, No. 1, 1993, and Milka Tyszkiewicz, "Jacek Kuron's New Economic Policy," *Labour Focus on Eastern Europe,* No. 3 in 1992, pp. 31–33.

41. It was the Solidarity parliamentary caucus that brought about the vote of "unconstructive no-confidence" (i.e., it did not have an alternative government in waiting) in the Suchocka government in May 1993, causing it to fall by 223 votes to 222 (198 in favor, 24 abstentions).

42. In 1993 he failed to receive an invitation and his relations with Solidarity became even more estranged. See Sabbat-Swidlicka, "Solidarity parts company with Walesa," *RFE/RL,* Vol. 2, No. 31, 30 July 1993, pp. 1–6.

43. Quoted from R. Wesolowski, "Solidarity warns Poland to check communist revival," Reuters, 11 June 1995 distributed on *Polish Cultural List, Berkeley.*

44. The Ursus tractor factory remains very symbolic for its involvement in the strikes of 25 June 1976, which halted proposed governmental price reforms, and the repression that followed. See M. Bernhard, *The Origins of Democratization in Poland* (New York: Columbia University Press, 1993).

45. See Moszczynski, "Assessment visit to Poland," op. cit.

46. For additional information, see L. Vinton, "Poland's Little Constitution Clarifies Walesa's Powers," *RFE/RL*, Vol. 1, No. 35, 4 September 1992, pp. 19–26. The power relationship vis-à-vis the president and the executive is obviously a very contentious issue, as can be seen in C. Bobinski and A. Robinson, "President at the eye of the storm," *The Financial Times*, 21 October 1994, p. 17.

47. A. Goszcynski, "Coalition Shifts Left," *The Warsaw Voice*, 20 February 1994, p. 4.

48. For such fundamental questions the *Sejm* and the Senate are sitting jointly as the National Assembly.

49. Przeworski, *Democracy and the Market*, p. 35.

50. For an overview of the role of the church in Polish society, see A. Sabbat-Swidlicka, "Church and State in Poland," *RFE/RL*, Vol. 2, No. 14, 2 April 1993, pp. 45–53.

51. See "The Sun Through Gathering Clouds," *The Warsaw Voice*, 28 May 1995, p. 7.

52. See *OMRI Daily Digest part II*, No. 62, 28 March 1995.

53. See V. Zubek, "The Fragmentation of Poland's Political Party System," *Communist and Post-Communist Studies*, Vol. 26, No. 1, 1993, pp. 47–71: p. 71.

54. L. Vinton, "Poland's Political Spectrum on the Eve of Elections," pp. 32, 39.

55. See *The Warsaw Voice*, 13 February 1994, p. 3.

56. *Rzeczpospolita*, 4 November 1994. Translated in the *Polish Cultural List, Berkeley*, 4 November 1994.

57. The BBWR promised to sort out the underdeveloped party system through its twenty-one-point program aimed at each of its four disparate pillars: employers, employees, farming communities, and local government.

58. There is a joke that President Walesa sided with the governing coalition three days a week; another three days he sided with the opposition; on the seventh day, Sunday, he rested. Taken from J. Zielonka, "New Institutions in the Old East Bloc," *Journal of Democracy*, Vol. 5, No. 2, April 1994, p. 98.

59. This became the new issue upon which the right attempted to create a new moral crusade. For additional information, see A. Sabbat-Swidlicka, "Walesa's Conflicts and Ambitions," *RFE/RL*, Vol. 3, No. 14, 8 April 1994, pp. 1–6.

60. Quoted in *BBC Summary of World Broadcasts*, 17 February 1994, p. 10.

61. Quoted in S. Majman, "The Terrible Effects of Too Much Time," *The Warsaw Voice*, 11 July 1993, p. 8.

62. Quoted in "Ex-Ally Heaps Scorn on 'Peasant' Lech," *Financial Times*, 9 February 1995, p. 12.

63. For an elaboration of these two schools of thought, see G. Pridham, "Democratic transitions in theory and practice: Southern European lessons for Eastern Europe?" in G. Pridham and T. Vanhanen, eds., *Democratisation in Eastern Europe: Domestic and international perspectives* (London: Routledge, 1994).

64. J. Valenzuela, "Democratic Consolidation in Post-Transitional Settings," p. 62.

65. R. Rose, "Escaping from Absolute Dissatisfaction," *Journal of Theoretical Politics*, Vol. 4, No. 4 1992, pp. 371–393: p. 381.

66. L. Morlino, "Consolidation and Party Government in Southern Europe," *International Political Science Review*, Vol. 16, No. 2, 1995, pp.145–167: p. 163.

67. See Gardawski and Zukowski, "What the Polish workers think," p. 37.

68. For a detailed analysis of public opinion within the post-Communist states, see R. Rose and C. Haerpfer, "Mass Response to Transformation in Post-communist Societies," *Europe-Asia Studies,* Vol. 46, No. 1, 1994, pp. 3–28; and R. Rose and W. Mishler, "Mass Reaction to Regime Change in Eastern Europe: Polarisation or Leaders and Laggards?" *British Journal of Political Science,* Vol. 24, No. 2, April 1994, pp. 159–182.

69. See Rose and Haerpfer, "Mass Response to Transformation in Post-communist Societies."

70. See R. Putnam, *Making Democracy Work: Civic Traditions in Modern Italy* (Princeton: Princeton University Press, 1993).

71. D. Gambetta quoted in Putnam, *Making Democracy Work,* p. 170.

72. R. Dahrendorf, *Reflections on the Revolution in Europe* (London: Chatto and Windus, 1990), p. 93.

73. R. Putnam, *Making Democracy Work,* p. 90.

74. Lipset, "The Social Requisites of Democracy Revisited," p. 13.

75. G. Ekiert, "Democratization Processes in East and Central Europe: A Theoretical Reconsideration," *British Journal of Political Science,* Vol. 21, 1991, pp. 283–313: p. 300.

76. Quoted in ibid., p. 300.

77. M. Krol, "Poland's Longing for Paternalism," *Journal of Democracy,* Vol. 5, No. 1, 1994, pp. 85–95: p. 90.

78. W. Wesolowski, "The Nature of Social Ties and the Future of Postcommunist Society: Poland after Solidarity," in J. Hall, ed., *Civil Society: Theory, History, Comparison* (Cambridge: Polity Press, 1995), pp. 110–135: p. 126.

79. T. Skocpol, "The Origins of Social Policy in the United States: A Policy Centred Analysis," in L. Dodd and C. Jillson, eds., *The Dynamics of American Politics* (Boulder: Westview Press, 1994), p. 204.

80. See R. Darendorff, "Europe's Vale of Tears," *Marxism Today,* May 1990, pp. 18–23.

81. Whether or not the criteria of a substantive democracy would make any difference is beyond the scope of this chapter. An exploration of some of these ideas can be found in S. Day, "Reinventing Politics: Future Orientations for the Left on the verge of the Fin de Siècle," working paper (The Centre for Studies in Democratisation: University of Warwick).

82. J. Valenzuela, "Consolidation in Post-Transitional Settings," p. 94.

6

The Roots of Reform in Albania

DAVID SEDDON
with Ruth Davey and Rachel Grellier

This chapter examines the roots of economic and political reform in Albania in the 1990s through an analysis of the dynamics of the Albanian political economy during the preceding decades. It identifies the growing internal contradictions and pressures for change as well as the so-called "revolution" of 1989 in Eastern Europe as major factors behind the introduction of reforms. It provides an introduction to the subsequent chapter, which examines the politics of economic reform during the first half of the 1990s.[1]

Albania's Struggle for Independence: 1912–1945

On 28 November 1912, after more than 400 years of Ottoman rule, Albania declared its independence under a provisional government. International recognition followed the London Conference of July 1913. During World War I, however, the armies of Greece, Italy, and Austria and, for a short while, the forces of Serbia and Macedonia, occupied Albanian territory. Italy continued its occupation until 1920, when it agreed to withdraw its forces and Albanian independence was reestablished.

In 1925 Albania was declared a republic and Ahmed Zogu was elected as president. He quickly established an autocratic, centralized state and in 1928 proclaimed himself King Zog I. But Italian intervention continued over the next ten years, and in 1939 Mussolini demanded a formal protectorate over Albania. When Zogu objected, the Italians invaded; Zogu fled into exile and Albania endured Italian domination for four years.

During the 1930s Communist cells had been established within Albania. Enver Hoxha, later to become head of state until his death in 1985, was elected leader of the provisional committee of the Albanian Labor (Communist) Party when it was formed in 1941. The Italian occupation gave radical groups the opportunity to mobilize patriotic elements into a national front dominated by the Albanian Labor Party (ALP), founded under the influence of the Yugoslav Communist Party leader, Tito. Throughout the war, relations remained close between the Yugoslav partisans and the Albanian Communists.

The People's Republic of Albania: 1946–1948

In 1943 Albania was occupied by German forces, but these withdrew after a year, allowing the Albanian National Liberation Front to take power in November 1944. The provisional government was headed by Enver Hoxha, the leader of the Albanian Communist Party. In December 1945 elections took place with a single list of candidates (all sponsored by the Communists), and the People's Republic of Albania was formed in 1946.

Prewar Albania had been one of the most backward economies in Europe, with a predominantly rural population and an economy heavily dependent upon agriculture. Industry accounted for 5 to 10 percent of national income. But if 90 percent or more of the population lived from agriculture, 3 percent of the population owned 40 percent of the arable land and 14 percent owned no land at all. Roughly three-quarters of the territory consisted of barren mountains and hills, although the western plains by the Adriatic were endowed with very fertile soil and Albania was rich in mineral resources. The smallest of the Balkan countries, it had an area of just over 11,000 square miles and a population of under 3.5 million.

In 1944–1945, land above what was considered sufficient for a family was confiscated and a program of land distribution was initiated. Private peasant farmers were subjected to compulsory delivery quotas. Collectivization began in November 1946 and continued through the 1950s. The process was completed in 1967, by which time all land was either collectively or state owned. In 1946 the government nationalized all public utilities and foreign capital. Local businessmen were taxed at prohibitive levels and their property was subsequently expropriated. By early 1947 the state controlled domestic industry and foreign trade.

The State Planning Commission, which was directly subordinate to the Council of Ministers, drew up the country's first plan, for April to December 1947. This plan was relatively simple, with no global indicators for the economy. Subsequent plans during 1948–1950 became progressively more complex, with macroeconomic targets for growth and investment, and detailed planning of physical output, material balances, and input norms for enterprises. A one-year plan was adopted in 1948, followed by a two-year plan for 1949–1950. The main objective of the latter was to repair war damage and restore the economy to its prewar level.

During the period 1944–1948 Albania maintained very close relations with Yugoslavia. Customs and monetary union was established and Albanian sovereignty effectively disappeared as its dependence on Yugoslavia grew.

When the Communist Information Bureau was founded in 1947, Albania was not represented; Yugoslavia acted as its advocate instead. Had it not been for the rupture in relations between Tito and Stalin in 1948, Albania might well have become Yugoslavia's seventh republic.

State Socialism Under Soviet Influence: 1948–1961

In 1948, following its break with the Soviet Union, Yugoslavia's leadership came to be collectively referred to in Albania as "anti-Communist renegades"; Yugoslav advisers were replaced by Russians and Albania turned to the Soviet Union for support. In 1949 Albania joined the Soviet-dominated Council for Mutual Economic Assistance (CMEA).

Hoxha now consolidated his political position with purges and repression. While ensuring political orthodoxy, the leadership embarked on a systematic transformation of the economy, progressively eliminating private ownership in industry and commerce and initiating collectivization in agriculture. By 1951, practically all forms of market mechanism had been replaced by central planning; all economic decisions were centralized and implemented within the context of five-year plans. The major preoccupation of the leadership at this time was the transformation of a predominantly agrarian economy and society into an industrial one. A program of rapid industrialization was launched.

The first five-year plan (for 1951–1955) was prepared with Soviet assistance and launched in 1951. There was a clear bias in favor of industry, particularly heavy industry and the minerals sector. By 1959 the complete Soviet system of plan indicators was adopted, including lists of projects, global output, output mix, input requirements, use of productive capacity, volume and structure of capital investment, labor productivity and employment, training of new workers, wage fund, average wages, unit production costs, and sales.

Between 1951–1955 and 1956–1960, aggregate percentage change in net material product (NMP) was 44 percent, but that for industry was 104 percent. By 1960, according to official figures, industry accounted for 20 percent of NMP, as compared with around 10 percent a decade earlier. At the same time, ambitious schemes in health and social policy had improved access to education and medical facilities, and there was a considerable improvement in levels of literacy.

Albania resisted Soviet pressure to specialize in agricultural production within the CMEA structure, and development of agriculture was given lower priority than industry. Growth in agricultural output was negligible: The aggregate percentage change in NMP between 1951–1955 and 1956–1960 was only 7 percent, an average annual growth rate of around 1 percent; population growth was already nearly double this. This was despite a massive extension in the area of land under cultivation. (Arable land expanded by more than 250 percent over the first 20 years of the republic through land reclamation, extension of irrigation and electricity services, and soil-improvement programs.)

Goods shortages were frequent and rationing was used to allocate goods among consumers. Before 1957 the government operated a dual pricing system for consumer goods whereby a ration could be obtained at a fixed price with further supplies available at a higher (albeit also fixed) price. In 1957, on Soviet advice, the government unified agricultural prices and raised them to a level between these two. These prices remained largely unchanged thereafter, setting the basis for increasing subsidies. A one-time wage adjustment was also given in 1957 to offset the impact of the price increases, and no significant price or wage policy changes occurred thereafter.

Soviet–Albanian relations began to deteriorate, however, after Stalin's death in 1953. Khrushchev's rapprochement with Tito in 1955 and his denunciation of Stalin the following year severely strained relations. In 1960 the Albanian leadership declared its support for the People's Republic of China in the Sino-Soviet ideological dispute; in 1961 diplomatic relations were severed and Soviet technicians were replaced by Chinese.

State Socialism Under Chinese Influence: 1961–1978

In the early 1960s the economy—which suffered immediately from serious dislocation after the withdrawal of Soviet assistance—experienced significant difficulties. Trade with the Soviet Union dropped from over 50 percent of all foreign trade to zero, and in 1962 Albania ended its participation in the CMEA. But by the beginning of the fourth five-year plan (1966–1970), in large part as a result of Chinese financial and technical assistance, Albania had substantially recovered. Through the 1960s Albania began to develop a manufacturing base, with an emphasis on heavy industry, and to transform an agrarian economy into an industrial economy. Indeed, the period between 1961 and 1978 as a whole was one of remarkable economic growth and structural transformation.

In the three plan periods between 1961 and 1975, the aggregate percentage change in NMP was 44 percent, with industrial growth varying between 78 percent, 66 percent, and 80 percent (in 1961–1965, 1966–1970, and 1971–1975, respectively) over the previous plan period. By the end of 1971–1975, industry accounted for 35 percent of national NMP.

Agricultural development was less rapid, largely because of the priority accorded to industrial development. Here aggregate percentage growth in NMP over the previous plan period was 27 percent in 1961–1965, 19 percent in 1966–1970, and 19 percent in 1971–1975, according to official figures. By 1971–1975, agriculture accounted for only 36 percent of total NMP (about the same as industry). By the end of the 1960s the process of collectivization of agriculture was effectively complete. Agricultural cooperatives or collective farms differed from state enterprises mainly in terms of their financial relationship with the budget (less than 10 percent of their "profits" were transferred to the budget while most of their investments either were financed by bank loans or were self-financed) and in terms of their wage policy (internally determined and a function of the revenues generated). Although plan targets set for the cooperatives/collectives were meant to be indicative, they were usually in fact compulsory.

Workers' dissatisfaction with the heavy-handed system of central planning led to attempts in the mid-1960s to increase incentives and streamline the planning process. From 1965 onward, instead of receiving a detailed plan from the state hierarchy, workers were induced to discuss broad plan targets, which would then be sent to the higher authorities for approval. (The ultimate decisionmaking power, however, remained with the central planners.) Some attempts at decentralization of decisionmaking were also introduced in the state hierarchy; primary responsibility in many areas shifted from the Council of Ministers to the branch ministries and then to local executive committees. In 1960, only 20 percent of enterprises were under the jurisdiction of executive committees; by 1969 the proportion had increased to 40 percent and by 1971 to 80 percent.

The position of enterprise managers, however, continually deteriorated. During the late 1960s and the 1970s, the typical manager faced several salary cutbacks; with the introduction of a degree of workers' participation, their authority over the activities of state enterprises diminished. Not only were managers under pressure from the state hierarchy and the workers' organizations to set high targets, but they were also held responsible for underachievement and poor performance. But conflict between managers and workers on questions of underachievement were strongly discouraged. Poor performance tended to be explained not by lack of economic incentives but by inadequate motivation or ideological commitment on the part of the workers.

The transformation of the Albanian economy during the 1960s and 1970s was largely made possible by a substantial inflow of Chinese capital and technology. The bulk of its imports of capital goods in the 1970s were of Chinese origin, largely financed by long-term credits. The Chinese influence was very strong not only economically but also socially and culturally. Political control was intense during the 1960s as Hoxha attempted to implement his own version of the Cultural Revolution. The Ministry of Justice was abolished in 1965, and in 1967 religious institutions and practices were banned and Albania was declared the world's first atheistic state. This last move was legitimized in the name of national unity to prevent potential conflict between Muslims and Christians within the People's Republic.

Relations with China deteriorated, however, after improvements in the latter's relations with the United States following President Nixon's visit to China in 1972 and after the death of Mao Zedong in 1976. Concern about reliance on foreign capital flows, and the growing dependency on China, led in 1976 to a constitutional ban on foreign loans. China was accused of taking the capitalist path and of "social revisionism." In 1978 China suspended all economic and military cooperation with Albania, after Albania had declared its support for Vietnam in the Sino–Vietnamese dispute.

State Socialism—the Albanian Road: 1978–1985

During the last seven years of Hoxha's rule, Albania's foreign policy was dominated by isolationism and the notion of development through self-reliance. But this was also a period during which economic growth began markedly to slow down and contradictions between the policy of self-reliance and the drive to industrialization became more acute.

Aggregate growth in NMP between plan periods declined from an average of 44 percent over the previous decade, first to 19 percent between 1971–1975 and 1976–1980, and then to 16 percent between 1976–1980 and 1981–1985. Industrial growth rates slumped from 80 percent between 1966–1970 and 1971–1975 to 37.5 percent between 1971–1975 and 1976–1980. Rates of growth in construction, transportation, and communications also declined, although agriculture held up relatively well. In general, economic growth decelerated substantially in the last years of the 1970s and the early part of the 1980s, averaging nearly 5 percent per year in the 1970s as a whole but slumping to an annual average of about 1 percent in the 1980s.

The explanation for this significant slowdown is debatable, but the IMF argues that

> Albania's distinctive experience began . . . in 1978, when it interrupted economic and financial relations with China and felt the full enforcement of the 1976 constitutional ban on all forms of foreign finance. Although many countries have been able to cope with the cessation of foreign financing, it usually requires macro-economic adjustments. Albania did not adjust to the new situation, and aggregate demand, fueled by monetary growth and fiscal imbalances, continued to grow rapidly. Moreover, to manage the economy in conditions of financial autarky, it was necessary to tighten state command of the system further, thereby aggravating the misallocation of resources.[2]

Factors that certainly contributed to a decline in productivity and increasing demands on the state budget were: the government's commitment to provide employment for a rapidly increasing labor force, and to maintain food subsidies to enable workers on low fixed wages to buy bread and other basic goods at low prices, combined with the continuous deterioration and increasing obsolescence of the capital stock (much of which had been outdated when installed). This in turn generated monetary growth and fiscal imbalances.

In the early years of the 1980s, however, the political leadership remained openly confident and optimistic about the prospects for economic growth and socialist development. In April 1983, for example, Ramiz Alia declared at the National Conference on Problems of the Development of the Economy in the Seventh Five-Year Plan:

> We have entered the third year of the seventh five year plan. The results achieved during the first two years (1981–82) regarding the increase of the social product and national income are among the greatest ever achieved in the last decade. Continuing on this road, our economy is underlining its distinctive features as a truly socialist economy of relatively high-rate development, an economy without crises.[3]

But whatever the situation in 1981 and 1982, there is no doubt that throughout the remainder of the decade the Albanian economy experienced a serious slowdown in almost all sectors. Referred to as a period of stagnation by some,[4] this could also legitimately be seen as a period of deepening crisis in the sense that the underlying structural contradictions within the economy were becoming more acute, even if they were perhaps less manifest than they might have been. The IMF argues that

> the crisis was able to be postponed for almost a decade because of the past accumulation of foreign exchange reserves, the ability to maintain a broadly based current account in non-convertible currencies, favourable developments in Albania's terms of trade, and new exports of primary commodities. But over time the accumulated repercussions from the intensified macroeconomic imbalances, along with growing fiscal deficits and rapid monetary expansion (especially in the second half of the 1980s) and increasing shortages of consumer goods, became fully apparent.[5]

Internal political orthodoxy was enforced with the utmost rigor. The security police, the *Sigurimi,* were vigilant in preventing the emergence of any opposition movement within the country, while volume after volume of Hoxha's collected works consolidated his cult of personality. By the mid-1980s, however, and particularly after the death of Hoxha, the political leadership was increasingly prepared to recognize that there were serious economic problems. Pressures for both economic and political change were to increase during the second half of the 1980s.

Growing Pressures for Change: 1985–1990

Enver Hoxha died in April 1985 and was succeeded as first secretary of the ALP by Ramiz Alia. Alia had played an important role in the development of post-1945 Albania as secretary for ideology in the ALP from the late 1960s onward. His rise to the leadership began after the death of Hoxha's expected successor, Mehmet Shehu, in 1981.

As first secretary, Alia adopted a less rigid style than Hoxha and the government began to distance itself gradually from the Hoxha legacy. The change was first noticeable in foreign policy and international relations. As Jeffries suggests, "since Ramiz Alia assumed power as First Secretary in April 1985, something of a foreign relations thaw . . . set in."[6]

Moves toward a strategic opening up were driven largely by the concern to expand international trade in order to upgrade technology and increase productivity (a concern shared by many Eastern European socialist regimes during the 1970s and early 1980s).[7] As the IMF has indicated, "in 1985, after decades of centralist rule, the Government started, albeit slowly, to move away from adherence to the principle of self-reliance";[8] but the objective was to strengthen state socialism, not to embark on a process of economic liberalization.

Trade links with China had already been restored in 1983, and Western companies were already helping to develop chromite and ferronickel processing. Relations with Greece improved following bilateral negotiations in 1984, and by 1987 Greece agreed to end the state of war that had continued technically after 1945. The status of the ethnic Greek minority in southern Albania remained a sensitive issue, as did alleged ill-treatment of the Albanian community in Yugoslavia; but relations with both Yugoslavia and Greece improved significantly. In 1988 Albania participated in the Balkan Conference of Foreign Ministers in Belgrade, the first official meeting of all six Balkan states in more than fifty years. This meeting aimed at increasing regional stability and cooperation in the spheres of economic and cultural relations, tourism, the environment, transport, and communications. Albania's representative, Foreign Minister Reis Malile, publicly declared that there was scope for improving economic relations through a limited expansion of cross-border trade and the removal of tariffs and licenses for some goods, and also through the development of links in respect to transport, communications, and water management.

During the 1980s as a whole, Albania's foreign trade grew slowly (generally recording a deficit); but from 1988 it increased rapidly—by 1989 imports from the West were worth about $165 million, and by 1990 an estimated $245 million. These were mainly capital goods such as locomotives, manufacturing machinery, some spare parts and, probably, armaments. Albania's exports were both agricultural and industrial, but the latter accounted for three-quarters of total exports and included petroleum, minerals, ferrochrome, copper wire, nickel, and electricity (from hydroelectric power). The major trading partners were Yugoslavia, Italy, Romania, Poland, Germany, Bulgaria, and France.

On the domestic economic front, there were cautious attempts at change and a degree of decentralization (although systematic reform from above—perestroika—was considered unacceptable). In his report to the ninth party congress in November 1986, Ramiz Alia acknowledged that economic performance over the period of the seventh five-year plan (1980–1985) had fallen well short of plan targets. National income had increased by only 16 percent (as against a target of 35 to 37 percent), an average annual growth rate of 3 percent, only just above the population growth rate. A serious drought in 1983–1985 had adversely affected agriculture, which grew by 27 percent instead of the planned 36 to 38 percent; petroleum extraction had achieved only half of the expected 58 to 60 percent growth over the previous plan period. He recognized that these failures in production had implications for the supply of goods to the population and that there had been "shortcomings in supplying goods for the people as envisaged in the plan."

Alia directed his main criticism at "management failure," arguing that "pre-industrial methods of management can no longer apply." A degree of decentralization in the decisionmaking process in enterprises was proposed, together with the linking of salaries and wages to output and quality. Already there had been some measures adopted in the late 1970s to provide bonuses for increased productivity. Now a more extensive system of bonuses was to be introduced for workers exceeding their targets, especially in important export industries. Before 1985 there were no penalties for enterprise losses, but thereafter a system of points was established, based on realized production, proportion of contracts met, costs incurred, and workers' productivity. If the enterprise recorded a number of points below a critical level, salaries could be cut by up to 10 percent annually. (There were, of course, no provisions for bankruptcy.) Vickers comments, however, that "such incentives, together with the diffusion of some economic responsibilities to local management and exhortations to the labour force to develop a more competitive spirit, were a response to dire necessity; but they produced few results."[9]

Although problems were recognized, and the need for more effective incentives appreciated, the commitment to the overall strategy remained firm. Alia explicitly ruled out the introduction of Soviet-type (perestroika) reforms. The Albanian leadership had observed with great concern the economic and political changes in the Soviet Union following Mikhail Gorbachev's rise to power, which roughly paralleled that of Ramiz Alia. Although many Albanians hoped that Alia would become "Albania's Gorbachev," there was little sign of any real commitment to reform—even of the "reform from above" variety. A leading article in the official journal *Zeri i Popullit* (The People's Voice) in 1988 indicates the official position until the end of the decade regarding economic reforms:

> It was Khrushchev who, at the 20th Conference of the CPSU, began the great counter-revolutionary transformation—that process of "reforms" which destroyed socialism, paved the way for the restoration of capitalism.

> . . . Perestroika is broader in scope than all the reforms undertaken by
> Gorbachev's predecessors . . . and aims to eliminate everything that hinders
> the complete transition to unfettered capitalism.[10]

The official government position linked Eastern Europe's internal problems with the "revisionism" and betrayal of socialism of the regimes of the
Eastern European states, and argued that the Communists in Albania had a
legitimacy that derived both from their having come to power on their own
(in contrast with the governments that were installed effectively by the Red
Army) and from their greater commitment to socialist theory and practice.

The aim of the eighth five-year plan (1986–1990) was to consolidate the
process of industrial development, devoting 51 percent of investment to
industry—with agriculture as a major, albeit secondary priority—with 32
percent of investment. In the industrial sector, priority was given to import
substitution (through the development of the engineering and chemical
industries) and export promotion. In 1987, light and food-processing industries accounted for 38 percent of gross industrial production and 40 percent
of total exports; they provided more than 85 percent of domestic requirements. The production of chemicals was seen as an adjunct to the development of the minerals sector and as being of potential benefit to the agricultural sector; engineering was to focus on producing spare parts for the many
types of foreign-made machines operating in the country (a historical legacy of the Soviet and the Chinese periods). Production of spare parts
increased by more than 25 times between 1960 and 1984. In 1990 Albania
was the world's second-largest producer of chromite (chromium ore), producing somewhere between 500,000 and 900,000 metric tons; but production consistently failed to meet plan targets and the management of the
industry was regularly criticized. Apart from management problems, the
industry suffered from antiquated Chinese equipment, a lack of refining and
processing plants, and inadequate transport facilities.

In agriculture, the aim continued to be to eliminate private farming by
the progressive transformation of cooperatives or collective farms—whose
members were permitted a private plot—into state farms in which all property would be state owned and where the loss of private plots would be com-
pensated for by job and wage security. The 1975 experiment of combining
family-owned livestock into joint herds was extended; but in 1986, pressure
to transfer livestock to the cooperatives led to the slaughtering of animals by
livestock owners and subsequent shortages. Agriculture performed badly
during 1986–1990, with aggregate percentage change over the previous plan
period of only 2.3 percent—a rate significantly lower than that of population
increase. A severe drought in 1987–1988 revealed the continuing reliance on
good weather, despite the fact that a high percentage of arable land (between
50 and 60 percent) was now under irrigation. The disastrous record of agriculture in the late 1980s was to have a dramatic effect on the availability of
food in the early 1990s.

According to one source,

> since the early 1950s, agriculture . . . received less support than industry, and within agriculture industrial crops . . . were favoured at the expense of foodgrain and livestock production. Although plans repeatedly emphasised the importance of increasing the output of foodgrains . . . the objective of attaining self-sufficiency in food production was rarely achieved and food has been intermittently imported.[11]

Albania claimed, however, at the end of the 1980s to be 95 percent self-sufficient in food, with agriculture accounting for up to a quarter of total exports.[12] The variation in agricultural output was considerable, and it is possible that both statements are correct.

By the end of the 1980s agriculture constituted roughly 33 percent of total NMP and employed nearly 50 percent of the total working population, of which 80 percent were in cooperatives and collective farms. The cooperatives (which covered roughly 75 percent of the arable land and produced 61 percent of total agricultural output) produced mainly cereals (75 percent of total cereal production), rice, tobacco, and livestock; the state farms (which covered roughly 22 percent of the land and accounted for 28 percent of output) produced mainly fruit and vegetables for the urban areas and for export. The rest was accounted for by private plots owned by members of the cooperatives and cultivated primarily for domestic consumption. Output per hectare in private plots was far higher than in the cooperatives or on state farms, but productivity was higher on state farms than on cooperative land.

Conclusion

The available data, taken together, indicate a serious slowing of economic growth and development during the 1980s, with a marked deterioration in the period of 1986–1990. Official figures for retail trade revealed increases in trading of only 3.3 percent in 1987 and 2.7 percent in 1988, suggesting that the supply of goods was barely keeping pace with population growth (estimated at over 2 percent a year by the end of the 1980s). Despite this, reforms remained extremely limited until the very end of the decade. The recognition of some of the problems facing the country's economy did lead to an incipient, hesitant rethinking of economic policy under Ramiz Alia, including a fledgling opening to the outside world and the recognition of the importance of effective incentives, along with a limited degree of decentralization. Yet the refusal to connect the recognition of these difficulties with any serious contemplation of dismantling central socialist control over the economy (with, for instance, the continued insistence on eliminating private farming), along with the rejection of any notions of significant political change until the very end of the 1980s, meant that the growing tensions in both economy and polity only continued to grow. This was particularly so in the context of events unfolding elsewhere in Eastern Europe. From the turn of the decade, as a result, even Albania began to find itself caught up in the current of change. The politics of this change will be examined in the following chapter.

Notes

1. In addition to the sources referred to in subsequent notes, the following were consulted or are useful for further reading: B. Backer, "Self-Reliance under Socialism—the case of Albania," *Journal of Peace Research,* Vol. 19, No. 4, pp. 355–367; E. Biberaj, *Albania: A Socialist Maverick* (Boulder, Colo.: Westview Press, 1982); *Europa World Year Book, 1991* (London: Europa Publications, 1990); N. Pano, *The People's Republic of Albania. Albania: Politics, Economics and Society* (Boulder, Colo.: Westview, 1985); S. Pollo and P. Arben, *The History of Albania* (London, 1981); P. Prifti, *Socialist Albania Since 1944* (Cambridge, Mass.: MIT Press, 1978); A. Schnytzer, *Stalinist Economic Strategy in Practice: The Case of Albania* (Oxford: Oxford University Press, 1982); O. Sjoberg, *The Agrarian Sector in Albania During the 1980s: A Changing Regional Focus,* Studies in International Economics and Geography, No. 4. (Stockholm: Stockholm School of Economics, 1989); id., *Rural Change and Development in Albania* (Boulder: Westview Press, 1990); O. Sjoberg and M. Wyzan, eds., *Economic Change in the Balkan States: Albania, Bulgaria, Romania and Yugoslavia* (London: Pinter Publishers, 1991); T. Winnifrith, ed., *Perspectives on Albania* (London: Macmillan: 1992); World Bank, *An agricultural strategy for Albania: A report prepared by a joint team from the World Bank and the European Community* (Washington: World Bank, 1993). In addition, see the Economist Intelligence Unit's quarterly reports on Romania, Bulgaria, Albania.

2. M. Blejer et al., *Albania: From Isolation Towards Reform* (Washington: International Monetary Fund, 1992), p. 3.

3. Quoted in I. Jeffries, "The People's Republic of Albania," in I. Jeffries, ed., *A Guide to Socialist Economies* (London: Routledge, 1990), pp. 77-84.

4. E.g., P. Sandstrom and O. Sjoberg, "Albanian Economic Performance," in *Soviet Studies,* Vol. 43, No. 5, 1991, pp. 931–947.

5. Blejer et al., *Albania,* p. 3.

6. Jeffries, "The People's Republic of Albania," p. 77.

7. D. Seddon, "The politics of reform in Central and Eastern Europe," in J. Walton and D. Seddon, eds., *Free Markets and Food Riots: The Politics of Global Adjustment* (Oxford: Blackwell, 1994), pp. 288–329.

8. Blejer et al., *Albania,* p. 55.

9. M. Vickers, "Albania," in *Eastern Europe and CIS 1994* (London: Europa Publications, 1993), p. 115.

10. Reported in *Albanian Life,* 1988, pp. 37–40.

11. Blejer et al., *Albania,* p. 16.

12. Economist Intelligence Unit, *Annual Economic Review of Rumania, Bulgaria, Albania, 1987–88* (London: Economist Intelligence Unit, 1987), p. 32.

7

The Politics of Economic Reform in Albania

DAVID SEDDON
with Ruth Davey and Rachel Grellier

This chapter examines the politics of economic reform in Albania during the 1990s, drawing on the analysis provided in the previous chapter.[1]

Perestroika, Albanian Style: 1990–1991

Albania had undoubtedly embarked on mildly reformist policies, largely for economic reasons, before the collapse of the Communist regimes in Eastern Europe in 1989. But during 1990 the pressures for change, both political and economic, were to grow enormously. The ALP leadership was obliged, largely by forces within the country, to move from cautious and limited changes to significantly more far-reaching reforms and, eventually, during 1991 to embark on a process of political as well as economic liberalization that had strong similarities with the process unfolding elsewhere in the former state-socialist countries of Eastern Europe.

The first signs of political liberalization appeared in November 1989, when an amnesty was announced for certain political prisoners. But on the eve of the violent overthrow and execution of the Romanian head of state, Nicolae Ceausescu, in December 1989, the president of Albania and first secretary of the ruling Labor Party, Ramiz Alia, assured the world that his country was immune to the dramatic developments that were reshaping the political landscape of Eastern Europe. Addressing a meeting of the Communist-controlled Trade Unions Council on 11 December, Alia confidently declared: "There are people abroad who will ask: Will processes like those taking place in Eastern Europe also occur in Albania? We answer firmly and categorically: No, they will not occur in Albania."

He observed that, after the break with the Soviet bloc in 1961 and the alliance with China during the 1970s, Albania had embarked on a distinctive path that meant that it was not faced with the same problems as the other Eastern European states.

> The crisis that is sweeping the countries in the East is the crisis of a definite community, the crisis of what used to be called the socialist community, but it is not the crisis of socialism as theory and practice. Consequently, the events taking place there have nothing to do with us.[2]

In January 1990, Ramiz Alia referred to the collapse of communism as "a tragedy" and convened a Central Committee meeting late in the month to assess the impact of developments in Eastern Europe. He rejected the possibility of political pluralism and declared that "the calls that are being made abroad for changes in our country, for a departure from the road we are following, do not find support in our country and are not in tune with the opinion and will of the broad strata of the working people."[3] Claiming that the domestic situation was "solid," he linked his opposition to the creation of other political parties to a broad concern that a multiparty system would undermine Albania's independence and stability. At the same time, he announced a cautious program of reforms.

In the political domain, the Central Committee decided that basic party structures would now hold open meetings, workers would play a greater role in the selection of party cadres, competition would be introduced in the election of cadres, and the terms of office of cadres elected would be limited. There would also be multicandidate elections to the People's Assembly.

In the economic sphere, the Central Committee approved a decentralization of decisionmaking, giving local authorities and enterprises greater autonomy. There would be a decentralization of light industry and transportation, more private housing, and productivity-linked wage increases. In order to stimulate agricultural production and deal with growing food shortages in the cities, cooperatives would be permitted to sell their surplus produce.

In a dramatic break with the legacy of Enver Hoxha, Alia reversed the government's policy on several major issues associated with external relations. He expressed his country's desire to normalize relations with Moscow and Washington and indicated that new laws would be promulgated to permit the government to accept foreign investment. In February 1990 the introduction of "a new economic mechanism" permitted foreign investment for the first time since 1976, and in June Albania began negotiations with a view to joining the IMF. In July private handicraft and family trading businesses were legalized and permitted to set their own prices and find their own suppliers. They were obliged to obtain licenses to work and could not employ any person outside the immediate family, but nevertheless there was a rapid response. By December 1990 there were some 1,500 registered private entrepreneurs, and some 7,000 service units had been privatized, including craft workshops, retail units, and restaurants.

In the context of Albania these were significant developments. Foreign journalists visiting Tirana in the spring of 1990 reported generally that Alia enjoyed considerable popular support, particularly in the rural areas, as he toned down the hard ALP rhetoric on ideological issues and allowed a greater measure of openness. At the same time, however, the secret police, the *Sigurimi,* intensified their activities against known dissidents. Whatever internal political reforms were envisaged would be limited.

The cautious pace of economic and political reform proved increasingly unacceptable to many Albanians in light of changes taking place elsewhere in Eastern Europe. In March 1990, several hundred young men took part in a demonstration in Kavaje, thirty miles south of the capital, Tirana, that was broken up by the police with batons and rubber bullets; in May, about 2,000 workers at one of the biggest textile factories in the city of Berat went on strike to protest against low wages; and in July there were demonstrations in Tirana itself calling for more far-reaching change. The official Albanian news agency ATA reported that demonstrators, numbering between 300 and 400, "including vagabonds and former prisoners, as well as some deceived adolescents," had clashed with security forces, throwing stones and breaking windows. Foreign diplomats referred to "large demonstrations" and reported at least thirty people injured in police shooting.

In August Alia met with a group of critical intellectuals and was faced with demands to abolish the one-party system and permit political pluralism. He rejected these demands but promised an increased role for elected bodies, including the People's Assembly, a greater separation between state and party, a relaxation of party control over mass organizations, and some refinement in the appointment of managers and cadres. The government also responded to the growing disaffection among workers by announcing wage increases. In September 1990 it raised all wages below 450 lek a month by 10 percent. But social unrest continued to mount.

In December thousands of students, academics, and workers staged a rally of unprecedented size, demonstrated over several days to demand greater political openness and the prosecution of those responsible for injuries to demonstrators during the previous popular protests, and clashed again with baton-wielding riot police. The ruling ALP held a special conference to prepare for economic reforms and to fight the first contested elections ever in the spring of 1991. The election manifesto adopted by the conference outlined a total reorganization of the party and the recognition of opposition parties, as well as new legislation, economic reforms, and a greater opening up to the outside world.

Meanwhile, popular unrest and opposition to the regime were growing. In Elbasan, Albania's major industrial city, tanks moved in to quell protests; in Kavaje a rally staged on Christmas Day by the newly established Democratic Party was attended by around 10,000 people; and in the northern town of Shkoder, where anti-Communist opposition was particularly strong, thousands turned out to attend Christmas Mass for the first time in decades. In early January 1991, miners at a pit just outside Tirana went on strike over wages and working conditions. Opposition reports suggested that the strike had spread to other parts of the country, with several thousand workers taking part. The reports added that transportation and other industrial workers were also threatening action and, like the miners, demanding wage increases of up to 200 percent. Under increasing pressure, the government agreed to pay raises of between 30 and 50 percent for the country's 30,000 miners, and promised further wage increases for other workers; by April 1991 the average wage was 650 to 700 lek.

The plea by the Democratic Party that the elections planned for February should be postponed in order to give it some time to organize was eventually agreed to by the Communist Party leadership. In exchange for this concession Ramiz Alia gained opposition support for an end to strikes and wage raises until May 1991.

In 1990 the economy registered an unprecedented decline of over 13 percent. A severe drought had adversely affected key sectors of the economy—agriculture, agribusiness, and agrobased industrial inputs and exports. Moreover, the industrial sector was subject to frequent power failures, and acute shortages in imported raw materials were caused by the curtailment of trade with Albania's major Central and Eastern European trading partners. By early 1991 the Albanian economy was on the brink of collapse. Increasingly, the government was obliged to concede to pressure for economic reform and inclined to look to cautious liberalization for a solution. In January Albania applied formally for membership in the IMF and the World Bank. This was a strong indication of a willingness to move toward economic liberalization. But the government still proposed the gradual introduction of "market mechanisms" into a largely state-controlled economy (a form of market socialism) although the democratic opposition was firmly committed to radical economic reform. During the latter part of January 1991 the Democratic Party held rallies across the country to gain support; its election manifesto called for "the creation of a share-owning democracy, the end of centralised communist control, and distribution of land to the peasants working it." As one commentator observed, "the opposition proposals on the economy are in line with the marketisation policies being carried out by post-communist governments in Eastern Europe; Mr Alia's recall the policies of Mr Gorbachev and pre-1989 Eastern Europe."[4]

The Deepening Crisis: 1991–1992

Elections were held at the end of March 1991. Eleven parties and organizations contested the elections, but the main struggle was between the old Communist ALP (now renamed the Socialist Party) and the Democratic Party. The Communists gained the majority (165 seats in the People's Assembly compared with the Democrats' sixty-eight) with overwhelming support (around two-thirds of the vote) from the rural areas. The towns, however, strongly supported the opposition; in many of the major centers they captured all of the seats. Ramiz Alia lost his own seat in Tirana, having obtained only 36 percent of the votes. The Communists offered the Democrats a role in a coalition government, but this was turned down. In several towns, notably Shkoder, there were demonstrations in protest of the election results, while on the streets of Tirana "people wept openly, rubbing their stomachs to indicate their belief that more hunger was in store."[5]

Despite the publication in April of a new draft constitution in which many of the central tenets of the previous orthodoxy were abandoned, and several major changes made in the structure of government, popular protest in the urban areas continued to grow. In early May about 100 miners at a pit outside Tirana undertook a hunger strike to support demands for improved wages and working conditions, and to call for the identification of those responsible for the deaths of anti-Communist protesters in Shkoder; this gave rise to calls for a general strike. In mid-May a general strike, called by Albania's newly independent trade unions, brought factories and public transportation to a halt in several major towns. Four days later, tens of thousands of workers marched through the streets of Tirana demanding pay raises of up to 100 percent. According to state radio, almost a tenth of the population was involved in the strikes, which had spread to all regions. "All forms of transport, mining, the oil sector, and other enterprises have been paralysed," it was reported.

President Alia appealed for an end to the stoppages, declaring that "economic and political life are almost at a standstill," and calling for dialogue and an end to violence. The government agreed to increase wages for all workers by between 15 and 80 percent. A week later, a rally by thousands of strike supporters in Shkoder, called by the trade unions in support of the miners' strike, was followed by a mass protest involving tens of thousands that clashed with security forces in the streets of Tirana. With the general strike entering its fourth week and massive popular unrest in virtually every town throughout the country, the government felt obliged to resign.

In June 1991, following nearly six months of social unrest, in a context of virtual economic collapse, and only two months after the Communists won their first contested elections, a new "national stability" coalition government was sworn in to end nearly half a century of Communist Party rule. The Democrats took control of most of the economic portfolios, Gramoz Pashko was made deputy prime minister with overall responsibility for the economy, and Genc Ruli was appointed minister of finance. Painting a grim picture of economic breakdown and mounting social unrest, the new prime minister, Ylli Bufi, appealed for foreign aid to help restore law and order, put the country back to work and introduce the basic elements of a market economy. He promised to devalue the lek, free prices (apart from those on basic foods), and close down unproductive plants and factories.

The new government inherited an economy in deepening crisis. Inflation was rising, output was falling, and unemployment was becoming a major problem; agricultural output had fallen by 20 to 30 percent between 1989 and 1991 and food shortages were becoming ever more acute, as were shortages of agricultural and industrial inputs. The effect of the earlier wage increases, given the growing shortage of goods, had been to push up inflation. The amount of money in circulation increased by 441 million lek through 1990, and by July 1991 the annual rate of inflation was estimated at over 25 percent. It was now recognized that there were many unprofitable enterprises that would have to be closed; other industrial plants were overstaffed. If industrial output were to increase, then industry must be made more efficient, but the economic and social costs in the short term were very severe.

Industrial production fell by over half in 1991, and by 1992 large industrial concerns were generally operating at only around 20 percent of capacity. Until 1991 the existence of unemployment had not been officially admitted, although absenteeism and effective underemployment were widespread. There were indications throughout the late 1980s of relatively high levels of disguised or hidden unemployment, with an average yearly labor force increasing in recent years by 3.5 percent, compared with growth rates for NMP of only 1.7 percent; this implied a declining rate of labor productivity of 1.7 percent a year. The Economist Intelligence Unit estimated in 1991 that unemployment might be as high as 35 percent of the labor force and commented that these levels of unemployment indicated a major economic crisis.

The 1991 plan (for 1991–1995) recognized the problem and stated that new mechanisms of social assistance would need to be introduced to give workers the time and opportunity to train for other jobs; but little seems to have been done to implement these proposals. In May 1991 it was announced that 50,000 were officially unemployed, while a further 40,000 were receiving reduced pay but had no work owing to lack of raw materials. Unemployment or underemployment—and the prospect of it—was a major reason for the large numbers of young men attempting to emigrate during 1991.

By the middle of the year, in several parts of the country the food situation had become critical and was still deteriorating. In Shkoder, thousands had been made jobless and even for those still in work pay remained low; the consequences included looting of shops and food stores, an increase in crime generally, and the sacking of the Communist Party headquarters. But the food shortages affected not only Shkoder. In July 1991, shocked by evidence of spreading hunger, the EC proposed a multimillion-pound emergency food and medical aid program for Albania. In mid-1991 some 30 percent of children under the age of three were reported as showing varying degrees of malnutrition, and in some areas, particularly the southeast, the figures were as high as 40 percent.[6] This apparently widespread problem was probably associated with a significant decline in per capita food production over the past three years, resulting from a combination of lower aggregate production and a continuing high population-growth rate, which the country has been unable to counteract with increased imports.

In the first half of the year, agricultural operations were disrupted by insecurity resulting from the proposed agrarian reform program. Confusion was caused by the sudden dismantling of the agricultural cooperatives that had held 70 percent of agricultural land, uncertainty over the future of the state farms, the scarcity of inputs and a lack of foreign exchange to purchase them abroad, and the breakdown of public distribution channels for agricultural inputs and outputs. This led to an estimated 55 percent decline in output.

Under the reform, introduced in July 1991, some 40 percent of state farms (which accounted for 30 percent of agricultural output in 1989) and nearly all cooperatives (which accounted for 60 percent of production) were to be broken up. Every family was to receive a plot of land of an average 1.5 hectares (and in some areas only 0.6 hectares). The sale of this land was prohibited for three years. Despite the law relating to the privatization of land, there were further disruptions to production due to delays in the distribution of land, partly due to efforts by landowners to repossess their property at once.

The land-distribution program became so problematic that the reform was temporarily halted and the land was increasingly occupied, illegally, by peasant farmers. Seeds, fuel, and transportation were all in short supply, although the government asserted that there was an adequate supply of farm machinery and fertilizer. Official figures for 1991 report grain production down by two-thirds from 1990 (wheat production falling from 600,000 tons in 1989 to 354,000 tons in 1991), milk output halved, acreage planted to cotton down by 80 percent, and that planted to tobacco reduced by about half. By early December only 45,000 hectares had been sown to wheat, less than 50 percent of the planned 100,000 hectares. Consequently the prospects for 1992 were even more serious.

The government was caught between the commitment to reform and the growing social and economic costs of its reform policies. In November 1991, to reduce the drain on its meager resources, the government withdrew subsidies from large enterprises and introduced price liberalization. The prices of vegetables, fruit, eggs, and lesser items were liberalized, although prices for bread, meat, and milk products continued to be fixed. Prices rose fourfold in five weeks and unemployment soared.

As food production fell, $1 million in food aid arriving every day, mainly from Italy, made it possible to avoid mass starvation. (Albania had been receiving emergency shipments of food aid since September, mainly from Italy and the EC.) By December food riots were becoming increasingly common and widespread; food distribution was hampered by racketeering and raids on convoys and warehouses. In mid-December thirty-two people died in a fire that swept through a food-aid depot as it was ransacked by looters in the northeastern town of Fushe-Arez. When, for the fourth day, bread failed to arrive in the town, 2,000 to 3,000 people marched on the central food and clothing depot. Sweeping aside the twenty policemen guarding the store, they entered the building with homemade rag-and-oil torches and, inadvertently perhaps, set it on fire. Earlier, a policeman and a girl of thirteen were killed in Lac, a town twenty-five miles north of Tirana, when crowds went on a rampage after bread trucks failed to arrive; the entire town was gutted, and water and power supplies wrecked, before troops were sent in to quell the disturbance. Meanwhile, food riots also took place in the capital itself as hungry protesters highjacked and ransacked trucks bringing bread into the city. According to some reports the riots were triggered by the announcement by the former prime minister that the country had only enough grain for six days.

At the end of 1991, as the economic and political situation became ever more desperate, the Democratic Party (itself increasingly divided over the autocratic ways of party president Sali Berisha) pulled out of the coalition government. The president, Ramiz Alia, at once appointed the former minister of food to head a caretaker government until new elections, scheduled for spring 1992, were held. The government was reported to favor a kind of "shock therapy," regardless of possible renewed social tension, to pull the country out of crisis: "We no longer have any choice," the minister of economy and finance declared.

In 1991 Albanian GDP contracted by 30 percent, after a decline of 10 percent in 1990, and was expected to fall an additional 23 percent in 1992.[7] The last of the socialist regimes of Central and Eastern Europe to embark on economic reforms entered 1992 apparently in the most desperate condition of all.

Shock Therapy: 1992 and After

At the beginning of 1992 the government committed itself to a package of radical economic reforms that the minister of economy and finance admitted would mean that "people will face fresh, acute shortages of all the most essential goods. . . . Even to survive will be tough. It will be difficult for the people not to react."[8] OXFAM described the Albanian economy as "teetering on the brink of collapse." "A chasm of poverty is opening beneath people's feet," according to OXFAM's emergencies coordinator, who warned that any break in emergency food supplies would lead to starvation on a massive scale, or violence, or both. "In political as well as humanitarian terms," he said, "this would be a catastrophe."[9] At the end of February thousands of young people were reported to have stormed the warehouses in Podradec, 90 miles southeast of Tirana; eight warehouses were emptied of food in three days of raids, and two rioters were crushed to death; similar attacks on warehouses took place in the central town of Lushnje.

In the spring of 1992 about half of the urban labor force was not working. In mid-February the rate of unemployment benefit stood at 750 lek (about $18) a month, while a family's bread ration alone cost 600 lek. With production generally in decline and the state enterprise sector yielding no surplus, government revenues declined by an estimated 25 percent of GDP, leading to a budget deficit in the first half of 1992 of about 50 percent of GDP. A large part of the budget deficit was financed by the domestic banking system. Inflation reached an annual rate of 300 percent (some sources suggest 500 percent) in early 1992. Confidence in the domestic currency vanished and the exchange rate collapsed; it only began to recover with the introduction of a free exchange-rate system in July 1992. Convertible currency exports fell to an estimated $65 million in 1992 (having fallen from $133 million in 1989 to $72 million in 1991).

Against a background of economic collapse and widespread social unrest, Albania went to the polls in March and threw out the ruling Socialist Party in favor of the Democrats under Sali Berisha. Within days of the result there were moves to give greater powers to the president and to replace Ramiz Alia with Sali Berisha. One of the new president's first tasks was to convince visitors from the IMF and the World Bank that the country was under control. But in June the new Albanian government was obliged to appeal to the UN for help in restoring law and order and resolving the growing ethnic problem. Meanwhile, the economy remained in dire straits, with mine workers on strike for substantial pay increases and agriculture officially admitted to be "in a state of complete paralysis." Food aid from abroad remained of critical importance.

Despite dramatically winning an absolute majority in the March elections, the Democratic Party was subsequently obliged, as a result of administrative elections, to form a coalition with the Social Democrats. The first government without ex-Communist Party members now embarked under Aleksander Meksi (and the overall supervision of President Sali Berisha) on a shock therapy reform strategy. The program was undertaken essentially under the guidance of the IMF.

The reforms included almost complete price deregulation, new pay scales, and the suspension of the 80 percent wage subsidy provided for the "technically" unemployed. It was argued that the wage suspension, which had been provided since 1990 as a form of social security to soften the hardship of mass unemployment, was too costly and tended to discourage "the necessary restructuring of the labor market."

The austerity measures adopted as part of the IMF-sponsored package had dramatic effects during 1992. The lek was devalued, and it fell from around 6 lek to the dollar (in mid-1991) to 80 lek (in mid-1992). The inflation rate—which had reached an annual rate of close to 300 percent in early 1992—dropped significantly. Over the next year, inflation ran at around 40 percent, but the currency remained relatively stable, the budget deficit was curbed (down from 50 percent to 20 percent of GNP during 1993, according to President Berisha), and the central bank was restructured—all bringing approval and a pledge of continued support from the IMF.

A macroeconomic restructuring program was introduced by the government under an IMF Stand-By agreement approved in August 1992. In that month the government liberalized the prices of domestic meat and milk but continued to maintain fixed prices for bread, sugar, cooking oil, and rice; the fixed prices, however, were increased by between 200 and 400 percent. The government continued with a policy of providing families with monthly food rations. In addition, from September 1992, imported meat, milk, butter, cheese, and eggs were sold at fixed prices to keep urban food prices low; as a result urban areas continued to depend on food aid, especially wheat and livestock products. However, given limited food aid supplies and the development of private food markets, market regulation became less effective. In September 1992, private market prices were up to 180 times higher than in official markets.

The fall in industrial production and in service-sector output during 1991–1992 had been dramatic (industrial production down 50 percent in 1991). As a result of the collapse of industrial production, agriculture came to account in 1992 for about 50 percent of GNP, with livestock production accounting for half of that. (In 1990 about 705,000 people were employed in agriculture and forestry, with an additional 100,000 in related sectors. The agricultural sector has accounted in recent years for about 50 percent of employment and some 20 percent of exports.)

In general, agricultural production appears to have been less adversely affected during 1992 than anticipated by the land reform, despite uncertainties created by the laws on property repossession and price deregulation. Indeed, one source suggests that by 1992 the land reform was 90 percent complete and relatively egalitarian.[10] The World Bank considers, more conservatively, that by August 1992, 79 percent of agricultural cooperative land had been privatized. However, the future of the 250 or so state farms, situated mainly in the coastal plains and covering 24 percent of good arable land, remained uncertain. In past years they accounted for 30 percent of the value of agricultural output and were the main suppliers of dairy products, fruit, and vegetables to the urban population; in 1991 their marketed surplus dropped sharply. The new small-farm sector continued to face serious challenges. Once the land-redistribution process is completed there will be some 380,000 small farms with an average size of about 1.4 hectares. In the lowland areas, where land has been distributed to individual farm households, a form of organization (the Private Farmers' Association) has emerged; some of these are private farmers' cooperatives, others are more like the former collective farms. The PFAs represent a response to the new private form of landholding with older forms of cooperative and collective agricultural enterprise. Nevertheless, the process of land distribution was reported in 1993 still to be causing problems, and there were rallies in some cities (such as Tirana) demanding the right to own land privately (implying that the process was still incomplete or was unsatisfactory for some).

Agricultural production estimates for 1992 showed some increases over 1991 but remained significantly below 1989 levels, with the exception of vegetables and livestock. Wheat and cotton production were expected to be 30 percent less than in 1991, with egg production falling another 14 percent. Other commodities probably maintained or exceeded their 1991 levels. Notable increases were in maize, vegetable, sunflower, and tobacco production, which were expected to be 70 percent above 1991 levels.

Despite a quick response by Albania's new private farmers to price liberalization and the freedom to grow what they want, Albania remains heavily dependent on food aid: Wheat imports during the first eight months of 1992 exceeded the year's harvest by 20 percent while domestic production of vegetable oil and sugar was estimated to cover only 6 to 15 percent of domestic needs. Grain production in 1993 was at least 30 percent down from 1990 and it was estimated that imports of between 200,000 and 300,000 tons would be required to meet the population's needs.

Food has historically held a very high (63 percent) share of household expenditures; lower real incomes, dwindling supplies in subsidized official markets, and increasing private sales at unregulated prices have driven this share even higher in urban areas and per capita food consumption is estimated to have declined.

Unemployment increased during 1992 and the first part of 1993, largely as a result of large-scale redundancies among public-sector employees (about 200,000 civil servants laid off), but the official number of unemployed declined during 1993, from about 465,000 in April[11] to under 300,000 in the second half of the year. The unemployment growth rate increased, according to the World Bank, from 29 percent in 1990 to 88.3 percent in 1992.[12] The unemployed accounted during 1993 for some 20 to 25 percent of the theoretical workforce. Between 70 and 75 percent of those received subsidies; in addition, at least 70,000 families, or a total of 300,000 people, received various kinds of state financial assistance. This means that, out of a resident population of just over 3 million, there were at least 600,000 people dependent on some form of social assistance.

Despite the evident problems, by mid-1993 it was possible for some to argue that "things remain bleak, but also hopeful."[13] International aid officials and development economists were reported to be unstinting in their praise for the reforms and optimistic that Albania was on the road to recovery. "They are over the curve from emergency aid to development," declared

Frederic André of the EC Task Force in Tirana. "I'm very impressed by what they've achieved in eighteen months. They doubled the price of bread last week, and there was barely a murmur of protest."[14]

Certainly, the incidence of strikes, which were widespread during 1992, declined markedly during 1993. But while some opinion-poll evidence suggested that a majority expected things to get better over the next year and agreed that the new political regime was better than the previous one, this does not necessarily indicate the "solid base of public support for market reforms" that some identified. The growing authoritarian tendencies of the Berisha regime, combined with continuing economic and social hardship (and the rising unemployment itself), provide perhaps a more convincing explanation for the muted response to further price increases. But at least part of the explanation must lie in the extraordinary exodus from Albania that took place during 1991–1993.

Between 250,000 and 300,000 people left the country, either legally or illegally, to Italy and Greece in particular, as conditions generally deteriorated and hardship increased. These Albanian migrants have come to contribute, through their remittances, some $400 million a year (one estimate suggests an average of $1.5 million a day) to the national economy. This amount is around four times the value of Albania's total exports, which at some $100 million barely reach a quarter of the value of exports during the last years of the Communist regime. It is claimed that although about half the working population is theoretically unemployed, many are actually working in the informal private sector. Government officials claim that some 100,000 people are now employed in the rapidly expanding private sector. Whether this situation indicates the recovery some have identified remains opens to debate.

There were certainly some positive indications by 1994 that the reforms were bearing fruit. Albania was one of the very few economies in transition that could record economic growth in GNP during 1993; initial estimates for the year of 3.5 percent were later revised upward to closer to 8 percent. The positive effects of the government's policy included a threefold increase in foreign investment during 1993 to more than $205 million, while the number of joint ventures doubled to around 150. (Investments were predominantly Italian, Greek, Austrian, and German.) A third, more liberal version of the law on foreign investment was introduced in November 1993 to encourage further inward flows of capital, although the risks of a wider Balkan conflict continued to deter many. The balance-of-payments deficit had fallen by the end of 1993 to under 50 percent of GNP, to recreate some modest reserves and to stabilize the exchange rate of the lek at around 100 to the dollar. The construction sector in particular was doing well as remittances from abroad were channeled into residential and office building. Some 30,000 private businesses were said to be operating in Tirana alone.

On the other hand, Albania undoubtedly remained one of the poorest and most precarious of the former state-socialist economies, highly dependent on aid from the West (despite the comments of the representative of the EC task force cited above). At the end of 1993, economic output represented only about 60 percent of its 1989 level. The most marked signs of recovery were in the agricultural sector, but substantial food imports remained necessary. The decline in industrial production appeared to have stopped and in some cases there was an upward trend, but many enterprises were producing below capacity and yet others had been obliged to close down. Reduced state subsidies and credit restrictions (with interest rates at around 40 percent) increased indebtedness. Hard-currency exports appear to have declined while imports rose (largely as a result of demands from the growing private sector). The foreign debt increased to reach $850 million by the start of 1994. And while the ruling Democrats have been generally praised, both inside the country and abroad, for their efforts to promote growth in the economy, they have done little to repair the crumbling infrastructure. A Western observer is quoted as noting that Albanians "have grown impatient with having to suffer basic hardships, like the power cuts and almost no running water in their homes."[15]

Another foreign observer reported in early 1995 that "in the depths of a fourth winter of economic hardship, Albania is a dark place, and disgruntlement towards President Sali Berisha is growing at an alarming rate."[16] Concern is now growing that President Berisha may be establishing a new form of authoritarian regime while at the same time encouraging economic liberalization. Since the March 1992 elections, support for the Democrats has been diminishing. Indeed, even in the July 1992 elections for the local municipalities and village councils only four months later, the Socialists received over 50 percent of the vote. In part there is growing anger and outrage at the deterioration in the living standards of the majority of the people; in part there is growing concern at the increasingly authoritarian rule of President Berisha. The popular rejection of the president's draft constitution in Albania's first-ever referendum in November 1994 has led to a series of increasingly authoritarian measures. "The No vote Berisha received in the referendum was in many ways a protest against our very bad economic situation," claimed the deputy leader of the opposition Socialist Party (the former ALP) at the beginning of 1995. But concern at the increasingly authoritarian regime of Berisha is shared by former allies of the president: "Without doubt we are seeing the revival of a police state," argued one of the leaders of the Democratic Alliance Party (which worked alongside the Democrats to overthrow the former Communists) in February 1995; this view is supported by the fact that the numbers of the police increased tenfold in the two years between the end of 1992 and the end of 1994.

If there were some signs of economic recovery, the political future for Albania looked uncertain in 1995, as the Albanian people struggle to retain the limited political freedoms achieved over the past few years and to safeguard their basic livelihoods. The dangers of a continuing process of economic liberalization combined with a form of authoritarian nationalism, and the prospects for entanglement in a regional Balkan conflict, threaten the achievements of the reforms and the sacrifices of the Albanian people.

Notes

1. In addition to the sources referred to in subsequent notes, the following were consulted (not including those already listed in note 1 to the previous chapter): E. Biberaj, *Albania: A Socialist Maverick* (Boulder: Westview Press, 1990); B. Hamilton, *Albania: Who Cares?* (Grantham: Autumn House, 1992); N. Stavrou, "Albania," *International Communist Affairs,* 1990, pp. 296–308; F. Tarifa, "Albania's Post-Communist Transition: Can Democracy Thrive?" *Balkan Forum,* Vol. 1, No. 5, December 1993, pp. 123–133; id., "Albania's Exit from Communism: Political and Social Change During 1990–1993" (unpublished paper, 1994); T. Winnifrith, *Perspectives on Albania* (Warwick Studies in the European Humanities) (London: Macmillan Press, 1992). In addition: The Economist Intelligence Unit's quarterly reports on Romania, Bulgaria, and Albania to 1994/1995, as well as its *Romania, Bulgaria and Albania: Country Profiles,* various years.

2. E. Biberaj, "Albania: The Last Domino," in I. Banac, *Eastern Europe in Revolution* (Ithaca: Cornell University Press, 1992), pp. 188–206: p. 188.

3. Ibid., p. 192.

4. *The Guardian,* 19 February 1991.

5. *The Guardian,* 2 April 1991.

6. S. Benson and E. Clay, *Eastern Europe and the Former Soviet Union: Economic Change, Social Welfare and Aid* (London: Overseas Development Institute, Special Report, 1992), p. 12.

7. World Bank, *An Agricultural Strategy for Albania: A Report Prepared by a Joint Team from the World Bank and the European Community* (Washington: World Bank, 1993).

8. *The Guardian,* 1 July 1992.

9. *The Guardian,* 17 February 1992.

10. D. Lewis and J. McGregor, *Change and Impoverishment in Albania: A Report for OXFAM* (Bath: Centre for Development Studies, University of Bath, 1993), p. 4.

11. S. Cani, "Albania Towards a Free Market Economy," *Balkan Forum,* Vol. 2, 1994, No. 1, pp. 207–216.

12. World Bank, *Albania—Country Economic Memorandum* (unpublished document) (Washington, D.C.: World Bank, 1994).

13. *The Guardian,* 24 July 1993.

14. Ibid.

15. *The Guardian,* 9 February 1995.

16. Ibid.

PART 3

THE MIDDLE EAST

8

Democratization in the Middle East: The Evidence from the Syrian Case

RAYMOND A. HINNEBUSCH

Economic liberalization may be on the agenda of every Middle Eastern state, but the "third wave" of global democratization appears to have spent itself on Middle Eastern shoals; a major study of new democracies judged Middle East countries to "have little prospect of transition even to semi-democracy."[1] Syria appears to be an exemplary case of such Middle East exceptionalism. Yet the Syrian Ba'th regime, far from being immune to the forces of political liberalization, is actively seeking to manage them. The Syrian case provides evidence for a critique of major explanations of political liberalization and democratization or their absence in the Middle East, and particularly of cultural exceptionalism.[2]

State-centric Approaches: The State as Obstacle to Democratization

Why is the Middle East state relatively invulnerable to the forces of democratization? In the culturalist "neopatrimonial" view, a primordial group is said to seize the state apparatus for self-aggrandizement and knows democratization would merely weaken it in the struggle with rival *asabiyya* (a term that in this context refers to kinship-based—or tribal—group feeling). In the Marxist view, the state is a creature of class—a state bourgeoisie aligning with a revived private bourgeoisie—behind a capitalist revival that requires the rollback of populist rights and hence political exclusion of the working and peasant classes.[3] However, such narrowly based, exclusionary models are too simple to capture the complexity of the Syrian regime or adequately explain its remarkable durability and resistance to change.

Authoritarian Populism

The Syrian state is best conceptualized as a Bonapartist authoritarian-populist regime that, like its French prototype, is a product of nationalism, war, and revolution. Revolution from above decimated upper-class economic power while creating and incorporating a large state-dependent peasantry and salaried middle class. This fluidization of the class structure was a perfect social terrain for the construction of a Bonapartist state above social forces that is very resistant to countervailing class power.

Authoritarian regimes with such populist social origins seem less vulnerable to political liberalization than others. The conservative authoritarianism typical of Latin America originates in the repression of the masses on behalf of the bourgeoisie and liberalizes under pressure from the bourgeoisie once the threat from below is mastered. By contrast, liberalization of populist regimes like Syria's would strengthen the bourgeoisie, a historical rival, unless the regime transforms its social base by striking an alliance with this class. In fact, as Syria's power elite became bourgeoisified, it sought a modus vivendi with the bourgeoisie. However, to avoid becoming dependent on a class it still cannot trust, it seeks to maintain its populist constituency and preserve its autonomy by balancing between rival bourgeois and popular social forces.

The structures of the Bonapartist state also resist liberalization. Asad concentrated power in a "presidential monarchy" by balancing between the army, the party, and his *jama'a*—a trusted core built from personal, kinship, and sectarian affinities—and he has no intention of unraveling the regime he built. The Alawi core around him has a special stake in regime survival and the firepower to defend it.

Reliance on Alawi *asabiyya* stimulated sectarian animosities that could conceivably "Lebanonize" the country under democratization; however, this danger is mitigated by the fact that—contrary to the neopatrimonial view—the regime elite is a cross-sectarian coalition. Elites have multiple identities beyond that with their primordial group, including nation, ideology, class, and institution, and multiple ties to society that cut across sectarian cleavages. Such multiple ties can be a strength: The reliability of the army is ensured by the intertwining of Alawi solidarity, military discipline, and Ba'thist ideology. This also ensures that the army has relatively few non-politicized professional officers who could be expected to be constitutionalists.

The institutional pillars of the state, being of Leninist lineage, do not lend themselves readily to democratization. Where liberal institutions persist under authoritarian rule, as in Latin America, liberalization rapidly develops into democratization; in Syria, a parliament exists but has little tradition of independence. The Ba'th party apparatus is, in fact, the most well-institutionalized political structure. It incorporates some 500,000 members, overwhelmingly state-dependent classes—teachers, students, state employees, cooperatized peasants, and public-sector workers—with a stake in the populist-statist status quo. Asad cannot shunt the party aside because it is the regime's main connection to the provinces—its original power base and crucial to its support among the Sunni majority. The regime is also linked to society by "populist corporatism"—an array of mass syndicates, such as the peasant union through which it incorporates a village base. Its ability to repress the formidable Islamic uprising of 1978–1982 was due, not just to the reliability of its Alawi security units, but also to the ability of its institutions—army, party, and bureaucracy—to keep its cross-sectarian coalition together and incorporate the village, thus depriving the largely urban opposition of the ability to mobilize a broad antiregime coalition.[4] These same institutions also obstruct mobilization of the masses for democratization.[5] The democratization literature tends to revert to early modernization theory in its dichotomous conceptualization of authoritarian regimes as wholly closed and uninstitutionalized, ignoring subsequent work that showed they can accommodate *limited participation* sufficient to incorporate a constituency.[6]

The legitimacy and strength of the Ba'th regime's political institutions are declining but there is no evidence they are on the verge of disintegration, as in the case of Eastern Europe's Communist regimes. However, the regime's exclusion of significant sectors of the bourgeoisie, urban middle class, and Islamic petite bourgeoisie deprives it of the broad legitimacy that would allow democratization at reasonable risk. Without significant alteration in its base, the regime incorporates enough of society to resist democratization but not enough to readily survive it.

The formation of this state cannot be understood in isolation from the external arena. The Middle East is the world subsystem wherein conflict and insecurity remain the most undiminished and war is the crucible of state power concentration. Asad built the Bonapartist state to achieve the autonomy and mobilize the power necessary to confront Israel, while nationalism legitimated it. This national-security state would have been impossible without Arab aid and Soviet arms—functions of regional conflict and global bipolarity. The current third wave (1974–1990) of democratization owes much to the demonstration effects of Communism's collapse and to the end of bipolar patronage of authoritarian states. However, the former is diluted in Syria by the Arab–Israeli conflict's legitimation of the national-security state, and the regime has adapted to the latter by diversifying its alignments and resources through adherence to the anti-Iraq Gulf coalition.

Rentierism and Its Limits

Another theory sees resistance to democratization in the Middle East as a function of the *rentier* economic base of the state: Rent allows regimes to control the economy, dispense with taxation, and substitute economic handouts for legitimacy and political rights; its decline could require them to seek legitimacy (and taxes) through democratization.[7]

In Syria, oil and Arab transfers have certainly enhanced the state's autonomy from the bourgeoisie and provided a revenue source crucial for a regime that did not want to tax its modest income constituency and could not readily tax a hostile bourgeoisie skilled at evasion. It has therefore had less need of a social contract facilitating taxation of the bourgeoisie (hence representation for it) while public-sector patronage (contracts and commissions) allowed it to co-opt elements of it. Its autonomous economic base also allowed the regime to service a social contract with its own constituency: socioeconomic opportunities in return for support.

However, the explanatory capability of rent has been exaggerated. Land reform, education, and state employment were the key redistributive measures that initially incorporated a populist constituency and, together with nationalism, legitimated the regime. This helped it to survive a decade of decline in rent (the 1980s); without it even vastly greater rents would arguably have failed, as they did in prerevolutionary Libya or Iraq, to stabilize the state.

Change in rent levels has not successfully predicted liberalization tendencies in Syria either. Its decline in the 1980s resulted in austerity and some economic liberalization to encourage the private sector, accompanied by hard authoritarianism, while a revival of rent in the 1990s has been associated with political decompression and further economic liberalization.

Societal Theories and Pressures for Political Liberalization

Modernization and the Secular Middle Class

Early modernization theorists believed that economic growth, social mobilization, and differentiation created participatory demands and complexity that required democratic adaptation. Syria's GDP per capita is apparently just below the threshold at which most states have recently been democratizing.[8] But social mobilization, as measured by education, literacy, urbanization, and the nonagricultural proportion of the work force, has greatly expanded under the Ba'th. The proportion of the labor force with secondary or university education climbed from about 5 percent of the population in 1970 to about 28 percent in 1989, and literacy climbed from 36.6 percent in 1960 to 77.2 percent in 1989.[9] Syria now has a significant educated middle class. Social differentiation is reflected in large membership increases in unions, professional associations, and business groups. However, the threshold beyond which social change requires political pluralization varies, in good part depending on social forces' independence of the state; in Syria the government employs perhaps 40 percent of the work force, including a large part of the educated and professional classes. Arguably, these classes constitute a civil society but—their professional organizations and unions being government controlled—a state-penetrated one.[10] However, as social mobilization and demographic pressure on the labor market exceeded economic growth, the state could no longer absorb new graduates, who have become a potential political threat. While this prescription for instability may not provide propitious conditions for democratization, the regime is seeking to deflect discontent by allowing more economic and personal freedom, and as its ability to provide economic benefits declines, more autonomous small enterprises are forming among the middle class. The regime could satisfy some pent-up middle-class participatory desires by allowing greater autonomy and power to its syndicates in a liberalized corporatist system. The new wine in these old bottles could in the long run make them vehicles of authentic pluralization.

Middle-class intellectuals are typically in the vanguard of discourse associated with democratic transformations. In the Middle East this is also true, but the middle class is not united behind democratization and is typically fragmented, cut off from the masses, and unable to mobilize them for democracy. In Syria the secular middle-class opposition has not challenged the regime and is associated with nationalism and socialism; no credible liberal parties (comparable to the Egyptian New Wafd) survived Ba'thism as potential vehicles of middle-class democratic mobilization.

No doubt, as critics of the regime argue, its intolerance of opposition and middle-class dependence are partly responsible for this situation. Nevertheless, these conditions have held in many regions, and Diamond et al. claim that the Islamic world is the only place where democratic ideology has not delegitimized all nondemocratic models of government.[11] While the existence there of a legitimate alternative model—an Islamic state—is unique, equally striking is the lack of ideological commitment to democracy among many secular intellectuals. In Syria, the loss of credibility of both Ba'thism and Marxism has revived liberalism among some; but the association of democratization with Western global hegemony, and an economic liberalization that affronts populist social justice, weakens democracy as a credible ideology of mobilization for either intellectuals or a mass constituency. Liberalism has been successful when associated with nationalism (as in the French and American revolutions); it is its association in the Middle East with imperialism, still an unresolved challenge there, that more than any cultural anomaly explains liberalism's weakness as an ideology.

State–Class Relations and the Bourgeoisie

For Barrington Moore, state–class relations are the key to democracy.[12] It is facilitated by a *balance* in which state power is checked by a dominant class, allowing space for civil society to emerge. Historically such a balance has been lacking in Syria. The Ottoman regime obstructed the rise of independent propertied classes that could extract power sharing from the state; when a landed class emerged coincident with the post-Ottoman state, the latter was so weak it was easily captured by this oligarchy, and thus lacked the autonomy to incorporate the rising middle classes. Under the Ba'th, the equation shifted again toward a dominant state. Salamé observes that political pluralism is facilitated where a stalemate between oligarchic segments in a premobilized society requires power sharing.[13] But in Syria the stalemate was broken by a "reform coup" and the mobilization of a populist middle–lower class coalition that swamped the incumbent oligarchy. The Ba'thist state defeated its main rivals—the bourgeoisie in the 1960s, the Islamicists and middle-class opposition in the 1980s. If stalemates between social forces provide the requisite conditions, the regime has had no immediate need to democratize.

Huntington observes that the recent third wave of democratization is associated not with modernization alone but with the combination of a period of sustained growth followed by statist economic failure that forced austerity, a retreat of the state, economic liberalization, and the resurgence of a more autonomous bourgeoisie.[14] This revision of modernization theory, combined with the concept of state–class relations, may give a more powerful key to democratization prospects.

In Syria, state-led economic growth in the 1970s fostered bourgeoisification of the political elite, a state-dependent bourgeoisie, and alliances between them and elements of the surviving private bourgeoisie. Then, when the expansion of the state ended with the decline of oil prices, and the state economic sector stagnated in the 1980s, private business had to be given concessions to fill the economic gap. The state now seeks economic partnership with the bourgeoisie.

An independent bourgeoisie able to check state power has not, however, been reconstructed. It is not yet strong enough to force greater economic liberalization than the state wants. It presents no common front for liberalization since much of it is dependent on state contracts, monopolies, and protection. However, two bourgeois factions, relatively independent of the state, have potential to widen the market and civil society. New industrial entrepreneurs have risen from the petite bourgeoisie. The regime's desire to attract expatriate capital gives it leverage to press for liberalization. The bourgeoisie as a whole, accumulating its own assets, is becoming less state-dependent, while the state is becoming more dependent on the bourgeoisie as the source, in place of the state budget, of a majority of investment. This has made a return to populist repression against the upper classes impossibly costly and may well lead to patterns of institutionalized bargaining between state and private sector and the balance needed to check state power.[15]

A major issue in Syria is whether the dual Alawi/populist bases of the regime can gradually be replaced with a bourgeois class base to lend it durability under liberalization. The state and private wings of the bourgeoisie are nowhere close to amalgamating into a new reconstructed bourgeoisie comparable to Egypt's, precisely because this cleavage partly overlaps with the communal Alawi–Sunni cleavage. However, strengthening alliances between the two are generating a growing sense of common class stake in the status quo that could result in power sharing rather than sectarian civil war if authoritarian power were to be dismantled.

While it may be true that democracy is unlikely without a bourgeoisie, capitalism is not inevitably associated with democratization in the Third World. Since capitalist development often initially increases inequality, hence popular discontent, neither state nor bourgeoisie might want democratization. Whether economic liberalization will foster democratization or its opposite may depend on whether it leads to such growing inequality or a greater dispersion of assets, perhaps through small-scale capitalism. There is cross-national evidence that where, as in Syria, reforming regimes redistribute assets, especially land, and increase access to empowering resources such as education, while tolerating the small-scale private sector, more equitable growth is possible. Democratization should be more viable in such a setting than where wealth distribution is highly unequal (such as Latin America).[16] But small-scale capitalism would have to be well organized to check the state; could Islam be the cement that forges it into an autonomous civil society with some countervailing power?

Islamic Civil Society?

The failure of modernization to translate smoothly into democracy in the Third World inspired thinking about additional requisites; *political culture* was identified as a crucial variable that could delay democratization and Huntington thought this likely in the Islamic Middle East.[17] By contrast, writings on *civil society* in the area see the struggle of voluntary associations for autonomy of both primordial community and the state as potentially democratizing indigenous culture.[18] Is the persistence of Syrian authoritarianism due to the lack of an autonomous civil society—either stifled by the state or nonexistent in a primordially segmented society, as the neopatrimonial model suggests? Is Islam an *obstacle to* or the *basis of* a civil society autonomous of the state?

Syria's *suq*—where merchant, mosque, and traditional quarter come together—constitutes a civil society still quite alive in spite of thirty years of Ba'thist authoritarianism. Far from declining under the Ba'th, the merchant petite bourgeoisie flourished in the vacuum left by the demise of the haute bourgeoisie. The political expression of the *suq* was Syria's Islamic movement, the only political force that effectively challenged the socialist state in the name of a free-enterprise Islamic economy. Though the Islamic rebellion was crushed, the traditional quarters, having a partially autonomous economic base and a counterideology, remain resistant to state penetration. The cleavage between state and *suq* in Syria is the closest thing to the stalemate Salamé regards as a facilitating condition of democratization.

Nevertheless, that the main opposition in most Arab countries is an Islamic movement lacking democratic credentials is often taken as a major obstacle to democratization. Certainly, there is little prospect that stability or political liberalization can advance in Syria without a historic compromise between the state and political Islam. Political Islam is an obstacle to liberalization insofar as it rejects secularism in a multisectarian society. Yet it is not necessarily incompatible with pluralist politics: In the pre-Ba'th era, the Syrian *Ikhwan* (Muslim Brotherhood) participated in electoral politics rather than creating secret organizations as in Egypt; in the 1980s it advocated a semiliberal, not a theocratic, state. The notion of violent revolution has now been discredited in most Islamic circles. To the considerable extent that the Islamic movement expressed the reaction of the *suq* to Ba'thist socialism, economic liberalization could advance a détente with the regime.

Contrary to neopatrimonial models, the state has not wholly suffocated the ingredients of civil society in Syria and indeed has actually fostered some of them, such as the salaried middle class. This, together with a resurgent bourgeoisie and the persistent *suq,* makes up a partly autonomous civil society that is likely to grow parallel to a greater state–class balance.

Leadership Theories: Regime Strategies and Societal Actors

Leadership Motivation

Leaders' values, their relation to societal actors, and the calculations of their own ability to resist or benefit from democratization provide the most immediate motives that may precipitate political liberalization from above. Syrian elites do not value democracy, because they were socialized in a period when liberalism was discredited; the generation that built the Ba'th state is still in power and is loath to repudiate its own work—which it insists is an alternative "popular democracy."

According to one argument, however, political liberalization, at least, is possible without a democratic-minded elite if the elite believes it stands more to gain from widening inclusion. This is most likely when stalemates precipitate coalitions between regime reformers and opposition moderates, if a pact with the opposition on rules limiting democracy will protect elite interests, or if elite rivalry leads a faction to bid for popular support.[19]

There seems little for the Syrian elite to gain from democratization and, indeed, even political liberalization holds many political dangers. The Ba'th might well not survive free elections, and even an Egyptian-type opening could unleash uncontrollable forces, at least until the cleavage between regime and political Islam is bridged. Until the social cleavage between state and bourgeoisie is fully bridged, the Alawis would be threatened by a possible return to power of Sunni interests under democratization. The regime's own weaknesses thus deter liberalization: While the Egyptian regime could rely on a homogeneous elite and the deference of a hydraulic society (i.e., one based on centralized maintenance of an irrigation system) to contain the risks of liberalization, the Ba'th cannot. But, unlike the Eastern European apparatchiks, the Syrian elite has not lost its will to power and is determined to prevent a repetition of the Algerian and Eastern European scenarios.

In some cases (such as Jordan and Algeria) popular riots convinced regimes that liberalization was in their interest and the Ba'th regime has not been immune to such pressures. In 1970 a regime split, partly precipitated by urban opposition, resulted in a tacit alliance between Asad, then a "reformer," and the "moderate" Damascene bourgeoisie, in which Asad came to power and initiated limited economic and political liberalization. During the 1978–1982 Islamic uprising, reformers wanted to satisfy the secular opposition with greater political liberalization, but the latter allied with the radical Islamicists and an assassination attempt on the president allowed regime hard-liners (Rif'at al-Asad) to deploy massive repression instead. Democratization is very unlikely when hard-liners dominate both regime and opposition.[20]

A democratic coalition of the secular middle class, moderate Islamicists, and the bourgeoisie could conceivably pressure the regime into liberalization, but the opposition is split between secularists and Islamicists. Although events in Eastern Europe, Algeria, and Jordan stimulated some public yearning for democracy, the accompanying disorder and Islamic fundamentalism made democracy's natural constituents—businessmen and intellectuals—wary of it in Syria.

Today the political elite is united and faces no unmanageable societal pressure for democratization from a divided society. Nevertheless, economics could provide the motivation for limited liberalization to broaden support and responsibility for continued economic reform as in Jordan. Syrian elites, however, plan only limited economic reform that preserves a division of labor between the public and private sectors. They believe stimulating the private sector requires political relaxation and greater political access for the bourgeoisie, but not democratization, and that incremental reform requires a strong governmental hand.

Changes in the regime's international environment, notably the decline of bipolarity and the winding down of the Arab–Israeli conflict, provide a more compelling rationale for political reform. The regime needs a new basis of legitimacy, given the increasing irrelevance of Ba'thism's nationalist-socialist mix and, except for political Islam, there is little alternative to liberal ideology. The foreign-policy calculations that most shape Asad's decisions dictate détente with the United States and opening to the international market. These may require some internal political liberalization, while the maximum flexibility in foreign policy needed for such adaptation requires enhanced presidential autonomy from sources of constraint—the party and the army.

Asad's Strategy

Asad is, however, the most cautious of liberalizers. His goal is to preserve the system through incremental adaptation, not to democratize it. He is using controlled liberalization to co-opt the bourgeoisie and mainstream Islamicists and lessen his dependence on the army and party, thereby facilitating limited economic reform and foreign policy realignment. Political decompression has relaxed the draconian controls of the 1980s: The security forces are being reined in, there is greater press freedom, and ministers may now be criticized. The downgrading of the Ba'th party in policymaking signals a subtle shift in the regime's social base. The party is ideologically exhausted and no longer a threat to private business; an informal revision of doctrine stresses Ba'thism's long-neglected liberal component, which had accepted democracy, freedoms, and a private sector. The Sunni bourgeoisie has been included in the formerly populist-dominated corporatist system through the chambers of commerce and industry. There has been a modest upgrading of the regime's liberal institutions: Parliament may not question the president or foreign policy, but can criticize government management of the economy and services, and promote the particular interests of its constituents. Parliamentary elections have been opened to more independents, including businesspeople, religious leaders, and free professionals. This signifies the legitimation of interests outside the regime's original social base and its attempt to politically incorporate a more complex social coalition.

Liberalization and the Islamic Opposition

While elsewhere Islamic resurgence has stalled liberalization amid secular–Islamic mistrust, paradoxically the Syrian regime's earlier smashing of radical Islam and proven ability to prevent an Islamic takeover may provide conditions for Islamic incorporation. Repression allowed the regime to divide the movement as security baron General Ali Duba negotiated a modus vivendi with moderate factions. That Islamicists in Syria favor economic liberalization rather than speak for its victims also makes Islamic inclusion easier than in countries where radical populists are strong.

Asad is seeking to co-opt the Islamic mainstream while marginalizing radicals. He is "playing the Islamic card"—downplaying secular Ba'thism while adding Islam to the regime's legitimacy formula by building mosques, patronizing the ulama, and propagating Islam in the mass media. Asad has also tried to bridge Alawi–Sunni differences by building mosques in the

Alawi mountains to bring Alawis into the Islamic mainstream. Islamicists are allowed to publish a magazine, some have been co-opted into Parliament, and thousands have been released from prison. The regime tolerates a nonpolitical movement fostering pious personal behavior as a safety valve.

But can Islamicists be incorporated without allowing them to organize politically? The scenario most favorable to liberalization would be parliamentary elections that resulted in power sharing between the regime and moderate Islamicists. Although Islamicists would probably sweep many urban areas, the Ba'th could arguably win a significant share of seats, especially in rural areas, given its record in mobilizing blocs of votes through its corporatist syndicates. It could also count on the support of many Westernized Sunnis and working women fearful of an Algerian scenario. Islamic resurgence is limited by a large (25 percent), influential non-Sunni population and a consequent tradition of secularism and religious coexistence. Islamic modernists are strong, if the popularity of a book by a leading Islamic liberal, Muhammad Shahrour, is any indicator. Given this relative secular–Islamic balance, the outcome of such an Islamic incorporation could be a milder version of Egypt's limited Islamization of the state. The regime has toyed with encouraging a moderate Islamic party as a way of taming political Islam through participation (as in Jordan). Nevertheless, its current line is that no party can claim a monopoly over Islam. It still evidently fears that an Islamic party could cast the Ba'th as un-Islamic and become a channel of real opposition.

However, the alternative to co-optation could be the renewal of political Islam as an opposition movement. A wing of the movement, recruiting from the marginalized and preaching a populist counterversion of Islam, could oppose the new alliance of regime and bourgeoisie. Capitalist penetration, combined with the less than honorable peace settlement with Israel that seems to be in the cards, could provide oppositionist Islam with fertile ground for proselytization.

The Bourgeoisie and the Masses

Rather than leading a democracy movement, the dominant segments of the Syrian bourgeoisie value stability first and are prepared to defer political power in return for business freedom and security. Asad has appeased the bourgeoisie by distancing himself from the Ba'th, co-opting some of its members into government, and according it greater political access. The regime's solidifying alliance with the bourgeoisie makes it easier for it to initiate limited liberalization yet avoid democratization.

In the longer term, capitalist development will strengthen the bourgeoisie's ability to construct a business-centered civil society. Business confidence will require curbs on arbitrary state power, more judicial independence, and an Egyptian-style upgrading of Parliament for regime power sharing with the bourgeoisie. Since the Ba'th party is, unlike Egypt's National Democratic Party (NDP), ill suited to incorporate businessmen, it is questionable that they can be satisfied without their own party and, thus, a serious multiparty opening.

This scenario may foster political liberalization but not necessarily democratization. The rule of law desired by the bourgeoisie puts the rights of property over those of labor, reversing current populist biases. Such a form of class law can readily evolve from upper-class states but to accomplish it in a populist regime would likely require the political exclusion of the masses. Diamond argues for gradual democratization in which elites first learn democratic habits before extending the experiment to the masses.[21] The Egyptian precedent, however, suggests that a limited liberalization of a populist regime, which increases the clout of the bourgeoisie over the state while opening no comparable opportunities for the lower strata, actually reduces the relative political power of the lower strata. The increasing power of the bourgeoisie gives it the potential to check the state that is necessary to the rule of law, but may also lead to mass exclusion from the state.[22]

Whether liberalization leads to democratization will depend on worker and peasant political mobilization. These classes have not been advocates of democracy, since they are regime incorporated and likely to be victims of the economic liberalization that accompanies it. Yet, as capitalist development forces the regime to renege on the social contract whereby the masses accepted its rule in return for populist rights, trade-union leaders have started to demand more autonomy from party control. Asad has rejected this; in part because of the Ba'th role in organizing popular syndicates, the regime has tighter control over them than in many other states. However, if Ba'thist corporatism is not to be redeployed to discipline the masses on behalf of capitalism, labor and peasant syndicates must acquire more autonomy to defend their interests in a postpopulist era. This would advance contestation and democratic inclusion, thereby guarding the autonomy of the state from capture by the dominant class.

In the short term, the regime's "decompression" strategy is sufficient to contain liberalization pressures: It co-opts a significant portion of the bourgeoisie while retaining control over the state's mass constituency. Rather than creating a stalemate, the strategy enhances Bonapartist balancing above classes. Other facilitating factors are needed to shift elite calculations and usher in the deeper forms of liberalization discussed earlier.

In the intermediate term, much depends on a peace settlement with Israel: If it becomes an issue that could be used against the regime, it will obstruct liberalization. Leadership change often precipitates political liberalization. Until Asad departs, change will remain incremental, but rivals for the succession will need to bid for support. The winner may have an interest in building a base beyond the core Alawi–army–party complex, requiring concessions to the bourgeoisie and possibly the mass syndicates.

Conclusion

Syria's resistance to democratization reflects no cultural peculiarity. Contrary to the neopatrimonial school, the state obstructs democratization not because it is the mere instrument of sectarian *asabiyya* but because incorporation of a rural base gives it enough strength to resist democratization while urban opposition makes it dangerous. It is true that, lacking a stable base in a dominant class, the regime had to find a substitute. It did rely on *asabiyya* to solidify the elite core but also—contrary to the neopatrimonial view—on Leninist/corporatist structures to incorporate multiple interests with a stake in the statist/populist status quo. This mix of patrimonialism, Leninism, and corporatism is resilient enough to delay political pluralization much as the totalitarian model presumably did in Communist states.[23] Combined with populist leveling, these structures gave the political elite autonomy from the dominant classes, precluding the Marxist scenario of a bourgeois recapture of state power as the road to liberalization. This state was also a function of the nationalist legitimation and external resources inseparable from regional conflict and bipolarity; the regime has so far proven able to adapt to the transformation in this international environment.

The regime is also resistant to democratization because in a late-developing leveling state, autonomous classes are insufficiently crystalized. As modernization theory expected, economic growth fostered an educated middle class and a semi-independent bourgeoisie that, together with the persisting autonomy of the *suq* petite bourgeoisie, make up an increasingly mobilized, complex society. To be sure, Syria's bourgeoisie, weak and leveled under the Ba'th, has not become a force for democratization. But statist economic failure has forced economic liberalization, and as this permits the bourgeoisie more autonomy from the state, a greater class–state balance will advance the prospects of political liberalization. The *suq* and the middle-class syndicates have potential to be components of a stronger, more autonomous civil society. As socioeconomic development advances these tendencies, the regime's structures may be increasingly inadequate to avoid political pluralization.

The current stalemate between forces for and against political liberalization will, in the long term, tilt toward the former, but in the meantime elite strategies determine the extent of liberalization. Syrian elites are not democrats and they give priority to the unsettled national issue of democratization; but the need for legitimacy renewal and economic liberalization, and the new possibilities of incorporating once-excluded groups like the bourgeoisie and the Islamicists without regime destabilization, may give it an interest in some political liberalization. However, there will be no major democratization until the rise of demands from below coincides with the interest of some elite faction in capitalizing on such discontent for major regime change.

Notes

1. The idea of a "third wave" of global democratization is explicated in S. Huntington, *The Third Wave: Democratisation in the Late Twentieth Century* (Norman, Okla.: University of Oklahoma Press, 1991); skepticism regarding Middle East democratization is found in L. Diamond, J. Linz, and S. Lipset, *Democracy in Developing Countries* (Boulder, Colo.: Lynne Rienner, 1988–1989), four volumes, Preface.

2. To the extent political liberalization can be viewed as a form of limited democratization (which may well develop more fully), explanations for one tend to hold for the other and the distinction between the two can be blurred with little risk. However, in certain contexts the distinction is important. In this chapter, political liberalization denotes the relaxation of state control over society, greater political pluralism and more rule of law, but *not necessarily* the *mass inclusion* of the whole citizenry in the political process, particularly in competitive elections of leadership, which is denoted by democratization.

3. For the patrimonial view, see G. Salamé, "Introduction: Where are the Democrats?" and O. Roy, "Patronage and Solidarity Groups: Survival or Reformation," both in Salamé, *Democracy Without Democrats? The Renewal of Politics in the Muslim World* (London: IB Taurus, 1994), pp. 9–16, 270–281. A sophisticated Marxist analysis is found in S. Farsoun and W. Carroll, "State Capitalism and Counter-Revolution in the Middle East: A Thesis," in B. Kaplan, ed., *Social Change in the Capitalist World Economy* (Beverly Hills: Sage Publications, 1978).

4. For the argument on multiple identities and the army, see A. Drysdale, "Ethnicity in the Syrian Officer Corps: A Conceptualisation," *Civilisations*, XXIV, 3–4, 1979, pp. 359–373. The authoritarian-populist conceptualization of the regime is fully developed in R. Hinnebusch, *Authoritarian Power and State Formation in Ba'thist Syria: Army, Party and Peasant* (Boulder, Colo.: Westview Press, 1990).

5. For Richard Cottam, the key to democratization is a liberal elite's incorporation of the masses into democratic institutions as they achieve political consciousness; however, in Syria this opportunity was missed and they were incorporated by authoritarian nationalism. See R. Cottam, *Nationalism in Iran* (Pittsburgh: University of Pittsburgh Press, 1978).

6. S. Huntington and J. Nelson, *No Easy Choice: Political Participation in Developing Countries* (Cambridge, Mass.: Harvard University Press, 1976).

7. G. Luciani, "The Oil Rent, the Fiscal Crisis of the State and Democratisation," in Salamé, *Democracy Without Democrats?* pp. 130–155.

8. According to Huntington, *Third Wave,* p. 63, the largest percentage of countries that democratized in the 1974–1989 period (76 percent) were in the range of $1,000 to $3,000 per capita in 1976 dollars. According to World Bank figures, Syrian per capita income in 1978 was $930 (World Bank, *Syrian Arab Republic Development Prospects and Policies,* Vol. 4, p. xix).

9. Syrian Arab Republic, *Statistical Abstract,* 1976, pp. 90–91, 144; *Statistical Abstract,* 1991, pp. 62, 74–75.

10. V. Perthes, "The Private Sector, Economic Liberalisation, and the Prospects of Democratisation: The case of Syria and some other Arab Countries," in Salamé,

Democracy Without Democrats? p. 269.

11. Diamond et al., *Democracy in Developing Countries,* p. 2.

12. B. Moore, *The Social Origins of Dictatorship and Democracy* (Boston: Beacon Press, 1966).

13. G. Salamé, "Small Is Pluralistic: Democracy as an Instrument of Social Peace," in Salamé, *Democracy Without Democrats?* pp. 84–111.

14. Huntington, *Third Wave,* p. 72.

15. John Waterbury, quoted in "Civil Society and the Prospects for Political Reform in the Middle East" (New York University: Civil Society in the Middle East Project, 1994), p. 7.

16. B. Moon and W. Dixon, "Basic Needs and Growth-Welfare Trade-offs," *International Studies Quarterly,* Vol. 36, June 1992, pp. 191–210; S. Kuo, G. Ranis, and J. Fei, *The Taiwan Success Story: Rapid Growth with Improved Distribution in the Republic of China* (Boulder CO: Westview Press, 1981); on the possible contradictions between economic and political liberalization, see D. Pool, "The Links Between Economic and Political Liberalisation," in T. Niblock and E. Murphy, *Economic and Political Liberalisation in the Middle East* (London and New York: British Academic Press, 1993).

17. S. Huntington, "Will More Countries Become Democratic?" *Political Science Quarterly,* Vol. 99, No. 2, Summer 1984, pp. 205–207.

18. See the introduction by A. Norton in his edited work *Civil Society in the Middle East* (Leiden and New York: Brill, 1995).

19. D. Rustow, "Transitions to Democracy: Toward a Dynamic Model," *Comparative Politics,* No. 2, 1970; G. O'Donnell et al., *Transitions From Authoritarian Rule: Comparative Perspectives* (Baltimore, 1986); for these theories applied to the Middle East, see J. Waterbury, "Democracy without Democrats? The potential for political liberalisation in the Middle East," in Salamé, *Democracy Without Democrats?* especially pp. 34–42.

20. Huntington, *Third Wave,* p. 123.

21. L. Diamond, "Beyond Authoritarianism and Totalitarianism: Strategies for Democratisation," *Washington Quarterly,* Vol. 12, No. 1, 1989.

22. R. Hinnebusch, *Egyptian Politics Under Sadat: The Post-Populist Development of an Authoritarian-modernizing State* (New York and London: Cambridge University Press, 1985).

23. This is no Middle East exceptionalism: Huntington (*Third Wave,* p. 47–48, 116–121) observes that everywhere the regimes most resistant to liberalization are personalist dictatorships and single-party regimes legitimized by ideology and nationalism that rose out of a revolution. Syria combines these two forms. For another argument against Middle East exceptionalism, see H. Deegan, *The Middle East and Problems of Democracy* (Buckingham and Philadelphia: Open University Press, 1993).

9

Syria's Private Sector: Economic Liberalization and the Challenges of the 1990s[1]

SYLVIA POELLING

Present-day Syria remains a predominantly socialist secular state with a centrally planned or "command" economy. However, the private sector has been allowed to play a limited role in the last two decades. Since the late 1980s government policy has been directed at opening up the Syrian economy, moving toward a more market-oriented system, and promoting a more active involvement of the private sector. The informal sector, or what is now called "parallel market activity," grew particularly fast in the crisis years of the mid-1980s. Its dynamics helped in part to prevent a collapse in the economy during that period, when official economic indicators showed a disastrous economic performance.

President Asad's official policy for his fourth seven-year term of office (1992–1998) is economic pluralism. In official terms it is a continuation of the "corrective movement" (*haraka tashihiyya*) initiated in the early 1970s, which Asad also referred to as "perestroika *à la Syrienne*." This current policy is designed to provide complementary roles for the public, mixed, and private sectors and to engage in gradual economic liberalization. The public sector is to retain its monopoly of strategic industries and, although the loss-making public-sector enterprises are to be rationalized, no privatization of state assets has been envisaged for the time being. However, the private sector is likely to be allowed to operate in the less strategic areas of the economy; this will inevitably lead to a shrinkage of the public sector in the face of stiff competition, greater private-sector efficiency, and the poaching of qualified government employees by the private sector.

Despite the earlier 1970s corrective movement, which had already defined a limited private-sector role in the economy, and despite the laws passed in the late 1970s setting up mixed-sector companies in tourism and tourism transportation and, in the mid-1980s in agriculture, it was not until the late 1980s that the private sector was effectively afforded a more substantial role in the economy.

The Political Background

These changes in economic policy, and the improvement in the economy that began at the end of the 1980s, occurred against a backdrop of a changing international power constellation. The breakup of the Soviet Union—Syria's erstwhile main strategic, military, and material ally—and the collapse of totalitarian and socialist regimes in Eastern Europe and the USSR, brought the Cold War to an end. On the regional front, Syria realigned its foreign policy by moving back into the Arab mainstream. Diplomatic relations with Egypt were resumed in December 1989 after a ten-year hiatus.[2] This followed on the August 1988 cease-fire agreement in the eight-year Iran–Iraq war, during which Syria had been a loyal ally of Tehran.

This new balance of power largely prompted Syria's U-turn in foreign policy during the 1990–1991 Gulf crisis. Following Iraq's invasion and annexation of Kuwait in August 1990, Damascus sided with the U.S.-led coalition against Iraq, signaling the Syrian leadership's launch of a "Westpolitik" in a dramatic policy reorientation. This move came in the context of President Bush's call for a "new world order" and in response to the fact that the United States was now the only remaining superpower. This Syrian stance, in turn, led to a resumption of generous Arab aid flows from the anti-Iraq coalition partners, a high level of direct inward investment, and an upswing in tourism.

However, it should be borne in mind that President Asad's strategies were conditioned to a large extent by economic and financial constraints: Since the ex–Soviet Union had fallen by the wayside as a material supporter of the cash-strapped Syrian economy, Saudi Arabia and, to a lesser extent, Kuwait and the UAE, remained the country's most reliable financiers. This is probably as important a reason behind Asad's economic policy decision as the rapprochement with the United States.

Official Promotion of the Private Sector

In the late 1970s and mid-1980s a number of presidential decrees and state laws had opened the areas of tourism, tourism transportation, and agriculture to private-sector participation in the form of mixed-sector companies, that is, joint ventures with the government. However, it was not until the early 1990s that a bolder attempt at liberalizing the economy was made by the Syrian leadership. This was illustrated by the passing of a favorable legal framework for private-sector productive investment: Law No. 10 of 1991.[3]

The May 1991 investment law was designed to encourage private-sector activity at a time when the public sector, which suffered from structural deficiencies, bureaucracy, and political interference, was failing to perform, and it has had a very significant impact on economic activity. It must be stressed that behind this move lay regional and international developments that prompted internal changes. The new legislation was passed in the wake of the Gulf War, when oil prices and revenues were high but uncertainty surrounded the future of transfers and remittances. (The latter, mainly from the Gulf, are Syria's major sources of foreign exchange revenues apart from oil.) Also, the economy had to absorb some 100,000 returnees who fled Kuwait following the Iraqi invasion in August 1990.[4] The returnees only partly represented a burden on the Treasury, but their hurried departure from Kuwait caused Syria a major loss in private transfers and, hence, depressed domestic demand. At the same time, however, the returnees' expertise and business contacts in the Gulf and worldwide, together with repatriated assets, provided added value. Many of the new boutiques and shops that have opened in Damascus since 1991 belong to the former expatriates; for them the new investment legislation provided a favorable legal framework that gave them added business opportunities.

The 1991 law sets out the conditions and objectives for private-sector productive investment. Project applications must be in line with the government's development plan and must use a large local component. The investment schemes must generate growth and create jobs; they must be export-oriented and promote import substitution; and they must contribute to the transfer of technology and managerial expertise. They require a minimum investment of S£10 million (at the S£42:$1 rate, equivalent to about $240,000) (subject to amendments by the cabinet). In return, Law No. 10 offers a wide range of fiscal and regulatory exemptions, incentives, and privileges. It guarantees the free transfer of profits and capital employed and offers tax- and duty-free imports; this includes tax exemptions on profits for up to seven years. Investors under Law No. 10 are exempted from Foreign Exchange Law No. 24 (passed in 1986), which imposes severe prison sentences on violation of its regulations. They can open foreign-exchange accounts and retain 75 percent of their export earnings for their own import/reinvestment requirements. The remainder has to be surrendered to the Commercial Bank of Syria (CBS) at the rate "prevailing in neighboring countries." They can also sell their foreign-exchange receipts to other Syrian importers via the CBS at a market rate.[5]

However, because of its fiscal and administrative exemptions, the new legislation does not translate into increased tax revenues for the Treasury, which is thus bypassed in favor of a more autonomous private-sector role. Nevertheless, job creation will raise employees' contributions to the Treasury.

The corporate tax exemptions, granted for the first five to seven years of a company's operations, can be extended for another two years if 50 percent of the revenues are earned from exports, that is, create foreign exchange. The law had originally excluded Syrian residents because the main rationale was to attract foreign capital to boost domestic growth and compensate for a nonperforming public sector. However, this decision aroused major concern among the local business community and sparked a political controversy. It was subsequently amended to include Syrian residents with "no questions asked" as to the origin of their foreign-exchange holdings.

The institutional setup for the implementation of the new law is a ministerial Higher Council of Investment, to which is attached an Investment Bureau charged with processing project applications (to be completed within one month) and with monitoring performance. Available statistics so far do not provide a breakdown for the source of foreign investment. There is some fear, also, that projects remain mere paperwork exploiting legal loopholes in fiscal and foreign-exchange regulations. The Investment Bureau is charged with monitoring implementation to provide a follow-up: If a project has not been started within one year, the rules stipulate that the license is withdrawn.

Results of the New Legal and Policy Environment

There is no doubt that the new legislation, and in particular Law No. 10, accelerated private-sector participation in the economy and had a significant impact on Syria's economic performance. Since the beginning of the 1990s the private sector has overtaken the public sector in its share in imports, in nonoil exports, and in fixed investment (at least on paper). Private-sector contribution to gross capital formation rose from a mere 34 percent in 1985 to 64 percent in 1992, while its share in import expenditure rose from just around 20 percent to more than 50 percent in the same period.[6]

The results of the law have on the whole been encouraging, despite its partial abuse by private-sector investors (who circumvented the state monopoly on car imports, for example, by setting up car-leasing operations, importing private cars on a large scale).[7] The government allocated a total of S£60 billion for the investment budget in 1991–1992. This compares with the private sector's total investments under the new law of S£93.4 billion by the end of 1992. (Of this, S£72 billion was the foreign-exchange element, or $1.7 billion.) Private-sector input in fixed investment, therefore, was about one-third higher than that of the public sector. The breakdown of private-sector project applications in this period (May 1991 through the end of 1992) perhaps illustrates some of the abuses referred to, but at the same time demonstrates a more widespread success: Out of 732 projects valued at a total of S£93.4 billion, 397 schemes covered the transportation sector, accounting for 46 percent of the total investment value. However, projects covering food processing (107 projects at S£19.4 billion), textiles/clothing (62 projects at S£7.9 billion), and chemicals/pharmaceuticals (67 projects at around S£7.9 billion) had clearly also made significant headway.[8]

In addition, private-sector job creation was estimated at around 56,400 jobs for both years (assumed rather than empirical). The 1993 budget envisaged the creation of some 68,000 jobs. (Such budget figures should be taken with caution, though, since there is a delay of at least two years before figures for the budget outcome are published.)

By early 1994 the value of total private-sector project applications had more than doubled the value in 1992, reaching S£152.7 billion ($3.6 billion at the exchange rate prevailing in neighboring countries). The foreign-currency element accounted for 81 percent of the total. This means that in 1993 alone, private-sector investment projects amounted to around S£60 billion—almost equivalent to the S£62 billion government budget for 1993 (which in itself represented a 70 percent increase over 1992 made possible by exceptional circumstances, namely concessionary funding from Saudi Arabia, Kuwait, and the United Arab Emirates for infrastructural and industrial projects).

Meanwhile, the private sector's share in total import expenditure exceeded 50 percent in 1992 and was reported to account for around 65 percent of the total in 1993. This largely reflects strong domestic demand for industrial inputs in response to the private sector's investment activity.

Another factor that illustrates heightened private-sector activity during that period was the rise in domestic liquidity: The banking sector recorded a rise in demand deposits from S£36 billion in 1990 to S£53 billion in 1992. Time and savings deposits nearly doubled, rising from S£28 billion to S£55 billion, and claims on the private sector (which represent bank lending) rose from S£20 billion to S£36 billion. Foreign assets held by the state-owned banks showed a nearly 140 percent increase, from S£11 billion in 1990 to S£26 billion in 1992.

The main rationale of the law, apart from its contribution to growth and job creation, is to attract private, direct inward investment on a large scale. Although it is directed not only at Syrian residents and expatriates but also at other Arab and foreign nationals, the positive response to it has been largely limited to Syrian and other Arab (especially Gulf) capital. However, this might well be the government's intention because it is not eager to see the country inundated by foreign interests, given the prevailing political sensitivities and the vested interests of the establishment. Such an inundation, moreover, would imply an erosion of state control and sovereignty.

Syrian expatriate assets held abroad are assumed to be running in tens of billions of dollars.[9] The repatriation of part of these sums would be largely sufficient to sustain growth in Syria's economy in the second half of the 1990s. However, many in the Syrian expatriate community remain reluctant to commit themselves to investing in their home market because of reservations about the seriousness of the regime toward economic liberalization, distrust of Asad's one-man rule and of his power base (the Alawite minority, the Ba'th party, and the security and military apparatus), and concern about contradictory legislation (for example, investors under Law No. 10 are exempt from the 1986 foreign-exchange regulations). Members of the old merchant class who left the country in an early 1960s exodus, prompted by the large-scale nationalization and expropriation following the takeover by the socialist Ba'th Party, complain about the restrictive and arbitrary legislation that applies to real estate (particularly Law No. 60).

The Need for Further Economic and Legal Reforms

The main structural shortcomings of the new environment remain conflicting legislation (especially with Foreign Exchange Law No. 24) and poor infrastructure. In order for the new legal framework to become fully operational, further market reforms are needed to underpin effective private-sector involvement in the economy. This would have to include speeding up the unification of the multitier exchange rate, as well as an urgently needed overhaul of the financial and banking sector. The archaic state banking sector is unable to provide the services required for a properly functioning market economy, whether in terms of credit allocation, interest rate policy, or interbank funding. The state banks offer no incentive to the individual saver to deposit money with them, and do not fulfill their role of mobilizing private funds in order to channel them into productive investment. In this area the government's half-hearted approach, reflected in a seemingly piecemeal liberalization program and a reluctance to open up the banking sector to private-sector participation, presents one of the main obstacles on the path toward a properly functioning market economy. A small step in the right direction was the establishment in 1992 of two investment banking branches attached to the Syrian Commercial Bank with offices in Damascus and Aleppo that are to facilitate operations of investors under Law No. 10. However, the government's procrastination on requests to allow private banks or mixed-sector joint ventures to open in Syria has led to similar projects being diverted to Beirut, where all the attractions of a free-market economy are being offered. In the longer term this means that many, if not most, of the financial and banking transactions of Syrian entrepreneurs are likely to be conducted via Lebanon, circumventing to a large extent the domestic banking sector. This development will be further boosted by the strengthening economic cooperation and coordination between the two countries following the 1991 Treaty of Fraternity, Friendship and Cooperation. It is questionable whether the Syrian authorities are fully aware of the implications of this trend, or whether conflicting interests within the power structure prevent a timely adjustment to the new circumstances and changing environment. It seems unlikely that the authorities would allow private banks to open offices in the country in the short term. The most obvious reasons behind this attitude were that the state would lose its foreign-exchange monopoly and that private-sector competition would most probably put state banks out of business.

Meanwhile, a controversial draft law for the opening of a Damascus stock exchange has, since 1993, been ready for submission to the People's Assembly. The scheme does not appear to be viable, however, given that no privatization of state assets is envisaged for the time being and that there are only a few long-standing mixed-sector companies whose shares could be floated on the exchange. This would mean that activity on the stock market would be dominated by primary issues, that is, shares of the newly set up companies under Law No. 10 that would be offered for public subscription. This involves high risk and speculative transactions, without a track record of past performance upon which to assess future returns, and without means to protect small investors. It would also give rise to the few big operators' playing the market at the expense of the small shareholder. Meanwhile, the issuance and trading of treasury bonds and bills could easily be handled over the counter by the state banks and would not need an open exchange for trading.

Other issues that need to be, and in part are being, addressed by the government cover the reform of labor law (unions, employment, job security, and social and national health service contributions); the updating of commercial law; further trade liberalization and lifting of price regulations to allow for a proper response to market forces of supply and demand; a reduction in government subsidies, an improvement in monetary and fiscal policies, and greater transparency in the government's economic and fiscal management; and the restructuring and eventual privatization of the inefficient and lossmaking public-sector enterprises.

Prospects for Private-sector Development

The key prerequisites for continued direct foreign investment and a higher level of private-sector activity in the Syrian market are (1) prevailing political stability; (2) confidence in the economy; and (3) a legal framework that allows business to operate efficiently and provides legal protection and commercial arbitration free from government intervention. Still lacking are consulting services that offer market research, feasibility studies, and management and accounting/audit services. Also needed are training courses and facilities, including business-management programs at the universities, to prepare the next generation for the challenges of a competitive market environment.

What the private sector has to offer in comparison with Syria's public sector is greater efficiency and profitability, work incentives (performance-related financial and career rewards), and better training and pay (the equivalent of up to ten times the salaries in the public sector). This has, in the recent past, led to the poaching of qualified officials in the administration (an internal brain drain), a trend that will contribute to the natural shrinkage or paring down of the public sector.

Against the background of continuing limited market reform, and despite uncertainty surrounding the issues of Asad's succession in the medium term and the outcome of the Middle East peace process, the reemerging business class is likely to assume a higher profile and have a greater say in economic policy formulation through lobbying and representation in the People's Assembly and in the chambers of commerce and industry.

The assumption here is that entrepreneurs are more interested in political stability than in party politics and wider political participation, as long as they can operate in an environment of minimum restrictions. Another assumption is that economic reform initiated by an authoritarian regime from the top has greater chances to succeed if it precedes political liberalization than if these two trends occur simultaneously. This has been amply demonstrated by the developments in Eastern Europe and the former Soviet Union, where the collapse of totalitarian regimes and the sudden change to a free-market economy from a state-managed system has caused economic chaos and political turmoil.

As to the challenge for the private sector in Syria to generate enough foreign exchange to finance its import requirements in the long term, the prospects are good. Unlike the government, the private sector has access to international capital markets and commercial borrowing via family links or intermediaries and a wide network of contacts abroad. Private business will also be able to tap the substantial foreign assets held by Syrian expatriates abroad. The slow pace of economic reform and the remaining restrictions on trade, pricing, and private-sector operations will not deter the local business community; it has been accustomed to operate under a much more restrictive system and tougher conditions in the years of socialist rule and a centralized, state-managed economy. Remaining handicaps in infrastructure, such as the chronic power cuts and a poor telecommunications system, are now being addressed by the government.

Prospects for improvements in Syria's economic management are also boosted by indications that the younger, Western-educated generation is returning to Syria. They see opportunities in the new market environment, where good growth prospects and a more relaxed political climate combine with domestic stability, against the background of world recession and an international scene marked by the collapse of totalitarian states and the ideologies of socialism and communism. However, some critics, especially those among the expatriate community, are wary about this trend. They claim that it only applies to the offspring of the establishment, the sons of the members of the nomenklatura, including the military and security services, who are well placed to go into business and secure lucrative commissions in public-sector industries. Nevertheless, it can be argued that this generation's exposure to Western values and education will change its perception of how its home country is run and how business is generated. In contrast to Eastern Europe, a merchant trading tradition prevails in Syria, and the region at large, that has never been eradicated by the imposition of a command economy. Even public-sector employees hold at least one private-sector job in the parallel market to make ends meet, a fact that can be called entrepreneurship on a small scale. (This phenomenon did not, for example, exist in the former Soviet Union and the Eastern European countries, where full-time employment and a rigid bureaucracy did not allow for the development of moonlighting and parallel-market activity.) The more flexible approach also reflects a mentality that is likely to benefit the development of a market economy in the region.

The main question will be whether the private sector, called upon to generate growth and employment in the economy, will be able to meet this target in the face of half-hearted government reforms. So far, government policy has excluded the privatization of state assets and has been slow to restructure the lossmaking public sector, while moving only reluctantly on market deregulation in the financial sector, as well as on the easing of trade restrictions and the freeing of prices.

Technology plays an important role in the Syrian business community. It is certain that the rapid computerization of business operations in the private sector and the increasing and now authorized use of fax machines (which circumvent control and supervision by the Syrian *mukhabaraat,* or security services) will erode state control and will also strengthen the universal trend in which the service industry assumes a dominant share in national output.

However, the new and more open business climate evident since the passing of the 1991 investment legislation will also *reinforce* the trend of growing polarization between the reemerging class of entrepreneurs, who are seizing the opportunities offered to enrich themselves, and those in the society who do not dispose of the capital to participate in the investment boom, and thus remain outside the class of privileged business and capital. There is the danger that reforms *à la Syrienne* could turn into another *infitah* (opening) *à l'Egyptienne,* which led to a widening gap between rich and poor. Any growing disparity will fuel social discontent and could easily undermine any attempt at political liberalization, however hesitant. A balance needs to be struck between business interests and social concerns to guarantee social peace and political stability.

A question mark hangs over the possible solution of the main problems and weaknesses in Syria's social and political system. These include opposition to economic liberalization and market reforms from the Ba'th Party and the military and security establishment—the political elite that is not ready to forgo its vested interests. It will be difficult to dismantle an inefficient and oversized bureaucracy fraught with widespread corruption. But the prospect of an "honourable peace" with Israel, which President Asad called for in his January 1995 summit with Bill Clinton, will pose a challenge to Syria's leadership and political establishment. The government will no longer have the pretext of the Arab–Israeli conflict to maintain a state of emergency at home and to spend at least 40 percent of its current budget on defense. The transition to a peacetime economy will only be peaceful if Hafez al-Asad makes the needed economic and political concessions to the private sector, which is the only indigenous Syrian resource able to generate and sustain growth in the economy.

Maintenance of social peace, which would also contain the threat of Islamist militancy, is only possible if jobs can be secured for the fast-growing population and if economic growth guarantees a minimum standard of living. The prospects for the Syrian economy will depend on the successful settlement of the Arab–Israeli conflict and on regional stability. The economic outlook in the medium term is fair to good. The rapid development of the hydrocarbons sector will slow, but the exploitation of the country's natural gas reserves will boost sectoral growth rates. Foreign exchange will be largely generated by oil, agriculture (textiles, cotton, vegetables, and fruit), tourism, and direct foreign investment. Gulf aid and Western concessionary funding will be largely project related. The switch of the Gulf aid and development agencies away from balance-of-payments support to project finance also implies that the funds are less likely to disappear into the pockets of the nomenklatura and can be more easily monitored.

In view of these fairly favorable economic prospects, the Syrian leadership should be in a position to accelerate economic liberalization. However, at a certain stage of this process it will become inevitable for the Syrian president to allow for the kind of wider political participation that the business community, having grown confident of its success, will claim beyond the domain of economic management and policy formulation. Enhanced prospects for a comprehensive peace agreement with Israel will further add to popular pressure for economic and political liberalization and the lifting of the state emergency law.

Notes

1. In addition to the sources referred to specifically in subsequent notes, this chapter has drawn on the following published material: *Syria: Country Profile 1992* and *1993* (London: EIU); *World Bank Debt Tables* (Washington, D.C.: The World Bank, annual); *World Development Report* (Oxford: Oxford University Press for the World Bank, 1988); Bank for International Settlements, *International Banking and Financial Market Developments* (Basle: BIS); the Syrian newspapers *Tishreen; Ath-Thawra;* and *Al-Ba'ath;* and the international Arab daily *Al-Hayat* (London). In addition, the author drew on reports of the IMF delegation to Damascus (confidential); a number of confidential diplomatic reports in Damascus in the course of 1992 and

1993; and personal interviews with Dr. Mohamed Al-Imady, Minister of the Economy and Foreign Trade; Mr. Zuheir Taghlibi, Director of the Investment Bureau (the executive organ of the Higher Council of Investment); as well as with the Damascene entrepreneurs Dr. Osmane Aidi; Dr. Saeb Nahas; Dr. Abdul-Rahman Attar; and Rateb Challah (now head of the Damascus Chamber of Commerce).

2. They had been broken off after President Sadat's separate peace treaty with Israel in the Camp David accords (along with relations between Egypt and most other Arab countries).

3. The original version of Investment Law No. 10 of May 1991 for the encouragement of investment and its executive regulations is: *Al-qaanun raqm 10 li tashjii' al-istithmaar min 4/5/1991 wa'l ta'limaat al-tanfiziyya min 28/5/1991* (Damascus: *Al-Jumhuriyya al-'arabiyya al-suriyya, Wizarat al-iqtisaad wa'l-tijaara al-kharijiyya* [Syrian Arab Republic, Ministry of Foreign Affairs], 1991); Also: *Al-qaraar raqm 7 m.w. bi ta'limaat al-tanfiziyya li'l qaanun raqm 10 li-'aam 1991* (Damascus: *Al-Jumhuriyya al-'arabiyya al-suriyya, Ri'aasat majlis al-wuzaraa'* [Syrian Arab Republic, Prime Minister's Office], 1991).

4. Interview with Dr. Mohamed Al-Imady; Reuters News Agency; various EIU Country Reports.

5. See the sources listed in note 3.

6. EIU, *Country Report: Syria* (quarterly), various issues, 1992 and 1993; *Statistical Abstract 1992* and *1993* (Damascus: Office of the Prime Minister, Central Bureau of Statistics, Syrian Arab Republic); IMF, *International Financial Statistics Yearbook* (various issues, 1990–1994); IMF, *International Financial Statistics Yearbook,* various issues.

7. EIU, *Country Report: Syria* (quarterly), various issues, 1992 and 1993.

8. Information obtained from the Investment Bureau, Damascus.

9. Interview with Dr. Mohamed Al-Imady.

10

The Initiation of Economic Liberalization in Algeria, 1979–1989

Emma C. Murphy

After the death, on 27 December 1978, of President Houari Boumedienne, who had come to personify Algeria and its political system since 1965, his successor Chadli Ben Jedid immediately declared that he considered Boumedienne's policies of socialism and national independence to be irreversible in both political and economic terms. In an interview, however, he also added: "We have a duty to evaluate regularly what has been achieved"—and hence introduce improvements where such evaluation indicated they were necessary.[1]

Chadli's re-evaluation took its early form in the political sphere, with the introduction of measures of apparent political liberalization as well as a cleanup campaign against increasingly frequent mismanagement, nepotism, waste, and corruption. An initial climate of political relaxation would, however, prove of limited impact (see also Chapter 11).

On the economic side, significant change became apparent with the announcement of the 1980–1984 development plan. This revealed a shift away from the mammoth industrial schemes favored by Boumedienne's strategy of building up the so-called industrializing industries, and toward agriculture, smaller industries, and welfare provision. This was to prove only the start, however, of a much more profound alteration in the character of the Algerian economy during the first decade of Chadli's rule.

The 1980–1984 Development Plan

Adjusting the Economy and Restructuring the Public Sector

Chadli's first development plan was intended to iron out some of the structural distortions created by his predecessor's economic policy. These included the chronic decline of agriculture and resultant food-import dependency; the poverty of distribution networks, with attendant shortages and bottlenecks; the overemphasis on heavy industry with its implication of dependence on import of capital, technology, and expertise; and the prevalent inefficiency and underutilization of production capacity. Vandewalle comments that Chadli's was "an ambitious overall three-legged reform plan that would quickly move the country toward a more market-oriented economy." The three legs were (1) the pursuit of greater efficiency through decentralization, rewriting of commercial and investment codes, and reform of banking, finance, and import; (2) minimizing projected losses of revenues through austerity and stabilization; and (3) creating supplementary sources of income such as nonoil exports and agriculture.[2]

The first five years of Chadli's rule saw policies geared toward decentralization of state-owned enterprises (*Entreprises Publiques Economiques,* or EPEs) and a new emphasis on efficiency, the rooting out of corruption, and reorganization into smaller, more task-centered units. Chadli's commitment to improving people's quality of life was greeted with some enthusiasm—even if the promise of a cleanup was received with skepticism.

The plan still envisaged devoting about 40 percent of investment to industry, but social spending increased to nearly a third; AD60 billion (over $15 billion) was allocated to new housing—second only to industry. Among other things, over $11 billion was set aside for professional and managerial education.

In March 1980 the government decreed that wages would henceforth be set according to production levels in each industry, with workers being entitled to a bonus of up to 100 percent depending upon whether they reached full production capacity.[3] Worker profit-sharing schemes were introduced, and in 1982 prices were adjusted to reflect true production costs more realistically. Price controls on fruits and vegetables were lifted in 1981, contributing toward an increase in inflation to 14 percent. Additionally, customs procedures were simplified and extra money allocated to imports by state enterprises to relieve shortages and bottlenecks.

Toward the end of 1982 a special price stabilization fund was set up by the government for basic consumer goods, when the black market threatened to push their prices to between three and five times what was considered to be their real price. It was clear, however, that the government would prefer to let enterprises set their own prices. In the event, the same could not be said of wages. The confused system of wage setting, combined with the discrepancy between private- and public-sector wages, led to an attempt in April 1983 to establish a national pay scale for public-sector workers—the *Statut Général des Travailleurs.*

The policy of decentralizing and restructuring EPEs was meanwhile taking root. The first to be tackled was the state fishing company, which was replaced in April 1980 by two new companies. In May it was announced that Sonatrach, the state hydrocarbons monopoly with over 85,000 employees, was to be split into three; the establishment of four more independent firms to take over some of Sonatrach's responsibilities was announced in November 1982. Such restructuring continued apace, and by 1987 the sixty-one state companies that had existed in 1980 had become over 350 smaller units.[4] This reorganization was accompanied by the relocation of many enterprises away from Algiers.

Frank criticism of the inefficiency of public-sector enterprises also began to appear in the French-language daily *El-Moudjahid*, often considered to function as a forum for the ruling party, *Front de Libération National* (FLN), and the government.

The Private Sector

In May 1980 a National Chamber of Commerce was set up by the government to promote more discussion between the government and both public and private traders. The new emphasis on light as opposed to heavy industry necessitated a rapprochement with the private sector, which was virtually excluded from the heavy-industry sector but accounted for up to half of the country's light-industry plants and 60,000 of the 134,000 workers employed in light industry.[5]

Private firms were to allowed to develop in a "controlled way."[6] At the sixth annual session of the FLN's Central Committee in December 1981, it was decided that the private sector was officially to be allowed new opportunities, although it was to remain subject to proper rules of conduct. A New Investment Code—replacing the rigid code of 1967—was adopted by the government on 13 March 1982, along with a new law to promote the growth of small-scale privately owned handicraft industries. The code did away with the notion that the private sector could only be parasitic. The official hope was that the new code would mobilize domestic savings as well as attract expatriate and migrant labor remittances for investment in the Algerian economy. The following month a further law was approved (enacted on 26 July) on joint ventures between Algerian EPEs and foreign companies, such ventures not having enjoyed legal status before. Incentives were held out for such investments, including tax holidays.[7]

A United States Embassy report in 1983 reported evidence of the implementation of new government initiatives to encourage the private sector, including the establishment of industrial parks. However, an inability to import privately raw materials and equipment, and an inability to transfer dinar profits legally into foreign exchanges remained, in this assessment, major inhibitions to private enterprise.[8] These problems were partially resolved in November 1983 when import regulations were further relaxed to allow the private sector to import equipment directly, up to a value of AD100,000, toward the production of goods and services for the Algerian market.

In the oil and gas sector in particular, a new emphasis was placed on encouraging increased foreign participation. Joint ventures with Elf, CFP, Getty Oil, and Hispanoil already existed, but the government was now offering five-year supply contracts and up to 40 percent stakes in exploration contracts. The first new deal was signed with Standard Oil in May 1980.

Finance

Prior to 1981 Algeria's banks were 100 percent state owned. In that year, however, a major reshuffle of the top management of the main financial institutions indicated that the financial sector was also being considered ripe for reorganization. In 1983 foreign nationals living in Algeria were allowed to open foreign-exchange accounts in Algerian banks, to be used for payments abroad as well as, among other things, land and housing. It was hoped that this would attract expatriate savings.

The early 1980s also saw Algeria move toward the international loans market, after a substantial break. Falling hydrocarbon revenues and the prospect of a return to austerity in 1983 encouraged EPEs to consider seeking financial support from outside the government. The decline in oil revenues after 1982 affected the country's capacity to service its outstanding debts. Algeria in 1981–1982 ranked fifth on the OECD's list of developing countries with the largest debt-service payments. Debt servicing in 1982 equalled $3.9 billion.[9] Yet by 1983 it was clear that, even as reduced oil revenues made debt servicing more difficult, new debts were likely to be incurred as EPEs raised funds abroad to make up for government unwillingness to invest. At the same time, the terms of the new debt, as well as the interest rates on existing debt, became less favorable. The financing of continued imports was pushing the government toward renewed international borrowing, due to its inability to increase export earnings significantly.

The Algerian government chose to respond to these difficulties during the 1982–1984 period with import cuts, austerity budgets, and curtailed public investment, as well as a greater role for private and foreign investment, and freer domestic markets. In 1984 it was announced that the prices of basic foods would increase between 10 and 30 percent. This move, which entailed the removal of government subsidies on bread, cooking oil, and eggs, among other things, was intended to reduce pressures on the budget, redress imbalances in the market, and reduce imports by promoting national products through improving farmers' profit margins.

Borrowing, however, was unavoidable. A Sonatrach Euro-loan of $700 million (subsequently raised to $800 million) approved in June 1983 was considered by many to be effectively balance-of-payments support for the government.[10] The state banks raised a second Euro-loan for $750 million, and the government itself during that year also negotiated project loans totaling close to $300 million with the World Bank.

Agriculture

The evidence of decline in the agricultural sector under Boumedienne was overwhelming. In 1980, despite employing 42 percent of the working population, agriculture accounted for only 7 percent of GDP. Low rural incomes, moreover, had contributed to a rural-to-urban drift, and food imports had reached alarmingly high levels: By 1986 Algeria was importing three-quarters of its food requirements, up from just over a quarter in 1969.[11]

In the wake of the destructive war of independence, when French colonial owners and farmers had left the land, agriculture was left devastated. The peasants occupied the land themselves, and then president Ben Bella accepted this fait accompli, announcing that while abandoned farms would be nationalized, de facto rights would be given to farmers already occupying them. These farms were to be run collectively by the farmers themselves (*autogestion*) under comprehensive government regulation. Boumedienne replaced Ben Bella's agrarian showpiece with state-owned heavy industry as the number-one priority of development policy. In an attempt to underpin his urban-industrial strategy with subsidized food he instigated the Agrarian Revolution of 1971. Extensive land redistribution was set in motion; maximum landholdings were limited to some 43 hectares, which was deemed sufficient to supply a farmer with the minimum wage. These holdings were to work together as cooperatives, and "1,000 socialist villages" were to be built at the center of the cooperatives. In fact, fewer than a quarter of that number actually materialized, and by 1979 some 24 percent of cultivable land remained to be distributed, that is, remained in private hands.[12]

These reforms failed to improve production. Distribution was inefficient; the extensive government intervention in production, marketing, and distribution had created bureaucratic bottlenecks and contradictions; price controls had affected wages adversely; and the rural-to-urban drift had not been halted. As Swearingen put it:

> By 1978 . . . it was clear that government agricultural policy was a fiasco. Discontent was growing in the countryside, urban consumers were complaining about empty food shelves, and food imports had reached alarmingly high levels. Furthermore, through its chronic inefficiency, the state agricultural sector had become a major drain on the national treasury.[13]

Chadli, then, embarked upon a series of reforms aiming to liberalize the agricultural sector and to relieve the government of the enormous bureaucratic structure that managed it. A measure of decentralization was introduced and extended to the fisheries sector. In addition, the 1980–1984 Plan envisaged a doubling of government investment in agriculture compared with the previous plan, or just under a third of the allocation for industry. At the May 1980 meeting of the FLN Central Committee, the government was called upon to restructure the state agricultural sector, particularly organiz-ing the self-management farms into smaller, more manageable units. By 1985 the self-management and Agrarian Revolution farms, covering over 2.8 million hectares, had been restructured into 3,429 state farms called *domaines agricoles socialistes* [socialist agricultural domains] (DASs). A further 700,000 hectares of Agrarian Revolution land were privatized. However, even in principle the new rights of ownership remained nontrans-ferable and nonassignable. They equated in reality to rights of usage, not ownership, and therefore did not represent privatization in a true sense.[14] The impact of this failure to clarify the legal status of land ownership meant that farmers continued to feel insecure and had little incentive to invest in their land.

In August 1983 the government announced a new law regarding land transactions. This greatly loosened regulations on such transactions, remov-ing the restrictions on the sale or purchase of private land and the extent of maximum holdings. In addition, homesteaders were encouraged with loans and subsidies to develop previously unused land.

Yet in spite of declared intentions to liberalize production, marketing, and distribution, there was little action to pursue this. The price of meat was indeed allowed to be determined by the market, but it is unclear to what extent free-market principles applied to fruit and vegetables.[15]

The government also established a new agricultural development bank in 1982, designed to provide more low-interest credit than had been avail-able and to do so both to private (previously very much neglected in these terms) and public-sector agriculture.

At the same time, as already mentioned, the government announced in the summer of 1983 that the price paid to farmers for wheat was to rise by 15 percent, while the price for basic foods for consumers was to rise by between 10 and 30 percent. The intention was to encourage domestic pro-ducers by offering more realistic prices for their produce—as well as reduc-ing government outlay on subsidies.[16] Even though Algeria also made a modest return to food exports around that time, the food import bill appeared set to rise further.

1979–1984: A Summary

Chadli's first years in government indicated a commitment to economic reform within certain parameters that included maintaining economic inde-pendence as far as was possible; transferring investment concentration away from heavy industry, which had proved to be inefficient and bureaucratic, toward light industry; encouraging rather than castigating the private sector so as to mobilize domestic savings and remove the investment burden from government; increasing agricultural production to reduce the food imports bill; and restructuring and decentralizing state-owned enterprises in an effort to make them more productive and efficient. As hydrocarbon revenues held steady relative to other exporting states—largely due to liquefied natural gas (LNG) and refined product sales—international confidence in Algeria's economy was expressed in the willingness of the major international commercial banks to participate in syndication of two massive Euro-loans. In addition, despite austerity measures in budget allocations to imports, the government attempted to redress the balance of government spending by increasing housing and welfare allocations, mindful of its 1982 slogan, "For a better life."

In the January 1984 presidential elections Chadli was returned unopposed for a second term in office with a turnout of over 96 percent of voters. He had used his first term in office to consolidate his own power by dismissing prominent Boumedienne-era personalities; slimming down the FLN's Political Bureau (the party's highest organ) from 17 to 7 members; reducing its powers as compared with that of the presidency; introducing a strictly limited political liberalization program that helped disguise clampdowns on more serious (Berber and Islamic) opposition; and appointing sympathetic army commanders to sensitive posts.

As the 1985–1989 Development Plan was being drafted he was in a strong position to impose his own ideas for further and accelerated reform upon planners. In a January 1984 cabinet reshuffle, Chadli brought in his former planning minister, Hamid Brahimi, as prime minister. Brahimi had a U.S. doctorate in planning and financial management and was known for his tough line on austerity as Chadli's chief economic architect. His appointment was an indication of the shape of economic policy to come over the succeeding years.

The 1985–1989 Development Plan

A Plan for Change

The 1984 FLN Congress outlined the themes for the 1985–1989 Development Plan as being agriculture, privatization, economic efficiency, and increased nonhydrocarbon exports (which at that time totaled only 2 percent of exports).[17]

According to the plan, agriculture would be made a priority, with further restructuring as well as privatization of land. A rise in agricultural productivity was also aimed for by greater investment in irrigation and training. Overall, agriculture and irrigation were set to receive 14 percent of investment, up from 11 percent under the previous plan. The private agricultural sector was to be revitalized and given incentives.

This policy of increased state credit and assistance to private-sector agriculture also extended to other businesses. Prime Minister Brahimi stressed the now "dynamic" role of the private sector in, among other things, replacing foreign consultants and contractors, although private exporters would not be allowed to use cheap labor or to bypass the state importing monopoly where this applied. The government hoped to see the private sector help push up the share of nonhydrocarbon exports in total exports. Additionally, the state banking monopoly was to be broken up, and the joint ventures between EPEs and foreign capital were to be encouraged by preferential treatment in government or EPE contracts.

Industrial policy would concentrate upon finishing existing industrial projects, job creation, the provision of consumer goods, and transferring economic activity away from the coastal strip to the high plateau of the south. In the hydrocarbons sector, investment would concentrate on maximizing output in existing establishments rather than embarking on expensive new building schemes. All of this went hand in hand with further administrative decentralization, with seventeen new *wilayat* (governorates) being set up in accordance with a 1984 decree.[18]

With Algerian debt being considered to have peaked (the debt-servicing ratio was expected to fall from 36 percent in 1984 to less than 30 percent after 1985), the country faced the second half of the decade with optimism. The first problem arose, however, as early as 1985, when expected hydrocarbon revenues failed to materialize and the import program and subsidy system had to be adjusted accordingly. It also became clear that new borrowing would now be necessary to service the $15 billion total foreign debt. In the event, Algeria incurred new debts totaling $1.3 billion in 1985. As the grace period for the 1983 debts moved closer to its end, international banks began to show signs of nervousness about negotiating new loans, projecting Algeria's total foreign debt to rise to about $20 billion by 1990.

The 1986 budget included a 20 percent increase in projected spending, over half of which was due to the government's having to fulfill promises to regularize public-sector wages with a 10 percent increase. Because 1985 had seen two hikes in food prices, as well as a 12 percent inflation rate, this did little to offset the problems facing public-sector workers. Disturbances in the poorer quarters of Algiers in 1985 were indicative of the contradictions between declining imports, local shortages, rising prices, and low public-sector wages.

In the light of declining oil and gas revenues, austerity measures were introduced, the permission to import foreign spare parts by mail (introduced under the previous plan period) was all but revoked, and the foreign travel allowance was halved.

A two-pronged strategy was employed to head off potential discontent, both within the party and among the population at large. On the one hand, what effectively amounted to an ideological shift was legitimized by revisions to the National Charter that both formalized the shift and tried to offer reassurance to more traditionalist elements in the party. On the other hand, social spending was increased. The 1985–1989 Plan expected spending on building and improving social infrastructure to increase to over 30 percent of the total investment budget.

Chadli sought to reform the 1976 National Charter—which enshrined clear secular socialist principles—in line with his own economic policies. Hardliners within the FLN were expressing public disagreement with his position. In December 1985 an extraordinary congress of the FLN approved draft revisions to the charter that would legitimize Chadli's reforms, giving priority to light and medium industries, to agriculture, and to a redefined role for the private sector. To reduce resistance within the FLN Chadli explicitly promised not to reduce the state's control over key sectors of the economy such as foreign trade, and not to challenge the role in society of the party and the army, which were very much linked in Algeria's independent history. On the other hand, more emphasis was placed on the role of Islam in society, and less on doctrinaire socialism.

The revised National Charter was adopted on 16 January 1986 after a national referendum in which over 98 percent of the voters approved the changes. Chadli accompanied this with a number of cabinet and military reshuffles, placing supporters in key positions and keeping any one figure from becoming too powerful.

The 1986 Oil-Price Slide and Difficulties with the Liberalization Effort

By mid-1986 the slide in oil prices was causing serious problems. While the plan had projected annual economic growth rates of some 6.5 percent, observers were now projecting rates of around 2 percent—not enough to keep pace with the needs of Algeria's rapidly expanding population, which was growing at over 3 percent per year. The government still needed to borrow up to $2.5 billion just to service existing debt in 1986, and at the same time was facing European demands for renegotiating LNG prices. In a revised 1986 budget, some 20 percent was cut from expenditure (split between investment and current spending) to help cope with hydrocarbon revenues 40 percent lower than projected. This left a deficit of some AD3 billion, or under 5 percent of GNP.[19]

While this appeared to deal with the financial situation, however, the government's liberalization efforts received a blow when, in July 1986, the National Assembly rejected a proposal to increase maximum foreign-company stakes in joint ventures to 65 percent. This was meant to make such ventures more attractive, only one, with Germany's Siemens, actually having been set up since the 1982 law. A watered-down version of the proposal was eventually adopted in August, accepting guaranteed transferability of profits but maintaining the 49 percent limit. On the other hand, some other measures were successfully passed, including allowing local residents to hold foreign-currency accounts and somewhat loosening the 1980 law covering foreign firms in oil and gas exploration.[20]

A further blow came in October 1986 when government hopes of raising a $300 million loan through Sonatrach were dashed. This reflected international unwillingness to lend to energy companies, as well as uneasiness over Algeria's general economic health.

By the end of 1986 the twin priorities of avoiding recourse to the IMF for debt rescheduling, and maintaining economic independence throughout the oil-price slide, had resulted in an economy of rising prices, acute shortages of imported consumer goods, and growing opposition within FLN ranks to policies of liberalization. November also saw student riots in Setif and Constantine. Foreign investment was put off by the terms under which it was allowed to operate, notwithstanding the slightly more attractive hydrocarbons law of late 1986.

It was becoming clear that the reformists needed a freer hand to introduce reforms beyond simply cutting imports and spending. The dinar was patently and vastly overvalued, and the banking laws and currency regulations clearly needed to be overhauled. In August 1986 a new banking law was introduced to begin a five-year schedule of reforms, including granting the commercial banks more autonomy and the central bank greater freedom from administrative control.

In a November speech to the assembly of regional governors, Chadli made it clear that he intended to push ahead with reform, reducing lossmaking elements in the public sector and encouraging private enterprise.[21] Tackling FLN and Islamicist criticism of his reforms head-on, he opened the campaign for the parliamentary elections with a speech defending his economic policies.

Yet, mindful of the November 1986 student riots, the 1987 budget included a commitment not to remove any more food subsidies. Shortages, meanwhile, were likely to be increased by a 17 percent reduction in imports compared to 1986 levels (35 percent when compared to 1985). The need to cut public-sector losses was continuously reiterated in Chadli's speeches during November, December, and January. Public-sector enterprises were promised more freedom in their investment and sales strategies, and support for the private sector was strongly emphasized.

Borrowing was now becoming a serious problem, however, as was the total level of foreign debt, which had reached an estimated level of $20 billion even earlier than expected.[22] Algeria was finding it increasingly difficult to tempt creditors, even with more generous pricing of loans. This was partly due to the confusion caused by the reform of the Algerian banking system,[23] but largely to nervousness over Algeria's ability to sustain repayments and impose austerity at home.

Improved Oil Prices and Continued Reform

In fact, a recovery in Algerian crude-oil prices in early 1987 allowed the government to increase its imports budget, especially for spare parts for industry; the lack of these was seriously hampering production. At the same time, an attempt was made to counter at least some of the lenders' concerns and internal confusion, by the establishment in July 1987 of the *Conseil National du Crédit* [National Credit Council] (CNC), to determine the government's borrowing strategy and coordinate the applications of the commercial and central banks. Meanwhile, IMF and World Bank suggestions that the dinar should be devalued continued to be adamantly rejected—but the discreet effective devaluation that the currency underwent in the course of the year was interpreted as an indication of the government's intentions.

Reform of the public sector was now also on the table. Proposals were put forward for public companies to be more directly responsible for their own borrowing from the commercial banks, taking investment decisions for themselves but equally being subject to the banks' new ability to reject borrowing requests from the public sector. Public-sector reform was approved by the cabinet in July 1987 and passed in September, allowing the EPEs to manage their activities "with full commercial powers"—that is, to manage their own budgets, fix their own prices, and invest their own profits. The new freedom to fix wages (in contrast to the *Statut* of 1983) that was also granted was, however, likely also to fuel already rising trade-union rejection of the liberalization program.

Further reform of the public agricultural sector was announced, with provision being made for the restructuring of 200 public units into smaller ones, formalizing the move away from collectivism. Farmers were to be able to lease land in units called *groupements des producteurs agricoles* and thereafter have as much control as the private sector over decisions regarding the farm. The state would still formally own the land, but after five years leases could be transferred or renewed. Although there was some concern about possibly rising prices, it was generally acknowledged that Chadli's previous agricultural reforms had helped to control the massive food import bill.

Significant joint ventures, meanwhile, were being set up with foreign investors in tourism and car production. Yet criticism of foreign firms also increased regarding their failure to complete contracts on time and to employ Algerian consultants and contractors.

In the course of 1987, in order to consolidate his position and continue his reform program, Chadli again instigated reshuffles in the armed forces and the cabinet. In July a reshuffle intended to professionalize the army and withdraw it from politics was equally aimed at ensuring that, as opposition to economic hardships increased, so would the president's control over the security forces. Changes in the cabinet in November and the following

February helped to surround Chadli with younger technocrats, to reduce direct government involvement in the economy (by abolishing three ministries and two deputy ministers' posts, including the planning ministry), and to reduce opposition to the 1988 program for economic reform.

Austerity remained the watchword of the 1988 budget, but the centerpiece of the year's reform was the law on company autonomy. While freed public and private enterprise were expected to increase nonhydrocarbon exports substantially, the government pledged to keep control over imports to prevent any balance-of-payments crisis if industry and agriculture failed to perform.

Significant joint ventures between foreign and Algerian companies were beginning to be established in hotel building, oil exploration, telecommunication, and car production. The increased confidence on the part of foreign venture capital was gradually reflected in renewed interest in the loan markets. This was helped by the news that domestic savings had risen and that there had been a small trade surplus in 1987.[24]

June brought the announcement of further reforms in both the public and private sectors that built upon the previous ones. Holding companies were established to take shares in those EPEs that neither had large debts nor required further structural reform and could therefore be moved into the new autonomous regime. Legislation was promised for 1989 to change the state's monopoly on trade. The rules on exporters' foreign-currency accounts were changed, with public companies able to retain up to 10 percent, rather than 4 percent, of their foreign-currency earnings. In July Parliament approved a new law affecting the private sector. Incentives were introduced such as access to hard currency through bank accounts and an end to the AD30 million ceiling on investment. Residents were also allowed for the first time to hold credit cards, including VISA International and American Express, if they held a foreign-currency account—as 300,000 did.

Additionally, the dinar was allowed to devalue unofficially by over 30 percent against the U.S. dollar in the first seven months of the year; this was explained as the result of changes in a basket of currencies against which the dinar was valued. Although this went in the direction of what the IMF had been suggesting, it also added to the price rises that were beginning to rock Algerian society because it made imports more expensive. Combined with other measures that were being experienced by poorer Algerians as a cut in their standard of living, the price rises helped set the stage for the disturbances that marked the country's sociopolitical scene in the autumn.

The November 1988 Riots and Constitutional Reform

Reforms and the higher cost of imports pushed up food prices by the summer of 1988. A wave of strikes and violent protests had already greeted the cuts in premiums paid to public-sector employees. Public anger was stirred particularly by announcements that bread prices were to rise by 250 percent. Even so, Chadli insisted on re-emphasizing the need for further austerity measures.

In October fierce rioting shook Algeria—not to mention international confidence. These riots were far more severe and widespread than those of 1986, and indicated that there was a limit to the willingness of ordinary Algerians to tolerate austerity. The riots have been attributed to economic discontent by some, to political dissatisfaction by others. Both clearly played a role, and for many Algerians they were probably connected. In any case, in a 10 October address to the nation, Chadli promised political reforms alongside a continuation of economic reform.

The urgency of further economic reform had been highlighted over the second half of the year. The short-term debt incurred in the previous few years, in an attempt to maintain imports and relieve the government of some of the direct investment burden, was coming due in 1989–1990. Estimates of debt servicing by the end of 1988 ran at some $5.4 billion—a ratio of over 60 percent. To keep any respectable degree of international confidence in the economy Chadli had to convince creditors that he was not intending to reschedule his debts and that his reform program would be continued with sufficient haste to begin relieving bottlenecks in the system fairly soon. Recourse to the IMF, meanwhile, was still being rejected as a submission to "economic imperialism"—in the words of *El-Moudjahid.*

In a move that could be seen as an attempt both to consolidate the economic reform path and to appease the political grievances of the population, Chadli also appointed a new cabinet and pushed through a number of constitutional reforms. Parliament was strengthened at the expense of the FLN—a move seen by many as an attempt to bypass institutional resistance to continued reform. The new prime minister, Kasdi Merbah, in November 1988 presented a package of emergency measures designed to relieve public pressure: across-the-board wage increases of 33 percent, employment creation (unemployment being estimated at around 25 percent), and a number of educational, judicial, and health-care reforms. The new government also began negotiations with the trade-union movement, the *Union Générale des Travailleurs Algériens* [General Union of Algerian Workers] (UGTA), to try to reduce its support for the wave of strikes. At the same time, Chadli gave a commitment to public-sector workers that the constitutional reforms would grant them the right to strike. There was considerable opposition to this from the FLN, as well as from a number of reformers who feared it might reduce foreign confidence in the economy.

While the UGTA generally supported the constitutional reforms, it remained stubbornly opposed to much of the economic liberalization program. Fears that liberalization was creating a new middle class at the expense of the poorer sections of society were reflected in the union's opposition to unrestrained private-sector activity and to a downgrading of the

FLN, its political patron. There was a general feeling that the government had failed to sufficiently explain its policies to the public, expecting them to swallow shortages, price rises, declining real wages, and intensified social-infrastructure problems in return for political reform, without real consideration for the impact on ordinary families.

The Constitution of 1989, as it became known, in the event did encompass Chadli's intended reforms. Most strikingly, the word "socialism" was removed from the constitution. The timing coincided with the arrival of IMF officials on an "advice-giving" mission to Algeria.[25]

News that Algeria had drawn upon its SDR188 million reserve tranche with the IMF provoked new concerns that ideological tradition would be broken and that the government would indeed opt for an IMF rescheduling agreement. In July 1989 the announcement finally came that a one-year IMF standby agreement had been reached, timed to precede a further round of economic reforms. Michel Camdessus, the IMF director-general, expressed the IMF's confidence that Algeria would continue to service its debts on time and in full, and its support for Algeria as one of the few countries that had imposed upon itself a genuine structural-adjustment program without prompting from the IMF and not simply in order to attract foreign aid.

Conclusion

The first decade of Chadli's rule in Algeria saw a profound reversal in the character of and policies toward the economy. It was his misfortune that his good intentions foundered under the pressures of the decline in oil prices just when he needed the associated revenue most. His predecessor had accumulated a national debt that, while not outstanding given reasonable hydrocarbon revenues, became painfully difficult to carry as low revenues combined with the structural deficiencies of Boumedienne's legacy to squeeze government spending power.

Chadli operated his policies under intense political pressures. To go too quickly in the first five years would have wholly alienated the governing infrastructure—those old men of the FLN who perceived in his reforms the beginning of their own end. His first development plan therefore introduced reform relatively slowly, giving him time to adjust the structure of power in his own favor and to remove some of those personalities most closely associated with Boumedienneism. Because his own roots were in that very same structure, however, he was forced to restrict his reforms in terms of maintaining the guiding principle of the state: economic independence. His efforts to encourage nonhydrocarbon exports did not come in time to stave off the effects of the fall in oil prices of the mid-1980s. Instead, they contributed to the economic problems as the new emphasis on profitmaking raised both prices and unemployment. Economic independence also necessitated directing government spending toward prompt debt servicing and repayment. Investment was neglected relative to previous years, and the increased priority given to providing consumer goods and improving the quality of life could never overcome the imposition of austerity that was necessitated by the intense pressure not to reschedule debts.

As his personal position appeared to become consolidated, Chadli accelerated the reform process. Although his efforts were rewarded in terms of increased efficiency and production in both agriculture and industry, growth in those sectors was too slow to fill the shortfall in imports. The contradictions resulting from Chadli's need to compromise politically (illustrated by the limits on foreign-investment stakes and the failure to release land-ownership documents) hindered the economy's ability to respond to the reforms and prevented popular confidence in them. In particular, private enterprise was obstructed from seizing the development initiative by continued restrictions on its contacts with foreign investment, by severely limited access to foreign currency, and by restricted access to public-sector purchasing.[26]

The reformers pursued a policy that did not carry with it the understanding and support of the people whose short-term interests would most likely be damaged by it. The cause of the 1988 riots was neither solely political nor solely economic. The failure of the government either to carry out policies wholly and committedly, or to communicate its actions to the population, would inspire neither economic nor political confidence. Observers reported the widening gap between rich and poor, pointing out the increasing tendency of the new middle class toward corruption and flaunting its new wealth. In 1990, 5 percent of the population was said to be earning 45 percent of the national income. At the same time, there was a chronic housing shortage of over 2 million units, shortages of even basic foodstuffs in the shops, derelict social services, and high unemployment.[27] Though these figures are from after the 1988 riots they were the accumulated result of the previous years.

It is no wonder that the impact of Chadli's policies, made many times worse by the prevailing oil-market conditions, the legacies of the Boumedienne era, and the burdens of debt, led the country to erupt in violence. Benachenchou has observed that during the period from 1954 to 1984, the effects of inflation and ever-growing consumption were moderated by increased job opportunities, subsidies, and state provision. Salarization and modernization of life were in effect state supported, although much of the salarization was engendered by employment through emigration.[28] When emigration tailed off, oil revenues fell, and the state ceased to fulfill the expectations created by the system, workers became alienated from a government they perceived as having broken a social contract. Chadli may have been trying to stave off the worst of the inevitable through his reforms, but the timing of the oil-price collapse undermined his efforts by necessitating austerity at a time when it would have been more convenient to ease the population into the changes with continued but carefully directed state investment.

Notes

1. *Middle East Economic Digest (MEED),* 9 November 1979.
2. D. Vandewalle, "Breaking with Socialism: Economic Liberalisation and Privatisation in Algeria," in I. Harik and D. Sullivan, *Privatization and Liberalization in the Middle East* (Bloomington, Ind.: Indiana University Press, 1992), pp. 189–209.
3. *MEED,* 7 March 1980.
4. *The Middle East,* November 1987, p. 26.
5. *MEED,* 3 April 1981. The 1980–1984 Plan envisaged 328 new light-industry factories being established.
6. *MEED,* 12 June 1981, quoting Light Industry Ministry officials.
7. These tax holidays were five years for land tax, three years with a further two at discounted rates for profits tax, 20 percent tax for reinvested profits, and no tax on additional payments by the joint venture to its foreign partner. *MEED,* 30 July 1982, pp. 3–5.
8. *MEED,* 13 May 1983.
9. See K. Pfeiffer, "Algeria's Implicit Stabilisation Program," in H. Barkey, ed., *The Politics of Economic Reform in the Middle East* (New York: St. Martin's Press, 1992), pp. 153–181.
10. *MEED,* 3 June 1983.
11. See *The Middle East and North Africa 1994* (London: Europa Publications, 1993), p. 261; and *MEED,* 8 February 1980.
12. For more information, see W. Swearingen, "Agricultural Policy and the Growing Food Security Crisis," in J. Entelis and P. Naylor, eds., *State and Society in Algeria* (Boulder, Colo.: Westview, 1992), pp. 117–127.
13. Ibid., p. 129.
14. J. Brule, "Algeria: The Situation of Agricultural Land Privatisation," paper presented at the conference on Privatisation and Economic Liberalisation in Socialist Countries of the Arab World, University of Erlangen, Banz Castle, Germany, February 1994.
15. Brule, ibid., claims that the free market operated only for meat, while Swearingen ("Agricultural Policy and the Growing Food Security Crisis," p. 129) insists it included fruit and vegetables. *The Middle East and North Africa 1994* (p. 261) states that the government did indeed relax price controls and allow farmers to sell directly to markets or to private vendors, and to do so across *wilaya* boundaries.
16. *MEED,* 5 August 1983.
17. *MEED,* 23 March 1984.
18. For more on these features of the plan and its early execution, see *MEED,* 30 March 1984 and 3 May 1985.
19. See *MEED,* 26 April 1986.
20. *MEED,* 2 August 1986.
21. *MEED,* 22 November 1986.
22. *MEED,* 14 March 1987.
23. In March 1987, both Sonatrach and *Crédit Populaire d'Algérie* appealed to the loan market, giving the appearance of uncoordinated borrowing. The Sonatrach

loan failed to materialize—the third Algerian bid to do so in a year—adding to the insecurity of the Algerian borrowers.

24. Algeria's *Direction Générale des Douanes* reported a surplus of just over $1 billion, but the IMF put it at $177 million. See *MEED*, 6 May 1988.

25. *MEED*, 17 March 1989.

26. T. Zeuner, "Promotion of Small- and Medium-Scale Industry in Algeria," paper presented at the conference on Privatisation and Economic Liberalisation in Socialist Countries of the Arab World, University of Erlangen, Banz Castle, February 1994.

27. *The Middle East,* March–April 1990, p. 16.

28. A. Benachenchou, "Inflation et Chômage en Algérie: les aléas de la démocratie et des reformes économiques," in *Monde arabe—Maghreb Machreq,* No. 139, January–March 1993, pp. 29–41.

11

Algeria's Troubled Road Toward Political and Economic Liberalization, 1988–1995

Michael Willis

Few countries in the Arab world appeared to be as close to economic collapse and violent political chaos as Algeria had come by 1995. Foreign observers increasingly spoke of the country being in a state of near civil war, and bleak analyses were made about the condition of the country's economy. For some observers these parallel crises afflicting the Algerian state were a result, directly or indirectly, of policies of liberalization that Algeria had pursued for varying periods over the last decade and a half, in both its political life and in the management of its economy. For some, it was the application of liberalization in one or both areas that precipitated the crises; for others it was the failure to apply liberalizing measures fully and consistently that led to the existing and chronic impasse. More so than in any comparable country, the interaction between the two processes of political and economic liberalization, their relative timing, and the extent to which one spurred or held back the other are vital to an understanding of Algeria's predicament.

One can undoubtedly trace the origins of Algeria's political and economic liberalization back much earlier, but it is the period since the death of the country's second but overwhelmingly influential president, Houari Boumedienne, in late 1978, that witnessed the most significant developments and substantial moves on the part of the Algerian regime toward liberalization. The state Boumedienne left behind, forged largely in accordance with his own vision, was one characterized politically by a centralized bureaucratic structure under the auspices, theoretically at least, of a single party, the FLN (which had ruled Algeria since winning independence from France in 1962), and economically by centralized state ownership and socialist-style management.

Breaking with Boumedienne: Liberalization 1978–1988

Economic Liberalization and Political Control

The first substantial steps along the path of liberalization by Boumedienne's successors, headed by the new president, Chadli Ben Jedid, were taken in the field of economics. Politically there was no more than an initial, tentative change of atmosphere. Though these initial economic reforms introduced in 1980 represented a clear and conscious deviation from the radical socialist path that Boumedienne had increasingly trod in his latter years, they aimed only at restructuring and rationalizing his vision. However, the administrative breakup and geographic dispersal of many of Algeria's huge state-owned and -run industries, in an attempt to combat rising inefficiency and declining productivity, gave way by the mid-1980s to more thoroughgoing liberalizing reforms and an acceleration of the pace of existing reforms. The government deregulated domestic prices, revised investment codes to encourage foreign investment, and further encouraged the country's private sector. This quickening of the pace of reform partly reflected a desire on the part of the regime to combat new economic problems such as the country's mounting debt. The debt had been accumulated through both the purchase of capital machinery abroad during Boumedienne's concerted bid to build up Algeria's heavy industry, and through the country's increasing need to import food as the population expanded and the neglected agricultural sector failed to keep productive pace. It undoubtedly also reflected a growing conviction, present even before Boumedienne's death, within parts of the Algerian government itself, of the desirability and need for a shift to a more market-oriented economy.[1]

Yet, as already stated, throughout this period of economic reform there was no substantial initiative on the part of the regime to move toward a more liberalized political system. A more politically permissive atmosphere was experienced in the first few years of Chadli's government, during which various low-level political and social organizations and activity were tolerated if not legitimized; but as this activity became more pronounced, and as it was perceived to increasingly represent a challenge to the authorities, the most prominent groups were clamped down upon. Most notable of these were the Berberist movement, which was effectively repressed by the regime in 1980; the Islamists, who saw large numbers of their leaders and followers arrested at the end of 1982; and the far smaller but highly vocal women's movement.[2] All these groups had their own grievances and agendas to advance, but the perceived threat or challenge they presented to the regime ensured their repression. Chadli in the early 1980s seemed no more willing than his predecessors to alter the "iron triangle" of state, party, and army that made up the political structure of Algeria. Official experimentation with broader political participation in this period was also abandoned after the regime found its outcome unpalatable. The election of a Popular National Assembly in 1982 containing only one-third FLN members, ensuring that the experiment of allowing independent candidates to stand, was not repeated in the next set of elections in 1987.[3]

The Riots of October 1988: The Opening of the Political Field

The issue of political reform was pushed to center stage by the large-scale social disturbances and riots that occurred throughout Algeria in October 1988. These resulted in the deaths of several hundred people and shook Algeria's ruling political establishment more profoundly than any previous event in the country's independent history. Considerable debate has taken place about what precisely underlay these riots, what the protesters themselves hoped to achieve through their actions, and most importantly for current purposes, the extent to which this massive unrest reflected popular discontent with the government's stance on economic and political liberalization. In the immediate aftermath of the disturbances, the implications of which had arguably been deepened by the brutality with which the police and eventually the army dealt with them, most observers pointed to the declining social and economic conditions ordinary Algerians had increasingly had to endure. For some observers this decline was a direct result of the liberalizing policies the Chadli regime had pursued in the economic sphere over the preceding period: restructuring of state enterprises, leading to substantial layoffs among employees (overall unemployment increased from 11 percent to 25 percent between 1984 and 1988);[4] reductions in state subsidies, causing soaring prices for some goods; and the deregulation of distribution channels, resulting in a greater volume of trade but not in greater equity of distribution. However, as Lynette Rummel has observed, such problems were due as much to factors unrelated specifically to the regime's liberalization program (drought in the summer of 1988 had contributed to rises in prices for foodstuffs, for example), and political grievances were increasingly acknowledged as making an equally important contribution to popular anger as more tangible economic hardships. Such a conclusion, Rummel goes on to argue, is borne out by the fact that institutions of the state, such as government ministries, government-run shops, and FLN party offices, rather than smaller businesses and shops that had benefited from the liberalizing policies, appeared to be the main and initial targets of protesters' and rioters' anger, indicating that it was dissatisfaction with the ruling political establishment that primarily motivated the people on the streets.[5]

Though Rummel's thesis is difficult to prove or disprove, given the difficulty in making a distinction between discontent with government policy and with the government itself, it certainly appears that President Chadli chose to view the crisis in political terms. In a nationwide address on 10

October, in the immediate wake of the riots, he promised political reforms and greater political freedom. Within four months Algeria had a new constitution, approved by referendum, that swept away the old single-party monopoly of the FLN and accorded Algerians the right to form "associations of a political character." Five months later, in July 1989, political parties began to be officially registered, and by the following June Algeria was staging its first ever multiparty elections.[6]

Such a startlingly swift about-face by the regime was attributable in part to a recognition by Chadli that some form of political safety valve was needed to prevent a repetition of what became known as "the events of October," and perhaps to a prescient belief on the president's part that single-party states were a political form soon to be eclipsed. But presidential motivations for the changes were arguably more complex. It seems clear that Chadli chose this particular path of political liberalization as a means of combating internal enemies he faced within the FLN and indeed the government apparatus itself. It is equally clear that the principal issue dividing Chadli from his opponents within the regime was his pursuit of the program of economic liberalization. Motivated both by an ideological desire not to see the statist project of Boumedienne destroyed, and, for some, by a more basic desire to prevent the erosion of long-standing personal financial (read: corrupt) and political power bases, Chadli's opponents fought increasingly hard against the president's reform program.[7] Chadli saw political reform as a means of recruiting new allies to his economic reforms outside the structures of the regime (among the growing private-business sector, for example) and as a tool for putting pressure on the old guard of the FLN, where resistance was concentrated, by depriving them of their political monopoly. At the same time he insulated himself from what one writer has termed the "quasi-destruction of the FLN"[8] by ensuring that his powers as president in the new constitution remained substantial and distinct from those of the party. In distancing himself from the FLN, Chadli sought, as Robert Mortimer explains, "to establish himself as an arbiter above the arena in which future party competition would take place."[9]

Full Speed Ahead: Liberalization, 1989–1991

The Acceleration of Economic Reform

In the economic field such comprehensive ruptures with the political past inevitably distracted critical attention, both within and outside the regime, from the economic policies Chadli and his allies pushed forward with renewed vigor in the aftermath of the October crisis.[10] This did not mean, though, that the reform program was implemented more covertly. In the immediate wake of the riots Chadli reaffirmed his commitment to the process of economic reform, and thus appeared to implicitly couple the two processes of economic and political liberalization.[11] This linkage was further confirmed by the noteworthy absence of any reference to socialism (historically a touchstone of Algeria's political, social, and economic life) in the new constitution of February 1989 that formally heralded the end of single-party rule in Algeria.

The acceleration of the reform program after 1988 built on reforms already in place, and pursued the two fundamental reform aims of increasing the autonomy of state enterprises and allowing greater private-sector involvement in the economy.[12] The government's commitment to reform was underlined by the conclusion in July 1989 of an agreement with the IMF to which few conditions were attached. This was a clear signature of approval, from a body increasingly seen as a bastion of economic liberalism and free-market economics, of the reforms planned and instituted by the Algerian authorities. Two months later Chadli reshuffled his government to give the key portfolios of the economy, foreign affairs, and the prime ministership to proven supporters of his economic reform program.[13]

Thus Algeria entered the 1990s with programs of liberalization in the fields of politics and economics that together were arguably more comprehensive than any others in the Arab world. Yet the early years of the decade were to prove, for different reasons, to be a time of crisis for Algeria in both the political and economic spheres.

The Debt Crisis and the Imperative of Reform

The crisis that progressively overtook the Algerian economy was one that had been long in the making but appeared to become more chronic with each year, until by the 1990s it became unavoidably the primary concern of the country's economic policymakers. Algeria's international debt had, as has been explained, been of some concern to the government since the early 1980s, but although some measures were taken, such as switching more state funds to the agricultural sector to cut down on the need for food imports, little real effort was made to tackle the problem. This apparent complacency on the part of the government was due to its belief that the debt could be funded by the increases in revenues it expected to get from its already considerable oil and gas (collectively referred to as hydrocarbons) sales.[14] However, the inherent vulnerability of this strategy was revealed when the international price of oil collapsed in 1985–1986, cutting Algeria's revenues from oil and gas by nearly 40 percent in one year and depriving the state of close to $5 billion in anticipated revenues with which it had planned to service its debt. Compounding the problem still further was the fact that at the time of the collapse, hydrocarbon sales constituted 97 percent of the country's total exports—a fact that severely limited Algeria's options in terms of finding alternative sources of hard currency with which to service its debts.[15]

The short-term response of Algeria's economic policymakers to the country's debt crisis was to restructure the shape and nature of the debt through the acquisition of further long-term loans to pay off the large number of short- and medium-term loans that began to mature in the early 1990s.[16] This did not of itself do much to reduce the overall size of the total international debt, which had grown from $15 billion in 1985 to $24 billion by 1990.[17] For President Chadli and his new proreform allies in the government, the increasingly dominant problem of the international debt further underlined the need for economic reform and thus contributed to the drive to increase the pace of reform from 1989. In their view economic liberalization would help reduce the debt in three ways. First, increased levels of efficiency and productivity, which it was hoped liberalization would produce in the domestic economy, would reduce the need for debt-swelling imports. Second, liberalization would serve to increase creditor confidence and thus make it easier for Algeria to continue to obtain further loans—particularly if liberalizing reforms had received the implicit approval of the IMF, as Algeria's had with the agreement of July 1989.[18] Third, and most important, liberalization served to bolster what Algeria's leaders saw as the long-term solution to the country's economic problems: the development of its hydrocarbon resources. This could only be done effectively by liberalizing the nationalistic investment laws to allow foreign participation in the gas and oil fields and thus, using their expertise, double the current recovery rate of the state energy company, Sonatrach.[19]

Consequently, much of the flood of liberalizing reform and legislation that occurred between 1989 and 1991 worked to serve these ends. In July 1991, for example, plans were announced to reform Algeria's 1986 hydrocarbons law to allow the participation of foreign companies in oil fields already in operation,[20] following legislation in 1990 that removed constraints on foreign investment in other parts of the economy. Other reforms in this period included, in 1990, legislation effectively ending the state's monopoly on credit (by allowing domestic and foreign investment in banking and financial institutions) and the relinquishing of government controls over export-import control and wage levels, both of which were henceforth to be determined by market forces.[21] By the autumn of 1990 the prime minister was confidently predicting the imminent achievement of a full market economy.[22]

The "Rebirth" of Political Life and the 1990 Local Elections

While economic liberalization appeared to forge strongly ahead, the process of political liberalization also proceeded apace in this period on its own and, for now, largely separate course. Twenty political parties officially registered themselves following the passing of the law on political parties in July 1989; with the first elections—those for local government—looming, most of these parties energetically set about organizing and promoting themselves in preparation. Robert Mortimer eloquently describes this period:

> Democratization came to Algeria with a flourish in the period preceding the June 1990 local elections. The new climate of free-flowing debate produced a torrent of political activity. The media showered the population with talk shows and interviews with the leaders of the new parties that continued to sprout across the political landscape. During spring 1990, marches, demonstrations and rallies became virtual daily occurrences. The rebirth of political life was exhilarating, especially for what Algerians call the "political class"—party leaders and activists—but, as the election drew near, the real options began to narrow.[23]

Indeed it was this narrowing of political options (in part exacerbated by the boycott of the elections by two of the more high-profile parties)[24] that produced the first potential test for Algeria's ambitious program of political liberalization. As the date of the election approached, it became increasingly apparent that the contest for control of the country's municipalities and provincial assemblies would effectively be between two parties: the old FLN, shorn of most of its constitutional privileges but relying on its long-established structures and historical legitimacy; and the *Front Islamique du Salut* [Islamic Salvation Front] (FIS), a party only formed in March 1989 and committed to the restoration of Algeria's Islamic identity.[25]

The triumph of the FIS, rather than the FLN, when the votes of 12 June were counted, had profound potential implications for Algeria's process of political liberalization, especially given the comprehensive size of the FIS victory. The party won over half the popular vote in both the municipal *communales* and the regional *wilayas,* taking full control of over half the councils in the former and nearly two-thirds of the latter.[26] The first major implication of the results was the effect of the comprehensive defeat inflicted on the FLN. Having expected to have taken something between 40 and 60 percent of the vote, the formerly dominant party took only 28 percent—barely half that of its Islamic rival.[27] For the regime this was a serious shock, since despite the changes announced in the new constitution of 1989, the whole machinery of government, including the entire Popular National Assembly and the presidency itself, was still clearly tied to the FLN. (Chadli had failed in attempts both to portray himself as being above the political fray and to seek alliances with other parties.)[28] Defeat on such a scale at a local level forecast political oblivion for virtually the entire existing political order if such results were to be repeated at the eventual national elections. More important still was the fact that it had been the FIS that had defeated the FLN: There was widespread unease, bordering on alarm, among other parties as well as the FLN that such a resounding victory should have been won by a party whose commitment to the whole democratization process seemed to be in doubt. (This issue will be looked at in more detail.)

Second Thoughts: Political Liberalization Compromised, 1990–1991

In the face of this unforeseen development President Chadli reaffirmed his commitment to the program of political liberalization and democratization by announcing in July 1990, only a month after the local elections, that elections to the far more influential Popular National Assembly (PNA) would take place sometime in the first three months of 1991.[29] However, despite this demonstration of his democratic credentials Chadli and the regime began to investigate ways of preventing a repetition of the outcome of the local elections. Some tactics, such as the encouragement of smaller, more moderate Islamist parties in order to splinter the potential FIS vote,[30] did not strictly run counter to the ideals of democratization, but others quite clearly compromised Chadli's commitment to free and unfettered elections. In March 1991, following the postponing of the elections to the first half of 1991 due to domestic upheavals resulting from the Gulf War, the government presented a bill to the soon-to-be-dissolved PNA to modify the electoral law under which the forthcoming national elections would take place. The bill contained two provisions clearly designed to maximize the vote of the FLN and limit that of the FIS. The first provision was a classic piece of gerrymandering that drew up electoral districts with widely varying numbers of electors, meaning that in some areas only 7,000 electors could elect one representative while in others it took 75,000 to do the same. Unsurprisingly, the low-population districts were drawn up in the areas where the FLN had performed relatively well in June 1990 (the rural south), and the FIS strongholds from those elections (the northern cities) fell into the most heavily populated districts. The second, less blatant, provision that the regime introduced to help the FLN was one that produced a two-ballot system in which the two leading candidates in an initial ballot would proceed to a second ballot to decide the result. Through this the government hoped that the FLN, as the closest challenger to the FIS, would receive full backing in the second ballot from supporters of the smaller secular parties.[31]

This backtracking by the Algerian regime on its commitment to more thoroughgoing political liberalization was eventually amended with a government decision to moderate some of the gerrymandering excesses of its original legislation. This could be seen as evidence of the extent to which democratization and pluralism had begun to take root in Algerian political culture. However, the decision arguably had as much to do with the economic reform–minded administration's ongoing battle with the old guard of the FLN, entrenched in the PNA (which supported and indeed had strengthened the March 1991 legislation),[32] as with concern for maintaining the integrity of the program of political reform.[33] Indeed, by the time the changes to the electoral law had been made in autumn 1991, the government already had two reasons for believing that the pattern of results produced by the local elections was unlikely to be repeated at the national level.

First, two public-opinion polls in May 1991 had suggested that the FIS would gain as little as a third of the vote, or less, in elections to the new PNA; the FLN actually placed ahead in one of the polls. Thus, even if the FIS remained the largest single party, the FLN as the second party was clearly much closer behind than had been the case in 1990 and thus stood to capitalize on the two-ballot electoral system, which had been left unchanged.[34] Moreover, the still significant showing by the FIS has been seen to be consistent with Chadli's aim of keeping his enemies in the government in check.[35] Second, and far more important, the government had successfully contained a protest campaign mounted by the FIS in May–June 1991 aimed at overturning the skewed electoral legislation of the previous month. Although the campaign had produced a considerable amount of unrest and violence on the street, it also revealed weaknesses and divisions within the party: A general strike call on 25 May was largely ignored and several senior FIS figures publicly denounced the leadership's confrontational strategy on national television in the wake of the crisis.[36] On 7 June, following the resignation of the prime minister on 5 June, the government offered an agreement to the FIS's demands in return for an end to the campaign of opposition (which had involved occupations of parts of Algiers). This offer could well be seen as a recognition by the administration of the FIS's strength and its own weakness.[37] However, the fact that the regime had imposed martial law two days earlier, eventually reneged on the FIS demand to hold presidential elections at the same time as those for the National Assembly, and arrested and imprisoned the party's two senior leaders following more disturbances later that month, indicated that the government had hardened its resolve.

Liberalization Abandoned: 1991–1993

The Victory of the FIS and the Reassertion of the Army

This new resolve on the part of the regime was undoubtedly due to the re-entry of the Algerian army into the political equation, with the declaration of martial law in Algiers on 5 June giving effective control of the city to the military. As one-third of the historic iron triangle of the Algerian state, the army had made a gradual withdrawal from political life during the early period of political liberalization, cutting its links with the FLN, as Chadli's presidency had done, by withdrawing its representatives from the party's central committee in March 1989.[38] However, the army remained, as indeed it had been since independence in 1962, the real embodiment of the Algerian state—far more so than the other two-thirds of the triangle and certainly more so than the FLN, which Hugh Roberts maintains had "never been more than a secondary apparatus" for the military.[39]

Opinion is divided on whether the army as an institution genuinely backed the Chadli democratization program. (He himself, it should not be forgotten, had been a senior military officer.) But there is little doubt that the army continued to see itself as the guarantor of political stability, as indeed it had done since 1962. Its reappearance on the streets in June 1991 was evidence of its continued commitment to this role, and indeed Chadli frequently hinted at the possibility of military intervention if the political situation threatened to get out of control.[40]

The ultimate demonstration of this intent to maintain political stability came six months later when the military moved to draw an abrupt end to Algeria's brief but volatile period of democratization. On 12 January 1992 it was announced that the elections were canceled indefinitely; Chadli was ousted as president and replaced by a *Haut Comité d'Etat* [Higher State Council] (HCE) clearly dominated by the military and its supporters. However, this dramatic coup did not occur as reaction to mass civil unrest but as a response to the results of the first round of elections to the National Assembly that had finally been held on 26 December 1991.

Despite all the predictions that the level of support the FIS had gained would be severely cut back, whether through the presence of parties that had boycotted the 1990 elections or through public unease at the prospect of Islamic rule (fueled by the experience of the party's control of most local authorities since 1990),[41] the party once again triumphed at the ballot box. The FIS had not officially announced its intention to participate in the elections until only twelve days before the first ballot because it had been holding out for further concessions on the electoral law and for the release of its imprisoned leaders. Nevertheless, the FIS took just over 47 percent of the vote, this time more than double the vote of its nearest challenger, the FLN. The party won over 188 seats outright by gaining over 50 percent in those constituencies. Although this did not yet constitute a majority, it needed only to gain a further twenty-seven seats in the second ballot runoffs, a task made easy by the fact that all the other parties and candidates between them had only managed to win forty-three seats outright.[42] The stage looked set for a convincing FIS majority in the Assembly following the second ballot due to be held on 16 January. It was at this point, and for this reason, that the military stepped in.

The military's antipathy toward the Islamist movement and its party-political face, the FIS, dated back to before October 1988 and had increased over time. The army had opposed Chadli's controversial decision in September 1989 to recognize the FIS as a legitimate political party and thus allow it to compete in elections.[43] Tensions had mounted as the Islamists perhaps began to recognize the army, rather than the FLN, as their real political competitors in their struggle for the Algerian state. Motivated more by fears that a FIS-dominated PNA would seek swiftly to eliminate its enemies in the military leadership, than out of a concern for the survival of the democratization program, the army intervened in January 1992 to prevent a full victory for the FIS.[44] In so doing they forced the resignation of Chadli, who had believed continuation of his democratization program was possible through cohabitation with the Islamists. The army thus demonstrated that even the presidency, with whom it had increasingly been at odds over Chadli's attitude toward the FIS, had to bow to the military's will.

Even if the senior figures in the military had acted, at least partly, out of a desire to preserve Algeria's fledgling democracy, the intervention's net effect was to destroy it. The leadership attempted to appear to be guided by the 1989 constitution after it canceled the elections, but the constitutional provision that presidential elections must follow within forty-five days of the death or resignation of a president was clearly ignored by the provisional High Security Council, which itself appointed the new president and the new ruling HCE.[45]

The Economy:
The Impact of Politics and the Return to Boumediennism

At the beginning of this period of immense political upheaval, the economic side of Algeria's liberalization program continued to be pushed ahead. However, developments in the political field inevitably influenced the course of the reforms, and vice versa. President Chadli, for example, was aware that political uncertainty was likely to be a hindrance to economic policy. His announcement in April 1991 that the National Assembly elections would be held only two months later was partly aimed at companies that were thinking of investing in Algeria but waiting to see the outcome of the elections before committing themselves.[46] The political and security crisis of May–June, which arose from the FIS street protests of the election law, in turn had an impact on the prosecution of the economic reforms. The crisis forced the resignation of Prime Minister Mouloud Hamrouche, whose reformist administration had been responsible for the acceleration of the reform program since its appointment in September 1989. Aware that he had lost the architect of most of his more recent and radical reforms, Chadli was determined that Hamrouche's resignation should not send the wrong signals to the outside world. As Tim Niblock explains:

> The further unrest in June 1991 . . . added a new dynamic to the economic reform process, not because the popular demonstrations demanded it (they did not), but because the danger of falling credibility (in the eyes of creditors) demanded it.[47]

However, popular unrest and discontent did have a bearing on the economic reform program as well. The Chadli regime was well aware that the poor and declining social and economic conditions of the majority of the Algerian populace posed a constant threat to his policies and indeed to the whole regime. Such discontent, despite having a political character as well, was a major factor in the riots of October 1988. Although critics of the reform program blamed it for the unrest in 1988, supporters of the program argued that the unrest occurred because the reforms had not been pushed far or fast enough to produce the sort of benefits that would outweigh the negative short-term effects so much in evidence in 1988. This provides another explanation for the acceleration of the reform process after 1989. Dirk Vandewalle argues that "liberalization is essentially a race against time," particularly in Algeria where the possible consequences of failure to deliver economic progress for the general population are so visible.[48] Algeria's problem was how to contain political and social dissatisfaction with the reforms until the beneficial effects of liberalization could be felt. This task was made all the more difficult by political liberalization, which permitted organized opposition groups and strikes in industry for the first time. The victories of the FIS in 1990 and 1991, though obviously having a political and ideological dimension, were perhaps an indication that no such beneficial effects were yet being felt by the population.

The effective termination of the political reform program in January 1992 did not, however, mean that the process of economic reform would proceed henceforth in a more concerted fashion, its progress less impinged upon by upheavals in the political field. Sid Ahmed Ghozali, who succeeded Hamrouche as prime minister in June 1991, appeared to continue the process of reform by announcing an economic recovery plan at the end of March 1992 that, among other measures, included the freeing of prices on all goods with the exception of a few food staples.[49] Some observers nevertheless remained skeptical of the extent to which Ghozali and the whole Algerian regime were committed to economic liberalization since the departure from power of its two main proponents, Chadli and Hamrouche.[50] Indeed, some suspected that the Algerian military had never been truly supportive of the economic liberalization program and would seek to undermine it now that they had reasserted themselves politically.[51] Such doubts were fully confirmed by the nature of the government that was appointed after the assassination in June 1992 of Mohammed Boudiaf, the president chosen by the HCE in the previous January.

It became universally acknowledged that the assassination was due to alarm within the state machinery at the new president's vigorous anticorruption drive (another complicating aspect of the political and economic reform processes) rather than to more clearly political factors (such as the FIS).[52] The event led to the formation of a new government that almost brought a halt to the whole program of economic reform. The new prime minister, Belayed Abdessalam, had, as minister of industry and energy, been the architect of President Houari Boumedienne's heavy industrialization program in the 1970s, a central part of the planned economy that Chadli's reform program since 1978 had sought to dismantle and reverse. As Francis Ghilès remarked, Abdessalam "proved only too true to his past," reimposing tight state controls on foreign trade, rejecting devaluation of the dinar, and injecting large sums of money into unreformed state companies.[53] Furthermore, the new prime minister proved unwilling to come to a deal with the IMF, suspended key articles of the legislation passed in April 1990 that had opened Algeria to foreign investment, and even began to draw up plans to reincorporate autonomous state companies into their former state conglomerates, thus reversing one of Chadli's earliest reforms.[54]

Liberalization Revived?

Renewed Commitment to Economic Reform

Abdessalam and his "war economy" policies lasted just over a year. He was sacked as prime minister in August 1993 when it became clear to the HCE that his reversal of the reform process had not only failed to produce any degree of economic recovery but had actually deepened the dire state of the Algerian economy. Inflation had been pushed above 30 percent under his administration and a modest budget surplus had been turned into a significant deficit.[55]

The new administration under Prime Minister Redha Malek appeared to move swiftly to try to undo much of the damage done to the economy under Abdessalam. The new finance minister, Mourad Benachenchou, who had been Algeria's representative at the World Bank for several years,[56] stated that his aim was to create "a real rupture with previous economic policy."[57] Indeed, the government was keen to emphasize that the reform program was back on track. In a public statement at the end of January 1994, Benachenchou listed new measures he had introduced to stimulate the private sector, which included the lifting of various customs duties, reductions in tax rates on company profits, and provisions for the private sector to have access to hard currency and foreign finance. He stated that with other measures, "This policy constitutes a rational choice for a successful move to a market economy since numerous elements of such an economy have already been put in place."[58]

Obstacles to Economic Reform

Although they acknowledged the importance of the reforms, such as the partial deregulation of import controls and the easing of restrictions on foreign investment, most foreign observers remained skeptical about the impact they would have in terms of liberalizing the economy and improving economic performance.

By 1993–1994 Algeria's economic policymakers had arguably become hamstrung by two overarching problems, with the obvious potential solutions to one threatening to exacerbate the other. The first of these daunting problems that faced Algeria was the enduring size of its foreign debt, which had hovered around the $25 billion mark for several years. Managing this debt, as has been indicated, became the main preoccupation of Algeria's policymakers after 1989 while they waited for an upturn in hydrocarbon revenues. The repayment strategy received a severe blow during 1993 when falling oil prices meant that Algeria's existing hydrocarbon revenues would be cut by 20 percent in 1994.[59] Almost certainly as a direct result of this, Algeria slipped into payment arrears on its long- and medium-term debts in January and February 1994 as debt repayment threatened to absorb the entirety of the country's foreign-currency earnings.[60] Although they officially attributed these delays to "technical difficulties," the Algerian government was forced to contemplate, not for the first time, the option taken by most other countries in its position: a formal rescheduling of its debts and agreement to a standby loan with the IMF. The Algerian regime had historically steadfastly and consistently rejected rescheduling and the IMF option (except, as in July 1989, when few conditions had been imposed), mainly for the nationalistic reason of wanting to retain full control of its economy. (Formal rescheduling would give foreign creditors a say in economic policy.) But the government was increasingly aware that it was running out of options. There were fears that the sort of recommendations likely to be advanced by creditors and the IMF could only serve to fuel Algeria's other overshadowing problem—deepening social and political strife. Nevertheless, the government agreed to a £1 billion standby facility with the IMF in April 1994 that cleared the way for a rescheduling of part of its international debt with the "Paris Club" group of creditors the following month. The securing of the IMF loan had primarily been the work of Redha Malek, who, with his central task achieved, resigned as prime minister the same month. His successor, Mokdad Sifi, an acknowledged technocrat, signified his support for the agreement by claiming in an interview that it would result in Algeria's public and private sectors being "faced not only with internal competition but equally with international competition." In the same interview, however, the new prime minister argued that the relaunching of the country's economy was only one of his government's two main objectives, the second being the improvement of the "security situation," which he regarded as an "absolute priority."[61]

Escalating Political Strife and the Search for Consensus

This need to improve the "security situation" was a result of the political strife that had escalated in Algeria since the termination of the electoral process in January 1992 and became the main concern of the HCE regime from its installation. In the ensuing months the new government sought to repress the FIS, whose supporters moved to show, both officially and on the streets, their outrage at having been forcibly deprived of a near-certain victory in the National Assembly elections. The violent clashes that inevitably and increasingly occurred between Islamists and the security forces provided the regime with the opportunity to declare a nationwide state of emergency on 9 February 1992. Less than a month later, on 4 March, the FIS was officially ordered to dissolve—the authorities having already imprisoned most of its leaders and roughly 5,000 of its activists.[62]

The effective forcing of the FIS underground presaged the steady growth in a guerrilla and terrorist war waged by Islamists against the regime. The conflict spread from initial clashes between armed Islamists and the police and army to the specific targeting by the Islamists of politicians, intellectuals, foreigners, and indeed anyone seen to be supportive of the regime or opposed to the Islamist viewpoint. Guerrilla warfare had claimed perhaps as many as 40,000 lives by the beginning of 1995. For many foreign observers the survival of the regime continued to be in doubt.

The resumption of the process of political liberalization and a return to elections appeared to be an unlikely response from a regime that had been formed in January 1992 to forestall the sort of chaos and instability that Algeria, ironically, was now experiencing. However, the Higher State Council was increasingly aware that, as the period since the cancellation of the elections had shown, security measures alone would not restore stability to Algeria. There would need to be some promise, at least, of a return to elections as a means of both reducing the violence and boosting the regime's currently negative level of legitimacy in the eyes of ordinary Algerians. Popular disillusionment and disgust with the corruption and ineffectiveness of the regime had continued to increase since 1990 and 1991, when so many had registered their feelings by voting for the FIS.[63]

From mid-1993 the regime began to lay out its long-term plans for a "return" to the democratic process and began to attempt dialogue with the country's existing political parties. However, the reluctance of the regime to officially involve representatives of the banned FIS led most of Algeria's major political parties to ignore and boycott the dialogue, which, despite their own antipathy toward the FIS, they saw as hollow and disingenuous without the presence of the most popular party in the country. A National Conference of Reconciliation, which had aimed to bring together all the legal opposition parties to help select a new body to replace the HCE when it came to the end of its two-year "mandate," failed to attract any of the major opposition parties in January 1994. However, the "selection" at the conference of a new president, General Liamine Zeroual, though reinforcing popular and opposition-party perceptions of the regime as being run by a corrupt clique of generals, did herald a new initiative in the political field. Declaring in a speech soon after his appointment that dialogue should secure the "participation of the national and political forces *without exception,*"[64] Zeroual worked throughout 1994 to achieve some degree of involvement for the FIS in talks on Algeria's political future. Two attempts were made through the party's imprisoned original leadership to bring the ferocious armed conflict to an end and to bring the Islamists into national dialogue. However, both initiatives ultimately failed—the second, in the autumn of 1994, foundering on FIS demands to reconvene and consult the entirety of the party's ruling body, dispersed since 1992 between the armed underground, exile abroad, and the regime's prisons.

The failure of attempts at dialogue between the regime and the FIS in 1994 resulted in both sides launching separate initiatives to break the political impasse, both aimed at restarting Algeria's abandoned electoral process. From the government's side, President Zeroual declared at the end of October 1994 the regime's intent to hold presidential elections before the end of 1995. Despite the absence of any fundamental improvement in the security situation inside the country—hitherto a stated obstacle to the resumption of elections—the government pressed ahead and the elections were held in November 1995, in the face of boycotts by most opposition parties and threats by Islamist extremists to kill those who voted. The FIS remained banned.

The failure of the main opposition parties to join in the elections was linked to their earlier involvement, together with FIS representatives, in two conferences in Rome in 1994 and 1995, that resulted in agreement on a set of proposals representing the opposition's stance on Algeria's political future. Signed by parties collectively representing over 80 percent of the votes cast in December 1991, the platform called for "free and pluralistic elections which allow people the full exercise of their sovereignty."[65]

Both initiatives in fact had some elements in common, but failed to find mutual acceptance. The Algerian government rejected the Rome Declaration as an intolerable foreign interference in Algerian affairs and refused to unban the FIS, while the legal opposition parties who had signed the declaration stated their unwillingness to participate in the planned presidential elections unless the FIS were allowed to take part as well.

In the end, four candidates stood in the elections: Sheikh Mahfoud Nahnah, leader of the moderate Islamist party Hamas; Said Saadi, from the Kabylie region and strongly antifundamentalist; Nouredine Boukrouh, who advocated a moderate Islamic state; and Liamine Zeroual himself. Contrary to the expectations of many observers, and threats of violence and assassination notwithstanding, the government claimed a 75 percent voter turnout. Even though this may have been somewhat inflated, monitors from the Arab League, the Organization of African States, and the UN did not dispute the figure. While the turnout in itself could be seen as a victory of the government over the extremist Islamists, the final results similarly strengthened Zeroual's legitimacy: the official count gave him 61 percent of the vote, followed by Mahfoud Nahnah (25 percent) and Said Saadi (10 percent). Tellingly, the three losing candidates offered the president-elect their congratulations.[66]

The outcome of the elections was widely interpreted as indicating a shift in popular attitudes, including a rejection of the extremist and violent form of Islamist politics. At the same time, the result also strengthened President Zeroual's position, both with respect to the FIS and to the hardliners in the regime.

Prospects and Conclusions

The Economic Field

By 1995 sixteen years had passed since the death of President Houari Boumedienne and the shift in the direction of economic policy by his successors to one more characterized by market economics and economic liberalization. However, the impact of this shift on the structure of the economy, and particularly its beneficial effects, can only be regarded as being very limited. Algeria's economic reformers not only had to deal with substantial institutional, as well as at times popular, resistance to their plans, but they also sought to reform an economy its previous managers once proudly described as having the highest levels of state investment in the entire world. Despite a sometimes impressive array of liberalizing legislation (notably under Mouloud Hamrouche in 1989–1991) the effects of such policies remained limited. At the beginning of 1995 Algeria's public sector still accounted for 70 percent of the country's GNP, still employed probably a third of the workforce, and only managed to function at 50 percent of its capacity.[67]

Nevertheless, in January 1995 Michel Camdessus, managing director of the IMF, applauded the efforts the Algerian government had made to liberalize the economy, stating that the requirements attached to the fund's loan of April 1994 had been "scrupulously" adhered to. The fund pointed to reductions in the country's budget deficit and a level of inflation lower than forecast, and thus felt able to agree to a further $1.8 billion loan to Algeria in the form of a three-year extended fund facility at the end of May 1995.[68] But although the government had also secured a World Bank loan explicitly to support its reform program, and created a specific Ministry of Privatization in April, prospects for further reform still appeared limited.[69]

The sheer weight of Algeria's political and social crises continued to marginalize any advances that were made in the economic sphere. The continuing civil strife inside the country presented a clear disincentive to foreign investors, with foreign workers having been targeted and killed by elements of the Islamist opposition since 1993. Indeed, the whole privatization program that became central to the government's liberalizing reforms in 1995 rested on the fundamental but dubious premise that either domestic or foreign buyers could be found to purchase state-owned enterprises in such an uncertain and violent climate. Furthermore, it was suggested that even those advances that had been made in the areas of inflation and the budget deficit were, perversely, actually the products of the conflict: Government employees were too concerned with their own personal safety to request salary increases for themselves or supplies for their jobs.[70]

Even those reforms that were successfully implemented failed to achieve any advances toward the ultimate long-term aim of the program: the alleviation of the poverty and the resultant despair that had fueled much of the violent opposition to the regime. Indeed, they arguably worsened it. As one commentator observed in 1994 of the effects of the whole reform program on the general populace, "Algeria's economic managers have succeeded over the last three years in accumulating all the adverse effects of an economic readjustment programme and none of it benefits."[71] Unemployment, already at close to 30 percent in 1995, remained high and looked set to dramatically worsen with a possible quarter of a million workers to be made redundant as a result of the ongoing reforms.[72] Cuts in state subsidies in 1994 had raised prices on staple foodstuffs and a 40 percent devaluation of the dinar had further raised food costs, since Algeria imported two-thirds of its food needs—a proportion that expanded in 1994 due to a domestic drought.[73] (Despite having reduced state intervention in the agricultural sector to levels below those found in any other Maghrebi country by 1991, farming yields remained the lowest in the entire Mediterranean.)[74] GDP growth in 1994 had virtually come to a halt: At 0.1 percent it was well short of the IMF's forecast of 3 percent, and nowhere near the 6 percent level estimated to be necessary to maintain even the existing low level of living standards in the face of one of the world's most prodigious birthrates.[75] It remained to be seen if the loosening of Algeria's debt repayments, and a consequent $33 billion three-year domestic spending program announced in April 1995, would have any impact on the dire and clearly deteriorating situation.[76]

Nevertheless, the imperative of comprehensive economic reform remained, in the eyes of free market–oriented observers, essential if Algeria was to achieve long-term political and social stability. *The Economist,* for example, remarked: "Whatever palliatives may be adopted, unemployment and discontent will rise—rapidly, albeit for a short time maybe, if reform goes ahead, slowly but lastingly if not."[77] Moreover, the colossal size of Algeria's debt and the comprehensive nature of its agreements with its creditors in international institutions, commercial banks, and foreign governments had arguably locked the country into its program of reforms. As one Algerian daily newspaper commented:

> The government, facing payment dates bound to its international commit-
> ments with institutions like the IMF and the World Bank, considers liber-
> alisation in general and privatisation in particular as irreversible.[78]

The Political Field

The end result of Algeria's significant but brief moves toward political liberalization appeared, from the perspective of 1995, to be violent conflict and
political chaos—even if the presidential elections of November have nudged
the situation in a less negative direction. Other regimes in North Africa and
beyond that had experienced social, political, and economic problems similar to those faced by Algeria in the 1980s, congratulated themselves for not
having taken the ambitious steps Algeria had to liberalize its political system, and thus having saved themselves the upheavals and deepening crisis
that befell Algeria. For other observers, though, the central flaw in Algeria's
program of political liberalization was essentially the same as that in its economic liberalization program: that the reforms were never fully implemented, or rather, in the political field, they were abandoned midway, creating the
conditions of frustrated hope that could only lead to political and social
unrest.

Technically speaking, Algeria's political system had become more liberal than it had been before October 1988—political parties were legal and
the press, although facing increasing restrictions in 1995, was still much
freer—but the violent nature of the regime's struggle with its Islamist opponents had created an atmosphere that was far more politically repressive. Not
only did the regime increasingly employ torture and detention without trial
in its battle against the Islamist militants, but the Islamists themselves had
launched attacks and assassinations on anyone—including writers and secular politicians—not conforming to their prescriptions for Algerian society.[79]

Prospects for further political reform remain uncertain. Indications of
flexibility on both the government's and the opposition's side have been cut
across by instances of intransigence. The latter is evidence of the existence
of powerful opposing elements within Algeria that see only a military solution to the country's crisis, and to whom compromise and political solutions
are consequently anathema.

President Zerou.al's attempts at dialogue with the FIS in 1994 were
strongly resisted by important figures in both the government—notably
Redha Malek, who resigned as prime minister in April 1994 in protest at the
attempts—and, more importantly, in the military—notably Lieutenant-
General Mohammed Lamari, the chief of staff. On the Islamist side, the
three-year-old armed struggle had seen the emergence of radical groups
operating largely independently of the FIS and its armed wing, who viewed
any deal with the government as inimical to Islam and who threatened any

Islamists participating in dialogue with the authorities with "the worst of deaths."[80] These groups, collectively known as the GIA (*Groupes Islamiques Armés,* or Armed Islamic Groups), were responsible for most of the violent and bloody excesses of the Islamist armed campaign.

The result of the 1995 presidential elections appeared to increase the possibility of dialogue. President Zeroual, while vowing to fight terrorism, pledged his commitment to dialogue with all those renouncing violence. Nevertheless, at the end of 1995 key hard-line generals remained in place and it appeared that Zeroual was moving only cautiously. Yet the election result undoubtedly strengthened his hand vis-à-vis hard-line challengers.

The legal opposition parties that had boycotted the elections afterwards declared their willingness to hold talks with the president—in effect recognizing the election result. Most tellingly, the FIS's leader in exile, Rabah Kebir, wrote a letter to Zeroual in which he, too, appeared to recognize the election and reaffirmed the willingness of the FIS to try and find a solution in cooperation with the authorities. On this side, too, however, there were countervailing forces. A prominent FIS member and the party's former Washington representative, Anwar Haddam, attacked the Kebir letter. Meanwhile the GIA again stepped up their assassination campaign in December 1995. Yet the overall impression of the mainstream FIS at this time was one of a party eager "to ditch its image as a promoter of indiscriminate violence."[81] Haddam was openly criticized, and the GIA came under increasing rhetorical attack from the FIS leadership. The situation, then, remained in some degree of flux at the close of 1995.

The Future: Are Algeria, Islamism, and Liberalization Compatible?

Overall, it would seem that although Algeria does have the opportunity and, many would argue, the need to move further down the twin paths of political and economic liberalization, this possibility will be severely hampered by substantial social and political unrest and the sharply declining economic and social conditions in Algeria on which such unrest feeds. In return, the political conflict in Algeria is increasingly serving to feed economic collapse as mounting death threats and fatal attacks against foreigners by some Islamist groups have led to the flight of virtually all foreign nationals from Algeria since late 1993. The adverse effect this has had on the oil and gas sector, so reliant on foreign expertise, threatens to strike at the very source Algeria's rulers hope their economic and thus political salvation will come from.[82]

While most Western observers have consistently urged the continuation of both political and economic reform, there have been dissident voices both within and outside Algeria. Most criticism of the reform programs has been directed at those who sought to liberalize the economy, and has come largely from old supporters of Boumedienne's policies of state ownership and heavy industrialization, who blame the country's current economic travails on the abandonment of these policies by Chadli Ben Jedid.[83] However, there are those commentators who argue that Chadli's pursuit of political liberalization, of the largely Western-democratic type, was at best premature and at worst unsuitable. John Entelis, for example, has argued that the whole notion of democracy, as understood in the West, was "a truly alien culture in Algeria" and that even among francophone intellectuals, "liberal democratic principles . . . have never been taken seriously."[84] Indeed, it could be argued that the "exhilarating rebirth of political life" that Robert Mortimer observed in the run-up to the local elections in 1990 was shown to be fairly superficial given the fact that roughly three-quarters of the votes cast in both the 1990 and 1991 were for parties whose commitment to democratization was either grudging (the FLN) or extremely dubious (the FIS).

The issue of the FIS's attitude toward both economic and political liberalization is worth briefly addressing, since there is a significant likelihood that the party, or some successor grouping, will have at least some say in the governing of Algeria in the future.

Much attention has been focused on the extent to which the FIS was committed to democratic elections as a continuing and worthy end in themselves rather than a simple means to impose their own particular and austere ideal of Algerian life. The FIS leaders engaged in a curious doublespeak on this issue in the run-up to both the 1990 and 1991 elections: Its leader, Abbasi Madani, stressed the party's commitment to pluralism and tolerance, while his deputy, Ali Belhaj, equated democracy with unbelief and threatened to "trample on" and repress other political parties not based on Islam.[85] Despite such pronouncements, and the often horrific excesses of some of the armed Islamist groups, it is possible to point to the FIS's participation in the Rome Declaration as a possible indication of the conversion, at least of the party's leadership, to the main tenets of liberal democracy. By adding their signature to the platform the representatives of the FIS formally and for the first time committed the party to the principles of "multipartyism," "respect for popular legitimacy," change of government through elections, and "respect for the fundamental liberties . . . of sex, confession, and language."[86] That such an endorsement was fully backed by Ali Belhaj, with whom the representatives of the FIS had channels of communication, may be even more encouraging. The reaction of the FIS to the 1995 presidential elections, outlined earlier, again appears to confirm a majority view within the party leadership in favor of participation in a pluralist political process, with the attendant negotiation and compromise.

The progress of economic liberalization under any future government run by or including Islamists is similarly uncertain. Though the FIS did put out several successive documents on economic policy during its election campaigns, these have been rightly characterized as "general and vague," containing little real detail. Initial literature produced by the party supported the traditional "Islamic" preference for free trade—blaming state planning for the economic failures of the past and seeking to encourage private ownership and entrepreneurship.[87] Such a stance even encouraged economic reformists within the government to view the FIS as a possible ally in the struggle against their opponents in the FLN and the bureaucracy.[88] However, later statements by some party leaders took a far more critical line toward the government's reform program. Abbasi Madani, for example, in 1991 characterized the reforms as "nothing more than an operation to enable the regime to steal from the pockets of citizens." He also condemned the government's opening of the country to foreign competition, which he described as "a dangerous deviation from Algerian history."[89] Abdelkader Hachani, the FIS's provisional leader in the run-up to the 1991 elections, displayed a similarly hostile attitude toward foreign involvement in the Algerian economy. The key liberalizing reform—allowing foreign participation in Algeria's oil and gas fields—was denounced by him as a "transaction of shame" and he dismissed a recent ECU 400 million European Community loan to Algeria as a gesture "made by countries who are enemies of Islam." Furthermore, Hachani stated that although he was not opposed to privatization on religious grounds, he opposed it for "publicly owned strategic industries."[90] However, there was a parallel recognition that such sentiments would probably have to bow to the "realities" of international economics, just as the existing regime had had to abandon its nationalistic distrust of foreign involvement.[91] During the 1991 elections, leaders of the FIS stated their commitment to maintaining relations with the IMF and other foreign creditors and their intention of standing by Algeria's existing international treaties and agreements.[92] Discreet contacts had also been established by the FIS with foreign governments and multinationals to reassure them of the security of their investments in the event of an FIS victory.[93]

Overall, though, the major questions facing the Algerian state as it enters the mid-1990s do not concern the issues of political and economic liberalization so much as the stark and basic issue of survival. There will have to be substantial improvements in both the country's economic performance and its political consensus if it is not to slide into political and economic disintegration of the type witnessed in Lebanon in the 1970s and 1980s.

Three things need to be achieved in the shorter term to prevent this doomsday scenario prevailing in the longer term. First, there needs to be a significant rise in the revenues Algeria receives from its oil and gas exports; second, a degree of political and social peace needs to be reestablished; third, and perhaps most important, there needs to be a slowdown in the country's prodigious birthrate. Political and economic liberalization can help to achieve at least two of these aims. Whether Algeria's current or future rulers will prove to have either the will or the ability to achieve these goals, however, remains very much in question.

Notes

1. D. Vandewalle, "Breaking With Socialism: Economic Liberalization and Privatization in Algeria," in I. Harik and D. Sullivan, eds., *Privatization and Liberalization in the Middle East* (Indianapolis: Indiana University Press, 1992), pp. 189–196; J. Ruedy, *Modern Algeria: The Origins and Development of a Nation* (Indianapolis, Ind.: Indiana University Press, 1992), pp. 231–237.

2. For details on the Berberist, Islamist, and women's movements in this period see, respectively: S. Mehzoud, "Glasnost the Algerian Way: The role of Berber nationalists in political reform," in G. Joffé, ed., *North Africa: Nation, State and Region* (London: Routledge, 1993), pp. 142–169; H. Roberts, "Radical Islamism and the Dilemma of Algerian Nationalism: The Embattled Arians of Algiers," *Third World Quarterly* (Vol. 10, No. 2, April 1988); P. Knauss, *The Persistence of Patriarchy: Class, Gender and Ideology in Twentieth Century Algeria* (New York: Praeger, 1987).

3. C. H. Moore, "Political Parties," in I. W. Zartman and W. Habeeb, eds., *Polity and Society in Contemporary North Africa* (Boulder: Westview, 1993), p. 62. There was, however, legislation passed in 1987 that permitted the formation of associations concerned with such low-level political issues such as culture and consumer defense. See Y. Zoubir, "The Painful Transition from Authoritarianism in Algeria," *Arab Studies Quarterly* (Vol. 15, No.3, Summer 1993), pp. 86–87.

4. J. Entelis, "State and Society in Transition," in J. Entelis and P. Naylor, eds., *State and Society in Algeria* (Boulder: Westview, 1992), p.18.

5. L. Rummel, "Privatization and Democratization in Algeria," in Entelis and Naylor, *State and Society in Algeria*, pp. 55–60. Mahfoud Bennoune disputes this view of the riots, claiming that the primary motivation for the unrest was indeed economic and social factors: "During initial attacks and looting the rioters raised no slogans or political demands. When demands finally came, they were for jobs, housing and state services. . . . The demands never included calls for pluralism and democracy, as Benjedid later claimed." See M. Bennoune, "Algeria's Façade of Democracy," *Middle East Report,* March–April 1990.

6. B. Dillman, "Transition to Democracy in Algeria," in Entelis and Naylor, *State and Society in Algeria,* p. 32; R. Mortimer, "Islam and Multiparty Politics in Algeria," *Middle East Journal,* Vol. 45, No. 4, Autumn 1991, pp. 578–579.

7. D. Pool, "The Links Between Political and Economic Liberalization," in T. Niblock and E. Murphy, eds., *Economic and Political Liberalization in the Middle East* (London: British Academic Press, 1993), p. 52.

8. F. Burgat and W. Dowell, *The Islamic Movement in North Africa* (Center for Middle Eastern Studies at the University of Texas at Austin, 1993), p. 269.

9. Mortimer, "Islam and multiparty politics in Algeria," p. 579. Abdelhamid Brahimi, Chadli's prime minister from 1984 to 1988, argues that the whole run of events from October 1988, including the riots themselves, was deliberately orchestrated by the president to preserve his position, since he had begun to fear that the FLN would not nominate him again as president for the forthcoming presidential "election" in November 1988. By creating a political crisis, Chadli was thus able to ensure his reselection by portraying himself as a stabilizing force. However, the fact that these accusations were made by Brahimi, the undisputed architect of the economic reform program in the 1980s (he had been minister of planning before becoming prime minister and was sacked in the wake of the crisis), undermines the argument that Chadli had acted purely to defend his economic liberalization program. Author's interview with Abdelhamid Brahimi, London, 19 December 1994.

10. R. Payne, "Economic Crisis and Policy Reform in the 1980s," in Zartman and Habeeb, *Polity and Society in Contemporary North Africa,* p. 161. Indeed, Payne

argues that political events had little effect on the economic reform program at all, as was indicated by the passage of a reformist budget through the National Assembly in December 1988.

11. Ibid.

12. Dillman in Entelis and Naylor, *State and Society in Algeria,* pp. 41–42.

13. Vandewalle in Harik and Sullivan, *Privatization and Liberalization in the Middle East,* pp. 199–201.

14. J. Entelis, *Algeria: The Revolution Institutionalized* (Boulder: Westview, 1986), pp. 132–133.

15. T. Niblock, "International and Domestic Factors in the Economic Liberalization Process in Arab Countries," in Niblock and Murphy, *Economic and Political Liberalization in the Middle East,* p. 72. Algeria did not even have its revenues from natural gas to fall back on after the collapse in the price of oil, since the price of gas had been linked to that of oil in 1982, the result of a long, and now bitterly ironic, campaign by the Algerian government, and thus gas revenues fell with the price of oil in 1985–1986. See Entelis, *Algeria: The Revolution Institutionalized,* pp. 115–122.

16. *The Middle East,* October 1991.

17. Dillman in Entelis and Naylor, p. 41.

18. *Middle East Economic Digest* (MEED), 23 February 1990.

19. *MEED,* 9 August 1991.

20. Ibid.

21. Ruedy, *Modern Algeria,* pp. 247–248.

22. *MEED,* 2 November 1990.

23. Mortimer, p. 583.

24. The *Mouvement pour la Démocratie en Algérie* (MDA) and the *Front des Forces Socialistes* (FFS), both headed by one of the "nine historic chiefs" of the war of liberation, boycotted the local elections on the grounds that the parties had not been given enough time to prepare for the elections.

25. For a full account of the formation and nature of the FIS, see Burgat and Dowell, *The Islamic Movement in North Africa,* pp. 273–276; and M. Al-Ahnaf, B. Botiveau, and F. Frégosi, *L'Algérie par ses Islamistes* (Paris: Karthala, 1991), pp. 29–34.

26. K. Sutton, A. Aghrout, and S. Zaimche, "Political Changes in Algeria: An Emerging Electoral Geography," *Maghreb Review,* Vol. 17, Nos. 1 and 2, 1992, pp. 18–19.

27. Ibid., p. 9.

28. Mortimer, p. 584. Some observers have suggested that Chadli even contemplated forging an electoral alliance with the FIS (ibid.).

29. Mortimer, p. 586.

30. For details of this, see Burgat and Dowell, *The Islamic Movement in North Africa,* pp. 287–291.

31. Mortimer, pp. 588–589; Zoubir, "The Painful Transition from Authoritarianism in Algeria," p. 98.

32. Mortimer, p. 588. This highlighted the irony and contradiction of an exclusively FLN National Assembly voting to destroy itself.

33. For details of the battles between the government and the PNA, see *The Economist,* 28 September, 12 October, and 9 November 1991.

34. *Algérie Actualité,* 9 May 1991 and 30 May 1991. The relative scores for the FIS and the FLN, respectively, in the two polls were 33–24 and 29–36. No other parties recorded preferences of more than 10 percent in either poll.

35. F. Burgat and J. Leca, "La mobilisation islamiste et les élections algériennes du 12 juin 1990," *Maghreb-Machrek,* No. 129, July–September 1990, pp. 7–8.

36. *Algérie Actualité,* 27 June 1991.

37. Mortimer, p. 590.

38. Ibid., p. 583.

39. H. Roberts, "The FLN: French conceptions, Algerian realities," in Joffé, *North Africa,* p. 112.

40. J. Entelis, "The Crisis of Authoritarianism in North Africa: The Case of Algeria," *Problems of Communism,* May–June 1992, p. 79.

41. Differing views exist on the performance of the FIS in local government between 1990 and 1992. Though there were reports of FIS-run local councils clamping down on dress and entertainment and turning a blind eye to attacks on "improperly" dressed women (see Dillman in Entelis and Naylor, p. 39, and *The Independent,* 6 June 1991), other observers point out that many of these supposed incidents were government propaganda and many of the "changes" introduced by the FIS administrations were policies already introduced by the previous FLN administration (see Burgat and Dowell, *The Islamic Movement in North Africa,* pp. 284–285).

42. Zoubir, "The painful transition from authoritarianism in Algeria," pp. 101–102. For fuller details of the results of the first ballot, see A. Lamchichi, *L'Islamisme en Algérie* (Paris: L'Harmattan, 1992), pp. 81–83.

43. Zoubir, "The painful transition from authoritarianism in Algeria," p. 97.

44. P. Dévoluy and M. Duteil: *La Poudrière Algérienne* (France: Calmann-Lévy, 1994), pp. 45 and 47.

45. *MEED,* 24 January 1992; Burgat and Dowell, pp. 301–303. The High Security Council explained this deviation from the constitution by stating that the constitution made no provision for the simultaneous absence of a National Assembly and a president, so had temporarily taken on itself the role of legislature with the assent of the head of the Constitutional Council. Burgat and Dowell, p. 302n.

46. *MEED,* 21 June 1991.

47. Niblock in Niblock and Murphy, p. 76.

48. Vandewalle in Harik and Sullivan, p. 192.

49. *Financial Times,* 2 April 1992.

50. Opinions differ sharply on Ghozali's attitude toward reform. Vandewalle argues that he was sacked as Energy Minister in the 1970s for "promoting market-orientated policies" (Vandewalle in Harik and Sullivan, p. 201), while Entelis characterizes him as a "neo-Boumediennist" (Entelis in *Problems of Communism,* p. 79).

51. Francis Ghilès in *Middle East International,* 4 March 1994. Zartman argues, however, that economic and political liberalization might actually have helped to consolidate the power of the military by weakening that of the FLN. Quoted by Rummel in Entelis and Naylor, p. 64.

52. For fuller accounts of the Boudiaf assassination and the reasons behind it see Dévoluy and Duteil, op. cit., pp. 190–215; and *The Independent,* 24 July 1992.

53. *Financial Times,* 24 August 1993.

54. *Financial Times,* 24 August 1993; Economist Intelligence Unit (EIU), *Country Report: Algeria* 1993, No. 3.

55. *Financial Times,* 24 August 1993.

56. *MEED,* 17 September 1993.

57. EIU, *Country Report: Algeria,* 1993, No. 4.

58. *Summary of World Broadcasts* MEW/0318 WME/2, 1 February 1994.

59. *Financial Times,* 28 February 1994.

60. *MEED,* 25 February 1994; *Financial Times,* 28 January 1994.

61. *El-Moudjahid,* 3 May 1994.

62. *The Guardian,* 10 February and 5 March 1992.

63. A study carried out by the Algerian national research center on the results of the first ballot for the National Assembly elections in December 1991 found that

only 50 percent of those Algerians who voted for the FIS actually supported the party's main objective of "Islamic" rule—suggesting that they had voted more to block and defeat the FLN than to support the FIS. *Financial Times,* 30 January 1992.

64. *Summary of World Broadcasts* ME/1917 MED, 9 February 1994.

65. *Platform for a Political and Peaceful Solution to the Algerian Crisis,* 13 January 1995. The platform won the support of the FIS, the FLN (which as a party had become effectively estranged from the regime), the FFS, the MDA, the small legal Islamist party, Ennahda, and two smaller parties.

66. See *Middle East International,* 17 November and 1 December 1995; and reporting in *Le Monde, Financial Times,* and *Weekly Guardian* over the period 20 November–20 December 1995. Also see *The Middle East,* January 1996, pp. 6–7.

67. *Financial Times,* 24 February 1995. In the view of one diplomat, Algeria's state industries remained "semi-paralysed." *Financial Times,* 3–4 September 1994.

68. *Financial Times,* 19 January 1995; *MEED,* 2 June 1995.

69. *La Tribune,* 4 May 1995; EIU, *Country Report: Algeria,* 1995, No.1.

70. *Financial Times,* 19 January and 24 February 1995.

71. *Middle East International,* 4 March 1994.

72. *Financial Times,* 24 February 1995.

73. *Financial Times,* 13 March and 3–4 September 1994.

74. Vandewalle in Harik and Sullivan p. 192; *Financial Times,* 17 November 1993.

75. *Financial Times,* 19 January 1995; *Daily Telegraph,* 1 February 1994.

76. *MEED,* 21 April 1995.

77. *The Economist,* 15 January 1994.

78. *Liberté,* 3 May 1995.

79. See Middle East Watch, *Human Rights Abuses in Algeria,* January 1994.

80. *El Watan,* 28 February 1994.

81. H. Saleh, "Zeroual's Caution," *Middle East International,* 15 December 1995, p. 13.

82. *The Middle East,* March 1994; *Financial Times,* 29 October 1993.

83. See M. Bennoune and R. Tlemcani in *Middle East Report,* March–April 1990. Bennoune has also stated that the pursuit of economic liberalization has resulted in "the deterioration of the political and administrative environment as a whole"—the natural result of the withdrawal of the state from management of the economy. M. Bennoune, *The Making of Contemporary Algeria 1830–1987* (Cambridge: Cambridge University Press, 1988), p. 271.

84. Entelis in *Middle East Insight,* Vol. 6, No. 3, 1988, quoted by Rummel in Entelis and Naylor p. 68; Entelis in Entelis and Naylor, pp. 20–21. Such an opinion is disputed by M. Benoune, who argues that pre-Arab society, as well as early resistance and the war against the French (with its values of freedom and popular sovereignty), indicated that democratic values were indigenous to Algeria and had played a key role in the country's development. See Bennoune, *The Making of Contemporary Algeria.*

85. *Middle East Report,* September–October 1990; *Financial Times,* 11 January 1992. For a more detailed analysis of the FIS's writings on and attitude toward *democracy,* see Al-Ahnaf in Botiveau and Frégosi, pp. 87–103.

86. *Platform for a Political and Peaceful Solution,* op. cit.

87. A. Layachi and A. Haireche, "National Development and Political Protest: Islamists in the Maghreb Countries," *Arab Studies Quarterly,* Vol. 14, Nos. 2 and 3, Spring/Summer 1992, p. 79.

88. Ghazi Hidouci, the Algerian economics minister and a leading reformer, was reported to have remarked of the FIS in 1989 that "they are more liberal than us."

Algérie Actualité, 11 June 1992. For a fuller analysis of this issue see H. Roberts, "Doctrinaire Economics and Political Opportunism in the Strategy of Algerian Islamism," in J. Ruedy, ed., *Islamism and Secularism in North Africa* (London: Macmillan, 1994), pp. 123–147.

89. *Horizons,* 5 May 1991.

90. *Financial Times,* 8 January 1992. For a fuller analysis of the FIS's attitude toward the economy see Al-Ahnaf, Botiveau, and Frégosi, pp. 150–203.

91. The circumspect attitude of the FIS toward particularly foreign involvement in the Algerian economy arguably owed more to nationalistic traditions present within the party than to any more theological position or reasoning. Abbasi Madani had been a member of the seminal FLN at the beginning of the independence struggle against France in the 1950s and Hachani belonged to a faction of the party that put more emphasis on Algeria's national identity.

92. *Financial Times,* 8 January 1992; *The Independent,* 30 December 1991.

93. *Financial Times,* 30 December 1991.

PART 4

EAST ASIA

12

The Origins of Economic Liberalization and Democratization in South Korea

TAT YAN KONG

Continuous and Discontinuous Transitions

The 1980s and 1990s witnessed the demise of various systems of authoritarian industrialization in Latin America, Northeast Asia (Taiwan and South Korea), and Eastern Europe. By "authoritarian industrialization" I refer to closed political systems in which the government exerts a high degree of economic control for the sake of accelerating industrialization. Such control may be market-conforming as in Northeast Asia, but could also bypass market signals altogether as in Eastern Europe.[1] Nevertheless all three cases share one common important feature, namely the view that bureaucratic action plays a vital role in the modernization of society.

Experience suggests that the transition from authoritarian industrialization is usually followed by a combination of democratization and economic liberalization. The transition may take either a discontinuous or a continuous path.[2] The collapse of the authoritarian regime represents the discontinuous path. On the other hand, authoritarian leaders may remain in power and gradually modify their political and economic practices (the continuous path). In the former path, democratization precedes economic reform and arrives suddenly as authoritarianism collapses amid public disapproval. This is followed by pressure to quickly reverse the authoritarian economic agenda. On the continuous path, however, the transformation is altogether less dramatic because economic and political reforms are interwoven over a long period as the authoritarian leaders dictate the pace of change. Having initiated much of the process of change themselves, they also develop a positive stake in the final outcome. The principal determinant of whether a continuous or a discontinuous transition is made from authoritarian industrialization is economic performance. Rapid political disintegration is normally associated with economic failure and deteriorating living standards. By contrast, those regimes that preside over economic success are in a better position to take the continuous path of gradual reform.

229

In a discontinuous transition, democratization brings with it powerful pressures for economic reform because economic failure and its social costs is usually one of the factors that spark political dissent against authoritarianism. At the practical level, democratization also undermines the bureaucratic mechanisms (for example, the capacity to enforce distributional outcomes) on which the authoritarian economic project depended. On assuming power, democratic-opposition leaders are compelled to follow the reform route by past promises, expedience, and genuine belief. But why should economic reform take the form of liberalization? That the economic failings and political costs of authoritarian industrialization become an indictment of government intervention per se is one answer—here, Eastern Europe after 1989 is a good case in point. Another answer lies at the international level. The wave of transitions from authoritarian industrialization mentioned above occurred in the context of the global ascendancy of free-market ideas reflecting both disillusionment with the results of economic intervention and the new opportunities posed by growing integration.

In the continuous transition from authoritarian industrialization, the background of successful economic performance allows the authoritarian leaders greater room for maneuver, and to implement reforms piecemeal and consistently with their own long-term interests. If any sequence exists, it is the preference for economic reform first. This is based on the observation that a growing economy provides the means for the alleviation of social discontent, and the belief that growth helps to stave off democratization pressures or allows the incumbents to relinquish power at a favorable moment. If the danger of imminent political collapse is absent, then what motivates the transition from authoritarian industrialization? The answer is that having delivered economic success, authoritarian industrialization is no longer sustainable for the following reasons:

1. Existing policies no longer fit the changed external environment.
2. Having achieved its objective, a policy may then be discontinued.
3. Success has raised new problems and calls for new policies.

The case of South Korea (hereinafter Korea) falls into the category of the continuous transition from authoritarian industrialization. Although democratization in 1987 was forced on the regime by mass popular protests, it had been preceded by a period of political accommodation characterized by constitutional dialogue and semicompetitive party politics (there was an election in 1985). Economic liberalization was announced in the early 1980s (when political repression was at its height) and is still continuing today. Nevertheless, the 1980s marked the transition to a democratized polity and a liberalized economy from the authoritarian industrialization pattern established under President Park in the preceding two decades. This chapter will focus on explaining the origins of that process, namely the factors that impelled Park's successors to embark on a course of reform.

The economic success (GNP growth of 9.5 percent per year from 1962 to 1978) delivered by authoritarian industrialization in Korea during the 1960s and 1970s could be explained by the following institutional features:

1. Discipline over the private sector through economic and administrative controls with incentives exchanged for high performance from the business sector[3]
2. Mobilization and control of high-quality labor[4]
3. An authoritarian political system that precluded economic alternatives[5]
4. Creation of the conditions for mass political compliance by meeting the aspirations for material improvement.

The three factors listed earlier underlying the policy change can be used to explain why Korea's authoritarian industrialization pattern had become unsustainable by the end of the 1970s.

Promoting Economic Growth

The basis of economic intervention under Park was the policy of targeted subsidies. Firms were given subsidized credit and other incentives in exchange for the fulfillment of performance criteria, notably export growth and capacity expansion.[6] In this way, infant industries received the necessary subsidies but at the same time derived the benefits of international trade such as competitiveness and economies of scale. With its export orientation, Korean industry avoided the problem of inefficiency that plagued the subsidized industries of most developing countries. Through its control of the financial system, the Korean government would reward companies in the strategic industries, namely export winners and potential winners. On the other hand, recalcitrants could be punished (for example, by being denied credit and having to borrow at exorbitant rates from the unofficial financial sector or "kerb" market). In the 1960s this system was responsible for the development of light industry (textiles, garments, footwear, toys, etc.) into export winners. Investment priority was given in the 1970s to heavy and chemical industry (HCI) with a view to developing the export winners of the future: steel, machinery, shipbuilding, chemicals, electronics, and cars. By 1978, most of manufacturing output was accounted for by HCI.

Without the incentive system it is doubtful that Korea would have developed such a vast HCI capacity (the sectors that constitute its present-day export successes) in the space of a decade. In hindsight the program was undoubtedly a success. Even though the gloomy prognoses of the early 1980s (when HCI was uncompetitive and working well below capacity) were dispelled, the experience of HCI in the 1970s pointed to the limitations of the authoritarian industrialization pattern in the face of a changing external and domestic policy context.

External Economic Conditions

The rising cost of imported oil undoubtedly contributed to the Korean economy's experience of negative growth in 1979–1980. For the nascent capital-intensive sector the problem was particularly serious. Not only did expensive oil raise production costs but it also helped to push Korea's principal export markets (the United States and Europe) into recession. Another source of the recession that had more profound implications for Korean economic policy was the deflationary strategy adopted in the industrialized countries. The resurgence of neoclassical economics in the 1970s as the orthodoxy of the industrialized economies put price stability and sound public finances (rather than growth) at the core of economic policy. It preached that government should confine itself to creating the conditions for private enterprise to deliver growth by macroeconomic stabilization—beyond that government risked overreaching itself and stifling the private sector (the real source of wealth creation) in the process. This was highly significant for Korea. The new orthodoxy permeated the international agencies (the World Bank and the IMF) upon whose financial assistance Korea depended. The country assessments made by these agencies also affected creditworthiness with international bankers. Along with other developing countries requiring refinancing, Korea had to demonstrate commitment to the tenets of the new orthodoxy with which the growth policies of the 1970s (detailed interventionism, financial repression, overvalued exchange rate, tolerance of high inflation) were at variance.

Even had there been no oil shock or recession, there were other international processes pushing Korean economic development along a new trajectory in the 1980s. The election of a conservative government in the United States in 1980 was a political boost for the new military rulers in Seoul but also a source of economic pressure. The 1980s marked a new U.S. approach to trade reciprocity: Politically indispensable allies (notably Japan and Korea) would no longer be allowed to get away with protectionism.[7] The United States was and remains Korea's biggest export market. The neoclassical resurgence in economics was also an indication of the acceleration of international economic integration made possible by new technology: Production and finance would increasingly take place on a global scale. These trends presented enormous opportunities for meeting the resource requirements (finance from capital markets, technology transfer from multinational joint ventures, etc.) of the next stage of Korean industrialization. To capitalize on these potential benefits required further opening up of the Korean economy to international capital and investment flows. But this also heightened the risk of foreign control over domestic industry, a problem over which Korean policymakers have consistently shown concern. From the perspective of policy, the implication of integration could not be ignored: Past policies designed to promote national economic interests would now have to be modified and rendered consistent with intensified liberalization pressures.

From "Big Push" to Efficiency

Government support for the rise of HCI and its consequences raised important issues about the appropriate role of intervention in a maturing industrial structure. The need for macroeconomic stabilization (a process keenly watched overseas) and the problems associated with the promotion of HCI (notably underdeveloped economic infrastructure, and business concentration) pointed toward more market-consistent policy reforms. Because of its long gestation period, HCI could only be expected to fulfill an import-substitution role during its infancy. In contrast to the labor-intensive sectors where government support was linked to export growth, incentives for HCI were linked to the expansion of productive capacity and not international competitiveness. The aim of the HCI development program was to establish productive capacity first through the Big Push, a policy also dictated by military requirements. Less attention was paid to efficiency, and quantitative targets determined the allocation of finance. (In the highly capital-intensive industries such as petrochemicals, Korea was simply not suited to international competition.) This encouraged companies to make unsound investments and to duplicate facilities. It questioned the wisdom of credit allocation by official fiat and opened up a debate concerning the efficiency of continued official dominance of the financial sector, the cornerstone of government economic leadership. Moreover, once the original aim of building up capacity was achieved, the agenda logically turned toward efficiency.

Apart from the faster rate of world-trade growth in the 1960s, it was much easier for standardized labor-intensive items (such as textiles and footwear) to penetrate Western markets by virtue of lower prices. In contrast, achieving export competitiveness in HCI depended heavily on the quality factor. This necessitated government intervention in the provision of economic infrastructure—technology, research and development, and human-resource development—a function well suited to government in that it requires vast resources and yields long-term social payoffs. The appropriate role for government in the 1980s seemed to be shifting toward indirect intervention.

Rise of the Chaebol

The problems associated with the rise of big business were further stimulus to economic-policy reform. Those companies that had achieved impressive export records were selected by the government to be the agencies of heavy industrialization in the 1970s. The chosen companies diversified quickly and became the multifaceted industrial conglomerates known as *chaebol* (such as Hyundai and Samsung).[8] Diversification was a sensible option for individual *chaebol* because cheap credit provided a cost-free opportunity to become established in the "frontier" industries, especially since rival conglomerates were doing the same. The result, however, was the creation of industrial groups far more diversified than Western multinationals. They tried to enter such a wide variety of activities that they ended up in many to which they were unsuited. Smaller companies that might have been more efficient were crowded out by the *chaebol*'s financial muscle.[9] While the *chaebol* were large by international standards in terms of overall size, their individual subsidiaries were weak in relation to their foreign competitors from the industrialized countries. Far from spreading their risk, the policy of diversification actually raised the specter of chain-bankruptcies as the financially vulnerable subsidiaries of the dominant groups were interconnected by cross-holding and centralized ownership. Clearly there was a pressing need to rationalize the industrial structure by giving more opportunities for small- and medium-sized industry (SMI) and separating the *chaebol* from the "peripheral" activities to which they were not suited.

The involvement of the *chaebol* in the unproductive forms of investment also cast doubt over the government allocation of finance. Very low rates of interest meant that there was credit rationing, with the losers (smaller companies lacking collateral and those lacking government backing) having to borrow at very high rates (20 to 50 percent per year) from the unofficial financial market or kerb market.[10] This enabled the recipients of official credit to make enormous profits by relending on the kerb.[11] Alternatively, there was the option of investing in Seoul real estate, the demand for residential and commercial property there being insatiable due to the pace of urbanization. The dynamic of *chaebol* expansion, their benefiting at the expense of smaller companies and households, and lopsided industrial structure raised efficiency and equity questions about the nature of government intervention.

From the perspective of national development it was necessary for the Korean government to intervene, to ensure that HCI got the funds for rapid expansion and to create companies of comparable size to those of the established multinationals. The market on its own was incapable of bringing such a transformation about. But by the end of the 1970s the development agenda had shifted. With the much-needed productive capacity having been created, the question was now about making the investments pay. The question of efficiency (made even more pressing by the external economic factors) opened the way for market-oriented policies (for example, liberalization of the domestic market as a means of disciplining the *chaebol*) as well as alternative forms of government intervention.

Labor Controls

During the 1960s, waves of migration from the countryside provided the industrial sector with an unlimited supply of low-cost labor. The availability of basic education ensured that this labor was of a high quality. Exploitation was reinforced by the absence of labor unions, the background of rural poverty, the absence of social provision, and a political system that repressed the tiniest manifestations of socialism. With the installation of the dictatorial Yushin Constitution in 1972, labor controls were tightened further. Yet the 1970s witnessed the failure of these control mechanisms as wage increases outstripped productivity growth (reflected in rising unit labor costs of 14.5 percent per year)[12] and labor disputes accelerated (as shown in Table 12.1).

Table 12.1   Indicators of Labor Activism in South Korea, 1971–1980

	No. industrial disputes	No. workers involved	Days lost
1971	10	832	11,323
1974	58	22,609	16,831
1975	52	10,256	13,557
1976	49	6,570	17,046
1977	58	7,975	8,294
1978	102	10,598	13,230
1979	105	14,258	16,366
1980	206	48,970	61,269

Source: International Labour Office, *Yearbook of Labour Statistics,* various issues.

Underlying these phenomena was a reversal of the market and institutional conditions that previously enabled capital to dominate labor. In spite of the massive investment in HCI, the knowledge gap meant that Korean comparative advantage would depend on high-quality, low-cost labor for the foreseeable future. The policy implication was that in the long term, labor control would have to assume a more sophisticated, less coercive form, perhaps similar to the Japanese company unionism pattern that meshed labor and company interests.

Developments in the Labor Market

The stronger position of labor during the 1970s arose from a combination of market and institutional factors. The abundance of labor became a thing of the past as the rate of unemployment dropped to an all-time low of 3.2 percent in 1978. In particular, there was a shortage of skilled labor, whose supply failed to keep up with the pace of expansion of HCI. For example, while manufacturing capacity grew by an annual average of 15.7 percent for 1971–1979, the supply of educated workers (in the managerial, administrative, professional, and technical categories) expanded at the rate of only 4.3 percent per year.[13] But the labor shortage was not only confined to white-collar sections. The boom in overseas construction after 1974, employing about 250,000 Koreans, served to exacerbate the domestic labor shortage. Although shortages were far less pronounced in the labor-intensive industries that relied mainly on semi- and unskilled labor, the labor market was much tighter than it had been during the 1960s. This had adverse consequences for competitiveness. First, wages were driven up by companies attempting to outbid each other in the scramble for skilled workers (wage increases in the HCI sector being especially sharp). For individual companies, poaching skilled workers trained by others made economic sense. Second, there was the spillover effect from the HCI sector to less-productive sectors, with workers in the latter being set a target to aim for, creating inflationary pressure as wage increases exceeded productivity growth.

But why did labor supply fail to match demand? The shortage of skilled white-collar workers reflected the underdevelopment of an infrastructure capable of sustaining the expansion of productive capacity. It was also exacerbated by the gender segmentation of the labor force.[14] Apart from the shortcomings of labor development and R & D, the pattern of rural emigration had changed. The exodus into the cities fell sharply during the first half of the 1970s as government price supports boosted the terms of trade in favor of the rural sector; therefore the countryside could no longer provide the abundant reserves of labor for the urban sector.[15]

Institutional Conditions of Wage Repression

Rural emigration accelerated again after 1976 (from 67,000 that year to 252,000 in 1977). The bad harvest of 1978 led to an exodus of 430,000.[16] Yet this did not stem the continuous rise in manufacturing unit labor costs (ULC), suggesting that ULC was determined not only by market conditions but also by the changing institutional context in which wage bargaining took place. Foremost of these changes was the emergence of labor activation, a condition facilitated by the rise of industrial employment. Between 1971 and 1978 production workers in the total workforce grew from 19.5 to 29.3 percent. The growth of labor strength during the 1970s could be seen in the data on strikes.[17]

What were the conditions favoring the acceleration of labor protest? In the initial phase of industrialization, urban employment facilitated political stabilization by improving the living standards of rural migrants (who also remitted money back to the countryside). But as absolute poverty declined, the issue of *relative* poverty emerged. Criteria such as GNP growth, the appalling conditions of work, and the material progress made by other sections of society (such as employers and government officials) increasingly shaped workers' perceptions of their own condition.[18] The rapid spread of mass communication and education facilitated the exposure of alternative ideas. Opposition to the government was much stronger in the cities. There were also deliberate attempts by radical organizations, especially church-based ones (such as the Urban Industrial Mission, or UIM), to campaign for workers' rights and heighten consciousness. Government concern about the UIM suggests that these radical forces exercised growing influence in the workplace despite strict official sanctions.[19]

Accelerated economic growth depended on the exploitation of labor. By the end of the 1970s the market and institutional factors that facilitated labor subordination had been eroded. Tighter labor markets, higher expectations, and the beginning of collective organization attested to the social impact of industrialization. It also marked the transition from industrialization based on cheap, abundant labor to the capital- and skill-intensive stages, and called for a new role for government in the management of labor–business relations. The shortage of skilled labor reinforced the argument for a shift in the direction of economic intervention toward the provision of infrastructure. In the changed social environment, industrial relations reliant on political coercion were unsustainable and pointed to the necessity of finding new ways in which labor could be controlled and motivated.

Sociopolitical Foundations of Growth

The sources of labor activation were symptomatic of a wider crisis of political legitimacy facing the Park regime. In the 1960s, legitimacy was reflected in the electoral success of Park and his governing Democratic Republican Party. By 1972, however, semiopen politics was replaced by the dictatorial politics of the Yushin (Revitalization) Constitution. Political rule was now based on economic performance and coercion. Yet spectacular growth rates and tough political measures did not assure public docility; the 1970s saw an upward spiral of popular resistance. How can this paradox be explained and what were its implications for Korea's development trajectory?

Distributional Issues

One of the conditions of economic success was the ability to meet aspirations for material improvement. Rising social discontent in the 1970s could be traced to the failure of government to keep pace with these aspirations as income distribution deteriorated and low official priority was accorded to pressing social concerns.

Korea's egalitarianism has been widely praised from a comparative perspective. Export development promoted greater equality during the 1960s by reducing the high levels of unemployment through the creation of labor-intensive employment. Distribution deteriorated after 1970 (as shown in Table 12.2).

Table 12.2   South Korean Income Distribution by Decile and Gini Coefficient, 1965–1980

	Bottom 40%	Middle 40%	Top 20%	Gini coefficient
1965	19.34	38.85	41.81	0.344
1970	19.36	39.02	41.62	0.332
1975	16.85	37.81	45.34	0.390
1980	16.06	38.55	45.39	0.389

Source: H. Koo, "The Political Economy of Income Distribution in South Korea," *World Development,* Vol. 12 (1984) p. 1030.

A study using three measures of distribution (decile distribution, Theil index, Gini coefficient) indicates that the slight improvement in distribution in 1965–1970 was reversed thereafter.[20] The gap widened between white-collar (especially educated personnel such as managers and administrators) and blue-collar workers, between heavy and light industrial workers, and between large and small businesses (an indicator also of the rise of the *chaebol*).[21] These trends could be explained by the tight market for skilled labor discussed earlier, the higher productivity of capital-intensive sectors, and the high male concentration in HCI and top white-collar posts.

Social development became a sensitive political issue in the 1970s as the persistence of social deprivation contrasted with rapid economic growth. In fact, some social problems grew markedly worse while the public had reason to expect the government's problem-solving capacity to be enhanced by growth. Consequently, there were grounds for criticizing the government for paying insufficient attention to meeting basic needs and allowing the fruits of the country's development to be misappropriated (by corrupt officials, domestic and foreign capitalists, etc.). In terms of government spending, economic development continued to occupy a higher priority than social development through the 1970s.

One intractable and politically sensitive social problem was the housing crisis, which got worse with urbanization. The supply ratio of housing to households indicated that construction failed to improve despite the more active role played by the government (see Table 12.3). The housing shortage

Table 12.3   Housing Supply Ratio and Public and Private Construction in South Korea (%), 1971–1980

	Supply ratio (units/households)	Public-sector construction	Private-sector construction
1971	77.8	18.5	81.5
1975	74.4	35.0	65.0
1976	77.4	36.5	63.5
1977	77.2	39.4	60.6
1978	76.8	38.3	61.7
1979	76.5	47.0	53.0

Source: Economic Planning Board, *Korean Economic Statistics,* various issues.

was particularly acute in the cities, where the supply ratio was only 59.2 percent in 1980.[22] Rapid urbanization forced many families into makeshift housing (shantytowns on the outskirts of major cities) or into shared accommodation (with relatives or in the rented sector). Mills and Song quote a government estimate that there were 218,000 illegal households in 1973 (of which 70 percent were in Seoul and 22 percent in Pusan, Taegu, and Inchon), making up 4 percent of the total population and 8 percent of the urban population.[23] Even for the bulk of the country's middle classes, the absence of mortgage facilities for home purchasing made it difficult to acquire property. Government control of the regulated financial sector and credit rationing meant that lending for industrial purposes inevitably got first priority. Loans from the kerb market, bearing high interest and available only short term, were unsuitable to potential home buyers.[24] On the other hand, property provided generous payoffs for those with the resources to enter the market, be they wealthy individuals looking for a sound investment or *chaebol* engaged in real estate speculation.[25] The ability to afford property became an obvious divide between the disadvantaged and well-to-do. The housing crisis was a potent symbol of the contradictions of Korean development, representing the deterioration in the provision of a basic need amid unparalleled economic growth, and profiteering by the powerful at the expense of the poor. The difficulty of property acquisition also frustrated middle-class material aspirations (home ownership being the principal means of asset accumulation for those of moderate means).

For the majority of working-class households immediate survival remained the principal concern. A study of Korean health care in the 1970s found that although Korea was not suffering from the stark starvation that blighted the masses of most developing countries, the general population was suffering from many of the debilitating illnesses associated with malnutrition.[26] The same source noted that the underutilization of the country's medical resources was not caused by oversupply but rather by the lack of purchasing power among needy sections of the population.[27]

One can get some idea of workers' capacity to make ends meet from a comparison of manufacturing wages to average urban household consumption expenditures (see Table 12.4).

Table 12.4   Manufacturing Wages as a Percentage of Average Household Consumption Expenditures of Salaried Wage Earners in South Korean Cities, 1974–1979

	1974	1979
All manufacturing	73.4	82.2
Food, drinks, tobacco	77.8	97.3
Textiles, garments	62.6	63.6
Iron and steel	131.5	115.4
All chemicals	84.9	92.6
Industrial chemicals	142.6	144.8
Petroleum refining	224.5	237.8
All machinery	74.7	86.4
Electrical machinery	67.6	68.7
Transportation equipment	99.9	121.4

Source: Bank of Korea, *Economic Statistical Yearbook,* various issues.

Significant difficulties faced those employed in the traditional export sectors (textiles, garments, electronics, etc.) with earnings of 55 to 70 percent of average household consumption expenditure. Even the relatively well-paid workers in some heavy industries were making enough to cover the basic necessities but had little left over for discretionary spending. Macrodata conceal the even worse plight for the "social marginals" (composed primarily of recent arrivals from the rural sector), who were underemployed or were forced to work in the informal sector under squalid conditions.[28] A report by the Korean Development Institute found that the majority of those living below the poverty line consisted of "working poor," usually temporary and casual production and agricultural workers with inadequate incomes.[29] The declining poverty gap (i.e., the amount that must be spent in order to bring the poor to a level above the poverty line) to GNP ratio highlighted the growing capacity of the government to alleviate the problem.[30]

Weak Authoritarian Foundations

The dictatorships that emerged in the South American "Cone" countries during the 1960s and 1970s were underpinned by their appeal to big business and the middle classes, which were menaced by the distributional implications of popular mobilization.[31] With its own Communist threat, Korea would have appeared to be fertile ground for the consolidation of authoritarianism of the Yushin type. Why did middle-class support for authoritarianism not solidify?

Though there were apparent similarities (moderate to high inflation rates, student dissent, labor activation), the South American dictatorships actually emerged out of quite different conditions. The most significant difference was that distributional conflicts in Korea developed in a context of rising prosperity, which prevented the emergence of zero-sum conflict between the middle and working classes. When the Yushin was proclaimed in 1972, things had certainly not reached the stage in which the Korean middle class would wholeheartedly throw its weight behind the authoritarian cause. On the contrary, opposition leaders and other notables representative of middle-class interests became more aware of and sympathetic toward the plight of labor through the 1970s.[32] The security argument for dictatorship was unconvincing given that very powerful institutional safeguards (such as the Anti-Communist Law and the Korean Central Intelligence Agency) already existed.

Authoritarianism was ideologically weakened by the emergence of popular democratic alternatives. Kim Dae Jung's vision of a "mass democratic economy," evoking the possibility of high growth, political democracy, and fairer distribution, had widespread interclass support. Such a program offered the appealing combination of prosperity and rule by consent. Having not yet been tested, populism was not discredited in Korea (in contrast to the South American cases where its failure led the middle classes to embrace authoritarian alternatives). The campaign for constitutional reform by politicians such as Kim Dae Jung helped to rally all opposition groups, conservative and radical, behind a common theme.[33]

Such social and political trends contributed to the weakening of authoritarianism in Korea. These sources of public disaffection with the Park regime suggested that economic priorities had to be balanced against social and political ones. Industrialization engendered new expectations that any government concerned with legitimacy had to address. If the economic problems pointed toward less-interventionist government, the social contradictions of accelerated industrialization called for a more active government role in effecting redistribution (albeit by market-conforming methods). Whether the economic growth of the 1970s could have been attained without the dictatorial politics of the Yushin is a matter of debate. But the issue was that in contrast to Latin America, the "natural" mass followers of authoritarianism, the middle class, did not see democratic politics as either exhausted or nonviable.

Conclusion

The 1980s marked a transitional period in Korean history as the authoritarian industrialization pattern established under President Park gradually gave way to economic liberalization and democratization. This chapter has focused on how the pressures for change originated. Three dimensions were identified. First, international economic and political trends exerted positive and negative inducements for greater economic openness. Second, the high interventionism of the 1970s had accomplished its aim of giving Korea the productive capacity required for its future export and defense plans. The economic agenda shifted from the creation of capacity to making that capacity efficient, meaning that markets inevitably played a bigger role. Third, authoritarian industrialization unleashed popular expectations that undermined its foundations of political stability. Securing new foundations (a condition for sustaining growth in the 1980s) meant accommodating expectations for social development and democratization.

If Korea was evolving out of the authoritarian pattern, it was doing so in a continuous way. Continuity was reflected in the persistence of national priorities (national autonomy and ascendance to advanced industrial status) behind government policies, be they interventionist/liberalizing or repressive/democratizing. It was also reflected in the controlled nature of change. Economic liberalization in the sensitive area of finance, for instance, is still underway and is not expected to be completed until the end of the 1990s. Similarly, democratization was only effected gradually. Between the fall of the Park regime and Chun's surrender to democratizing pressures there was an eight-year period in which the authoritarian rulers had time to prepare themselves for competitive politics (a successful preparation judging by post-1987 events).

How do we explain the continuous pattern? Economic performance provides one answer. If Korean authoritarian industrialization stimulated the social changes that undermined its own foundations, its economic performance also provided policymakers with sufficient leeway to manage the transition. The legacy of the Cold War and colonial bureaucratic rule meant that the Korean state (bureaucracy and security apparatus) remained sufficiently powerful in the face of societal pressures to dictate the pace of change. Finally, the national priorities mentioned earlier remain far more deeply rooted in Korean society than the liberal impulse. Seeing the devastating human consequences of the sudden lurch to the market in Eastern Europe and Latin America, this reticence has been no bad thing.

Notes

1. G. O'Donnell et al., eds., *Transitions from Authoritarianism* (Baltimore: John Hopkins University Press, 1986); and A. Przeworski, *Democracy and the Market* (Cambridge: Cambridge University Press, 1992) represent the most important theoretical works on democratization and economic reform to appear in the last decade.

2. S. Han in "Bureaucratic-Authoritarianism and Economic Development in Korea during the Yushin Period: A Re-examination of O'Donnell's Theory," in K. Kim, ed., *Dependency Issues in Korean Development* (Seoul: Seoul National

University Press, 1987), distinguishes between continuous and discontinuous patterns in the transition *to*—as opposed to *from*—authoritarianism.

3. L. Jones and I. Sakong, *Government, Business and Entrepreneurship in Economic Development: The Korean Case. Studies in the Modernization of the Republic of Korea, 1945–75* (Cambridge, MA: Harvard University Press, 1980); A. Amsden, *Asia's Next Giant: South Korea and Late-Industrialization* (New York: Oxford University Press, 1989); R. Wade, *Governing the Market* (Princeton: Princeton University Press, 1990).

4. F. Deyo, *Beneath the Miracle: Labour Subordination in the New Asian Industrialism* (Berkeley: University of California Press, 1989).

5. Military-dominated authoritarian rule (under which economic takeoff began) lasted from 1961 to 1987 in Korea and from 1949 to 1988 in Taiwan.

6. Amsden, *Asia's Next Giant,* pp. 72–76.

7. J. Woo, *Race to the Swift: State and Finance in Korean Industrialization* (New York: Columbia University Press, 1991), pp. 187–189.

8. L. Jones, "Jaebul and the Concentration of Economic Power in Korean Development: Issues, Evidence and Alternatives," in I. Sakong, ed., *Macro-economics Policy and Industrial Development Issues* (Seoul: Korea Development Institute, 1981), pp. 84–94, describes the characteristics of the *chaebol.*

9. Woo, *Race to the Swift,* pp. 167–168, makes the point that financial repression encouraged bankers to lend to "known entities," namely *chaebol,* rather than to seek out the most profitable investments for their funds.

10. D. Cole and Y. Park, *Financial Development in Korea* (Cambridge, MA: Harvard University Press, 1983), pp. 128–133, 185–188, outline the lending rates on the kerb market.

11. W. Hong and Y. Park, "The Financing of Export-Oriented Growth in Korea," in A. Tan and B. Kapur, eds., *Pacific Growth and Financial Interdependence* (Sydney: Allen and Unwin Press, 1986), pp. 173–180, calculated that credit diversion (fungibility) was very high across the manufacturing sector, with the exception of the steel and cement industries, which were directly government run. Foreign loans were not so susceptible to such diversion.

12. Dollar unit labor costs accelerated at a higher rate reflecting the overvalued won.

13. From Bank of Korea, *Economic Statistical Yearbook,* various issues.

14. Women were excluded from white-collar supervisory as well as capital-intensive blue-collar work. See H. Cho, "Labour Force Participation of Women in Korea," in S. Chung, ed., *Challenges for Women: Women's Studies in Korea* (Seoul: Korean Women's Institute Series—Ewha Woman's University Press, 1986), pp. 165–168.

15. T. Castenada and F. Park, "Structural Adjustment and the Role of the Labour Market," in *Working Paper 8705* (Seoul: Korea Development Institute, 1987), pp. 15–17.

16. Ibid., p. 16.

17. F. Deyo, *Beneath the Miracle,* pp. 211–212, argues that of the East Asian cases, the structural position of Korean labor was most akin to that of the Latin American countries (stable proletarian communities, labor aristocracy employed in HCI, etc.), giving it greater independence from the state in contrast to labor in Taiwan, Hong Kong, or Singapore.

18. J. Choi, *Labour and the Authoritarian State: Labour Unions in South Korean Manufacturing Industries 1961–80* (Seoul: Korea University Press, 1989), p. 281, argues that in spite of their links to the government, the unions helped to transform workers' conception of the minimum wage from individual subsistence to the

level required for the maintenance of a family. According to Deyo, *Beneath the Miracle,* p. 212, the Korean government's control over the unions was the least penetrative of the East Asian countries. The attempt at incorporation could help to account for the rise in the numbers unionized—from 515,300 in 1972 to 1,054,000 in 1978.

19. J. Lee, "Dynamics of Labour Control and Labour Protest in the Process of Export-Industrialization in Korea," *Asian Perspective* Vol. 12, No. 1 (1988), pp. 146–147, notes the emergence of "core" groups (consisting of: charismatic individual leaders and their close associates; production-line team leaders associated with the UIM; union leaders educated by the central unions or Christian Academy; and students turned workers) at the head of worker protests in the 1970s.

20. H. Choo, "Economic Growth and Income Distribution," in C. Park, ed., *Human Resources and Social Development in Korea* (Seoul: Korea Development Institute, 1980), pp. 288–289.

21. Another significant development in the urban sector during the 1970s was the changing pattern of distribution among employer households, with a declining income share for the lowest 40 percent, which was being mirrored by concentration in the top 30 percent. See Choo, "Economic Growth and Income Distribution," p. 293.

22. Economic Planning Board, *Major Statistics of Korean Economy* (1989).

23. E. Mills and B. Song, *Korea's Urbanization and Urban Problems: Studies in the Modernization of the Republic of Korea 1945–75* (Cambridge, MA: Harvard University Press, 1979), pp. 137–138.

24. Mills and Song, *Korea's Urbanization,* p. 136.

25. B. Song and R. Stryuk, "Korean Housing: Economic Appraisal and Policy Alternatives," in C. Kim, ed., *Industrial and Social Development Issues* (Seoul: Korea Development Institute, 1977), pp. 131–132, notes that official land development programs often resulted in the sale of property to speculators rather than end users owing to the government agencies' desire to recover their investments quickly.

26. C. Park, "The Organization, Financing and Cost of Health Care," in C. Park, ed., *Human Resources and Social Development in Korea,* p. 144.

27. Ibid., p. 108.

28. C. Kim, "Marginalization, Development and the Korean Workers Movement," *AMPO: Japan–Asia Quarterly Review,* Vol. 9, No. 3 (1977), pp. 28–30.

29. S. Suh, "The Pattern of Poverty," in Park, ed., *Human Resources,* pp. 361–362.

30. Ibid., p. 352.

31. D. Collier, ed., *The New Authoritarianism in Latin America* (Princeton: Princeton University Press, 1979).

32. H. Sohn, *Authoritarianism and Opposition in Korea* (London: Routledge, 1989), pp. 132–136, notes the support for labor reform by the traditionally conservative civic and religious leaders by 1977. Committee for Justice and Peace of South Korea–National Organization of Catholic Priests to Realize Social Justice, "A Fact-Finding Survey on the Masan Free Export Zone," *AMPO: Japan–Asia Quarterly Review,* Vol. 8, No. 2, pp. 58–69, highlighted the plight of Korean labor in foreign-invested enterprises.

33. Sohn, *Authoritarianism and Opposition,* p. 144, notes the congruence of the views of the student movement with the principles of "democracy, nationalism, people, and unification" espoused by the broader reform movement. See also Korean Institute for Human Rights, *News Reprints and Other Materials on Kim Dae Jung* (Alexandria, VA: Korean Institute for Human Rights, 1984).

13

South Korean Liberalization Since 1993

STEPHEN KIRBY AND SALLY HARRIS

The South Korea of the mid-1990s was strikingly different from the same country a mere decade earlier. A former dissident was now president, and the democratic process was becoming increasingly entrenched. Economically, too, reform had made considerable strides. Although domestic dynamics were important, one of the themes of this chapter will be the role played by U.S. policy in forcing the pace of opening up the South Korean economy. To this end, the chapter starts out with a brief look at U.S. trade policy, and in particular its application to South Korea (henceforth also referred to as the Republic of Korea, or ROK).

U.S. policy under President Clinton has guaranteed a high profile for trading issues in the international security debate. It has also brought to the fore a more confrontational model of interstate economic activity. This model may be said to combine aspects of two perspectives on economic security, as outlined by Cable. These include the notion that power projection requires a robust domestic economy. Where poor economic performance is believed to be the result of unfair trading practices of other states, then "economic policy instruments" must be used "for purposes of aggression (or defense): trade and investment boycotts; the restriction of energy supplies . . . and specialized technologies."[1] Clinton's determination to keep domestic economic needs at the top of the U.S. foreign-affairs agenda, and to ensure that U.S. commercial interests and values are in the ascendant in the forging of regional and global trading agreements, has had a profound impact on states whose culture, history, and political and economic traditions do not easily fit into the Anglo-American philosophy on international trading.

The countries of the Asia-Pacific region, South Korea among them, are a clear example of such states. For the Kim Young Sam regime, this period has been an extraordinarily challenging one. The Seoul government, intent on making South Korea a key player in the global community, has been pursuing a highly ambitious internationalization program, with additional pressure from Washington, in a bid to prise open "one of the most shuttered economies and guarded national psyches in Asia."[2]

Seoul's successful bid to join the World Trade Organization (WTO), and its application to become a member of the OECD in 1996, mean that it has had to take some considerable steps toward liberalization of its economic and trading policy in order to be acceptable as a member of either. With its traditionally pronounced protectionist approach to overseas trading, the country has found it difficult over the years to accommodate to the GATT norms of reduced trade barriers, nondiscrimination, fair trade, multilateralism, reciprocity, and economic development. The Uruguay Round (1986–1993), with its emphasis on intellectual property, standards harmonization, foreign direct investment, and trade in services, proved to be particularly demanding for Seoul. This is primarily because of the ROK's overregulated and closed financial system, and because its economic wealth has been concentrated mainly in the hands of a few large *chaebol*. Even as of 1995, thirty large corporations generated 82 percent of South Korea's GNP.[3] While Seoul has been eager to take steps that will bring its standards into line with those required for membership in the WTO and the OECD, its government has been forced into even more rapid and extensive liberalization by the U.S. administration. The South Korean leadership is in an awkward position: It has no wish to have a submissive relationship with Washington on this score, but the unpredictable political situation on the Korean peninsula, and Seoul's perceived military dependence on Washington for its survival, tend to dictate a degree of obsequiousness. This problem is further compounded by additional South Korean anxieties. First, the uncertain and changeable nature of U.S. military support for the ROK as part of its current "win-hold-win" strategy, in which the United States, if confronted with two serious regional conflicts, would hold the enemy at bay in the second conflict until it had secured victory in the first[4]; and second, Pyongyang's preoccupation with isolating South Korea in pursuit of improved bilateral relations with Washington and Tokyo, thus engendering widespread South Korean fears that "Washington is alienating itself from Seoul."[5] The quandary confronting Kim Young Sam has been, and remains, to try to maintain internal political and economic stability while forging ahead, in some haste, with wide-ranging reforms in the quest for globalization, or *segyehwa*. In this respect he has something of a tightrope to walk: He must balance the need to respond positively to U.S. demands that he accelerate the liberalizing process, against domestic opposition and the crescendo of anti-Americanism that such deferential behavior generates.[6]

U.S. Trade Policy

President Clinton came to power in November 1992 on a campaign pledge to concentrate resources on domestic needs in a bid to revive the U.S. economy, and to ensure that foreign-policy goals matched domestic priorities. In the firm belief that Washington's external deficit stemmed from a highly unequal trade playing field, Clinton declared just prior to being elected that the only way to balance trade was to force open overseas markets, or, where this was not successful, to introduce import restrictions. He told U.S. trading partners: "Either you play by our rules, or we will play by yours."[7]

Even though the Clinton administration's foreign policy received criticism for being strong in rhetoric but weak in practice, especially in trade matters (for example, over separating the human rights question from Most Favored Nation [MFN] status for China, and decoupling security and trade in relations with Tokyo), the contrast with the Bush presidency was tangible. While the latter had been reluctant to apply rigorous commercial sanctions that might trigger a spate of retaliatory protectionist measures, the Clinton administration displayed far less reticence. Some notable developments highlighted the new emphasis on trade. First, there was the importance attached to the U.S. Commerce Department; its secretary was brought into Clinton's cabinet through the upgrading of the Trade Promotion Coordinating Committee (TPCC), which now includes the heads of twenty-five government departments. The Commerce Department's main priority is to strengthen America's commercial footing in ten Big Emerging Markets (BEMs). These include greater China, India, Indonesia, Brazil, Mexico, Turkey, South Korea, South Africa, Poland, and Argentina. These countries have been chosen because they have the most swiftly growing economies in the world, and because their rapidly developing status means that they will require goods and services such as information technology, financial services, telecommunications, power generation, medical and health equipment, and transportation, which "promise to be the top growth sectors for U.S. exports, where Americans enjoy comparative advantages." The U.S. leadership believes that its BEM strategy, if successful, will lead to the creation of millions of new jobs in the United States, reduce the trade deficit, and restore public confidence, over the course of one or two decades.[8] The U.S. undersecretary of commerce for international trade commented that "the aggressive commercial policy adopted by the Commerce Department is being integrated into U.S. foreign policy as never before."[9]

A second change concerns the U.S. shift toward multilateralism during the Clinton presidency. Trading disagreements between the United States and allies such as Japan, South Korea, Australia, Indonesia, and Thailand, coupled with a reduced U.S. military presence in the Asia-Pacific region, prompted countries in the vicinity to look more toward regional and global multilateral frameworks such as ASEAN, APEC, GATT, and the OECD as a means of safeguarding their trading interests.[10] Under Clinton, the United States, responding to these developments, is also now relying more on such institutions to protect its defense and trading interests in the area. Clinton stressed this approach when addressing the South Korean National Assembly in July 1993.[11]

It is also through multilateral frameworks that Washington under Clinton has sought to promote its own vision of trading norms and rules, and to harmonize world commercial and economic relations based on formulas and standards accepted by all states. In targeting specific developing states for its trade expansion over the next two decades, Washington requires that those states achieve and maintain political stability, pursue open-market policies, and strive for regional peace. As the United States seeks to foster these ideals, and to handle with care its increasingly complex relationships with such states, it has become apparent that to rely solely on traditional bilateral channels is no longer adequate. Even where bilateral contacts are concerned, the military aspect is becoming relatively less important.[12]

The third major development on trade was Clinton's hard-won agreements on NAFTA, GATT and the WTO, and APEC (Asia-Pacific Economic Cooperation). The NAFTA agreement, which took effect in January 1994, actually improved on the Uruguay Round provisions with respect to services, investment, intellectual property, agriculture, and nontariff barriers; its members aimed at free trade by 2005.[13] The Uruguay Round of the GATT was formally concluded on 15 December 1993, after seven years of intensive bargaining, followed by a major Clinton effort to have it ratified in Congress. The APEC summit in Seattle in December 1993 was deemed a success in that it assured the organization's future as a respected regional institution. In 1994, at the APEC summit in Indonesia, Clinton won resounding endorsement for his initiative for the introduction of free trade among all members by the year 2020.[14]

U.S. Trade Liberalization Pressure on South Korea, and the Korean Response

The U.S. attitude toward international trading is best summed up by the guiding neoclassical economic principles on which the GATT regime is founded. That is to say, free trade and open markets are the means to greater wealth and more efficient goods and services, and the economy thrives better where there is minimum governmental interference. It is this ideology that underlines Washington's approach to its trade relations with South Korea and other Asia-Pacific states. (This is not to say, of course, that the fair trade argument does not at times bring effectively protectionist instincts to U.S. policy.) The United States's trading relationship with South Korea—its eighth-largest trading partner—is of great importance to Washington. U.S. exports to the ROK amount to around $18 billion per year, and support approximately 350,000 U.S. jobs. Therefore, Washington's trade with Seoul is on a par with U.S. trade with all the oil-exporting states of the Middle East put together. The United States ardently seeks to keep and increase this level.[15]

The United States has been applying pressure on South Korea for years to comply more fully with the rules of GATT (of which both were members) in a number of different ways. In terms of reducing visible trade barriers, Washington's persistence led to a cut in general South Korean tariff levels from 25 percent in 1980 to 13 percent in 1989. Quotas were lifted in 1991 from 243 agricultural South Korean products but continued on fruits, grains, beef, pork, and paper.[16] Regarding nondiscrimination, Section 1302 of the 1988 U.S. Omnibus Trade and Competitiveness Act (the "Super 301" clause) called upon the Office of the U.S. Trade Representative (USTR) to name those states that imposed the most pernicious trade barriers against U.S. trade. In order to avoid being named on this list, Seoul felt obliged to adjust its product standards and regulations policy. In May 1989 Seoul signed an agreement promising to accept internationally agreed standards and certification, and to inform GATT of any new or changed trade-related procedures and regulations that conflicted with the international norm.[17] Again under pressure from the USTR, Seoul agreed to accede to the Tokyo Round Government Procurement Code, in June 1990, by liberalizing some government procurement policies, especially in the field of telecommunications. The threat of the Super 301 also led Seoul to make moves toward opening up South Korean markets to foreign direct investment. By the beginning of 1992 almost 98 percent of manufacturing sectors and 62 percent of service sectors had been opened up.[18]

Life insurance is another area in which Washington demanded access by foreign firms, or threatened trade sanctions, during the Reagan presidency. In 1988 an agreement was reached whereby the ROK would open up its life insurance market to more foreign competition. Since 1988 U.S. and ROK firms have set up six joint ventures, but as of mid-1995 only one of these ventures was having any success at all and the remainder looked ready to break up.[19] This at first appears surprising, given that the life insurance market in the ROK is buoyant and growing fast. The reason for the setback, however, is that the Korean decision to approve licenses to foreign firms was little more than a gesture to satisfy U.S. critics. The Ministry of Finance, in an attempt to block foreign competition, at once issued a flood of licenses to domestic insurance firms so that their number rose from six to thirty-two; this reduced the market share for foreigners. In addition, the government maintained tight controls to make sure that "all companies offer identical products at identical prices." Because one domestic firm, the Six Sisters, still controls 85 percent of South Korea's life insurance market, foreign firms experience great difficulty in competing by providing better products at lower prices. They have also been hampered by a law forbidding foreigners to own real estate.[20]

Under the Clinton administration the pressure placed upon Seoul to further liberalize its markets has gathered momentum; but this has occurred in conjunction with the arrival of the Kim Young Sam regime, which is dedicated to a program of trade globalization and opening. Throughout the autumn of 1992 and the early months of 1993, a dispute raged between the United States and South Korea over allegations that Korean semiconductor firms were "dumping" chips on the U.S. market at reduced prices. In October 1992 the U.S. Commerce Department had imposed antidumping charges of between 6 and 87 percent on dynamic random-access memory chips exported by South Korean firms. In the absence of an agreement over the antidumping lawsuit brought by a U.S. firm, Micron Technology, the Commerce Department decided to retain the charges, despite a Seoul government comprehensive pricing offer.[21] A deal was concluded in mid-March, but not on Seoul's terms. South Korea had sought a bilateral semiconductor deal based on the U.S.–Japan one, in which South Korea would promise the United States a specified share of its semiconductor market in return for a lifting of antidumping measures. However, Washington opposed this, levied additional penalties of $446 million on the three ROK firms involved, and warned South Korea to reduce its share of the U.S. market and to maintain prices.[22]

In April 1993 the USTR, taking a tough approach and complaining of the United States' "complete exclusion" from South Korea's telephone market, threatened to impose trade sanctions if the U.S. firm AT&T was not allowed to bid for a $100 million telephone switching contract. Seoul again relented. On 26 June, Washington persuaded Seoul to agree to increase beef imports from the United States by 7 percent per year between 1993 and 1995, and to allow U.S. exporters to sell a larger percentage of their beef directly to wholesalers instead of to government agencies.[23]

In December 1993 President Kim Young Sam was forced by Clinton into making a dramatic U-turn in the GATT negotiations, by conceding to the opening of South Korea's rice markets against all former pledges to protect farmers from foreign rice imports. The decision led to widespread, angry domestic protests. In an attempt to mitigate opposition, Kim Young Sam promised to re-export all imported rice as a means of protecting the domestic rice market.[24]

During 1994 and into 1995 Washington intensified its demands that South Korea fully open up its meat, automobile, financial services, and telecommunications markets. The United States does not maintain a large trade deficit with South Korea; its intention to extract additional concessions toward liberalization is in no small part due to its distaste for what Washington regards as Seoul's shady trading practices and sly negotiating methods, which it deems to be wholly untrustworthy.[25] In response to this pressure, the Seoul government declared in June 1994 that it would attempt to lower the import tariff on automobiles before the agreed deadline of January 1996. South Korea succeeded in gradually opening its capital markets through a three-phase program, called the "blueprint program," from 1993 to 1997, and a three-stage program to reform its foreign-exchange system from 1994 to 1999. Nevertheless, Washington bitterly complained in February 1995 that Seoul's attitude toward opening its financial market was much too "defensive." South Korea has been threatened with exclusion from MFN status unless it includes its financial deregulation and liberalization programs in the list of offers to be submitted to the WTO, making them irreversible under any circumstances.[26]

Clinton's 1995 trade policy aimed at creating a much closer link between trade and nontrade issues in U.S. commercial dealings with other states. Washington is now attaching more weight to antitrust practices, environmental protection, and labor standards, and Seoul has had to take account of this. The USTR at the time of writing (mid-1995) was threatening Seoul with the Super 301 over continued restricted access to imports of sausages and automobiles. Seoul reacted in a minor way to reduce the tangle of tariffs, taxes, and licensing fees imposed upon foreign cars that made them twice as expensive as comparable domestic models. In January 1995 the government lowered import tariffs on all cars to 8 percent from 10 percent. It also cut acquisition taxes to 2 percent from 15 percent on models costing more than $89,000, and lifted a ban on television advertisements for foreign cars. The government also agreed to remove nontariff trade barriers—for example, requiring tax auditors to visit people who buy foreign vehicles.[27]

Washington's chief motive for wanting South Korea to become a signatory to the 1993 GATT, the WTO, and the OECD was so that it would be forced to accede to the codes of international behavior that these institutions demand, particularly in relation to trading. The Kim Young Sam regime regarded South Korea's membership in the OECD as essential to advance its globalization policy and to heighten its international stature. In May 1994 the Economic Planning Board was given the task of promoting Seoul's membership in the OECD as one of twelve special projects. Specifically, the vice economic planning minister, Han I-hon, was given overall responsibility for raising South Korea's economic standards to meet the OECD's requirements, and for preparing the country for entry. His Economic Globalization Committee and forty-one subcommittees were tasked with matching domestic economic systems and regulations with international norms, and his Deregulation Committee was in charge of removing bureaucratic barriers and unnecessary red tape.[28] At the time of writing, preparations for joining the OECD in 1996 were well under way. Seoul had submitted its official application to join the organization in March 1995; by midyear it was able to confirm that it had accepted 27 of the 178 OECD Acts, and that by August it would be able to accept 43 more. A year-long consultation with the OECD was to follow. Failing upsets, South Korea was scheduled to be accepted as a member in June 1996, after which the Seoul General Assembly must ratify the agreement.[29]

South Korea's passage toward acceding to the Uruguay Round Final Act was not smooth, and was made no easier by sustained U.S. insistence that it conform closely to the rules. The decision by Seoul to bow to U.S. demands to open up its well-protected rice market, thus overturning President Kim's promise not to do this, led to a huge outpouring of public disquiet and to the resignation of the prime minister and the entire cabinet on 16 December 1993. This reversal was considered to have been prompted by the requirement to stay on amicable terms with Washington during a time of growing tension with North Korea.[30] For Seoul, the GATT agreement meant reducing agricultural subsidies by 13.3 percent over a ten-year period, beginning in 1995, on rice, barley, beans, corn, and rapeseed oil. This was in contrast to previous practice, when the government upheld agricultural prices through the purchase of such items at a set price, and made up the price difference. The Ministry of Agriculture, Forestry, and Fisheries stated that tariffs and tariff equivalences would be reduced on fourteen basic farm products, and on 1,312 additional farm products, by an average of 24 percent by 2004.[31]

During the year following the GATT agreement, opposition and dissent were rife in South Korea. Students, farmers, and others demonstrated throughout the spring and summer. Prime Minister Yi Hoe-chang issued a formal apology following public uproar over confusion concerning the exact agricultural measures taken by the ROK to conform to the accord. In January 1994 President Kim indicated that he was introducing a Rural Development Tax to assist agriculture; the tax was intended to bring about structural adjustment and a rationalization of the farmland ownership system, and to improve farm administration. In May he announced additional specific measures to assist the farming and fishing industries in meeting the GATT agreement. Although South Korea signed the Final Act of the Uruguay Round in Marrakesh on 12 April, it could not sign the mandate for the WTO until the General Assembly ratified the Final Act. Indeed, when parliamentary agreement was reached in December 1994 on ratifying the accord, it came as something of surprise.[32]

At the beginning of 1995 South Korea had to focus on additional liberalization of its financial services and telecommunications to meet the June 1995 deadline under the provisions of the Final Act. Meanwhile, U.S. pressure did not slacken: Washington promised it would carefully monitor Seoul's observance of the new GATT rules, and warned that it would not hesitate to take antitrust proceedings in instances where market access was not forthcoming. In March 1995 the assistant USTR told the Seoul leadership that the United States would certainly apply the Super 301 clause to economic sectors not covered by the WTO. He said that the Seoul government was not removing invisible trade barriers or liberalizing investment quickly enough and he warned that "resistance to global liberalization will lead to greater bilateral trade conflicts and lost investment." He added that "the Korean marketplace has a reputation for being an unfavorable environment to do business among U.S. investors." In April the USTR informed

Seoul that it would file a complaint with the WTO over South Korea's unwieldy quarantine and testing procedures for imported agricultural products, and for its wholly inadequate shelf-life standards for various types of frozen, chilled, and vacuum-packed meats.[33]

South Korean Globalization and Democratization Since 1993

President Kim Young Sam, in a 1995 interview, defined what he meant by *segyehwa* (globalization), which he was striving to achieve for South Korea:

> *Segyehwa* means not just opening Korea toward the outside world. It also means our engaging other countries more actively. Our people want to go outside, to explore and to understand their foreign partners. Our businessmen are already globe-trotting to look for business opportunities. So it means both openness and also an active attitude on the part of the Korean people. Through this effort Korea can be reborn as a country that is in the middle of the action not only in the Asia-Pacific region but also in the entire international community.[34]

Once elected to office, President Kim lost no time in embarking upon reforms toward greater liberalization that have covered several different areas. In his inaugural address he proclaimed the arrival of "a new Korea that will be a freer and more mature democracy." He promised a government that would focus upon justice, the economy, ministerial discipline, and elimination of corruption, as top priorities. Phase One of his reforms (1993–1994), during his first year in office, broadly covered political reforms to eliminate military rule and authoritarian methods; reforms focusing on rationalization and liberalization of the financial and economic sectors; and measures to boost economic growth. Phase Two (1994–1995) was concerned with expanding some of these reforms and channeling further reform into specific sectors, such as administrative, political, and educational. Phase Three, begun in 1995, is concerned with maintaining the momentum of reform while preparing South Korea, commercially and diplomatically, for its new status in world affairs.[35]

Economic Reforms

The surge toward change.   Financial and business reform began even before Kim took office on 25 February 1993. In January he requested the Central Bank to free interest rates from the government-regulated level and to lower them, in return for a commitment from the Ministry of Finance to implement further deregulation. This move was intended to begin the erosion of the ROK's command-capitalist system, and to enable firms to compete more freely for cash rather than having to rely on bureaucratic and political leverage. President Kim wanted to end the government's direct support for industry through its control over the banking system and to bring about a financial system more sensitive to the market.[36] On 17 June 1993 a five-year economic plan reflecting the New Economic Policy was unveiled by the Economic Planning Board. The plan promised commitment to deregulation of interest rates; liberalization of foreign exchange and capital markets; and the removal of direct controls on money supply and capital flows. At the same time, an easing of regulations on foreign-exchange transactions was announced, to take effect in July.[37] From 1 November 1993 all lending rates and deposit rates were deregulated except those associated with government policy loans, deposits with maturities of less than two years, and corporate bonds with maturities over two years. In January 1994 the government introduced a package of measures to deregulate the capital market and liberate business operations in the private sector. These included (1) an end to government-set targets for growth, inflation, and balance of payments; (2) the provision of facilities to enable firms to pay bonuses in shares of convertible bonds, not cash; and (3) further deregulation of the capital market to give listed firms easier access to markets for rights issues and corporate bonds. Six months later an Economic Internationalization Planning Corps was created at the Economic Planning Board to oversee the realization of twelve projects designed to promote internationalization of the ROK economy. In addition to preparing for OECD membership, the projects included: improvement of the ROK's banking system; the creation of rural development programs; expanded participation in international bodies; overseas advancement strategy; hastening the development of key technologies; a change of direction for industrial policy; and small-industry support policy.[38]

In the autumn of 1993 the Administrative Reform Committee was set up under the leadership of the deputy prime minister with the specific remit of Easing of Economic Regulations, in order to relieve the ROK economy of some of the vast network of red tape that had long engulfed it. The Ministry of Finance and the Ministry of Trade, Industry, and Energy then set up committees of their own designed to assist in the removal of controls. Between October 1993 and July 1994 the Seoul government produced a plethora of deregulatory measures covering a total of 1,128 cases, while the Administrative Reform Committee achieved (de)regulations in 1,684 mainly noneconomic areas. Early in 1994 the government selected twenty-two targets for deregulation, relating chiefly to customs clearance and distribution. By mid-July 1994 it had revised 168 statutes in these and other target areas. In the same month it announced the easing of twenty-six administrative regulations in relation to construction and distribution businesses, including the licensing standards for landscaping firms. However, most of these measures were so insignificant as to be meaningless.[39]

Policies toward foreign direct investment. At the beginning of 1994 the government revealed deregulation measures that aimed at encouraging foreign direct investment by attempting to provide opportunities that were as attractive as those available in the People's Republic of China (PRC) and the ASEAN countries. Accordingly, it was announced that (1) the Foreign Exchange Control Act would be abolished in 1999, by which time all controls on foreign exchange would be removed; (2) the Ministry of Finance would no longer control the business plans of major state-run banks; (3) no foreign commercial loans would be allowed; (4) all restraints on banking, securities, and insurance would be lifted. In July 1994 there was an additional move toward freeing the financial institutions from control with the announcement that foreign-exchange business would no longer be handled exclusively by the banks. Official permission was granted to eleven leasing firms to handle foreign-exchange business. Earlier in the year the Ministry of Finance abolished the regulation limiting a person's foreign-currency holding to $10,000; from 1 June 1994 there was to be no limit on the holding. From 1 July there was a small concession toward opening up the ROK's $140 billion bond market, when foreigners were permitted to buy nonguaranteed convertible bonds issued by small- and medium-sized firms listed on the Korea Stock Exchange.[40]

However, continued restrictions meant that foreign investors would be able to buy bonds issued by large firms only indirectly, and not until 1995. By then a few government bonds were open to foreign direct investment but offering lower coupons than those available on the domestic market. The ROK government has been careful to allow only a very gradual opening of its bond market in order to avoid a situation in which overseas investors pour foreign currency into the Korean market to take advantage of its higher-than-average interest rates. The likely consequence of more rapid opening would have been heightened inflation and a steep rise in the value of the Korean won. From 3 January 1995 some regulations were lifted on domestic and foreign securities, and individuals were allowed to increase their maximum investment in foreign securities from 100 million to 500 million won. From 1 July 1995 the ceiling on foreign ownership of local stocks rose to 15 percent from 12 percent.[41]

Privatization. A privatization strategy featured prominently in President Kim's package of reforms. At the close of 1993 he announced the privatization of public corporations, with the object of increasing productivity by eliminating the widespread inefficiency of government-owned businesses. In March 1994 the government initiated its program to transfer 68 out of the 133 public corporations to the private sector through open competitive tendering over a period of four years. However, it was not long before the program began to run into trouble. It became clear that the *chaebol* were the only businesses that could actually afford to buy these corporations, therefore more and more of the economic power of the country was going to be concentrated in their hands.[42] The government then took remedial action, announcing on 6 July 1994 a supplementary measure that excluded the thirty top conglomerates from participating in the purchase of the public corporations. Yet this, in turn, drew fire from the managing director of the Federation of Korean Industries, Chon Tae-chu; he argued that the public corporations would thrive no better in the private sector unless their new owners had extensive managerial and financial resources, which only the *chaebol* had.

The government encountered similar criticism following its declaration of May 1994 that the banking system was to be privatized over a period of a few years. Among the candidates for transfer were the Citizens National Bank, the Industrial Bank of Korea, the Korea Exchange Bank, and the Korea Housing Bank. In June 1994 the deputy prime minister stated categorically that these would be transferred only to enterprises "engaged exclusively in financial services," thus restricting the participation of *chaebol* industries in the bidding. There were accusations that this constituted another form of administrative interference, and when the Ministry of Finance also became involved in the criticism, the deputy prime minister had to withdraw his statement and revise the policy.[43]

Another privatization move that ran into difficulties of this nature arose as part of the nation's social-overhead capital scheme. Following the Uruguay Round agreement there was concern that the ROK's competitive position in world markets would deteriorate without a huge program of investment in infrastructure, which had been badly neglected. Accordingly, a scheme was put forward by the government at the conclusion of the agreement, calling for the ROK's trunk road capacity to be quadrupled to reach the levels of advanced nations, and for a vast expansion in airports and harbors. The only way the authorities could finance such schemes themselves would be through raising taxes, issuing public bonds, or acquiring foreign capital. The government decided, therefore, to bring in legislation for attracting private investors with tax concessions and other financial incentives; such investors would also be given ownership and control over any auxiliary facilities that were constructed, such as highway services, distribution outlets, department stores, and fueling stations. The same dilemma that had marred other privatizations now beset the plan: Only the large conglomerates could afford to participate. It was feared that the *chaebol* would grow richer and larger; because this ran counter to the government's policy of taming their power in the economy, the legislation had to be delayed. (This was followed by the announcement of another infrastructure expansion plan in July 1994, and a renewed government call for the "systematic construction of major transportation networks," in January 1995.)[44]

Business reforms. The central principles guiding reform of the business sector were (1) that the close ties between politics and business must be severed; and (2) that the rash of direct restrictions and regulations on business activity, financing, and planning must be lifted, and substituted with fair-trade laws that would give a boost to small- and medium-sized firms and limit the growth of the *chaebol*.[45] As part of President Kim's drive to curtail the power of the latter and bring them under control, he sought to disperse their ownership. He also called upon the Fair Trade Commission to monitor their business practices, warning that penalties could be levied against unfair commercial activity. On 27 October 1993 the Ministry of Trade, Industry, and Energy announced its industrial specialization plan. The plan called for the nation's top thirty conglomerates to state by the end of the year which three industries (excluding financial services) they wished to specialize in as their "core" activities; these industries would then be eligible for special credit facilities. Attempts were made by the government in power in 1995 to boost the fortunes of smaller firms by offering them preferential programs, such as the recent 1.3 trillion won subsidized loan program.[46]

President Kim promised to withdraw government financial support from firms with poor labor-relations records. However, he pledged to give generous support to ten advanced-technology industries to enable them to become world class by the year 2005. This includes the production of semiconductors, textiles, home appliances, cars, electronics and information devices, optical fibers, precision chemicals, new materials, mechatronics, and aircraft.[47]

Educational reforms. Kim's reforms also included a concerted drive, begun in the autumn of 1994, to raise the standards of South Korea's colleges and universities in order to improve the country's global economic competitiveness. Teaching English was made a key priority. In the spring of 1995 President Kim ordered an assessment of the ROK's entire education system, saying that it needed a major overhaul to overturn its rigid and outmoded methods. A comprehensive reform plan was required, he argued, to bring schools into line with the ROK's need to become much more competitive.[48]

Political, Governmental, and Administrative Reforms

Political liberalization. Politics in South Korea has gone through a transformation since 1987. The significance of the peaceful transition in 1988 from General Chun Doo Hwan to the first elected president, retired general Roh Tae Woo, was confirmed by the election in 1992 of Kim Young Sam—a former dissident—as the first civilian president. This democratic change was subsequently consolidated and developed in a number of ways.

On 5 March 1994 the National Assembly passed three laws designed to make South Korean politics more democratic, transparent, and fair. The

Public Election and Election Irregularities Prevention Law and the Political Funding Law were, between them, designed to set limits on the amount spent on election expenses, abolish the salaried campaign-worker system, and eliminate bribery, corruption, and illegal electioneering. The Local Autonomy Law was intended to give local government greater independence from central government and more authority over regional affairs. Local government now has charge of, among other things, local transport and roads, regional welfare and economic matters, and promoting local customs and culture. The government began establishing regional economic centers and diverting more funds to the regions to help consolidate their independence and new powers.[49]

The anticorruption drive and a shake-up of the military were further contributions to, and illustrations of the extent of, the democratization process in the country.

A resounding confirmation of this process came in the shape of the local elections of 27 June 1995. As one observer commented, "for the first time in thirty-four years, local democracy had come to South Korea."[50] Fifty-seven thousand previously appointed posts were fought over in generally free and fair elections. At one stage the president, fearing that his Democratic Liberal Party (DLP) would lose heavily, considered making candidates stand as independents rather than on party platforms, but strong popular protest scuppered this suggestion. In the event, a de facto alliance between the center-left Democratic Party (DP) and the strongly conservative United Liberal Democratic party (ULD) did result in the DLP's losing ten of the fifteen most important electoral battles for mayor or governor. While this no doubt came as a serious shock to President Kim, there was never any likelihood or suggestion that the results would not be accepted or honored.[51]

Administrative and government reform: Toward greater efficiency. President Kim's administrative and government reforms were directed toward producing less government and more efficient rule, and eliminating corruption and waste. In January 1994 the Board of Audit and Inspection (BAI) was empowered to conduct a thorough investigation into budget wastefulness in every government department and every state-financed institution. Plans were introduced in January 1994 for reorganizing and downsizing the Trade, Industry, and Energy Ministry and the Foreign Ministry, following the Uruguay Round agreement, in order to sharpen their performance in promoting South Korea's economic and political position globally. By the spring of 1994 a program of streamlining and revamping was well under way at all of the government ministries. In December 1994 the Ministry of Finance was merged with the Economic Planning Board to create a "super ministry" with the task of speeding up the ROK's economic globalization process. In the same month the Legislation Ministry was charged with overseeing a major restructuring of eighteen ministries by removing at least ninety divisions and 700 personnel.

The Agency for National Security Planning was reorganized to improve South Korea's international competitive situation by collecting information on developments abroad, and to strengthen its counterespionage operations to protect national trade secrets and advanced technological information.[52]

The anticorruption drive. The police also came under scrutiny, with the National Police Agency launching its own investigation and audit inspection on police personnel in all the major cities. The goal was to eliminate irregular and corrupt practices, such as taking bribes, conducting biased investigations, and neglecting duties.[53]

In a different field, President Kim promised in February 1993 that investors would no longer be able to avoid paying taxes by using fictitious names for their financial holdings—the so-called false name accounts. The practice of using false names in transactions, which dated back to the 1960s, had given an impetus to personal corruption by facilitating insider dealing and allowing public officials to conceal cash they had accepted as bribes. The "real-name system," which Kim said was to be one of his key domestic reforms, had to be established before full interest-rate deregulation could be introduced. On 12 August 1993 Kim signed a national decree prohibiting the use of aliases in all financial transactions. The deadline for compliance with the decree was 12 October, by which time all bank accounts had to be registered in their real owners' names. In the summer of 1994 the government announced that it would set up a real-name land-transaction system that would come into force on 1 January 1995. Its purpose was to assist a land reform program intended to promote better use of landholdings by businesses and farmers, and to weed out property speculators.[54]

Rules on disclosure of assets were further weapons in the anticorruption drive. Kim introduced a series of laws in the course of 1993 that required government personnel, civil servants, politicians, the military, and the judiciary to disclose the full details of their personal wealth. He set an example on taking office by revealing his own and his family's assets in terms of property and savings. As a result of these disclosure measures, 243 persons resigned when they were unable to explain their assets, and 1,363 more were forced to leave their posts.

In the military, 62 percent of South Korea's corps commanders and 39 percent of its division commanders were removed from office.[55] This had strong political implications: A former editor of *Dong-A Ilbo,* Park Kwon Sang, in applauding the changes, is reported to have commented that Kim Young Sam "succeeded in the demilitarization of politics."[56] Indeed, there appears to have been little serious resistance to this sharp and unprecedented civilian intervention in the military's fortunes.

The Arrest of Roh and Chun.   The most dramatic illustration of South Korea's changing political mores came as a result of the rules on asset disclosure. In November 1995, former president Roh Tae Woo became their most prominent victim, being arrested on charges of corruption, and indicted the following month. There had been rumors for some time that Roh had amassed a political "slush fund," but it was only the ban on false-name accounts that led to the revelation that the former president had at least some funds thus administered. In response to opposition accusations in the National Assembly, Roh publicly confessed to having accumulated a $650-million fund from donations from the leaders of some of the top *chaebol.* He admitted having kept $221 million for his own use, while the rest had been destined for handouts to other politicians. Roh and Kim's Democratic Liberal Party itself was said to have received $72 million, used in support of Kim's own presidential campaign. The president denied, however, having received any money personally. Opposition leader Kim Dae Jung admitted having received $2.6 million but denied personal gain or wrongdoing.

With Roh under arrest, and Kim himself under attack by the opposition and under some suspicion by many, the president appears to have decided that he could no longer afford to be seen as shielding either his own predecessor and former colleague Roh, or the latter's own predecessor Chun. For corruption was not the only accusation made: the involvement of the two former generals and presidents in the massacre at Kwangju in May 1980, after Chun's accession to power, had been left unexamined under an understanding that the past would not be raked up. President Kim stated several times that the two former leaders should be judged by history, rather than a court of law.

The president's reversal in 1995, while triggered by the Roh scandal and arrest, must also be seen against the background of increasingly open discussion in the public and the media about the 1979 coup and the Kwangju massacre. The new mood culminated in early December in student riots and an attempt by some to march on Chun's home to effect a citizens' arrest. In response to these public and political pressures, President Kim reversed his earlier position and announced that prosecutions over the 1979–1980 events would be started "to show the people that justice, truth and the law are vividly alive in this land."[57] On 3 December, former president Chun was arrested.[58]

Limitations to the democratization process.   Not all of South Korea's authoritarian heritage has yet evaporated; nor are political and electoral dynamics yet quite those of a mature nationwide democracy. Notwithstanding the independent press, the popular protests, the removal of the military from direct involvement in politics, the free elections, and the arrest and prosecution of Roh and Chun, two features of South Korea's political scene qualify the democratizing picture.

The first is President Kim's own style of rule, at times reminiscent of earlier authoritarian attitudes. His presidency has been referred to as "imperial."[59] The conviction over campaign finance regulations of Hyundai founder Chung Ju Yung, after the 1992 elections in which he had stood against Kim Young Sam, was seen by some as a case of political intimidation. The abandoned attempt to change the local election law was another indication of Kim's less than wholly democratic reflexes. Perhaps most tellingly, the National Security Law, a holdover from the previous regime that gives the government wide-ranging powers of arrest, remains in force and has indeed been made use of. According to Amnesty International, almost 500 political prisoners were being held in 1995—more than under Kim's predecessor.

The second feature is the regional factionalism of South Korean electoral politics, which, though largely divorced from the actual running of the country, in fact further detracts from its democratic credentials. People from the southeastern city of Taegu have a tradition of pre-eminence in power and business dating back to the era of President Park. That the bias persists and causes resentment in other regions was revealed in the local elections. The DP, for instance, is mainly based in the poorer southwestern Cholla region. This situation and its implications have been perceptively summed up in *The Economist:*

> South Korean elections are not about big national questions; they are expressions of regional jealousy. . . . South Korea's imperial presidency encourages regionalism, since rule by one man necessarily prevents rule by a coalition of leaders from different parts of the country. At the same time, regionalism encourages imperiousness, since it reduces party politics to squabbles that have nothing to do with national issues. The assembly cannot play its . . . role of balancing the president's power. So South Korea is run by ministers who the president hires and fires. . . . This creates a damaging divide. The business of government is carried by brainy backroom boys. Politics and elections run on a largely separate track, which has little to do with policy.[60]

Assessment

The reforms of the past three years have led to a more liberal and democratic South Korean state. Kim's campaign against privileges and corruption in every sphere of public and private life, his attack on vested interests, and his consolidation of civilian control over the military have combined to alter, arguably for good, the manner in which authority is conducted in South Korea. The experience of the 1995 local elections confirmed and consolidated this change, and the arrest and prosecution of two former presidents in late 1995 on charges of corruption and involvement in the 1979 coup and the 1980 Kwangju massacre demonstrated how dramatically different South Korean politics had become.

Yet the development of democratic politics has not yet completed its course. It is complicated by the tradition of regionalism and by the problematic relationship with North Korea, which resonates in the domestic scene. On the left (at times most strikingly represented by students) there is pressure for a more conciliatory policy toward the North, while on the right this remains anathema. The president's strong stance against student demonstrations over this issue, and indeed the persistence of the National Security Law, could perhaps be seen as largely a means of maintaining support from the right of the political spectrum. None of this, however, detracts from the fact that South Korea has in many ways become one of the more vigorous democracies of East Asia.

Economically, President Kim's wide-ranging program of reforms toward liberalizing and globalizing the ROK's trade has undoubtedly met with success. In 1994, after a lull of some three years when economic growth was sluggish compared to the heady years of the 1980s, economic growth rose to 8.4 percent from 5.8 percent in 1993, and inflation was kept at 5.6 percent. The ROK economy is booming: Per capita income has reached $10,000 a year and there is full employment. South Korea is now the world's fifth-largest car manufacturer. Samsung leads the world market for dynamic random-access memory chips. The big conglomerate Cheil Foods and Chemicals stated in 1995 that it was paying $300 million for an 11.1 percent stake in DreamWorks SKG, Steven Spielberg's new Hollywood studio.[61]

However, some of the financial, business, and economic reforms appear to have been less successful, and sometimes more apparent than real. A number of reasons may be put forward to explain this. First, many of the deregulation measures relating to business activity have been insignificant or restricted to nonessentials, and because actual policy has not changed, little progress has been made in some quarters. Business owners and managers would have infinitely preferred that the government focus its deregulatory efforts on quality rather than quantity, and on areas that would make a practical difference to business and consumer interests—which it has not.[62]

Second, the government has introduced a spate of financial reforms covering deregulation, and foreign-exchange and capital-transaction liberalization. Some of these are only minor changes, but they have been so numerous and were brought in so quickly that the banks have not been able to keep pace. In addition, although the government has passed reforms in different areas of the financial market, it has not liberalized the monetary institutions that must carry them through, nor removed the methods of control that they use. Some of the changes therefore have the effect of relaxing and tightening restrictions at once. And despite the rapidity and quantity of the financial reforms, South Korea still has the most tightly closed financial market; foreigners can hold only 15 percent of listed shares on the stock market and the won has yet to be made convertible.[63]

Third, the bureaucracy has displayed an obstinate resistance to all the reforms and has indulged in persistent foot dragging, aimed at slowing the process of implementation and thus retarding progress.[64]

Fourth, the power of the *chaebol* in the economy continues to soar despite Kim's reforms. It is their expertise and wealth that the ROK relies upon to boost economic growth, and all attempts to check the overconcentration of power in the *chaebol* have failed. Their success has continued unabated, while bankruptcies among small and medium-sized industries and firms are running at a record level. So important are the *chaebol* now to the Seoul regime's globalization program that President Kim's policy of cutting links between business and politics has been reversed.[65] There is little doubt that the present regime has been facing a dilemma with respect to managing the *chaebol,* as have its predecessors. According to one view, however, it has been approaching the problem in exactly the wrong way:

> Overregulation is not a problem that can be solved with regulation. For almost a decade, Korean governments have tried to rein in the chaebol with no success. Tighter regulations on ownership will simply drive the process deeper underground by creating an artificial paper trail. A far better solution would be simply to open up the economy and get the government out of the business of allocating credit. A chaebol competing at home for market share—with no hope of a government bailout—would concentrate on its core strengths quickly enough. . . . As Mr Kim wrestles with preparing his country for the 21st century, our advice would be to leave Korean business alone. It's Korea, Inc. that needs reforming.[66]

Finally, the government is still showing reluctance to relinquish its control over sections of the economy.[67] Price policy has yet to be reformed. The government continues to resort to "administrative guidance" to prevent price rises in goods and services, and to prop up insolvent businesses with large injections of cash. Competition in the financial and key industrial sectors has not materialized because administrative controls still persist. The business community has complained that President Kim has actually extended government intervention into the private sector by preventing private firms from investing in new industry, by artificially manipulating production, and by overseeing the facilitation of investment.

In the field of the economy, then, the verdict must be mixed as well. Features inherent to the economic system will, for the foreseeable future, continue to combine with political considerations to place limitations on the extent and speed of further liberalization.

Notes

1. V. Cable, "What Is International Economic Security?" *International Affairs,* Vol. 71, No. 2 (1995), p. 307.

2. A. Spaeth, "He's Just Tough Enough," *Time,* Vol. 145, No. 26 (26 June 1995), p. 62.

3. Ibid.

4. S. Awanohara, "Win, Hold, Confuse: South Koreans Worried by New U.S. Military Strategy," *Far Eastern Economic Review,* Vol. 156, No. 28 (15 July 1993), p. 12.

5. "Ambassador Park Stresses Harmony In Ties With North Korea, U.S.," *Korea Newsreview,* Vol. 24, No. 5 (4 February 1995), p. 8.

6. K. Jinwung, "The Nature of South Korean Anti-Americanism," *Korea Journal,* Vol. 34, No. 1 (Spring 1994), pp. 36–47.

7. J. Stremlau, "Clinton's Dollar Diplomacy," *Foreign Policy,* No. 97 (Winter 1994–1995), p. 26; N. Dunne, "Clinton & Co Looks for Business," *Financial Times,* 24 February 1994.

8. Stremlau, "Clinton's Dollar Diplomacy," pp. 23–24.

9. N. Dunne, "'Bloody Fight' for Emerging Markets," *Financial Times,* 21 September 1994.

10. W. Tow, "Reshaping Asian-Pacific Security," *The Journal of East Asian Affairs,* Vol. VIII, No. 1 (Winter/Spring 1994), pp. 97–101; Kyung-Won Kim, "Korea and the U.S. in the Post–Cold War World," *Korea and World Affairs,* Vol. XVIII, No. 2 (Summer 1994), p. 228.

11. "Visit by U.S. President," *Keesing's Record of World Events,* Vol. 39, No. 7 (July 1993), p. 39,557.

12. Stremlau, "Clinton's Dollar Diplomacy," pp. 21, 28, 29; Dunne, "'Bloody fight.'"

13. S. Randolph, "Give NAFTA a Chance," *Far Eastern Economic Review,* Vol. 156, No. 33 (19 August 1993), p. 20.

14. F. Ching, "At APEC Summit, Everyone Won," *Far Eastern Economic Review,* Vol. 156, No. (9 December 1993), p. 48; A. Spaeth, "Dressed for Success," *Time,* Vol. 144, No. 22 (28 November 1994), pp. 34–35.

15. J. Laney, "The ROK–U.S. Relationship and the Test of Time," *Korea and World Affairs,* Vol. 18, No. 4 (Winter 1994), p. 664.

16. Office of the U.S. Trade Representative (USTR), *1992 National Trade Estimate Report on Foreign Trade Barriers* (Washington, D.C.: Government Printing Office, 1992), p. 158.

17. M. Ryan, "East Asian Political Economies and the GATT Regime," *Asian Survey,* Vol. XXXIV, No. 6 (July 1994), pp. 560–561.

18. Office of the U.S. Trade Representative (USTR), *1992 National Trade,* p. 165.

19. M. Clifford, "No Assurance: Foreign Insurance Firms Find South Korea Tough Going," *Far Eastern Economic Review,* Vol. 156, No. 26 (1 July 1993), pp. 62–63.

20. Ibid.

21. "U.S. Chip Talks Fail," *Far Eastern Economic Review,* Vol. 156, No. 9 (4 March 1993), p. 55.

22. S. Awanohara, "Chips with Everything," *Far Eastern Economic Review,* Vol. 156, No. 13 (1 April 1993), p. 80.

23. Business Briefing, "South Korea: AT&T Allowed to Bid," *Far Eastern Economic Review,* Vol. 156, No. 15 (15 April 1993), p. 67; Business Briefing, "South

Korea: Beef Imports Set," *Far Eastern Economic Review,* Vol. 156, No. 27 (8 July 1993), p. 55.

24. *Keesing's Record of World Events,* Vol. 39, No. 12 (December 1993), p. 39,777; "President: Nuclear Issue Must Be Solved," *FBIS (Foreign Broadcast Information Service)-EAS-94-001,* 3 January 1994, p. 47.

25. "U.S.–Korean Trade Relations Seen to Be Thorny in '95," *Korea Newsreview,* Vol. 24, No. 1 (7 January 1995), pp. 14–15.

26. "Seoul to Open Auto Market Ahead of Schedule," *FBIS-EAS-94-105,* 1 June 1994, p. 50; "Industrial Nations Demand Wider Opening of Financial Market," *Korea Newsreview,* Vol. 24, No. 7 (18 February 1995), p. 15.

27. "Seoul–Washington Trade Dispute Looms Large," *Korea Newsreview,* Vol. 24, No. 15 (15 April 1995), pp. 21–22; "U.S.–Korean Trade Relations," p. 14; M. Newman, "Start Your Engines," *Far Eastern Economic Review,* Vol. 158, No. 12 (25 March 1995), pp. 50–51.

28. "Seoul Expected to Join OECD by End of '96," *Korea Newsreview,* Vol. 24, No. 10 (11 March 1995), p. 16; "Government Promotes Economic Internationalization," *FBIS-EAS-94-085,* 3 May 1994, p. 48; "Economic Official Details Outlook," *FBIS-EAS-94-192,* 4 October 1994, pp. 58–60.

29. "Government Decides to Accept 27 OECD Acts," *FBIS-EAS-94-138,* 19 July 1994, p. 48; "Government Applies for Admission to OECD," *Korea Newsreview,* Vol. 24, No. 14 (8 April 1994), p. 14.

30. "Dismissal of Government," *Keesing's Record of World Events,* Vol. 39, No. 12 (December 1993), p. 39,777.

31. "Government to Reduce Agricultural Subsidies," *FBIS-EAS-94-030,* 14 February 1994, p. 59.

32. "Over 30,000 Protesters Oppose Uruguay Round," *FBIS-EAS-94-069,* 11 April 1994, p. 45; "160 Said Injured in 'Violent' Anti-UR Rallies," *FBIS-EAS-94-118,* 20 June 1994, p. 32; "Prime Minister Apology for Uruguay Round Issue," *FBIS-EAS-94-065,* 5 April 1994, p. 46; "Deputy Prime Minister on Opening, Deregulation," *FBIS-EAS-94-006,* 10 January 1994, p. 33; "Chongwadae Defines 11 Issues as 'Core Tasks,'" *FBIS-EAS-94-097,* 19 May 1994, p. 35; "Opposition Launches Offensive Over UR Accord," *FBIS-EAS-94-070,* 12 April 1994, p. 47; "DLP, DP Agree to Ratification of WTO Accord," *FBIS-EAS-94-241,* 15 December 1994, p. 39.

33. "US–Korean Trade Relations Seen to Be Thorny in '95," *Korea Newsreview,* Vol. 24, No. 1 (7 January 1995), p. 14; "Seoul–Washington Trade Dispute," pp. 21–22; "U.S. Continues to Wield 'Super 301,'" *Korea Newsreview,* Vol. 24, No. 12 (25 March 1995), p. 16.

34. "'I Feel Very Proud,'" *Time,* Vol. 145, No. 26 (26 June 1995), p. 65.

35. "President's 'Phase-Two Reform' Criticized," *FBIS-EAS-94-062,* 31 March 1994, p. 27; "Kim Substantiates Vision of Globalized Diplomacy," *Korea Newsreview,* Vol. 24, No. 2 (14 January 1995), p. 5.

36. E. Paisley, "Kim the Broker," *Far Eastern Economic Review,* Vol. 156, No. 5 (4 February 1993), p. 36; E. Paisley, "Wounded Tiger," *Far Eastern Economic Review,* Vol. 156, No. 25 (24 June 1993), p. 22.

37. "Five-year Economic Plan," *Keesing's Record of World Events,* Vol. 39, No. 6 (June 1993), p. 39,509.

38. "Rates Deregulated," *Far Eastern Economic Review,* Vol. 156, No. 45 (11 November 1993), p. 75; "Government to Develop Measures to Fight Inflation," *FBIS-EAS-94-005,* 7 January 1994, p. 24; "Government Promotes Economic Internationalization," *FBIS-EAS-94-085,* 3 May 1994, p. 48.

39. "Deregulation: Fall in the Momentum Fuels Anxieties for Backfire," *FBIS-*

EAS-94-204, 21 October 1994, p. 45–46; "Midway Assessment of Kim Yong-sam's Economy," *FBIS-EAS-94-204*, 21 October 1994, p. 45.

40. "Finance Minister: Deregulation to Accelerate," *FBIS-EAS-94-002*, 4 January 1994, p. 31; "Financial Group's Business Barriers Attacked," *FBIS-EAS-94-131*, 8 July 1994, p. 29; "Foreign Currency Holdings Limit Abolished," *FBIS-EAS-94-075*, 19 April 1994, p. 37; "Finance Ministry Moves Towards Open Bond Market," *FBIS-EAS-94-085*, 3 May 1994, pp. 48–49.

41. E. Paisley, "The Final Frontier," *Far Eastern Economic Review*, Vol. 156, No. 29 (23 July 1993), p. 58; "Ministry to 'Drastically Ease' Regulations," *FBIS-EAS-94-246*, 22 December 1994, p. 42; "Business Briefing," *Far Eastern Economic Review*, Vol. 158, No. 20 (18 May 1995), p. 63.

42. "Administration Not to Favor Large Companies," *FBIS-EAS-94-008*, 11 March 1994, p. 31.

43. "Finance Ministry to Begin Privatizing Banks," *FBIS-EAS-94-085*, 3 May 1994, p. 48.

44. "Incentives Sought for Public Project Investment," *FBIS-EAS-94-006*, 10 January 1994, p. 35; "Private Participation in Infrastructure Encouraged," *FBIS-EAS-94-173*, 7 September 1994, p. 63; "Up-to-Date Transportation Networks Slated," *Korea Newsreview*, Vol. 24, No. 3 (21 January 1995), pp. 7–8.

45. Shim Jae Hoon, "Rich Men and Politicians," *Far Eastern Economic Review*, Vol. 158, No. 18 (4 May 1995), p. 36.

46. "Ruling Against Chaebol," *Far Eastern Economic Review*, Vol. 156, No. 37 (16 September 1993), p. 79; "Rules of Conglomerates," *Far Eastern Economic Review*, Vol. 156, No. 45 (11 November 1993), p. 75; "Government Unveils 9-Point Aid Package for Small Businesses," *Korea Newsreview*, Vol. 24, No. 7 (18 February 1995), p. 14.

47. "Strike-Ridden Firms To Lose Support," *FBIS-EAS-94-010*, 14 January 1994, p. 22; "Government to 'Intensively' Support 9 Industries," *FBIS-EAS-94-207*, 26 October 1994, p. 55.

48. "President Kim Stresses Educational Reform," *FBIS-EAS-94-173*, 7 September 1994, p. 58; "Globalization Drive Stresses Early English Education: A huge upsurge in the learning of English," *Korea Newsreview*, Vol. 24, No. 19 (13 May 1995), pp. 10–11; Shim Jae Hoon, "Option B: Education Reform May Cross Off Multiple-Choice Tests," *Far Eastern Economic Review*, Vol. 158, No. 14 (6 April 1995), p. 18.

49. "Articles Discuss Political Reform Developments," *FBIS-EAS-94-098*, 20 May 1994, pp. 38–46; "Government Plans to Transfer Tasks," *FBIS-EAS-94-116*, 16 June 1994, p. 39; "Fostering of local Economic Autonomy Stressed," *FBIS-EAS-94-227*, 25 November 1994, p. 54.

50. *The Economist*, 1 July 1995, p. 57.

51. Ibid.; see also "The House That Park Built: A Survey of South Korea," *The Economist*, 3 June 1995, pp. 14–16.

52. "BAI to Investigate Government Budgets," *FBIS-EAS-94-002*, 4 January 1994, p. 32; "Trade, Industry, Energy Ministry on 'Revamp,'" *FBIS-EAS-94-002*, 4 January 1994, p. 33; "Yonhap Speculates on Foreign Ministry Restructuring," *FBIS-EAS-94-008*, 12 January 1994, p. 26; "Government Accelerates Reorganization Work," *FBIS-EAS-94-044*, 4 March 1994, p. 45; "Ministries Instructed To Form Downsizing Plans," *FBIS-EAS-94-070*, 12 April 1994, pp. 5051; "NSP Changing Role in Era of 'Internationalization'," *FBIS-EAS-94-009*, 13 January 1994, p. 19; "Government Decides to Restructure Administration," *FBIS-EAS-94-233*, 5 December 1994, p. 56; "Government Virtually Confirms Restructuring Plan," *FBIS-EAS-94-239*, 13 December 1994, p. 46.

53. "Police Agency Launches Internal Audit Inspection," *FBIS-EAS-94-169*, 31 August 1994, pp. 72–73.

54. "Prohibition of Anonymity in Financial Transactions," *Keesing's Record of World Events*, Vol. 39, No. 8 (August 1993), p. 39,598; Ed Paisley, "What's in a Name?" *Far Eastern Economic Review*, Vol. 156, No. 10 (11 March 1993), p. 55; Takashi Oka, "Confucian Reform," *Time*, Vol. 142, No. 15 (11 October 1993), p. 37; "Real-Name Land Transaction System Planned," *FBIS-EAS-94-149*, 3 August 1994, p. 50.

55. Shin Jae Hoon, "The Outs Are In," *Far Eastern Economic Review*, Vol. 156, No. 10 (11 March 1993), p. 12.

56. A. Spaeth, "He's Just Tough Enough," p. 63.

57. Quoted in *Time*, 11 December 1995, p. 46.

58. Good contemporary coverage of these events can be found in the *Financial Times*, *International Herald Tribune*, and *Washington Post* of 20 November to 11 December 1995; *The Economist*, 2 December and 9 December 1995; and the *Far Eastern Economic Review*, Vol. 158, 30 November, 7 December, and 14 December 1995. Also E. Desmond, "Legacy of Blood and Greed," *Time*, 11 December 1995, pp. 44–49.

59. See "The House That Park Built: A Survey of South Korea," *The Economist*, 3 June 1995, p. 15.

60. Ibid., pp. 15–16.

61. "Korean Economy Grew 8.4 percent in '94," *Korea Newsreview*, Vol. 24, No. 12 (25 March 1995), p. 12; "Kim Spearheads Reforms in His Two Years in Office," *Korea Newsreview*, Vol. 24, No. 8 (25 February 1995), pp. 4–5; Spaeth, "He's Just Tough Enough," p. 62. See also *The Economist*, "The House That Park Built: A Survey of South Korea," 3 June 1995.

62. "Divorced from Reality: Why?" *FBIS-EAS-94-024*, 21 October 1994, p. 45; "Suggested Prescriptions," *FBIS-EAS-94-204*, 21 October 1994, p. 46.

63. "Banks Lost Amid Reforms, Adding to Confusion," *FBIS-EAS-94-204*, 21 October 1994, p. 54; "Why the Delay in Reform?" *FBIS-EAS-94-204*, 21 October 1994, p. 54; Spaeth, "He's Just Tough Enough," p. 65.

64. "President's 'Phase-Two Reform' Criticized," p. 28; M. Clifford, "Control Freaks: South Korean Firms Challenge Business as Usual," *Far Eastern Economic Review*, Vol. 158, No. 19 (11 May 1995), p. 73; "Concern Over Prime Minister's Lack of Authority," *FBIS-EAS-94-107*, 3 June 1994, p. 35.

65. Clifford, "No Assurance"; Shim Jae Hoon, "Rich Men and Politicians," p. 36.

66. "The Will To Fail: South Korea Versus its Chaebol," *Far Eastern Economic Review*, Vol. 158, No. 6 (9 February 1995), p. 5.

67. "Regime Back to 'Old Methods' of Price Control," *FBIS-EAS-94-006*, 10 January 1994, pp. 32–33; "Government Criticized for Interfering in Business," *FBIS-EAS-94-179*, 15 September 1994, p. 57.

14

"Opening Up" China: Liberalizing International Economic Relations[1]

ALASDAIR I. MCBEAN

Under the Maoist regime China sought to minimize its dependence on the rest of the world. Imports were determined by a central plan and closely followed China's domestic investments. Exports were either planned to pay for capital-goods imports deemed essential, or a residual after domestic needs had been satisfied. No attention was paid to considerations of efficiency in terms of the relative costs of domestic versus foreign sourcing of goods or services. Contact between Chinese and foreigners was minimized, and after the break with Russia in the late 1950s China borrowed little from the rest of the world. Foreign investment was forbidden.

After Mao, in the mid-1970s, China's imports and exports rose sharply, but the real break with the past began in 1978 with a step-by-step process of opening up China's international economic relations. Like the domestic reforms, the process involved no grand plan. Indeed, it was characterized by pragmatism and experiment; by occasional retreats to central direction as well as progress toward greater liberalization. The reforms in China's policies toward foreign trade, finance, technology, and investment interacted with domestic reforms in macroeconomics, agriculture, rural industry, state enterprise, and decentralization of decisionmaking. It is difficult to discuss one kind of reform without the other. Peter Nolan, in his study for this volume, has concentrated on the domestic issues; this chapter will focus on international policies and their effects.

Judged by results the policies were remarkably effective. China's export success rivals that of the Asian dragons (South Korea, Singapore, Taiwan, and Hong Kong). Its share of world trade increased by nearly two and a half times between 1978 and 1995.

This chapter addresses five questions: (1) What were the aims of the government? (2) What policies did they adopt? (3) What is the record of economic progress? (4) Were the government's policies the cause of success? (5) What are the prospects for continued progress?

Origins of Liberalization: The Government's Aims

Prereform China's trade policies were basically aimed at independence. Two quotations stress this aspect. In 1955 the minister of foreign trade, Ye Jizhuang, said: "Export is for import and import is for the country's socialist industrialisation." The director of the ministry's Import Bureau put it more specifically: "The purpose of importing more industrial equipment from the Soviet Union is to lay the foundation of China's industrial independence, so that in the future China can produce all of the producer goods it needs."[2] In 1978 almost all trade took place through twelve State Trading Corporations organized along sectoral lines. Sino-Chem, for example, had a monopoly over exports and imports of chemicals. This meant that Chinese managers in manufacturing had little or no opportunity to meet foreign businesspeople. Most trade deals were struck at the biannual Canton Trade Fair.

The system was exceedingly rigid and highly inefficient. The yuan prices facing enterprises had no connection with world prices. Exports and imports were not determined by comparative advantage but simply as a means of obtaining essential imports, almost exclusively capital goods. Until the 1970s there was a high correlation between China's investment and imports.[3]

China did gain substantial flows of capital and technology from the USSR in the 1950s, but after the break in relations Chairman Mao placed his confidence in the development of indigenous technology. Despite some dramatic successes this proved illusory and after Mao's death the government swung to the opposite extreme in the mid- to late 1970s in a frantic attempt to gain Western technology. As part of the Four Modernizations program, which stressed the use of modern technology in industry, agriculture, defense, and science and technology, the government began massive importing of machines, power plants, and complete factories. The enthusiasm brought chaos in 1977–1978. There were bottlenecks, power shortages, duplications of orders, equipment left to rust at ports, and inflation as money incomes outstripped the supply of consumer goods. An unprecedented trade deficit of $1.1 billion precipitated a crisis leading to the abandonment of the Four Modernizations, canceled orders, strict import controls, abandonment of many projects, and retrenchment. This early attempt at opening China's economy contained no elements of liberalization. It was entirely carried out by command and was badly planned.[4]

These failures, together with the reinstated Deng Xiaoping's success in his political struggle with Hua Guofeng, the conservative chairman of the Chinese Communist Party, led to the recognition of the need for more fundamental economic reforms to improve efficiency and release the energies of China's workers and managers. Reformers blamed the bottlenecks on the overcentralization of Soviet-style planning, which put the economy in a straightjacket, discouraged initiative, and resulted in waste.[5] These led to the aims of decentralizing China's centralized planning system and reversing its policy of international isolation. Policymakers recognized that it would be necessary to encourage foreign investment in China and the importation of technology through joint ventures.

Motivation to modernize production and improve living standards was also influenced by the examples of China's close neighbors, especially Taiwan and Hong Kong. Indeed, the postwar success of Japan and the more recent outstanding growth of the East Asian economies attracted the attention of Chinese economists. The opening up let them compare economic growth and economic systems elsewhere in the world. Ideological liberation was also promoted by "the bitter experience of the Cultural Revolution" and Deng Xiaoping's insistence that "practice is the only criterion for judging the truth."[6] Experience and ideological change stimulated foreign-trade reform.[7] There was no blueprint, but broad aims included harnessing market forces to serve the ends of decentralization to enterprises, and to give incentives to farmers, managers, and foreign investors to produce for export. Subsidiary objectives developed as prompted by the success and failure of the policies, but all remained subject to maintaining the control of the Chinese Communist Party (CCP).

The Record

Following the leadership's shift toward liberalizing China's international policies on trade, finance, technology, and investment, what does the record show about the country's trade and investment performance and the degree of openness it achieved?

Overall Growth

China's trade and investment record is outstanding. Exports grew from about $15 billion in 1979 to over $115 billion in 1994.[8] At an average annual growth rate of 14 percent in real terms between 1980 and 1991 China's merchandise exports outstripped South Korea's 11 percent over the same period.[9] OECD imports of manufactures from China rose from $243 million to $59.5 billion between 1970 and 1992.[10] China moved from 20th to 10th in terms of its share of world trade. Its increased openness is shown in a trade ratio (exports plus imports to GNP) that has at least doubled. The data show an increase from 8 percent in 1978 to over 20 percent of GDP.[11] But this provides a somewhat exaggerated picture because GDP is underestimated at official rates of exchange, and recent exports contain many that are simply processed imports of which only wages and a share of profits accrue to China. The data show these as 23 percent in 1988 and 45 percent in 1991; for manufactured exports the processed share was 64 percent.[12]

Overall China's trade balance has generally been healthy, its reserves relatively high, and its foreign indebtedness low compared with most transitional or developing economies.[13]

Export Structure

The structure of exports shifted from primary products to labor-intensive manufactures. The share of all manufactures rose from 46 percent to 80 percent between 1960 and 1990, with a drop in primary commodity exports from 46 percent to 19 percent.[14] Labor-intensive manufactures rose by an average 23.6 percent from 1980 to 1990, and human capital–intensive manufactures rose by 25.3 percent, but from a relatively small base.[15] In 1991 China's share of world exports of travel goods was 30 percent, of plastic goods 20 percent, garments 14 percent, and footwear 13 percent.[16] Recent studies suggest that over the 1979–1990 period of reform China increased its international competitiveness in OECD markets relative to other East Asian economies.[17] Like its East Asian counterparts China is moving up the "ladder of comparative advantage" to more skill-intensive products. In 1994 electronics goods fetched $12.3 billion, about 11 percent of total exports.[18]

On the basis of these data, this huge country has consistently, over the last fifteen years, done what few would have predicted and many would have considered impossible. It has achieved a foreign trade performance that equals that of the East Asian "miracle" economies.

Investment

The cumulative total of foreign direct investment (FDI) in China was only $1 billion in 1979–1982, but a rapid growth in FDI up to 1993 brought that total to above $60 billion of actual investment. FDI in 1993 was about $26 billion and the contracted amount of FDI was over $110 billion.[19] Cable gives a figure of $28 billion disbursed in 1994, with $170 billion contracted. These figures compare with a cumulative total of FDI in India of just over $2 billion for the same period, and a mere $600 million actual and $2.5 billion contracted in 1993.[20] There were 20,000 Sino–foreign joint ventures operating in China in 1991.[21] In recent years Chinese companies have invested large amounts abroad, particularly in Hong Kong, but also in the United States, Germany, and the UK.

Over the period 1986–1992, between 60 and 70 percent of inward FDI came from Hong Kong and Macao. When Taiwan, Singapore, and the Chinese communities of East Asia are added, the "Greater China" share in 1992 was just over 80 percent. The share of OECD investment has been falling in recent years but it has continued to rise in absolute value from $917 million in 1989 to $1,594 million in 1992.[22] Japanese FDI seems to have been rising rapidly more recently, partly in an attempt to make up ground lost to Germany and the United States in the automobile industry in China.[23] South Korea is expected to emerge as a major supplier of FDI to China in the near future.

Almost 90 percent of FDI has been concentrated in coastal cities and Special Economic Zones (SEZs). Indeed, attracting FDI and new technology was one of the express purposes of these SEZs. Guangdong Province (Canton), with its high-profile Shenzhen SEZ, attracted 41 percent of China's FDI in 1986 and was still attracting 33 percent in 1992.[24]

Technology

Success in acquiring advanced technology through FDI in the 1980s has been limited. Most FDI has been in labor-intensive production, and a good deal of the ventures have been in simple processing in textiles, clothing, footwear, toys, intermediate products, and assembly operations for foreign companies.[25] Looked at more broadly, however, China has acquired much technology from abroad. Between 1952 and 1991 China concluded 5,300 contracts for imported technology to a total value of over $40 billion.[26] Between 1950 and 1959 China imported plant and equipment from the Eastern bloc to establish 156 manufacturing facilities, financed by a long-term loan of $1.9 billion from the USSR. Experts from the USSR flocked to China, and some 12,500 Chinese were trained in the USSR. Sharply cooling relations between China and the USSR, however, brought this aid to a sudden end, and from 1960 China turned to Japan and other OECD countries for imported technology. But the Cultural Revolution caused a sharp swing toward autarky in technology as well as investment and trade, and it was not until the early 1970s that China once more started importing foreign plants and equipment. This was done with a vengeance and culminated in waste and excesses in the late 1970s. But the demand for imported technology continued to rise, and between 1979 and 1991 China concluded over 4,400 imported technology contracts with a value of $26.75 billion.[27]

International Borrowing and Equity Finance

China has a relatively easy debt-servicing position and a reasonable credit rating that has enabled the government to sell bonds on the international markets. Since 1991 China has raised $8.5 billion in this way. Large Chinese enterprises such as CITIC Pacific raised $950 million through international sales of its shares. Other Chinese companies are being listed on stock exchanges in New York or Hong Kong.[28]

Given the extent of change illustrated above, it is worth inquiring in more detail what in fact the policies of the Chinese government have been, and to what extent they can be given credit for the results achieved.

Government Policies to Reform
China's International Economic Relations

Special Economic Zones and Foreign Direct Investment

While the authorities and intellectuals debated how to proceed with reform, the first investment initiative came in 1978 from a Chinese multinational company in Hong Kong. It sought permission to develop a small area of China, along the border with Hong Kong, in collaboration with foreign companies in joint ventures. This had the appeal that it could introduce foreign investors and their capitalist business practices into China, while isolating their activities to a confined zone and thus containing the possible spread of political contamination. In February 1979 the authorities permitted this development and created a "special municipality" on the Hong Kong border with the small town of Shenzhen as its center.

As with many reforms in China, action preceded legislation. The legal framework followed in July 1979 with the Law on Chinese–Foreign Ventures, which was the first step in the enabling legislation for foreign investment in China. It codified the rights of foreign firms and set out the types of foreign ventures that would be allowed in China.[29]

Subsequent legislation clarified property rights, sorted out tax matters, including preferential tax treatment and other incentives, relaxed foreign-exchange controls, and in 1982 made it clear that even wholly owned foreign subsidiaries, previously legal but frowned upon, were acceptable.[30]

The establishment of the Shenzhen Special Economic Zone was followed rapidly by three others, Zhuhai, Shantou, and Xiamen, and in 1988 by the large island of Hainan. There were later extensions of similar privileges to fourteen coastal cities from Beihai in the south to Dalian in the north and to the Pearl River and Yangtse River deltas. In 1990 Pudong in Shanghai was given special status, as were several cities on borders with Russia and other Commonwealth of Independent States (CIS) countries in 1991–1992.

The objectives of the SEZs were: (1) to attract FDI and especially advanced technology to China; (2) to increase exports; (3) to act as "windows and bridges" to the outside world; and (4) to act as laboratories where experiments with reforms could be tested safely before extending them to other parts of China.

The initial effects on FDI were slow, but starting to accelerate by the mid-1980s. In 1991 SEZs and coastal cities alone accounted for 62 percent of actual FDI in China. FDI is highly concentrated in the coastal areas. Nearly 90 percent in 1992 was in the coastal regions, with Guangdong alone accounting for a third of all FDI. By 1991 contracted FDI in manufacturing had risen to 80 percent.[31] Such a high concentration inevitably exacerbates the growing inequalities of income between the coastal and the interior regions of China, which causes social strains and could contribute to political instability. Questions also have to be raised about the opportunity costs to the rest of China of the domestic resources that were poured into infrastructure in the SEZs. Some of the investment has been in highly protected industries serving the domestic market; most has been in low–value added assembly and processing industries. It is not at all evident that the income streams directly generated by the SEZs would outweigh the costs.[32]

China is now a significant investor abroad. Most of its FDI, for obvious reasons, has been in Hong Kong where it now stands at $25 billion. Since the 1990s some of the investment in China has been "round tripping"— Chinese multinational enterprises export capital to subsidiaries who then invest in China to take advantage of the more favorable tax and foreign-exchange treatment afforded to foreign investors. Such activities are antisocial in terms of producing personal rents to managers and defeating the aims of the incentives for foreign investors.[33]

Disappointment with the ability to attract advanced technology led to laws in 1986 that gave differential incentives to encourage export enterprises and technologically advanced enterprises. Yet more guidelines were issued in 1995 to encourage investment in infrastructure and underdeveloped agricultural land while discouraging investment in retailing industries, where supply is outstripping demand. Investments in newspaper publishing, telecommunications networks, and environmentally damaging projects are prohibited.[34]

China has been immensely successful in attracting foreign capital, and the Chinese diaspora has been a major ingredient in this. Their family and other connections (*guanchi*), knowledge of the language and culture, and pride in the success of the land of their ancestors have certainly helped. But their proximity to Hong Kong and their ability to recognize a good investment opportunity probably counted for more. The contrast between the rapid development of Guangdong and the slower growth of Shanghai, an initially better-endowed area, is testimony to the benefits of proximity to Hong Kong. Businesspeople there have simply moved most of their manufacturing processes to Guangdong to take advantage of its drastically lower labor costs and the incentives offered by China. Hong Kong especially, but also Taiwan, Singapore, and the Chinese communities in Indonesia, Malaysia, the Philippines, and Thailand, have been an enormous benefit to China's exports in supplying both manufacturing expertise and marketing skills along with capital. Twenty-seven percent of Chinese exports were from foreign investors in 1993 and about a third in mid-1994.[35] A recent paper claims that China owes a great deal to "productivity gains from dynamic forces unleashed by the creation of an investment-friendly environment and the subsequent inflow of foreign capital, entrepreneurship, technology and market links."[36] Where the Chinese connection has been less successful is in bringing the advanced technology China sought in FDI. Eighty percent of inward FDI has been by overseas Chinese, but most has been in real estate or in labor-intensive exporting, neither of which met the objective of acquiring advanced technology.[37]

It is also a source for concern that the ratio of actual to contracted investment has fallen to 20 percent in the 1990s.[38] This suggests a certain overoptimism on the part of OECD investors who belatedly realize that many obstacles remain to be overcome after they agree to invest in China; the environment is not really as investment-friendly as they are led to believe. It may also suggest increasing political uncertainty about what to expect when Deng Xiaoping departs the scene.

In sum, the SEZs and China's policies toward investment have certainly succeeded in attracting a great deal of FDI, foreign loans, and equity finance. The quality of the FDI has not been ideal from the viewpoint of attracting advanced technology, but FDI has facilitated China's surging exports of manufactures through most of the 1980s and 1990s.

The "windows and bridges" function of the SEZs was particularly useful in the early 1980s when both foreigners and Chinese had to go through a learning process in developing economic relations. The SEZs were windows for foreigners to look in on China and for Chinese to look out on the rest of the world; they served as bridges for foreign capital and know-how to move into China and for exports to move out. SEZs fulfilled both roles admirably.

They also worked quite well as laboratories. Many reforms were first tried out in SEZs that have later been adopted elsewhere. FDI has spread throughout China and market reforms tried out in SEZs are now widespread. In the SEZs commodity markets were largely liberalized; market-determined prices and imports from abroad and from the Chinese hinterland were available without tariffs or restrictions. Now most prices in China are market determined. Experiments in the labor market have included the ending of lifetime employment and the substitution of contracts, increased labor mobility, easier hiring and firing, and a shift of social security provisions from the enterprise to central authorities. Labor markets remain highly controlled in China, but many of these reforms are being tried outside the SEZs. Foreign banks were allowed to operate in SEZs. Joint stock companies, stock markets, futures markets, and foreign-exchange markets were first permitted in Shenzhen and are beginning to spread to other parts of China. The extension of leases of land to enterprises started in SEZs. Other experiments include "a centralised social security system for urban workers in Hainan, the partial sale of state enterprises to foreigners in Xiamen . . . bankruptcy proceedings in Shenzhen," and so on.[39]

Trade Policy Reforms

China's prereform trade policy has been described as an airlock that sealed off the economy from the rest of the world. Almost all trade was controlled by a few state-owned foreign trading companies (FTCs) with monopoly control over specific products. The FTCs executed the central plan for exports and imports under the administration of the Ministry of Trade, later to become the Ministry of Foreign Economic Relations (MOFERT), and still later to be renamed Ministry of Trade and Technical Cooperation (MOTEC). They paid local prices that bore no relation to international prices for products for export, and sold at international prices. Because the exchange rate was overvalued they usually made losses on these transactions. Imports were bought at world prices and sold in the domestic market at inflated prices that again bore little if any relation to world prices. Any profits, and all foreign exchange earned, were remitted to the central government, and losses were met by subsidies from the government budget. Imports, mainly capital goods or essential inputs, were paid for by exporting commodities such as rice, petroleum, other minerals, and processed foods in which China could generate surpluses or divert supplies to the foreign markets. Export quotas had priority. The central plan aimed at importing the required capital goods that China could not produce for itself, balancing China's foreign trade, and avoiding international debts.

Decentralization and incentives. The basic aims of the reforms were to decentralize decisionmaking and introduce more reliance on market forces to guide decisions. Manufactured exports rocketed after 1985, about the time that China's main reforms took effect. These reforms were: (1) the decentralization of Foreign Trade Companies, dividing many of them on provincial lines, allowing new FTCs to be formed, and allowing some larger enterprises to trade directly; (2) increased incentives to export generated by foreign-exchange retentions for exporters; (3) the introduction of "swap markets" for foreign exchange and the depreciation of both the swap-market and the official rates of exchange; (4) the encouragement of foreign-invested firms in order to increase exports. Together the reforms removed the bias against exporting that existed in the old system, and made exporting an attractive option for enterprises and regional authorities.[40] Strikingly, most of the growth in exports was achieved during a period of slow world growth and rising protectionism in the OECD countries.

After 1978 the main thrust of China's trade reforms was to reduce the extent of command planning, but initially trade remained tightly controlled. The first step was to divide the plan for foreign trade into command-plan goods and guidance-plan goods. Exports in the former group were mandatory and governed by specific quotas designated for individual producers, who were allocated the input supplies they needed to meet those quotas. By 1988 some 112 commodities were still covered by the plan but only twenty-one remained in the command plan under the direct control of the State Planning Commission. Guidance-plan targets were fixed in value terms and provinces had discretion over how to achieve them. In 1991 all mandatory planning was supposed to be abolished, but goods designated to one category or the other continued to be controlled by being channeled through a few designated FTCs. In 1992 some 15 percent of China's exports remained in these two categories—down from some 3,000 individual commodities, 100 percent of exports, controlled in 1978.[41]

The planning to which imports were subject was also progressively relaxed, but they remained fairly tightly controlled. In 1984 seven key commodities—steel, chemical fertilizers, rubber, timber, tobacco, grain, and synthetic fibers—were controlled by a system of "unified management." In 1986 about 40 percent of imports were subject to the mandatory plan (down from 90 percent in the early 1980s), 30 percent were subject to foreign exchange allocation for priority projects, and the rest were financed from retained foreign-exchange earned by enterprises or through foreign borrowing by noncentral authorities. By 1992 mandatory planned imports were down to about 18.5 percent.[42]

While command planning declined, China continued to exert control over exports and imports through a system of licensing and the increased use of tariffs. This system served several aims. At the macroeconomic level the government could use these levers to balance the use of foreign exchange with the exchange received. But import licensing and tariffs could also be used to protect selected domestic industries. Imported cars, for example, carried a tariff of 220 percent, which was only recently cut to 150 percent.[43] There were three other main objectives. The first was to correct for domestic price distortions that could lead to excessive exports. For example, where domestic prices for some goods were controlled below world prices, export licenses could be used to make sure that excess exports did not create domestic shortages. The second was to limit exports of tungsten, antimony, tin, and rare earths where increased exports would lower world prices due to China's dominant share of the markets for these products. The third was to allocate subquotas to enterprises from China's quotas for goods restricted under the Multifibers Arrangement or under voluntary export quotas.[44]

The 1988 reforms also introduced the foreign-trade contract system, under which provincial authorities and specialized FTCs signed contracts with MOFERT. The contracts governed three targets that fixed the quantity of foreign exchange to be earned; the amount to be remitted to the central government; and the amount of subsidy for losses on exports that the center would provide. Later the targets were fixed in a "bottom-up" manner, with provincial authorities and FTCs proposing the targets. The amount of money available for subsidies was capped and in 1991 officially cut to zero. National and provincial FTCs became responsible for their own profits and losses, at least on exports.[45] Together with domestic price reforms, the removal or reduction of subsidies on imports such as chemicals, food grains, and coconut oil cut the budgetary costs of international trade and shifted the composition of exports and imports to reflect China's comparative advantage more than in the past.

Foreign exchange. China's real effective exchange rate (the official exchange rate adjusted for relative inflation and weighted by China's trade with partners) appreciated in the early 1980s but after 1983 depreciated markedly. As a result the competitiveness of China's exports improved against its main East Asian competitors. As most of China's manufactures compete on the basis of price this gave a substantial boost to China's exports.

Before 1979 all foreign exchange had to be handed over to the Bank of China in exchange for yuan. Exporters, like domestic firms, had to rely on allocations of foreign exchange through the State Planning Commission when they needed to buy imports; these had to fit the national import plan. After reform began, the government started to decentralize the administration of foreign exchange by letting local authorities and enterprises retain the right to buy back a proportion of their foreign-exchange earnings to use for approved imports. By 1988 foreign invested and domestic enterprises were given permission to sell foreign exchange in the newly established currency swap markets.

The introduction in 1986 of foreign-exchange adjustment centers (FEACs) or swap centers (initially only for foreign companies but later opened up to domestic enterprises) served to ease the difficulty of obtaining foreign currency for essential inputs, and acted as an incentive to earn foreign exchange that could be sold at a premium in the FEACs. Exporting was stimulated by both these effects. Originally firms were allowed to retain rights to only 25 percent of their foreign-exchange earnings, but the authorities adapted this mechanism to adjust incentives to achieve policy objectives. They raised the retention rates to 70 to 100 percent for priority sectors such as light industries, arts and crafts, clothing, machinery, and electrical goods. In addition, firms that exceeded their foreign-exchange targets were allowed to retain higher percentages until 1991, when mandatory planning ended. Higher retention rates applied to certain provinces and in the SEZs were 100 percent. The retention scheme was drastically modified in 1991 with the elimination of the different rates and the introduction of a uniform retention rate throughout China. This was set at 80 percent, divided into 10 percent to the local government, 10 percent to the producing enterprise, and 60 percent to the FTC.[46] In January 1994 the dual-rate system was abandoned. The official rate and the swap rates were merged at the average level in the swap markets. This enabled a devaluation of about 50 percent in the official rate, bringing it down to 8.7 yuan to the dollar. The new system was a managed float based on the market supply and demand for the currency. As of June 1995 it stood at Y8.3 to the dollar.[47] Companies were also freed from the obligation to sell a proportion of their foreign-currency earnings to the state.[48] These moves represent a step toward full convertibility for the yuan.

The role of the FTCs.   From 1979 the number of FTCs was allowed to expand progressively. Provincial branches of many of the specialized national FTCs were turned into provincial FTCs, trading in the same products at first, but sometimes diversifying into broader ranges, in some cases taking over factories whose trade they had handled in the past. Many new so-called general FTCs were created that had authority to deal in a broader range of goods. By 1988 there were over 5,000 FTCs as compared with twelve in 1978. Instead of simply meeting targets laid down for them they were increasingly given responsibility for their commercial performance.

Many FTCs proved inexperienced, incompetent, or untrustworthy, and foreign customers complained of unfulfilled contracts and lack of quality control. Some broke government regulations in their pursuit of business. As a result many lost their licenses to trade, were shut down, or merged with better-regulated FTCs. By late 1988 only some 3,600 remained in operation.

These were all publicly owned and apart from a few operated by sectoral ministries they continued to be supervised by MOFERT (later MOTEC) and its provincial and municipal offices. In addition, just over 500 large enterprises had direct trading rights by 1993. Foreign-owned and joint-venture firms can also conduct their trade independently of FTCs, though sometimes this is made difficult and they sell at least part of their exports through FTCs. This is also true of some large enterprises: In general they strongly prefer to deal directly with their customers, but for special situations such as barter deals with formerly Soviet economies they may choose to use a FTC because of the difficulty of selling goods received in exchange for their exports.[49]

The FTCs normally buy goods for export from enterprises at prices settled by bargaining, and then sell these goods in the world market for what they can fetch. The foreign exchange received is divided between FTC, enterprise, local authority, and central authority according to formulas that have changed over time. For imports, however, the normal method is the agency system, in which they act as agents for a fee that is a percentage of the value of the transaction. It brings domestic prices closer to international prices and makes them more responsive to changes in the latter. This ought to improve resource allocation and competitive efficiency in China. About 90 percent of imports are handled in this way, but relatively few exports, which is hardly surprising given the premiums that could be obtained for foreign exchange, and the lion's share of exchange retentions received by the exporter. As of the early 1990s FTCs were still selling about 80 percent of China's exports and buying about 90 percent of imports. Although this might seem to suggest that they are doing a useful job, not unlike the giant trading companies of Japan and South Korea, that would be too favorable an assessment.[50] Reforms in 1994 have increased the number of enterprises allowed to manage their own foreign trade, and equalized income tax rates to produce equal competitive conditions between foreign trade enterprises and others.[51]

Appraisal.   The rate of growth achieved by China's manufactured exports since the mid-1980s seems evidence enough of the success of the institutional and commercial policy reforms undertaken in opening China, but what role did the reforms in fact play? The correct answer is probably that the role was substantial.

Under the command economy there were no incentives to export. A continuation of that system could not have released the energies of rural industries or attracted the huge inflow of foreign investment. In 1991 exports from rural industries and foreign-invested enterprises were $10 billion each.[52]

The old FTCs were a brake upon foreign trade. Their whole culture was against enterprise and most enterprises were dissatisfied with the services they provided. Their breakup and reform has not been a complete answer to the needs of enterprises, most of whom would prefer to handle their exports and imports themselves, but it is a great improvement on the situation before 1988. Many have retained some monopoly over their suppliers, but most enterprises now can probably shop around for a FTC and obtain competitive bids for their work. Managers have been retrained and many now have foreign experience. More companies are being given the right to trade directly. With a few exceptions the handling of foreign trade is now much more competitive.[53]

Trade barriers are lower and China is much closer to meeting the standards for admission to the WTO. If China's were not so vast an economy, with such a potential impact on world trade, the country would probably have been accepted as a full member of the GATT. Many developing countries became members with less GATT-conforming commercial policies. While under pressure from the World Bank and the OECD nations to do more, China has moved far in the direction of orthodox opinion on trade policy by devaluing and removing barriers to trade and investment. When combined with domestic reforms, particularly those that decentralized decisions to provincial and local authorities and encouraged the development of township and village enterprises, China's foreign-exchange and commercial-policy reforms probably explain most of the country's exporting success in the face of stagnant world growth and rising protectionism in the industrialized nations.

The extra ingredient, which other countries can only envy, was the proximity to Hong Kong and the gains from the diaspora of Chinese throughout East Asia. With about half of investment in China coming from Hong Kong, and nearly half of China's exports passing through Hong Kong, it would be hard to deny the tremendous benefit these links have brought. The enormous growth of Guangdong makes it abundantly clear how important the Hong Kong link has been. Without the reforms this would not have happened, but without the links the export success would have been much less spectacular.

Prospects: Questions of Stability, State Industries, Labor Markets, and Inflation

From the viewpoint of the foreign investor China represents enormous opportunity combined with great risk. The track record has been excellent, but serious problems are emerging. Political instability represents the greatest threat to continued success. But economic policies and their effects contribute powerfully to disaffection that could undermine the central authorities.

So far China has postponed many of the problems that have been faced at high cost in the European transitional economies, such as liberalization of labor markets, social security reform, bankruptcy proceedings, and genuine privatization of at least some of the state-owned enterprises (SOEs). But the threat to the budget from continued SOE losses cannot be allowed to continue much longer. So far the authorities have made promises to tackle these issues, but with little progress, and they have retreated from attacking the problem of loss-making SOEs. Employment in the state sector has risen by 20 percent since 1985. The state currently employs about 70 percent of China's industrial workers, and 70 percent of industrial investment was in SOEs in 1993—up from 61 percent in 1989.[54]

To continue its success in foreign trade and attracting investment China will have to remain competitive. The basis of its comparative advantage, and one of its main attractions to FDI, is its low labor costs. To keep these costs low requires that wages rise no faster than productivity, but because China still has a huge reserve of underemployed workers in rural areas and in old SOEs this should not be difficult, provided labor is mobile. However, many obstacles to labor mobility remain.

Labor-market reform is a high priority. The majority of workers are still tied to their work unit by employment security, housing, child care, schools, and health services provided by enterprises. Not only does this prevent labor from moving to more profitable enterprises, but many SOEs stay in business only because they are fed subsidies or soft loans. Their lack of profits deprives the government of a major source of revenue and causes rising budget deficits and a banking system riddled with bad debts. These in turn weaken the ability of the government to control inflation, which distributes real income arbitrarily, increases uncertainty, and creates disaffection among the many losers. A real threat to China's stability is that inflation could become endemic, bringing with it the problems that have afflicted many

Latin American and Eastern European economies.

It would be a mistake to continue benign neglect of the SOEs in the hope that the growth of township and village enterprises and the private sector will solve the problem. Some are already performing well and others may be salvaged by reform, new managers, or mergers. Many will simply have to close. But that could throw thirty million workers out of their jobs, according to some estimates.[55] Adequate housing, social security, and retraining provisions at the provincial level need to be put in place soon to reduce the social cost and instability that could result. Until now the authorities have not faced up to this challenge.

China's rapid development has been extremely unequal in its effects. Although up to 1985 reform narrowed the gap between urban and rural incomes, the last ten years have seen urban incomes grow much faster than rural. Inequality of incomes between the coastal regions and most other areas of China has also increased. Ending or reducing subsidies to food, transportation, and housing and undermining job security tend to hit the poor. The contrast between their decline and the conspicuous consumption of successful businesspeople, well-connected individuals, and corrupt politicians and officials exacerbates an already stressful situation. So far China has not effectively confronted these growing inequalities and injustices.

Further trade liberalization, along with fiscal reform, would help with most of these problems. As long as some prices are controlled, some products can be sold at different prices in different markets, as continues to be the case, and people with good connections can exploit these differences to make large personal gains. Continued licensing and regulations nourish corrupt practices.

Such reforms are the objectives laid down by the Central Committee of the Communist Party in 1993. Their "socialist market economy" aims at the establishment of nationwide integrated and open markets and at further reform of the foreign-trade and investment regimes.[56] If they implement these reforms the chances are that they can avoid the perils of instability. Returning to a centrally controlled economy is no longer a viable option. The Chinese people have tasted the benefits of opening and liberalizing China's economy. They do not want to turn back.

Notes

1. I am grateful to the Economic and Social Committee on Research of the Overseas Development Administration for research grant R 4847, which helped to support research on China's Foreign Trade Corporations on which I have drawn in this chapter. They bear no responsibility for any of the analysis or opinions expressed here.

In addition to the sources referred to in subsequent notes, this chapter has drawn on the following: A. Singh, "The Plan, The Market and Evolutionary Reform in China," UNCTAD Discussion Paper No. 76, Geneva, December 1993; World Bank, *China: Between Plan and Market* (Washington, D.C.: World Bank, 1990).

2. F. Mah, "Foreign Trade," in A. Eckstein, W. Galenson, and T. Liu, eds., *Economic Trends in Communist China* (Chicago: Aldine Publishing Company, 1968), pp. 672–673. Quoted in N. Lardy, *Foreign Trade and Economic Reform in China, 1978–1990* (Cambridge: Cambridge University Press, 1992), p.16.

3. J. Hsu, *China's Foreign Trade Reforms: Impact on Growth and Stability* (Cambridge: Cambridge University Press, 1989), Figure 1.1.

4. Ibid., pp. 20–23.

5. G. Lin and R. Wang, "Restructuring of the Economy," in Y. Guang Yuang, ed., *China's Socialist Modernisation* (Beijing: Foreign Languages Press, 1984), quoted in P. Nolan, "Introduction," in P. Nolan and D. Fureng, eds., *The Chinese Economy and its Future* (Cambridge: Polity Press, 1990), p. 13.

6. X. Zhou, "Foreign Trade," in Nolan and Fureng, *The Chinese Economy,* p. 248.

7. Ibid., pp. 248–250.

8. K. Fukasaku and D. Wall, with M. Wu, *China's Long March To An Open Economy* (Paris: OECD Development Centre, 1994), Figure III.1; *China–Britain Trade Review,* April 1995, p. 19.

9. World Bank, *World Development Report 1992* (New York: Oxford University Press for the World Bank, 1992), Statistical Appendix, Table 13.

10. World Bank, *World Development Report 1994* (New York: Oxford University Press for the World Bank, 1994), Statistical Appendix, Table 16.

11. V. Cable, *China and India: Economic Reform and Global Integration* (London: The Royal Institute of International Affairs, 1995), p. 18.

12. World Bank, *China: Foreign Trade Reform: Meeting the Challenge of the 1990s,* Washington, D.C.: World Bank, 1993.

13. *World Development Report 1994,* Statistical Appendix, Tables 17, 20, and 23.

14. People's Republic of China, *Statistical Yearbook,* various issues.

15. World Bank, *China: Foreign Trade Reform,* Table 1.3.

16. Cable, *China and India,* Table 13.

17. Fukasaku, Wall, and Wu, *China's Long March,* p. 69 and the studies cited there.

18. *China–Britain Trade Review,* June 1995; see also A. Yeats, *China's Foreign Trade and Comparative Advantage* (World Bank Discussion Papers, No. 141) (Washington, D.C.: World Bank, 1991).

19. Fukasaku, Wall, and Wu, *China's Long March,* Table III-5.

20. Cable, *China and India,* pp. 40–42.

21. World Bank, *China: Reform and the Role of the Plan in the 1990s* (Washington, D.C.: World Bank, 1992), p. xvi.

22. Fukasaku, Wall, and Wu, *China's Long March,* Table III-6.

23. See *Financial Times,* 22 June 1995.

24. Fukasaku, Wall, and Wu, *China's Long March,* Table III-7.

25. World Bank, *China: Foreign Trade Reform,* p. 73.

26. H. Zhao, "Technology Imports and Their Impacts on the Enhancement of China's Indigenous Technological Capacity," *Journal of Development Studies,* April 1995, Appendix I.

27. For a recent description and analysis of China's technology imports see H. Zhao, "Technology Imports."

28. Cable, *China and India,* pp. 44–45.

29. Fukasaku, Wall, and Wu, *China's Long March,* p. 42.

30. A detailed list of China's legislation governing FDI is set out in Fukasaku, Wall, and Wu, *China's Long March,* Appendix 1.

31. Ibid., p. 76.

32. See World Bank, *China: Foreign Trade Reform;* Fukasaku, Wall, and Wu, *China's Long March,* and references cited there.

33. A. MacBean, *China's Foreign Trade Corporations: Their role in economic reform and export success,* Lancaster University, Management School Discussion Paper, 1993.

34. Fukasaku, Wall, and Wu, *China's Long March,* p. 37; *China–Britain Trade Review,* April 1995, p.17.

35. Cable, *China and India,* p. 41.

36. A. Panagarya, "Unravelling the Mysteries of China's Foreign Trade Regime," *The World Economy,* January 1993, p. 66.

37. Fukasaku, Wall, and Wu, *China's Long March,* Table III-6.

38. Ibid., p. 73.

39. Ibid., p. 47.

40. See Lardy, *Foreign Trade and Economic Reform in China;* World Bank, *China: Foreign Trade Reform.*

41. World Bank, *China: Foreign Trade Reform,* Chapter 2.

42. Ibid.

43. *Financial Times,* 20 January 1994.

44. Lardy, *Foreign Trade and Economic Reform in China,* Chapter 3.

45. Ibid.

46. World Bank, *China: Foreign Trade Reform,* pp. 28–32.

47. Fukasaku, Wall, and Wu, *China's Long March,* p. 35; *The Economist,* 10 June 1995.

48. *Beijing Review,* 30 January 1995, p. 8.

49. See MacBean, *China's Foreign Trade Corporations.*

50. See World Bank, *China: Foreign Trade Reform,* Chapter 3.

51. *Beijing Review,* 30 January 1995, p. 8 ff.

52. D. Perkins, "China's 'Gradual' Approach to Market Reforms," UNCTAD, Discussion Paper No. 52, Geneva, December 1992, p. 13.

53. MacBean, *China's Foreign Trade Corporations;* World Bank, *China: Foreign Trade Reform,* Chapter 3.

54. World Bank data quoted in *The Economist,* 10 June 1995.

55. For instance, *The Economist,* 10 June 1995.

56. Fukasaku, Wall, and Wu, *China's Long March,* p. 111.

15

China's Post-Mao Political Economy: A Puzzle[1]

PETER NOLAN

The Consensus on Post-Communist Reform

China's approach toward economic reform contrasts markedly with that of most other former centrally planned economies (CPEs). Eastern Europe and Russia tried to move rapidly toward a market economy after 1989 ("one cut of the knife"), whereas after Mao's death in 1976 China adopted an incremental reform path ("touching stones to cross the river"). Many observers considered the program to be poorly designed. China's economy seemed to have been led to an unsatisfactory "halfway house" that was neither capitalism nor socialism, an institutional framework that perpetuated bureaucratic interference in the economy and therefore should have produced poor results. Moreover, in 1989 China experienced the terrible upheaval of the Tiananmen massacre, the demonstrations leading up to which were connected closely with the tensions of economic reform. It was widely felt that this signaled the end of reform, and that China would lapse into low-growth authoritarianism.

China confounded the consensus of critical opinion. Even after the Tiananmen massacre neither reform nor economic growth was halted. In most important respects the halfway house economy performed extremely well over the whole period of a decade and a half since 1976.[2] This is a puzzle that presents problems for mainstream economic theory and policy.

Although there has been a dissenting minority, it is rare in economics for there to be such agreement about a fundamental issue of economic policy. One can identify several broad areas of agreement about basic propositions among economists advising the former Communist countries in the early phase of post-Communism:[3]

- *"Market socialism" cannot work.*

  In Hungary, and also in a number of the other socialist countries, the principle of "market socialism" has become a guiding idea of the reform

287

process. . . . Under this principle, state firms should remain in state ownership, but by creating appropriate conditions, these firms should be made to
act as if they were a part of a market. . . . I wish to use strong words here,
without any adornment: the basic idea of market socialism simply fizzled
out. Yugoslavia, Hungary, China, the Soviet Union, and Poland bear witness to its fiasco. The time has come to look this fact in the face and abandon the principle of "market socialism."[4]

• *Institutional reform cannot be successful unless there is macroeconomic
stability.*

It is difficult to think of an economist who would disagree with this
proposition.

• *Enterprises will not respond in desirable ways to market signals unless
private-property rights are established.*

Stabilisation and price reform together will only set the scene for a meaningful supply response if they are accompanied by the establishment of private ownership rights and elimination of the panoply of controls which currently prevent competition and discourage the efficient use of resources.[5]

• *Enterprises' attempts to make profits will not produce socially desirable
outcomes unless prices are determined by market forces.*

Markets cannot begin to develop until prices are free to move in response
to shifts in demand and supply, both domestic and external. . . . Price
decontrol is essential to end the shortages that . . . afflict the economy.[6]

• *Economic progress will be greatly inhibited unless there is full integration into the world economy.*

It is. . . essential to move as rapidly as possible to a transparent and decentralised trade and exchange rate system, in order to hasten the integration
. . . into the world economy. . . . The exchange rate [needs] to be moved to
market clearing levels. [Only] a few sectors [need to be shielded] for a
short time from intense competition of international markets.[7]

• *The pace of the transition from central planning needs to be rapid.*[8]

Common sense suggests that if you are sliding into a chasm, you should
jump quickly to the other side . . . and not tread cautiously. There is no theory supporting a gradual switch of system.[9]

• *Democratic political institutions are a necessary condition for success of economic reform.*[10]

> To survive and successfully evolve as a living social organism, the system of free markets, private property, and contractual buyer–seller transactions must operate within a legal order and a politically democratic environment.[11]

The Chinese Approach Toward the Political Economy of Reform

Market Socialism

Market socialism was the overarching philosophy of the economic system in the 1980s, albeit that the term "socialist market economy" was not enunciated formally as the guiding principle of economic organization until as late as 1992. The overall framework strongly resembled that of New Economic Policy (NEP) in the Soviet Union in the mid-1920s and in China itself in the early 1950s. The old Stalinist system of direct administrative planning was rejected decisively in favor of one in which markets and their related incentives were viewed as necessary to the effective functioning of the economy. In the 1980s public enterprises were given greatly increased independence in production, marketing, and the disposal of their income. However, since then key Communist Party documents have unremittingly spoken of the economy as one in which public ownership, planning, and socialist values are central to socioeconomic life. Throughout the reform period there has been continual reference to the need to combine the virtues of market and plan. This was in striking contrast to the economic ideology of post-Communist countries in Eastern Europe and Russia, in which the economic functions of the state were looked upon with hostility from the moment the Communist parties were overthrown.

For a large number of observers of the Chinese economy this mixture of market and plan under a system in which the Communist Party remained in power made it impossible to imagine that the economy could perform well. China in the 1980s, like post-1968 Hungary, was regarded as a negative example for the reforming Eastern European countries and for the former USSR after their anti-Communist revolutions:

> The sad chronicle of China's post-Mao attempt to introduce a modern economic system contains a useful lesson which others, notably the East Europeans are taking to heart. The lesson is that to address the economic problem in a modern way in the context of a low calibre, inefficient, slothful, wasteful, cronified socialist system, one must go all the way to the market system. Do it quickly, and not stop anywhere on the way. To go part of

the way slowly, "crossing the river while groping for the stones" as the Dengists put it, is to end up the creek to nowhere.[12]

Property Rights

Instead of rapidly moving toward a system in which private property became the dominant form of ownership, China in the 1980s was committed to experimentalism and gradualism in ownership reform. In all important areas of the economy, transparent, legally protected individual property rights were the exception, and public ownership with confused property rights was the rule.

In agriculture, the "decollectivization" of farmland was not followed by the establishment of private property rights in land. The Chinese Communist Party (CCP) did not wish to allow the emergence of a landlord class, and therefore land could not be bought and sold. Rather, the village community remained the owner of farmland, controlling the terms on which it was operated by peasant households, endeavoring to ensure that farm households had equal access to farmland,[13] and obtaining part of the Ricardian rents from the land to use for community purposes. The relative equality in local access to farmland was a major reason that the Gini coefficient of rural household income distribution remained so low.[14] The rural reforms of the late 1970s and early 1980s left property rights in land unclear: "Every member of a village community has a share in the property rights to the land of his/her community but the share is not embodied in any tangible form, such as a title deed or stock, *so it seems that no-one is a real owner of land*" (my emphasis).[15] Moreover, even the way land was used remained heavily influenced by state instructions. The state's compulsory deliveries remained in force for some key products, notably grain, so that providing grain for self-consumption and compulsory delivery pre-empted around 70 percent of farmland.[16]

In industry, although the reforms allowed individuals to set up businesses, there was a strong preference for the publicly owned sectors in state policies (e.g., the allocation of credit, power supplies, public transportation, and foreign exchange). Public ownership of industrial assets took both the "all people" (state) and the "collective" (often the local community) form. Still at the end of the reform decade, around 55 percent of industrial output came from the all people–owned sector and 36 percent from the collectively owned sector (see Table 15.1). The genuinely privately owned sector occupied only a tiny fraction of total output.[17]

The reforms decentralized control over financial capital. A rapidly growing share of industrial enterprises' finance came from the enterprises' retained profits, from banks, and from other sources, such as interenterprise investment and investment by groups of enterprise in joint projects. Furthermore, much of the control that had formerly been in the hands of central or provincial authorities was decentralized to local authorities, often with ill-defined rights to claim a share of enterprise profits.

Table 15.1 Share of Industrial Output (Gross Value) Produced in Chinese Enterprises by Type of Ownership (%)

	1981	1985	1990
State	78.3	70.4	54.5
Collective	21.0	27.7	35.7
Individual	neg.	0.4	5.4
Other	0.6	1.5	4.3

Source: State Statistical Bureau, *Statistical Survey of China (Zhongguo tongji Zhaiyao)* (Beijing: Zhongguo tongji chubanshe) [henceforth SSB(ZTZ)], 1986, p. 49, and 1991, p. 68.
Note: Data for 1981 and 1985 are both at 1980 prices; data for 1990 are at current prices.

In its 1990 report on the Chinese economy, the World Bank laments the confused position with respect to property rights in the state-owned sector:

> *The ownership of Chinese "state owned" enterprises is becoming increasingly ill-defined.* Ten years ago, all industrial assets in the state run economy were clearly controlled, and effectively "owned" by various levels of governments, which exercised both ultimate management power and final claim on residual income. Today, managerial authority and claims on income are split between government and the enterprise itself, as well as, to a lesser extent, the banking system. *The uncertainty attending on the ownership system is putting serious obstacles in the way of improved performance* [my emphasis].[18]

Bankruptcy in the state sector was virtually unknown. The "soft budget constraint" was dominant, with a rapidly increasing share of finance coming from a highly politicized banking system.

The rural collective sector[19] was the fastest-growing part of the Chinese industrial economy in the 1980s. The vast bulk of assets in this sector were owned by the local community, with the community's asset-management board arranging on the community's behalf the key aspects of the use of the property under their control. The World Bank's study of this sector concluded:

> *[This is] an environment in which ownership and property rights with respect to industrial assets are not clear and pure private ownership is rare except in the smallest concerns.* . . . Thus, the most powerful reward for small-scale entrepreneurs in other countries—the ability to reap large gains from the "capitalisation" of entrepreneurial success in their firms—is absent or at least sharply circumscribed [my emphasis].[20]

Price Reform

By 1984 the Chinese government had become convinced of the necessity of comprehensive price reform. However, its approach was to give social stability a high priority. "Social tolerance" (*shehui chengshouxing*) was a key criterion by which reform was to be judged. The government decided to reform only gradually the structure of relative prices and to do so in a controlled, planned fashion:

> There is much confusion in our present system of pricing. . . . This irrational price system has to be reformed . . . otherwise it will be impossible to assess correctly the performance of enterprises. . . . As the reform of the price system affects every household and the national economy as a whole, we must be extremely prudent, formulate a well-conceived, feasible programme based on the growth of production and capability of the state's finances and on the premise that the people's real income will gradually be increased, and then carry it out in a planned and systematic way.[21]

In the late 1970s virtually all prices were directly controlled by the state. By the mid-1980s there had been a large growth in the role of free markets, but even by 1990 it was still the case that no more than around one-half of the value of marketed goods was sold at free-market prices (see Table 15.2). Not much above one-third of industrial means of production was sold at free-market prices. Moreover, for much of the second half of the 1980s a large part of marketed output was sold under the "dual track" system, with different prices for the same product in parallel markets (state-controlled, "state-guided," and free).

The International Economy

The value of the yuan was slowly brought closer to its free-market rate, but even at the end of the 1980s it had not become a freely convertible currency. Innumerable bureaucratic restrictions pertained at different points in the 1980s to access to foreign currency.

Table 15.2   Proportion of Products Sold at Different Types of Prices in China (%)

	1978	1986	1990
Share of total retail sales sold at:			
state-controlled prices	97.0	n.a.	29.7
state-guided prices	0.0	n.a.	17.2
market-regulated prices	3.0	n.a.	53.1
Share of total sales of agricultural products sold by farmers at:			
state-controlled prices	94.4	37.0	25.2
state-guided prices	0.0	n.a.	22.6
market-regulated prices	5.6	n.a.	52.2
Share of ex-factory means of production for industrial use sold at:			
state-controlled prices	100.0	64.0	44.4
state-guided prices	0.0	23.0	18.8
market-regulated prices	0.0	13.0	36.8

Sources: P. Li, "Price reform the progressive way," *Beijing Review,* Vol. 35 (1992) No. 18, 4–10 May, p. 17; and Y. Tian, "Prices," in P. Nolan and F. Dong, eds., *The Chinese Economy and its Future* (Cambridge: Polity Press, 1990), p. 143.

Unlike the Maoist period, in the 1980s the leadership was convinced of the necessity of integration into the world economy. However, in the same fashion as Taiwan and South Korea in earlier years, China pursued an explicitly mercantilist path: "In foreign trade our principle is to encourage exports and organise imports according to needs."[22] Exports were "promoted" through a wide variety of subsidies, so that they frequently were loss-making at world market prices while imports were tightly controlled by a wide variety of quantitative controls:[23] "The pattern of exports and imports appears to be determined more by administrative decisions at the industrial bureau or foreign trade corporation level than by incentives at the level of the individual enterprise."[24]

Politics

There were important changes in China's political system in the post-Mao period. The most significant of these was the attempt, spearheaded by Deng Xiaoping,[25] to create a professional bureaucracy. The intention was to dismiss into retirement the old guard of party officials in the government administration who did not possess high technical qualifications. This effort parallels those of Bismarckian Germany and Meiji Japan in the late nineteenth century, or Taiwan and South Korea in the 1950s, in which a key point of the modernization drive was the creation of a professional government administration that was responsible to an unelected executive authority rather than to an elected parliament. Much progress was made in the 1980s: "The speed of organisational turnover, and the relative ease with which it has occurred, has been impressive. . . . The Chinese bureaucracy now has a greater ability and willingness to bring technical competence to bear on competing policy alternatives."[26]

However, China in the 1980s remained a one-party state, with the CCP firmly in control of political life. The challenge to its authority in Tiananmen Square was repressed brutally.[27] Many analysts felt that the CCP could not lead the centrally planned economy more than a certain part of the way toward a market economy since further movement would threaten its power fundamentally.[28] It was felt widely that the CCP could not itself make the transition to secular rational rule. It had the double burden of highly centralized traditions of Leninism plus millennia of centralized rule in China. The CCP, it was thought, had to be removed from its monopoly of political power if the move to a market economy was to be put into effect:

> Deng Xiaoping tried to restart China's economy without affecting the dictatorship of its entrenched vanguard. . . . Although the term had not yet been invented, Deng sought *perestroika* without *glasnost*. This is not a particularly unusual project. There are innumerable examples of similarly placed monopolists of political power who wanted economic modernisation without political reform. . . . It does not work. . . . Instead of duplicat-

ing South Korea and Taiwan, China seemed to have taken as its model
Ferdinand Marcos's Philippines.[29]

In the euphoria of post-Communism, it was very difficult to believe that such
a brutal, undemocratic regime as China's could perform well economically.

The Results of China's Reform Path

In almost all key aspects of institutional arrangements and policy China's
postreform economy in the 1980s appears as the kind of interventionist
halfway house that most economists would predict would perform very
badly. Throughout the decade private-property rights existed in only a minor
part of the economy; the government continued to intervene heavily in price
setting; the economy remained substantially isolated from the impact of
world prices; the Communist Party continued to rule in a sometimes brutal
and always authoritarian fashion, and intervened at all levels of the economic process. Indeed, some observers believed that market socialism was
too charitable a description of this system and that "market Stalinism" was
more appropriate.

In fact, in the first decade or so of reform China's economic performance was much better than under Maoist policies. The rate of growth of net
national output accelerated sharply (see Table 15.3). China's system of
authoritarian political control enabled it to control population growth,
despite the bulge in the reproducing age cohorts in the 1980s, and in per
capita terms the annual growth rate of net national output more than doubled. A striking shift occurred in the pattern of growth, away from that characteristic of a Stalinist economy. The overall industrial growth rate, which
was already very rapid under Maoism, changed little. However, there were
important changes in the efficiency in resource use. In state-run industry
there was a sharp reversal of the long-run decline in productivity China had
experienced in the Maoist years,[30] and China's state-owned enterprises
began to behave in a cost-minimizing fashion.[31] Moreover, the typical
Stalinist relationship between the growth rate of heavy and light industry
was reversed (see Table 15.3), with explosive growth in light industry. The
agricultural growth rate accelerated much ahead of that achieved during the
Maoist period, and with much more economy in resource use.[32] The growth
rate of commerce and transportation increased sharply compared to the
Maoist years (see Table 15.3), reflecting the rapid rise in the market economy.

China outperformed almost all developing countries in terms of output
growth and export performance (see Table 15.4). Moreover, it remained relatively unburdened by foreign debt and achieved fast growth with relatively
low inflation. It cannot be argued that growth in the 1980s was achieved

Table 15.3   Changes in the Characteristics of Chinese Economic Growth: Average Annual Growth Rate (% per Year, at Constant Prices)

	1957–1975	1978–1990
Net material product total	5.3	8.4
agriculture	1.7	5.6
industry	9.8	10.1
construction	4.6	9.6
transport	5.3	9.4
commerce	2.3	7.2
Net material product per person	3.3	7.0
Gross material product of industry:		
heavy	11.2	10.3
light	8.3	13.9

Source: SSB(ZTZ), 1991, pp. 33, 55, and 79.

Table 15.4   Comparative Economic Performance of the Chinese Economy in the 1980s

	China	India	Low-income countries[a]	Middle-income countries[a]
Avg. annual growth, 1980–1989 (%):				
GDP	9.7	5.3	3.4	2.9
Agriculture	6.3	2.9	2.5	2.6
Industry	12.6	6.9	3.1	3.0
Services	9.3	6.5	4.4	2.8
Avg. annual real growth rate of exports,1980–1989 (%)	11.5	5.8	0.8	5.5
Avg. annual growth rate of population, 1980–1989 (%)	1.4	2.1	2.7	2.1
Avg. annual rate of inflation, 1980–1989 (%)	5.8	7.7	14.9	73.0
Debt service as % of exports of goods and services:				
1980	4.6	9.1	11.4	26.1
1989	9.8	26.4	27.4	23.1
Index of avg. per capita food consumption, 1987–1989 (1979–1981 = 100)	128	113	103	101
Daily calorie intake per capita				
1965	1931	2103	1960	2482
1988	2632	2104	2182	2834
Crude death rate (per 1000):				
1965	10	20	21	13
1989	7	11	13	8
Infant mortality rate (per 1000):				
1981	71	121	124	81
1989	30	95	94	51
Life expectancy at birth (years):				
1981	67	52	50	60
1989	70	59	55	66

Source: World Bank, *World Development Report 1983* and *1991* (Washington, D.C.: Oxford University Press for the World Bank).
Note: a. Excluding India and China.

at the expense of popular consumption. The 1980s saw a revolution in all aspects of real incomes (see Table 15.5). Remarkable improvement occurred in the diet of the Chinese population, with significant and easily observable improvements in the quality of produce. A vast new fashion industry developed in the textile sector. A huge increase occurred in consumer durable consumption, mainly met by domestic production, with huge new industries springing up where formerly there had been virtually nothing. Housing space per person more than doubled over the course of a decade. Large improvements took place in the availability of professional health care; a massive transformation occurred in the number and variety of services available. The reported improvement in the already exceptional figures for life expectancy and mortality rates (see Table 15.4) suggests that the growth in living standards affected most social strata, even if there was greater inequality in consumption than under the extreme egalitarianism of Maoism.

Table 15.5   Changes in the Standard of Living in China, 1978–1989

	1978	1989
Index of real per capita consumption	100	208
Consumption per capita of:		
grains (kg)	196	239
edible oil (kg)	1.6	5.7
pork (kg)	7.7	16.6
fresh eggs (kg)	2.0	6.3
sugar (kg)	3.4	4.9
cloth (meters)	8.0	10.6
Ownership of consumer durables (per 100 people):		
sewing machines	3.5	12.3
watches	8.5	51.6
bicycles	7.8	34.2
radios	7.8	22.0
TVs	0.3	16.2
Retail outlets, catering, and service trades		
no. of establishments per 10,000 people	13	104
no. of workers per 10,000 people	63	255
Doctors (per 10,000 people)	10.8	15.4
Hospital beds (per 10,000 people)	19.4	23.0
Housing space per capita (sq. meters)		
cities	3.6	7.1
villages	8.1	17.8

Source: SSB(ZTZ), 1990, pp. 40–42.

China's economic performance in the 1980s was much better than that in the most relevant comparator countries, such as India, and was vastly better than anyone in the late 1970s could have hoped. Were Eastern Europe and Russia to achieve remotely comparable advances in the 1990s, their reforms would be regarded as immensely successful.

Conclusions

The Chinese system of political economy in the 1980s was market socialist in any meaningful sense of the phrase, and yet its performance was one of the most dynamic in terms of both output and income growth that the modern world has seen. This presents economists with a puzzle: Why did China perform so well in the first decade and a half of reform, despite the fact that the economic institutions and policies were gravely inadequate in relation to mainstream Western economic theory and policy? There are a number of interrelated possibilities, of different orders of difficulty for mainstream Western economics to digest.

China entered its reform program with several important short-term economic advantages compared to Eastern Europe and Russia; these made the tasks of reform easier in China. Unlike the COMECON countries, China did not have to cope with the collapse of the system of international trade with which it was closely associated simultaneously with its post-Communist economic reform program. It did not have large foreign debt. Nor did China have the large "monetary overhang" that gave monetary stabilization a high priority in post-Communist Europe and Russia. However, these factors explain merely why China's apparently wrong choice of institutions and policies did not produce extremely bad results—they cannot be used to explain its success.

China enjoyed certain economic advantages that made it likely that almost any policies that produced some move toward a market economy would produce good results. Several factors can be identified. The first is the special role of Hong Kong and, increasingly, Taiwan. Undoubtedly, capital and expertise from these countries played an important part in enabling Guangdong province and, to a lesser extent, adjacent Fujian province, to grow rapidly in the 1980s. However, this is only part of the explanation. While Guangdong grew extremely rapidly in the reform period, other provinces with a much smaller role for foreign capital grew at least as fast.[33] Moreover, the mere existence of overseas Chinese with large capital resources was not sufficient to ensure that it was invested on the mainland. Domestic political and economic conditions needed to be such as to induce a large inward flow of investment.

A second important special advantage that China enjoys is the strong capitalist tradition stretching back at least a thousand years. The Jiangnan area (northern Zhejiang and southern Jiangsu provinces) and Guangdong province were advanced areas of capitalist-style production for many centuries before the European Industrial Revolution.[34] Even in the adverse political conditions of the first half of the twentieth century large industrial progress occurred in these areas.[35] Their huge growth potential was squashed under postrevolutionary Maoist planning,[36] and burst into life in the 1980s.

A third factor is that there may be more easily won gains from reform in a low-income, predominantly rural CPE. It is much easier to reform a simple labor-intensive agriculture through institutional change than it is to reform huge mechanized collective farms such as those in the former USSR. Peasants who take out leases on collective land in labor-intensive Chinese agriculture face smaller risks and require much less of a change in management skills than do Russian collective farmers. It is also the case that in an economy such as China's there is wide scope for expanding the small-scale, labor-intensive, rural nonfarm sector with all the multiple benefits this brings through the rapid growth of nonfarm employment, income, and export earnings.[37]

China's incrementalist path to reform may have been correct and the attempt in most other CPEs to move rapidly toward a market economy may have been a serious mistake.   China did not in the late 1970s put into place a stable set of market-socialist institutions. Although the pace of advance was uneven, there was a consistent push forward in reforms, broadening out from agriculture to the small-scale nonfarm sector and eventually penetrating the commanding heights of the large-scale state industrial sector. The Chinese experience demonstrates that it takes much longer to develop a market economy than was initially realized by most advisers to post-Communist governments. The undoubted costs incurred in a slower transition may tend to be outweighed by the benefits. If a former CPE is moved forward slowly toward a market economy by a clear-sighted leadership, there may be large efficiency gains at each step as the economy responds, like a slowly unwinding spring under pressure, to new opportunities for profitmaking. Economists advising formerly Communist countries may have been greatly overoptimistic about the time required for successful reform, and may have been led into serious policy mistakes as a result. This kind of "great leap forward" into a new socioeconomic system that allegedly will bring great benefits was, paradoxically, exactly that against which Popper warned in the late 1950s in respect to the Communist experiment:

> Every version of historicism expresses the feeling of being swept into the future by irresistible forces. . . . Contrasting their "dynamic" thinking with the static thinking of all previous generations, [the historicists] believe that their own advance has been made possible by the fact that we are now "living in a revolution" which has so much accelerated the speed of our development that social change can now be directly experienced within a single lifetime. This story is, of course, sheer mythology.[38]

Structural transformation of the former CPEs may require a lengthy period of extensive state intervention to cope with probable large areas of market failure.   The enthusiasm of post-Communist "capitalist triumphalism"[39] among advisers to Eastern Europe and the former USSR may have caused a major mistake in assessing not only the required speed of transition but also the desirable economic functions of the state over an extended period. As Adam Smith made clear, the degree of market failure is likely to be very different "in the different periods of society."[40] The huge tasks of structural transformation in the atmosphere of great uncertainty in the reforming CPEs is precisely a situation in which it is likely in principle that market failure will be especially large. Private agents will likely tend more than under other circumstances to look toward the short term and speculation rather than toward longer-term investment, so that the gap between private and social benefits may be especially wide.[41] Some obvious areas in which government intervention may be needed in such an economy include: constructing large, internationally competitive manufacturing companies where formerly there was no concept of a company;[42] managing labor markets to control the large inflationary pressures that emerge during the reform process;[43] expanding infrastructure;[44] funding research and development to enable rapid technical progress to occur; protecting infant industries;[45] promoting exports;[46] controlling the distribution of income and wealth; and providing for the basic needs of the poorest social strata.[47] The early stage of development economics in the 1940s and 1950s, and the practical experience of the Newly Industrializing Countries of East Asia,[48] may be more relevant to the enormous tasks of transition that these economies now face than the mainstream economics of the 1970s and 1980s that stressed the shortcomings of the state as a vehicle for achieving socially desirable goals.[49] In the case of the transition away from central planning, a "second-best" approach might be the most fruitful one. For all the faults that state action may have, in the transition from central planning these may tend to be exceeded by the costs of trying to minimize the economic role of the state.

The interaction of political factors with economic ones may be the crucial determinant of success in the transition from a centrally planned economy. A successful reform strategy may require a comprehensive perspective of political economy. A more successful transition away from a Communist economy may, paradoxically, be easier to achieve with a strong state that is able to place the overall national interest above that of powerful vested interest groups. A self-reforming Communist party may be the least bad vehicle available to accomplish this. To take the simplest examples, a strong state may be better able to raise the taxes necessary to fund an industrial strategy, to control growth of the money supply and restrain inflation, or to maintain the social order necessary to give investors confidence. The causes for China's success may lie above all in the set of historical factors that allowed the CCP to survive while Communist parties were overthrown in Eastern Europe and Russia, and to preside over the introduction of a genuinely competitive economy.

A key part of the explanation is the set of factors that caused China's

Communist leadership to persist in reforms beyond the point at which Eastern European market-socialist efforts ground to a halt. Two outstanding causes of this can be identified. The first was the impact upon the Chinese leadership of the collapse of Communism in Europe and Russia. This and the fear engendered by the Tiananmen massacre initially pushed the leadership into political and economic retreat in 1989–1990, but the reforms quickly got under way again. Paradoxically, the leadership was given confidence to press ahead with its move toward a market economy by the increased social stability induced in China in the medium term by the collapse of Communism in Eastern Europe and Russia, and the awful performance of these economies under the simplistic reform programs that immediately followed the end of Communist rule. It was widely realized by Chinese people both inside and outside the country in 1990–1991 that the leadership in the 1980s had in fact done extraordinarily well in comparison with the performances of the post-Communist leadership in Eastern Europe and Russia, and that the Chinese people had much to be thankful for, despite the authoritarian nature of political life in China. In 1989 many internal critics of the Chinese government had in mind a "counterfactual" of a prosperous free-market U.S. economy (powerfully symbolized by the Goddess of Liberty in Tiananmen Square). It became increasingly obvious that the most appropriate counterfactual was a post-Communist economic disaster. The government used this for propaganda purposes in a shameless fashion, but the underlying message was correct.

A second cause of the government's persistence with reforms was the intellectual impact of Hong Kong and Taiwan. They demonstrated to the Chinese leadership on their very doorstep the importance of the competitive market for economic dynamism. However, their function as role models was wider than this. Taiwan demonstrated the advantages of combining plan with market in order to achieve successful structural transformation. Indeed, Taiwan's leadership under the KMT (Kuomintang) described its economic system as a "planned free-market economy" (*jihuaxing de ziyou jingji*). Moreover, both Taiwan and Hong Kong were ruled in an undemocratic fashion for over three decades.[50]

The subtle changes in the mainland's ideology in the post-Mao period can be viewed as a journey back to the intellectual foundation laid by Sun Yatsen before 1949, which provides a unifying element to modernization in the whole of Chinese East Asia, including even Singapore. This in turn harks back to traditional Chinese statecraft and political culture, in which the state was massively dominant in overall social and ideological control, performed some important economic functions that were beyond the reach of individuals, and unhesitatingly placed national goals above those of individuals (the Western concept of individual rights in economic and social life was completely absent). However, large areas of grassroots economic life were left to be determined by individual decisionmaking in response to market forces.

This combination was at the center of China's medieval economic and technical revolution,[51] and is, equally, at the center of its revolutionary economic advance since 1976.

Notes

1. An earlier version of this chapter—based on the conference paper for the workshops underlying this book—was published in *Contributions to Political Economy,* Vol. 12 (1993), pp. 71–87. The author and editor are grateful to Academic Press and the Cambridge Political Economy Society for the permission to use and in part reprint this material here.

2. At each stage of the reform, critics argued that the reforms had run out of steam and that short-term gains had been won through "easy" institutional change that would damage long-term performance. After a decade and a half of sustained growth these arguments have worn thin.

3. The closest one can come to such a consensus is probably the combined IMF, World Bank, OECD, and EBRD report on the Soviet economy: IMF, World Bank, OECD, and EBRD, *The Economy of the USSR; Summary and Recommendations* (Washington, D.C.: World Bank, 1990).

4. J. Kornai, *The Road to a Free Economy* (London: Norton, 1990), p. 58.

5. IMF et al., *The Economy of the USSR,* p. 2.

6. Ibid., p. 17.

7. Ibid.

8. One could add a very long bibliography of economists who advocated high speed as the only "logical" way to achieve a successful transition. Kornai's account of the "failure" of Hungarian reform was deeply influential in the early days of thinking about reform in the post-Communist countries: J. Kornai, "The Hungarian Reform Process: Visions, Hopes, and Reality," *Journal of Economic Literature,* Vol. 24, 1986, pp. 1687–1737.

9. A. Aslund, "Gorbachev, Perestroika, and Economic Crisis," *Problems of Communism,* January–April 1990, pp. 13–41: p. 37. In their joint report on the Soviet economy the IMF, World Bank, EBRD, and OECD put their combined weight of opinion behind a rapid transition toward a market economy, despite explicitly acknowledging the risks involved: "The prospect of a sharp fall in output and rapid increase in prices in the early stage of a radical reform is daunting. . . . In advocating the more radical approach we are well aware of the concerns of those who recommend caution" (IMF et al., *The Economy of the USSR,* pp. 18–19).

10. In fact, few economists have dared to venture publicly into the arena of political theory and the reform of the former CPEs. However, there is a widely accepted, though rarely stated, belief that the reform of politics and the economy are causally linked.

11. J. Prybyla, "A Broken System," in G. Hicks, ed., *The Broken Mirror* (Harlow, Essex: Longman, 1990), p. 188. The view that democratic politics is positively and causally related to economic growth has gained widespread currency in recent years. For example, Dasgupta's influential article (P. Dasgupta, "Well-Being and the Extent of Its Realisation in Poor Countries," *Economic Journal,* Vol. 100, pp. 1–32: pp. 4, and 27–28) argues: "The choice between fast growth in income and negative liberties is a phoney choice. . . . Political liberties are *positively* and significantly correlated with per capita income and its growth. . . . Nations whose citizens enjoy greater political liberties and civil liberties also perform better in terms of . . .

improvements in life expectancy at birth, per capita income, and infant survival rates."

12. Prybyla, "A Broken System," p. 194.

13. A striking feature of the "land reform" of the early 1980s is that land was contracted to households mostly on an equal per capita basis within each village, so that equality of access rather than growth of maximization was the guiding principle.

14. The Gini coefficient of rural household income distribution reportedly rose from 0.21 in 1978 to 0.26 in 1985. R. Zhao, "Income Distribution," in P. Nolan and F. Dong, eds., *The Chinese Economy and its Future* (Cambridge: Polity Press, 1990), p. 193.

15. L. Zhu and Z. Jiang, "From Brigade to Village Community: The Land Tenure System and Rural Development in China," *Cambridge Journal of Economics,* Vol. 17, No. 4, December 1993, pp. 441–462.

16. Ibid.

17. Even in Guandong (adjacent to Hong Kong), the most rapidly reforming province in the whole country, in 1990 the all people–owned sector still accounted for 40 percent of the value of gross industrial output, and the collectively owned sector for 34 percent, leaving at the most 26 percent from the genuinely privately owned sector. State Statistical Bureau, *Statistical Survey of China (Zhongguo tongji zhaiyao)* (Beijing: Zhongguo tongji chubanshe) [henceforth SSB(ZTZ)], 1991, p. 69.

18. World Bank, *China: Macroeconomic Stability and Industrial Growth under Decentralised Socialism* (Washington, D.C.: World Bank, 1990), p. 149.

19. Its share of the gross value of industrial output rose from 12 percent in 1985 to over 19 percent in 1990. SSB(ZTZ), 1991, p. 68.

20. W. Byrd, "Entrepreneurship, Capital, and Ownership," in W. Byrd and Q. Lin, eds., *China's Rural Industry* (Washington, D.C.: World Bank, 1990), p. 189.

21. Central Committee of the CCP, "Decision on Reform of the Economic Structure," reprinted in S. Liu and Q. Wu, *China's Socialist Economy* (Beijing: Foreign Language Press, 1994), p. 683.

22. *Beijing Review,* Vol. 33 (44), 1990.

23. E. Vogel, *One Step Ahead in China* (London: Harvard University Press, 1989), Chapter 11.

24. World Bank, *China: Long-term Development Issues and Options* (Washington, D.C.: World Bank, 1985), p. 106.

25. The need to professionalize, reduce in size, and make more youthful China's government bureaucracy was a central theme of Deng's speeches in the early 1980s. See X. P. Deng, *Selected Works of Deng Xiaoping (1975–1982)* (Beijing: Foreign Language Press, 1984).

26. H. Harding, *China's Second Revolution* (Washington, D.C.: Brookings Institution, 1987), pp. 208–209. Harding (pp. 204–211) provides a careful account of the large increase in the proportion of technically qualified bureaucrats and the substantial decline in their average age during the early to mid-1980s.

27. Such violent repression of protest movements is normal rather than exceptional in developing countries. Similar actions in recent years include that in Thailand in 1976 (Thammassat University), in South Korea in 1980 (Kwangju), and in India in 1990 (Srinagar). None of these received remotely as much publicity in the West as the Chinese massacre, despite their great ferocity.

28. Kornai ("The Hungarian Reform Process") is scathing in his criticism of the "naive reformers" who believe that a Communist party can preside over a process that he considers will inevitably lead to its own demise.

29. C. Johnson, "Foreword" in G. Hicks, ed., *The Broken Mirror* (Harlow: Longman, 1990), pp. viii–x.

30. Careful studies of Chinese state industry show that after steady long-run decline from the mid-1950s to the mid-1970s, the pattern was reversed in the 1980s. Whereas from 1957 to 1978 there had been a decline of 0.2 percent per year in the reported average annual growth rate of total factor productivity (TFP) in Chinese state-owned industry, in the early 1980s (1980–1984) TFP reportedly grew by 3.5 percent per year and in the second half of the 1980s (1984–1988) the growth rate was reported to be 5.9 percent per year. K. Chen et al., "New Estimates of Fixed Investment and Capital Stock for Chinese State Industry," *China Quarterly,* No. 114, June 1988; G. Jefferson, T. Rawski, and Y. Zheng, "Growth, Efficiency, and Convergence in China's State and Collective Industry," *Economic Development and Cultural Change,* Vol. 40, No. 2, January 1992, pp. 293–266; G. Jefferson and W. Xu, "The Impact of Reform on Socialist Enterprises in Transition: Structure and Conduct and Performance in Chinese Industry," *Journal of Comparative Economics,* Vol. 15 (1991), pp. 15–64.

31. This is the conclusion of the study of 200 state-owned firms during the years 1983–1987 undertaken by D. Hay and G. Liu: "Cost Behaviour of Chinese State-Owned Enterprises During the Reform Period, 1979–1987," paper for the Institute of Economics and Statistics Oxford, April 1992.

32. From 1957 to 1978 agriculture's purchases of farm inputs (fixed and working capital) increased at a real average annual rate of growth that was five times that of farm output, but in the 1980s farm inputs and outputs increased at roughly equal rates. SSB(ZTZ), 1991, pp. 38, 53, and 90; and SSB, *Chinese Statistical Yearbook* (Beijing: Zhongguo tongji chubanse, 1990), pp. 35, 50, 254, and 622), suggesting a massive change in the efficiency of resource use.

33. The reported average annual growth rate of industrial output from 1979 to 1989 (gross value, constant prices) was 18 percent in Guangdong, compared to 12 percent across the whole of China, but in Jiangsu the rate was 17 percent, in Zhejiang 21 percent, and in Fujian 17 percent. SSB, *Compendium of Historical Statistical Materials [Lishi tongji ziliao huibian],* 1990, p. 50. The total population of these four very rapidly industrializing provinces is around 200 million, or roughly three times the combined population of the "Four Little Tigers" of Hong Kong, Taiwan, South Korea, and Singapore.

34. There is a large and growing scholarly literature in Chinese economic history on the so-called capitalist sprouts. See e.g., D. Xu and C. Wu, eds, *China's Capitalist Sprouts [Zhongguo zibenzhuyi mengya]* (Beijing: Renmin chubanshe, 1985).

35. T. Rawski, *Economic Growth in Pre-War China* (Berkeley, Calif.: University of California Press, 1989).

36. A major reason for the success of Taiwan and Hong Kong was the emigration of people and capital from these areas shortly before and after the 1949 Revolution on the mainland.

37. The share of China's rural township sector in total world exports from low income countries rose from 3.2 percent in 1985 to 8.0 percent in 1989 (SSB[ZTZ], 1991, p. 65; and World Bank, *World Development Report* [Washington, D.C.: Oxford University Press, for the World Bank, 1987], p. 230), a remarkable rise in such a short time. Full-time employment in this sector rose from under 30 million in the late 1970s to around 100 million in the late 1980s.

38. K. Popper, *The Poverty of Historicism* (London: Routledge and Kegan Paul, 1960), p. 160.

39. This term was coined by Professor Peter Wiles of the LSE.

40. A. Smith, *The Wealth of Nations* (Chicago: University of Chicago Press, Cannan Edition, 1976), Vol. 2, p. 244.

41. This applies a fortiori insofar as the reforms are accompanied by socioeconomic instability to which they may have themselves contributed.

42. The danger of simply privatizing individual enterprises is that it might take a long time for large competitive multiplant companies to emerge, yet it is the latter that are the basis of prosperity in the advanced capitalist economies. China's policy of encouraging the emergence of powerful "industrial groups" is in marked contrast to the laissez-faire approach toward the emergence of companies that has been dominant in post-Communist Eastern Europe and Russia to date.

43. It is an unpalatable fact that in China in the 1980s, just as in Taiwan and South Korea from the 1950s to the 1980s, the state intervened powerfully to prevent the development of an independent trade union movement. "Free" labor markets were maintained by force with large economic consequences.

44. China in the 1980s increasingly followed a highly pragmatic policy of combining government (central and local) and private capital to obtain rapid growth of infrastructure, which inevitably is a key bottleneck in an economy experiencing such rapid growth of the market.

45. The whole concept of what constitutes an infant industry needs to be thought through very carefully in this unusual context. The characteristic features of most industrial sectors of the former CPEs are that they have technically backward capital stock, poor entrepreneurial skills, and low workpace, but a high level of general education among the workforce, and widespread engineering and scientific-research skills. It is not obvious that there ought to be a "surgical operation to remove the outdated and inefficient industries" (as in S. Gomulka, "Shock Needed for the Polish Economy," *The Guardian* [London], 19 August 1989), as opposed to a planned attempt to restructure behind tariff barriers and make use of the advanced human skills they possess to create industries that in five or ten years will be able to compete on world markets.

46. In areas where the benefits (from access to foreign exchange and technically advanced imports, economies of scale, and learning effects from competition on the world market) can be demonstrated as being likely to exceed the static efficiency costs of neglect of short-term comparative advantage.

47. This is not simply a question of ethics but also of the objective impact on the economy of social disturbance stemming from the destabilizing effect of excessively large and rapid changes in the distribution of income and wealth that can result from an uncontrolled transition.

48. See especially A. Amsden, *Asia's Next Giant: South Korea and Late Industrialisation* (Oxford: Oxford University Press, 1989); and R. Wade, *Governing the Market* (Princeton: Princeton University Press, 1990).

49. Writing in respect to the economics profession's view of the role of the state in development economics, Stern comments: "The apparent swing in the profession from whole-hearted espousal of extensive government intervention to its rubbishing seems to be an example of unbalanced intellectual growth. . . . There are problems and virtues with both state intervention and the free market." N. Stern, "The Economics of Development: A Survey," *Economic Journal,* Vol. 99, September 1989, pp. 597–685: pp. 621–622.

50. Hong Kong is a colony and Taiwan was under martial law throughout most of its rapid modern economic growth.

51. See especially the account in J. Needham, *Science and Civilisation in China* (Cambridge, Cambridge University Press, 1954).

PART 5

CONCLUSION

16

Linkages Between Economic and Political Liberalization: Some Concluding Observations

Gerd Nonneman

At the end of this book, the answers to one question, implicit in the title, would seem still to require summing up: Can anything be said about the linkages between political and economic liberalization? Inconveniently, the question remains problematic. There is no definite, coherent set of answers—only a number of possible trends and likely scenarios, and a few empirically observed causations, all of which vary with the context considered. Yet the preceding chapters do contain ample material to suggest some of these. Here, a brief roundup of the most relevant is offered.

General

Whether they have occurred simultaneously or at different points in time, and whether or not they have had a direct impact on each other, the phenomena of political and economic liberalization—particularly in their shape of the last decade—often seem to share the same origin: a combination of (1) the failure of existing systems to perform, often with resultant upheaval; (2) the prevalent international intellectual climate regarding the "best" way to organize polities and economies; and (3) the increased integration of the world economy, with a mutually amplifying effect between these factors. If the political upheaval results in a total regime change, this dynamic of shared origins is likely to mean that political liberalization leads to economic liberalization, if the two do not actually occur at the same time (see the following section). Simultaneous occurrence of both processes as a result of upheaval does not, however, mean that both will necessarily proceed at the same pace or indeed come to full fruition. As von Beyme has pointed out:

> Only in the cases where a market economy and democracy were pushed through at one and the same time and supervised by the victors [in war]—

as in the case of Japan and the Federal Republic of Germany after 1945—
did both develop reasonably simultaneously. In all other cases . . . there
exists a relationship of asymmetric antagonism . . . : a market economy fosters the development of democracy but democracy does not necessarily
lead to a functioning market economy, as the example of India illustrates.[1]

Hamilton and Kim in their comparative study of Korea and Mexico perti-
nently highlight the fact that "those groups concerned with expanding
democracy and opportunities for political participation were often not the
same as those pressuring for economic liberalisation, and where they were,
one goal is often subordinate to the other."[2] There may in this sense be a link
("coincidence"), but where this is true one group's support for the other's
aims will often be utilitarian and subject to changing priorities. The length
to which political liberalizers will want to see economic liberalization go,
and vice versa, will usually differ markedly between the groups, as well as
within them. Among the country studies in this book, the examples of
Poland, Syria, Algeria, and South Korea are cases in point.

The concluding lines of Hamilton and Kim's article are appropriate here
as a summing up of the evidence throughout the literature as well as in the
present volume:

> Although political and economic liberalisation may occur simultaneously,
> they are not necessarily complementary processes, and the relationship
> between [them] may be accidental or negative. . . . [T]he relationship
> between economic liberalisation and democratisation is a complex one
> which challenges simplistic assumptions of a direct, intimate connection
> on the one hand as well as the premise that the two processes are totally
> unconnected.[3]

In the following sections some of the specific possible links in both directions will be reviewed.

From Economic to Political Liberalization?

Von Beyme, quoted above, asserted that "a market economy fosters the
development of democracy." Similar assumptions are widespread and shared
by Huntington and Diamond, among others.[4] This cannot, without considerably more evidence and the passage of time, be considered an iron law, but
it certainly appears to be a plausible trend. A number of reasons may be
advanced to explain why economic liberalization, in all its forms, should
produce this effect—even if often with a considerable time lag. The first is
simply that an economic withdrawal of the state is likely to reduce its capacity for sociopolitical control, patronage, and co-option. Indeed, as seen in
Chapter 2, several authoritarian or rentier-type regimes have proved reluctant to allow economic liberalization to proceed more than hesitantly for
those very reasons. In authoritarian systems,

there was less reason to expect that the directions of state intervention would reflect the popular will rather than the requirements of influential elites. Thus any "rolling back of the state," while it may cause hardship . . . , also represented an attack on the privileges of elites and, in countries . . . with more developed party systems, on the privileges of party functionaries and their clients.[5]

2. The second cluster of reasons concerns the effects such liberalization at home and in international trade tends to have on civil society. The different components of economic liberalization and their effects tend to help bring about some of the changes in social conditions and structures referred to by Pridham and Vanhanen (see Chapter 3), thus affecting what they call the distribution of power resources (economic, intellectual, and otherwise). New forms of wealth and its distribution, technological change, and changing education are all part of these resources, and are almost inevitably affected by a process of economic liberalization. It is plausible that political liberalization should be boosted by a wider distribution of such resources. One of the social effects of economic liberalization will tend to be the creation, expansion, or strengthening of a middle class with some degree of independence from the state. That such a class is likely to develop its own political demands, however gradually, is both conceivable and confirmed by the evidence (although, as indicated before, the form or extent of these demands with respect to political liberalization may vary greatly, along with the varying interests of different sections of the middle class, and its degree of dependence on the state). Ehteshami finds "impressionistic support for the modernisation paradigm" in the evolution of Taiwan and South Korea: "Political liberalisation has occurred only *after* a long period of economic growth and where relentless economic expansion and development had created a well-to-do and vocal middle class along with a mass consumer society."[6]

3. Economic liberalization may enhance opportunities for the development or emancipation of civil society in a different way as well. Such development will be fed by the greater openness to new ideas, influences, technologies, and people from abroad entailed by measures to open the economy. This openness may foster political demands directly; it may also do so indirectly, or after a time lag, as a result of its effects on civil society. At the same time, regimes' vulnerability to explicit and implicit international pressures for political liberalization also increases along with states' increased reliance on, and opening up to, world markets. For one thing, such integration with the world economy tends to bring increased outside attention to bear on domestic developments and to generate concerns that the regimes often cannot afford to ignore. The case of the 1988 Olympic Games in South Korea (a key step in the country's globalization strategy), and the attention for Mexican developments at the time of the NAFTA negotiations, are but two instances of these dynamics.

One specific example of regimes' vulnerability to outside pressures over political liberalization is the needs imposed on them by economic problems and the resultant need for foreign assistance of one sort or another. Economic problems at the same time create domestic dynamics. Such problems, of course, may find their origins in a variety of causes. But for the purpose of the present discussion it is worth drawing attention to the frequency with which economic-liberalization measures have resulted in economic hardships, even if not for everyone and even when only temporary (this has been the case especially in programs designed before protection for the most vulnerable sections of the population became more fashionable again). These hardships may themselves increase the need for foreign assistance, thus potentially increasing outside pressure for political liberalization. But such pressure will equally arise on the domestic scene, where demands for political change of some kind have often been seen to multiply at times of economic crises in part induced by liberalizing measures (this may be illustrated by the case of Algeria in this volume, as well as those of Mexico and Jordan). The regimes involved in economic liberalization programs often themselves react to, or try to preempt, such pressure by political "decompression" (which may or may not evolve into more extensive liberalization). The case studies on Albania and Algeria provide good examples of such dynamics. It is of course possible that the combination of economic liberalization, the economic difficulties that in part are its result, and the (limited) political liberalization that ensues, ends up producing a far worse crisis—witness, again, Algeria. This scenario, however, is neither necessary nor subject to general laws, only to the specific conjuncture of the country concerned.

There is one other way in which a concern with economic liberalization may translate into political liberalization from above. Quite apart from trying to diffuse popular antagonism to economic reforms by introducing a measure of political liberalization, economic reformers in some instances have used such political measures in order to circumvent resistance against their economic program within the regime itself. As mentioned earlier, examples of this could be found at different times in Algeria, Tunisia, Egypt, and Jordan. This particular dynamic could of course also be viewed as an example of political liberalization leading to (because allowing) economic liberalization. It is to this category of linkages that we now turn.

From Political to Economic Liberalization?

The most striking way in which political liberalization has been observed to lead to economic liberalization must be the dramatic shifts in political systems in Eastern Europe and the directly related subsequent shift in their socioeconomic systems. This represents Kong's "discontinuous" type of transition from authoritarian state industrialization (see Chapter 12).

Although the causes of such a transition in the first instance have been economic failure, domestic political pressure, and external pressure, it was the resulting political change (read political liberalization) that led to full-scale remodeling of the economy (read economic liberalization). This was true in varying ways in the Eastern European transitions—with the Polish case as analyzed by Gowan in Chapter 4 being a particularly good example. As Kong points out, the reasons that this should be the case in such discontinuous transitions, where previous regimes have dramatically failed to deliver, are (1) the state's limited ability to direct events; (2) the level of antistate feeling; and (3) the global climate. We should add Balcerowicz's concept of "extraordinary politics" (very much an instance, if a very special one, of political liberalization), which in such cases may allow a determined and coherent group of economic reformers to push through a comprehensive economic-liberalization program of the sort that might not otherwise have been feasible. It must again be stressed, however, that the precise way in which the linkage is given shape, and the form of its results, depend very much on the specific circumstances of the country in question.

As indicated earlier, even such dramatic initiations of the process of economic liberalization do not necessarily mean that it will proceed smoothly to a full market economy thereafter. This is all the more true of the cases other than these systemic "revolutions." India is only one of a range of examples in which democracy did not, until very recently, lead to any significant economic liberalization. Although there is circumstantial evidence that a dynamic linking a democratic system with the emergence of a market economy does increasingly tend to hold sway, "the time-gap between the achievement of democracy and of a market economy . . . is a fact that cannot be ignored."[7] Only in the prevailing international economic and intellectual climate of the 1990s is it reasonable to assume that this time lag might be growing smaller.

It is worth reexamining, at the end of this book, the controversial claim that democracy may in fact be an obstacle to successful economic liberalization rather than a precursor to it. The recognition that the interventionism of strong, even authoritarian states has been a feature in the economic success of at least some countries has been mirrored in an assertion that only authoritarian governments can push through the sometimes painful and politically unpopular measures entailed in economic reform. The experience of the military or otherwise authoritarian regimes in Brazil, Argentina, Chile, Uruguay, South Korea, Taiwan, and Singapore is usually referred to in corroboration of this thesis, and contrasted with the case of democracies such as India's. Peter Nolan's chapter in this volume posits the case of China as a further example.

First, it is worth reiterating that the evidence is not convincing for even the link between authoritarian rule and economic *development.* There is, in fact, "suggestive evidence that links features of democratic systems positively with overall aspects of development and welfare,"[8] in part because such systems tend to be associated with investment in education, greater equality, and other social policies favorable to economic development. The evidence equally "[does not] endorse the notion that authoritarian governments, on average, show greater promise for achieving rapid growth."[9] This corresponds with the increasing recognition in the 1980s that authoritarian regimes have all too often proved to be the epitome of ineptitude, corruption, and subjection to narrow group interests—the few exceptions notwithstanding.

In examining more specifically the possible link between authoritarian rule and successful economic (liberalizing) *reform,* two preliminary qualifications need to be made, both relating to the fact that a *general* assessment distinguishing only between authoritarian and nonauthoritarian systems is not very useful. First, an authoritarian regime with ample economic institutional capabilities and resources is likely to be better able to carry through economic reforms than one without such assets. Kong's category of "continuous transition" from authoritarian industrialization captures this difference. Second, and perhaps most basically, the *degree* of authoritarianism will be a crucial variable. The evidence is very strong that the dynamics of a dictatorship or autocracy run by a small group almost inevitably militate *against* far-reaching economic liberalization. On the other hand, if the level of authoritarianism is less severe or the autocracy less restricted, different dynamics may become possible. The debate really concerns this latter group, where there is a willingness to allow the emergence of a significant middle class with a degree of independence. Even in these cases, a hypothesis worth exploring further would be that far-reaching economic liberalization will more often be successful if such an authoritarian regime has in fact a wide basis of support—be it tacit or explicit. The striking extent of reforms that President Fujimori of Peru was able to implement in the first half of the 1990s would appear to point in that direction; so might the fact that in Chile significant sections of the middle class (as well as the armed forces) were supportive of the stability and economic reforms introduced by General Pinochet. It must be recognized, however, that the causes of successful or failed reform must be sought much more widely.

"On the whole," the World Bank has commented, "the evidence suggests that the democratic-authoritarian distinction itself fails to explain adequately whether or not countries initiate reform, implement it effectively, or survive its political fall-out."[10] Poland, and Portugal before it, are but two examples of a democratic system implementing thorough economic reform. The conclusion that the authoritarian-reform thesis is therefore not a tenable general rule also emerges from most of the country studies in this book and the analysis presented in Chapter 2, as well as other recent work on the subject.[11]

*   *   *

Even if economic liberalization can proceed without significant political liberalization in the first instance, and even if this may in particular cases be the preferred (and, temporarily, preferable) strategy (witness the Chinese success), any claim that economic reform will more often than not *necessitate* authoritarian rule is manifestly false. Political liberalization in the more dictatorial, corrupt, and economically mismanaging systems of the developing world would, just as in the case of Eastern Europe, most likely usher in more, rather than less, economic openness—as well as a more viable economy generally. In more competent authoritarian regimes the likelihood is that some degree of political liberalization *will* eventually follow economic liberalization, although this will vary in extent and timing, and although, as this volume has amply demonstrated, economic liberalization itself forms only part of the explanatory mosaic.

Notes

1. K. von Beyme, "Approaches to a Theory of the Transformation to Democracy and Market Society," in G. Parry, ed., *Politics in an Interdependent World* (Aldershot: Edward Elgar, 1994), pp. 126–145: p. 129.

2. N. Hamilton and E. Kim, "Economic and Political Liberalisation in South Korea and Mexico," in *Third World Quarterly,* Vol. 14, No. 1 (1993), pp. 109–136: p. 133.

3. Ibid.

4. S. Huntington, "Will More Countries Become Democratic?" *Political Science Quarterly,* Vol. 99 (1984), pp. 193–218; L. Diamond, "Introduction: Roots of Failure, Seeds of Hope," in L. Diamond, J. Linz, and S. Lipset, eds., *Democracy in Developing Countries,* Vol. 2 *Africa* (Boulder: Lynne Rienner, 1988), pp. 1–32.

5. R. Pinkney, *Democracy in the Third World* (Buckingham/Philadelphia: Open University Press, 1993), p. 113.

6. A. Ehteshami, *The Politics of Economic Restructuring in Post-Khomeini Iran,* CMEIS Occasional Paper No. 50 (Durham: CMEIS, University of Durham, July 1995), p. 7.

7. K. von Beyme, "Approaches to a Theory of the Transformation," p. 130.

8. World Bank, *World Development Report 1991* (New York: Oxford University Press, 1991), p. 134.

9. Ibid., p. 9.

10. Ibid., pp. 132–133.

11. See for instance R. Bates and A. Krueger, *Political and Economic Interactions in Economic Policy Reform* (Oxford: Blackwell, 1993); A. Przeworski and F. Limongi, "Political Regimes and Economic Growth," *Journal of Economic Perspectives,* Vol. 7, No. 3 (Summer 1993), pp. 51–69; and the collective work directed and edited by John Williamson, *The Political Economy of Policy Reform* (Washington: Institute for International Economics, 1994), especially the chapter by J. Williamson and S. Haggard, "The Political Conditions for Policy Reform'" pp. 527–596: pp. 568–569.

About the Contributors

Gerd Nonneman is lecturer in international relations at Lancaster University (UK), and has taught Middle East politics and the politics of development at the Universities of Manchester and Exeter and at the International University of Japan. His most recent publications include: *Development, Administration and Aid in the Middle East* (1988); *War and Peace in the Gulf* (coauthor, 1991); *Economic Liberalisation in the Developing World* (1993); and *The Middle East and Europe: the Search for Stability and Integration* (1993).

Stephen Day is research assistant at the Centre for the Study of Democratisation, University of Warwick, and Editorial Assistant for the journal *Democratization*. He has written several articles on democratization and party politics in Eastern Europe, including: "Poland's Post-Communism," in *The Chartist*, February 1994; and "Slovakia—The End of the Beginning or the Beginning of the End," in *Co-existence*, September 1995. He is currently preparing his doctoral thesis on the realignment of the post-Communist left in Poland and Slovakia.

Peter Gowan is principal lecturer in European politics at the University of North London. He is an editor of *Labour Focus on Eastern Europe* and has written extensively on both Polish politics and relations between the European Union and East-Central and Eastern Europe. He is completing a book on Western policy toward the region since 1989, to be published in 1996.

Sally Harris is research fellow in the Department of Politics, University of Hull. She has researched and written on security and defense issues relating to NATO and northeast Asia—especially the Korean peninsula—as well as on democratization in South Korea. Her most recent publications include: "Alternative security architectures," in S. Kirby and N. Hooper, eds., *The

Cost of Peace (1991); *Defensive Defence* (with S. Kirby), a report for the UK Ministry of Defence; and *The Union of Democratic Control and the Conduct of British Foreign Policy, 1914–1918* (1996).

Raymond A. Hinnebusch is professor of political science at the College of St. Catherine in St. Paul, Minnesota, and was Visiting Professor at the University of Durham during his participation in the project. In addition to numerous articles on Syria and Egypt, his publications include: *Peasant and Bureaucracy in Baathist Syria: The Political Economy of Rural Development* (1989); *Authoritarian Power and State Formation in Ba'thist Syria* (1990); *Egyptian Politics Under Sadat;* and *Syria and the Middle East Peace Process* (with A. Drysdale, 1992).

Stephen Kirby is professor of politics, Pro-Vice Chancellor, and Dean of Humanities and Social Science at the Manchester Metropolitan University. He has worked and published on various aspects of European and northeast Asian foreign policy and defense policy issues, including the United States/ Japan/Korea relationship. His most recent publications include: "The Korean Peninsula and the Emerging North-East Asian Order," in *Brassey's Defence Yearbook 1994;* and "Security and Nuclear Proliferation in North and Southeast Asia," in RUSI's *International Security Review 1994.*

Tat Yan Kong is lecturer in politics and development studies at the School of Oriental and African Studies (SOAS), University of London. His research focuses on the political economy of development issues, with particular reference to South Korea. His publications include *The Korean Peninsula in Transition* (1995).

Alasdair I. McBean is emeritus professor of economics at Lancaster University. He was a visiting Ford Foundation Professor in China, Fudan University, Shanghai (1990) and People's University, Beijing (1992). He has been a consultant on World Bank and European Union missions to the states of the former Soviet Union. Recent publications include: "GATT's last stand," *Journal of International Development* (1992); "Lessons of Trade Policy and Economic Reform in China," in P. Cook and F. Nixon, eds., *The Move to the Market?* (1995); and "China's Foreign Trade Corporations," in J. Child and Y. Lu, eds., *Management Issues for China in the 1990s* (1995).

Emma C. Murphy is lecturer in the politics of the Middle East at the Centre for Middle Eastern and Islamic Studies, University of Durham. Her publications include a wide range of articles on the area's political economy and on the Arab–Israeli conflict, as well as *Economic and Political Liberalization in the Middle East* (with T. Niblock, 1993). She is currently completing a book on economic and political liberalization in North Africa.

Peter Nolan is director of Studies in Economics, Jesus College, and Lecturer in the Faculty of Economics and Politics, Cambridge University. His most recent books include: *State and Market in the Chinese Economy: Essays and Controversial Issues* (1993); and *China's Rise, Russia's Fall: Politics, Economics and Planning in the Transition from Stalinism* (1995). He has edited, among other works: *Market Forces in China* (with D. Fureng, 1990); *The Chinese Economy and Its Future* (with D. Fureng, 1990); *China's Economic Reforms: The Costs and Benefits of Incrementalism* (with F. Qimiao, 1994); and *The Transformation of the Communist Economies: Against the Mainstream* (with H. Chang, 1995).

Sylvia Poelling is an Arabist and Middle East analyst, specializing in political and economic risk analysis. She is vice-president and managing editor of the London/Frankfurt-based consulting firm ASIM & C Ltd., leading the Euro-Mashreq Division, which publishes the bimonthly *Business Briefs Lebanon and Syria*. Until December 1994 she was the Economist Intelligence Unit's senior editor for the Middle East and North Africa, among other things writing the EIU's *Country Reports* and *Country Profiles* on Syria.

David Seddon is professor of development studies, and codirector of the European Development Centre, at the University of East Anglia. His research interests include the politics of reform in developing countries and states in transition. His most recent book is *Free Markets and Food Riots: The Politics of Global Adjustment* (coauthor). He is currently working with a Russian colleague on a book dealing with the politics of economic reform and social welfare in Russia.

Ruth Davey and **Rachel Grellier** are both graduates of the School of Development Studies, University of East Anglia, specializing in development issues in Eastern Europe.

Michael Willis, of the Centre for Middle Eastern and Islamic Studies, University of Durham, specializes in the politics of North Africa. He wrote his doctoral dissertation on *The Development of the Islamist Movement in Algeria,* to be published by Ithaca Press in 1996. His publications also include "The Islamist Movements of North Africa: Threat from the South?" in Niblock, Joffé, and Aliboni, eds., *Security Challenges in the Mediterranean* (1996).

Index

About the Book

It is almost universally agreed that political liberalization, or democratization, is a good thing. However, as Gerd Nonneman demonstrates in the first part of this book, the merits of economic liberalization are more controversial.

Explanations for the recent surge in the processes of democratization and economic liberalization, and for the forms they have taken, remain fragmentary. Likewise, the linkages between the two remain under-researched—despite many sweeping assertions of a positive relationship. Nonneman investigates these issues, providing a framework for the remainder of the book, in which diverse country studies are used to advance our understanding of the dynamics and complexities of these two intertwined processes.

GERD NONNEMAN is lecturer in international relations at Lancaster University, UK. He has written widely on Middle East politics and the politics of development.